Wilhelm Gräb, Lars Charbonnier (Eds.)

Secularization Theories, Religious Identity and Practical Theology

International Practical Theology

edited by

Prof. Dr. Chris Hermans (Nijmegen),
Prof. Dr. Maureen Junker-Kenny (Dublin),
Prof. Dr. Richard Osmer (Princeton),
Prof. Dr. Friedrich Schweitzer (Tübingen),
Prof. Dr. Hans-Georg Ziebertz (Würzburg)

in cooperation with the
International Academy of Practical Theology (IAPT),

represented by

Ruard Ganzevoort (President) and Claire Wofteich (Vice President)

Volume 7

LIT

Secularization Theories, Religious Identity and Practical Theology

Developing International Practical Theology
for the 21st Century

International Academy of Practical Theology
Berlin 2007

edited by

Wilhelm Gräb and Lars Charbonnier

LIT

Cover Picture: Berlin Dom, Alexanderplatz
  © Lars Charbonnier

Gedruckt auf alterungsbeständigem Werkdruckpapier entsprechend
ANSI Z3948   DIN ISO 9706

Bibliographic information published by the Deutsche Nationalbibliothek
The Deutsche Nationalbibliothek lists this publication in the Deutsche
Nationalbibliografie; detailed bibliographic data are available in the Internet at
http://dnb.d-nb.de.

ISBN 978-3-03735-991-4 (Switzerland)
ISBN 978-3-8258-0798-6 (Germany)

A catalogue record for this book is available from the British Library

©LIT VERLAG GmbH & Co. KG Wien,
Zweigniederlassung Zürich 2009
Dufourstr. 31
CH-8008 Zürich
Tel. +41 (0) 44-251 75 05
Fax +41 (0) 44-251 75 06
e-Mail: zuerich@lit-verlag.ch
http://www.lit-verlag.ch

LIT VERLAG Dr. W. Hopf
Berlin 2009
Fresnostr. 2
D-48159 Münster
Tel. +49 (0) 2 51-620 32 22
Fax +49 (0) 2 51-922 60 99
e-Mail: lit@lit-verlag.de
http://www.lit-verlag.de

Distribution:

In Germany: LIT Verlag Fresnostr. 2, D-48159 Münster
Tel. +49 (0) 2 51-620 32 22, Fax +49 (0) 2 51-922 60 99, e-Mail: vertrieb@lit-verlag.de

In Austria: Medienlogistik Pichler-ÖBZ GmbH & Co KG
IZ-NÖ, Süd, Straße 1, Objekt 34, A-2355 Wiener Neudorf
Tel. +43 (0) 22 36-63 53 52 90, Fax +43 (0) 22 36-63 53 52 43, e-Mail: mlo@medien-logistik.at

In Switzerland: B + M Buch- und Medienvertriebs AG
Hochstr. 357, CH-8200 Schaffhausen
Tel. +41 (0) 52-643 54 85, Fax +41 (0) 52-643 54 35, e-Mail: order@buch-medien.ch

Distributed in the UK by: Global Book Marketing, 99B Wallis Rd, London, E9 5LN
Phone: +44 (0) 20 8533 5800 – Fax: +44 (0) 1600 775 663
http://www.centralbooks.co.uk/html

Distributed in North America by:

Transaction Publishers
Rutgers University
35 Berrue Circle
Piscataway, NJ 08854

Phone: +1 (732) 445 - 2280
Fax: + 1 (732) 445 - 3138
for orders (U. S. only):
toll free (888) 999 - 6778
e-mail: orders@transactionpub.com

Contents

Preface — 9

Words of Welcome

Wilhelm Gräb, Host of the Conference and Dean of the Faculty of Theology at Humboldt-University Berlin — 15

Christoph Markschies, President of Humboldt-University Berlin — 17

Elaine Graham, President of IAPT — 20

Secularization Theories, Religious Identities, and Practical Theology: Main Lectures

Does modernisation lead to secularisation?
Hans Joas — 25

Do we live in a secular world? An African Perspective
Jaco Dreyer — 35

Why is Europe the most secularized continent?
Grace Davie — 63

Practical Theology and Secularization

Practical theology is a secularized world beyond the obsession with guilt and atonement. Towards a theology of blessing and its implications for our practices
Riet Bons-Storm — 77

Educating for Religious Identity in secularizing worlds
Thomas Groome — 85

Jose Casanova on Public Religions and Modernity: The Basis for a Practical Theological Agenda?
Lewis Mudge — 92

The Impact of Culture on Religiosity. An empirical study among youth in Germany and the Netherlands
Hans-Georg Ziebertz — 99

The Factor Religion in the Perspective of the Third Sector Comparative Studies: Where Practical Theology needs to speak out against methodological secularisation
Eberhard Hauschildt — 108

6   Contents

Natural Law in a Time of Secularization
Terence Kennedy   115

Highlighting children's spirituality in a de-traditionalised society: The challenge of theologising with others for religious education and pastoral care
Annemie Dillen   123

Secularization and Disestablishment of the Church: Theoretical and empirical discussion around the case of French Roman Catholics in Quebec
Solange Lefebvre   131

Secularization in Quebec: Phenomenon, Expression and Theory
Robert Mager   146

Postmodernism and Mennonites in the Netherlands
Lies Brussee-van der Zee   152

Practical Theology and Empirical Research

Empirical Research in the Service of the Church? The Evaluation of Ecclesial Praxis as a Task of Practical Theology
Friedrich Schweitzer   161

The gestalt of the Cross – phenomenological and theological remarks
Hans-Günter Heimbrock   167

Agency, Religion, and Hope: Palestinian Young Women Reflect
Raymond Webb   175

Research group on Post Traumatic-Spirituality:

'All things work together for good'? Theodicy and post-traumatic spirituality
R. Ruard Ganzevoort   183

Spiritual narratives of adolescent orphans affected by HIV and Aids and poverty
Julian C. Müller   193

Pastoral care and the meaning of touch in sexual abuse
Karlijn Demasure   205

Trend Research – a Tool for Pastoral Planning
Brigitte Fuchs   214

Redefining Children's Spirituality
Bonnie Miller-McLemore   223

Contents 7

Practical Theology and Liberating Practice

Social Suffering, Its Aftermath and Questions of Redemption
Nancy Pineda-Madrid 235

The Struggle of Practical Theology in its Search for Identity. A Latin American Perspective
Lothar Carlos Hoch 243

Gender Norms and Their Consequences for Body and Soul – a Challenge for the Christian Community
Isolde Karle 252

Creating Space within the Dynamics of Interculturality: The Impact of Religious and Cultural Transformations in Post-Apartheid South Africa
Johan Cilliers 260

Prayer as Liberating Practice: Theological Complexities in Two Case Studies
Claire Wolfteich 271

Theological Method – A Way of Life
Terry Veling 278

Youth and Spirituality in the Context of Internet: New challenges for pastoral practices
Valburga Schmiedt-Streck 286

Reframing masculinities and femininities in the gender debate. From the body as social text (narcissistic model tyranny) to the body as religious text (compassionate intimacy) in a practical theology of human embodiment and sensuality
Daniël J. Louw 293

How can Christian communities claim their "better truth" without violence against others, even more for the sake of solidarity with them? Some considerations reflected on Biblical traditions
Ottmar Fuchs 308

Southern Perspectives: Theological Education, Community Development and Leadership Empowerment
Susan Adams 316

Non-Theological Discourse in Theological Practices of Peacebuilding
Mary Elizabeth Mullino Moore 325

The Charismata of Women. An Empirical Case Study
Stephanie Klein 333

8   Contents

Practical Theology and Ministry Formation

Spiritual Care by Physicians: Maintaining the Integrity of Religion and Finding an Appropriate Form
Neil Pembroke   343

Ministerial integration
Edward Foley   350

Impossible Challenge between Church Institution and Society in Fribourg: Experience of the Ecclesial Power, Neglecting the Issues of Secularization
André Beauregard   356

Theological issues in fluid ways of being church
Cornelis de Groot   364

Ministry in Depth: Three Critical Questions in the Teaching and Practice of Pastoral Care
Rodney Hunter   372

Dialogue as a Reply to the Modern. The ideas behind the Church of Sweden closely related Sigtuna Foundation at the time of its establishment
Elisabeth Christiansson and Tomas Fransson   380

Social forms of the Church in relation to medial publicity. Do the media constitute or communicate "religion"?
Leo Karrer   388

Beyond Pastoral Theology: Why Catholics Should Embrace Practical Theology
Kathleen Cahalan   392

The Academic Paradigm and the Denigration of Practical Theological Know-How
Bonnie Miller-McLemore   398

Interfaith Pastoral Care in the Hospital: A Project in Practical and Pastoral Theology
Daniel Schipani   407

Interfaith Chaplaincy: Pastoral Care for all Religions and all Faiths A New Perspective for Clinical Pastoral Care in 21st Century Western Europe? A Swiss Protestant view
Tabitha Walther   415

Preface

This present volume contains a collection of lectures and papers with international contribution to practical theology. In their original form, these lectures and papers were presented at the eighth biennial conference of the International Academy of Practical Theology held at Berlin/Germany in April 2007. The purpose of this Academy is to support international dialogue and cooperation in all fields of practical theology. The contributions in this volume represent this purpose in a splendid way. The subject of the conference was "Secularization Theories, Religious Identity and Practical Theology"; for introduction a short note on its background and its relevance for practical theology.

Religion is undergoing a process of transformation. And in various ways also the Churches are being transformed and Christian communities with them. For a long time already, we have been observing the transformations of religious culture. Modernization does obviously not lead to the end of religion. Nevertheless, theories of secularization can still be found in scientific contexts. But what do people mean when they talk about secularization? Do they mean that the Churches lose members? That many services on Sundays are empty? That a great number of the population does not belong to any denomination of the religious communities? That the social and political influence of the Churches becomes weaker? All of these questions imply observable facts, in Germany as well as in many other European countries. At the same time, we have to do with the phenomena of individualized and privatized religion. We observe various types of fluid religion, different types of spirituality with people searching for God but not being engaged in or part of any religious community. We have to do with new Christian communities inside and outside the traditional denominations. How do religious identities have to be developed in a cultural situation like this? What could practical theology do in order to contribute to a better understanding of the cultural context in which the practice of the Churches and religious communities takes place today?

Theories of secularization are in conflict with theories of religious individualization and globalization. Also Churches and religious communities are concerned with the functional differentiation of modern societies: their direct influence on politics has totally faded. Conversely, they can still determine discussions about values and moral positions. In addition, the religious institutions are being transformed, also the Churches and religious communities. They are adapting to the modern, functionally differentiated society and cultural pluralism. The Churches are more and more successful in contributing to the formation of new religious identities, whenever they achieve a pluralistic point of view on the immense variety of life-styles and today's religious interpretations of life. As open Churches, they are learning to be neither doctrinaire nor dogmatically and liturgically inflexible.

It is obvious that the social and political influence of the Churches and their members is decreasing, at least in countries of the north-western hemisphere. Nevertheless, religious symbols and/or a certain contact with them are provoking conflicts worldwide. They are used for the articulation of last and universal truth, claims and values, e.g. when we think of the intensive discussions about cartoons of the prophet Mohammed in 2007. In modern culture, religious symbols and religious communities still represent those existential questions of meaning and fundamental values without which human life, even that that is conscious of it, is not possible at all.

Today, practical theology has to observe the transformations of religion in the modern world. Thus we can at the same time try to find out about the relevant stimuli of the biblical traditions to the religious practice in the Churches and Christian communities today. Theories of secularization do not have to keep the last word. Modern and post-modern societies rather show diverse tendencies of religious productivity than a loss of any religious affiliations. Although the Churches do find themselves in a pluralistic religious situation, they are nevertheless an important guarantor for values and meaning. Certainly, they are changing shape enormously. But those Christian communities that are ready for the modern culture are returning into the society.

Practical theology has to recognize these new challenges. So Churches and Christian communities might find out by themselves that they are able to achieve new influences also in politics and society.

The conference of the IAPT in Berlin 2007 was dealing with these challenges in the main lectures of the plenary sessions and the working group sessions. On the one hand, the conference discussed the transformation processes of religious culture, the secularization theories and their boundaries. On the other hand, it helped to clarify the challenges that arise for the religious institutions, in particular the Churches and Christian communities. In the working groups, especially as usually concerned with three different foci, we also dealt with other topics of practical theology that are of great interests for our research and work in the many different sub-disciplines.

The publication of a volume like the present one is not only the result of the editors' work. We are most grateful to the authors. Most of them have taken upon themselves the task of fulfilling a very harsh limit of pages and sometimes therefore of rewriting and reworking their contributions. Our colleague Raymond Webb has – once again – graciously done a language check and has greatly improved chapters written by non-native speakers. Our student assistants in Berlin have done a great job in revising the articles before publication – thanks to Cornelia Stock, Christina Klasink, Anna Hellmich and Thomas Thieme.

Preface

At last it must be said that it has not been possible to fully standardize the references and the style of all the presentations. At least to a degree, the individual contributions still breathe some of the atmosphere of their countries of origin. It is our conviction that this is not a loss. On the contrary, this variety and difference are fruitful components of mutual dialogue through which practical theology has once again been experienced during the time of the conference – and will hopefully be experienced by reading this volume.

Berlin, October 2008

Wilhelm Gräb
Lars Charbonnier

Words of Welcome

Wilhelm Gräb

Words of Welcome
By the Conference Host and
Dean of the Faculty of Theology at Humboldt-Universität zu Berlin

Mrs. President, Mr. President, Dear Members of the IAPT, Dear Guests,

Welcome all of you to the biannual meeting of the IAPT. I am glad that so many members of the academy and so many guests have accepted our invitation. I hope that all of you will enjoy your stay here in Berlin.

Our meeting takes place in the new building of the Theological Faculty. It is the first international conference in this house. You see everything is new and not fully completed. But we as the Theological Faculty are very happy that last December we could move from separate buildings into this house which is set in a fascinating environment and I hope that you will enjoy being here.

We find ourselves in the old centre of Berlin, a few steps from the "Berlin Cathedral" and the "Museum Island". In your conference file you'll find an article of the German weekly magazine "Der Spiegel" from last week with the leading article: "Berlin, the Comeback of a metropolis". It is a very interesting article describing the processes of transformation since the early nineties of the 20th century. It illustrates what happened after the fall of the wall and especially why Berlin is one of the most exciting cities of the world today. I hope that this will be your impression and experience in the next days, too.

The subject of our conference, "Secularization Theories, Religious Identities and Practical Theology", is in accordance with our location, Berlin. Already in the second half of the 19th century, Berlin was called one of the most secularised cities of the world. Over all, at the beginning of the 19th century, Friedrich Schleiermacher, the first Dean of the Theological Faculty in Berlin published an article with the title: "Some thoughts about how to stop the decline of religion". Schleiermacher became one of the founders of Practical Theology as a theological discipline. The article shows his motivation: It was his opinion that theology should improve the ability of Church leaders to make the practices of the Church and the congregations more attractive so they could match the cultural developments in the society of the early 19th century.

Nowadays the challenges are more comprehensive. In Schleiermacher's times there was still a Christian society. Today, however, more than 80 per cent of the population in the east part of Berlin and in East Germany as a whole are not members of the church at all. They don't belong to any religious community. So it is not possible to say that they have a religious identity. But at the same time we realize that there are more than one hundred small religious associations and a big Islamic community in Berlin. We cannot ignore either that the protestant church and on a lower level the Catholic Church are still well established as public churches in Berlin representing much more than the minority of the population. Considering basic values and issues of worldview churches play an important role in the German society of today. As a consequence, we have had controversial discussions about secularization theories for many years. Instead of using the term "secularization", many scholars today prefer to talk about the individualization and pluralisation of religious identities. During the last 10 or 15 years, we have witnessed a growing awareness among theologians and sociologists of contrasting developments in various regions of the world. The decline of the established Christian churches in many parts of Europe is in contrast with the increase of some kinds of religious movements which belong to traditions of Pentecostalism. For most of us it's obvious that modernization does not necessarily lead to secularization. Nevertheless, the interrelationship between religion, culture and politics has changed in modern societies. Their structure is determined by functional differentiation and consequently religion is not strictly interconnected with the other spheres of society.

But I don't have to discuss the topics of our conference now. I am very glad that Hans Joas, one the most important sociologists of religion worldwide, will introduce us to our topic after further words of welcome have been spoken, firstly by the president of the Humboldt-University Berlin and Professor of our Theological Faculty, Chair of the department of church history, Christoph Markschies, and secondly by the president of IAPT, Elaine Graham.

Christoph Markschies

Words of Welcome
By the President of Humboldt-Universität zu Berlin

The semester break, ladies and gentlemen, is a time where many seminars and conferences tend to take place at a university. This has led to the situation that two events are taking place at Humboldt-Universität zu Berlin on the same day, which deal with the same topic, namely secularization: In the early afternoon, we hosted a small-scale, but first-rate congress of young researchers who are connected with the collaborative research centre "Repräsentation sozialer Ordnungen im Wandel" – "Representation of changing social orders". Just afterwards, the larger conference of the "International Academy of Practical Theology" begins – to which I would like to welcome you warmheartedly. At the congress of the collaborative research centre, several academics, including some who came from Israel and the Arabic world, were discussing the long-standing dichotomy between the religious and the secular area. In the Arabic world, even an attentive traveller cannot simply speak of such a dichotomy, even though there are good reasons why states in the Middle East pay careful attention to the separation of these two areas irrespective of all interferences/interfaces. The comprehensive programme of the „International Academy of Practical Theology" conference contains a whole section about „Practical Theology and Secularization", which is due to be discussed over several days.

The coincidence that these two events are taking place at the same afternoon at the same institution is hardly surprising for the president of the university, who is simultaneously a church historian and a theologian – it is perhaps only the need to hasten from one event to the next that keeps him on his toes and calls for careful logistical planning. It could not escape the notice of the academic, whose regular occupation is the study of early Christianity, that there are considerable debates about the theory of secularization. Despite the well-known fragmentation of disciplines, which has resulted from the contemporary desire for demarcation of subject areas, the boundaries of disciplines are somewhat blurred and permeable. Here are two pars pro toto examples that stem from the reading material of the patristician in the office of University President: Hans Joas, the opening speaker at this conference of practical theologians, whom we all hold in very high esteem, has just published a substantial soft-bound book with the title "Secularisation and the Religions of the World" („Säkularisierung und die Weltreligionen"). In the introduction to this book, he has not only pointed out that the religion question and the debate about its relation to society has occupied a whole range of disciplines and public discourses since the eighteenth century. Joas also speaks of a crisis – or, as he phrases it: of the end of the theory of secularization – and of the difficulties that it presents in trying to find an all-encompassing explanation for developments that are taking place in quite differentiated regions in North America, South America, Western Europe and Eastern Europe. Furthermore, Talal Asad, who delivered the opening speech at the conference „Religion and its other", pointed out in his book „Formations of the Secular", which was published in 2003, that here, as is often the case, the dual of the coexistence of religious and political areas, which is a key characteristic of modernity, does not explain the existence of enlightened societies or those that are still in need of enlightenment. That, which we understand as secularization is, as Asad has observed very accurately, initially only the other part of a particular development in religion and theology. It is closely connected with this particular development of religion and theology and cannot be separated from it. The leading assumption of our understanding of "secularization" as a retreat from religion is, then, in precisely that sense nothing more than a theory, insofar as it describes the fixed notions of certain contemporary intellectuals, but not the multiple reality of European and non-European societies.

You know all of this of course, as well as the colleagues who are currently meeting in a different location in this university at another conference. For a historian, who is dealing with early Christianity, the recent discussion about secularization already seems a little stale: indeed, the notion that the theories about secularization say more about the intellectual situation of modernity than about its practical religious relevance has already reached our delimited circles, which deal with Greek inscriptions and ancient Syrian liturgies. If that is so, then please allow an amateur in the area of modernity to pose a few heretical questions. The ancient Christians, with whom I occupy myself day in, day out, attempted to dissolve the close interrelation of religion and public discourse. They argued that those who refused to wear a garland in honour of the Emperor's birthday could still be loyal citizens of the state. They were convinced that the refusal to perform sacrifices that were demanded by the state was not an act of disloyalty towards the emperor and the Empire. The church services of these Christians contained an intercession towards all forms of authority, which, in their eyes, was a far more real demonstration of loyalty. Is that not, ladies and gentlemen, an indication that Christian theologians of the antiquity can make an invaluable contribution to the theory that religion and politics should be demarcated (not separated)? The fixation onto the European modernity in the discussion about the theory of secularization is perhaps a similarly modern myth in the same way as the theory of secularization in the form as we know it.

Bishop Augustin, who is well known to experts of the antiquity and modernity alike, preached in the cathedral of a small North African town. He preached to an audibly applauding and protesting congregation who was used to lively worshipping with his thin, asthmatic voice. He spent a lot of energy on ensuring that Christians were recognisable as Christians in public. During Lent, they should eat only the intended foods – a thin soup with small bacon cubes in

Words of Welcome

the evening – and they were to avoid the wellness baths during the time of doing penance until the evening of Maundy Thursday in order to ensure that they did not prepare and cleanse themselves for Easter before the evening of the Last Supper. It is, therefore, hardly possible to say that Augustin intended a differentiation between the two areas of religion and public life. And yet, in his great work De civitate Dei from the beginning of the fifth century, he produced a theory of there being a dispute between the church and the secular world – between civitas Dei and civitas terrene. The two are interconnected and are often hardly recognisable as separate entities, but pursue very different paths.

It will hardly surprise you, ladies and gentlemen, that a patristician in the office of the university president is of the opinion that antique texts are of vital importance in order to deal with the theory of secularization and the therewith connected theoretical constructions in a differentiated way – at least, they are of greater importance than many colleagues tend to think.

The lively dates about religious practice of the ancient world are as relevant as the highly interesting attempts of Christian, Jewish and Muslim theologians of the antiquity to draw clear lines of separation between religion and politics, church and state, private and public lives, to differentiate between them, and yet to keep them in reciprocal reference to one another. How does one intend to describe the migration of peoples appropriately – to point out only one important aspect – without looking at the coherence between the key categories that form the foundation of the description?

In a simple greeting speech, I can hardly hold a lecture about the so far neglected importance of the imperial ancient world for research into tendencies of secularization – such an endeavour would go beyond the framework and the genre. I can, though, refer to brilliant academics and fellow historians of the Middle Ages who are working at Humboldt-Universität zu Berlin, such as Michael Borgolte, who have long since accepted such themes. It might also suffice for you to believe me at the beginning of this conference that it is my own personal belief that the topic "secularization" is not yet depleted by far, even though it is widely known. I regret not being able to participate at both conferences, as I will be on my way to Moscow very early tomorrow morning. Perhaps you are already anticipating what I am about to say next: in the third Rome it is, however, quite likely, that I will stay with the topic of secularization for a little longer – how could it be otherwise? The same is true for you, ladies and gentlemen, and with this I not only welcome you to this university, which is as rich in tradition as it is versed in modernity, but wish you fruitful and constructive lectures, discussions and conversations. Many thanks.

Elaine Graham

Words of Welcome and Opening of the Conference
By the President of the International Academy of Practical Theology

It is with great pleasure that I open these proceedings of the International Academy of Practical Theology for 2007 in this splendid new building of the Faculty of Theology at the Humboldt University in Berlin. Our meeting here in this city is significant for a number of reasons, all of which promise to make a significant influence on our discussions over the next few days.

For many Practical Theologians, especially those from German-speaking contexts, Schleiermacher's influence represents the beginnings of a public science of theological enquiry. It proceeded from an apprehension of the universal nature of human religious experience, in that he was concerned to retrieve theology from the margins of intellectual discourse in the face of challenges from the Enlightenment and reinstate it as a public, rational, discipline. He placed it in the context of the scientific study of religion, as the study of the exercise of the Christian faith in the world. This opened up the possibility for Practical Theology to move out of the seminary to take its place in the modern, secular (or certainly non-confessional) university curriculum. For many of us in Practical Theology, its location within the modern university alongside other disciplines, many of whom represent important opportunities for interdisciplinary collaboration, is a significant aspect of its identity.

It is also significant that we meet in this city, which demonstrates so many tangible signs of physical and economic regeneration since reunification. When I first visited West Berlin (for a committee of the World Student Christian Federation) at the beginning of 1984, my arrival necessitated taking a Pan-Am shuttle plane from Frankfurt, over East German airspace, into Tegel airport. I remember riding the U-Bahn and S-Bahn trains and it was via the underground train system that I first entered East Berlin. But now, the city is no longer divided, but united in a new confidence and welcoming new generations of visitors.

We are also within sight of the magnificent Berliner Dom, badly damaged during the Allied bombing of this city in the later stages of the Second World War, but now extensively restored at the heart of a city area that is still undergoing physical refurbishment to restore many of the fine public buildings to their former glory.

As is usually the case with international conferences, the opportunities fully to explore our location will inevitably be limited, as we have a full programme of events. But our setting surely reminds us of the contexts within which we conduct our work in Practical Theology, even though we all come from many different national, cultural and institutional backgrounds. We are indeed, at the axis of David Tracy's 'three publics' from which and to which he argued every theologian must refer. And Practical Theology, with its particular ways of engaging with academy, society and church is no less responsive – and responsible – to those realities.

Our theme for this week, of secularization, clearly also relates to these different aspects of our setting here in Berlin: what models of social change and what intellectual currents define our age as 'secular' or otherwise? What theoretical and empirical tools are at hand to make sense of the shifting patterns of believing and belonging in our world? Are societies driven by global or local forces in their trends of religious affiliation, growth or decline? In places where institutional, creedal religion is on the wane, are there signs of incipient religiosity or spirituality in areas such as popular culture? And how should institutions such as churches respond to the currents of religious change: by a return to traditional orthodoxies, or accommodation to secular influences?

These intersections of academy, society and church are therefore highly relevant to our theme, and the challenge for Practical Theology, and this Academy, is to make the most of our time together. We need to listen to our many different contexts, and learn to appreciate our diversity. We need to strive for greater understanding in rigorous yet collegial fashion, appreciative of the many epistemological and practical conventions that inform our discipline. If we are living in an increasingly 'secular' world, Practical Theology must justify its existence, even to those who share none of its presuppositions; but our location – as participants in this conference, and as Practical Theologians – at the interstices of the academic, the civic and the ecclesial, gives us ample opportunity to equip ourselves for this task.

Secularization Theories, Religious Identities, and Practical Theology:
Main Lectures

Hans Joas

Does modernisation lead to secularisation?[*]

The topic I am going to deal with in this talk is: Does Modernisation lead to Secularisation? I think it makes sense to begin my reflections with a few thoughts why this topic – which might sound like a rather abstract problem of the social sciences – currently attracts so much attention. I will then briefly clarify the ways in which I use the two main concepts 'secularisation' and 'modernisation', offer a sketch of a historical argument why the secularisation thesis is wrong, and derive some political conclusions from this argument.

There are four reasons for this attention, two more or less obvious, two others much less so and more in connection with profound cultural changes taking place in our time.[1] The two obvious reasons are of a political character, and you are all familiar with them. The spectacular terrorist attacks of 9/11/2001 have made it clear to all contemporaries that there are highly politicized forms of religion in the Islamic world and among alienated Muslims in the West today. This has intensified the interest in other forms of the politicisation of Islam and in the role of other religious justifications of violent political action, e.g. in the Jewish settler movement on the West Bank or in the connection between certain forms of Protestant fundamentalism in the US and the foreign policy of the Bush administration. The second context, particularly prevalent in Europe, is the problem of the integration of Muslim immigrants into European societies and, although definitely to distinguish from this, the question of the expansion of the European Union, particularly with regard to the possibility of Turkey joining the EU. Whatever one's perspective on these questions is, nobody denies that the immigration problems challenge the existing and very diverse arrangements between state and religion in Europe and that the problems of EU expansion challenge the self-understanding of Europeans and their definition of what constitutes European values and the European cultural or political identity. We can often observe rather paradoxical situations here, for example when intellectuals emphasize the Christian character of Europe against a Turkish membership without ever having positively referred to Christianity in their writings before. Or when completely secularised East German high school students whose deeply religious Muslim fellow students in Berlin ridicule them for having no religion at all suddenly develop an interest in the religious roots

---

[*] We thank the WRR/Scientific Council for Government Policy, The Hague, NL, for the right to reprint this article. It was first published in WRR/Scientific Council for Government Policy (ed.), Beyond the Separation between Church and State? WRR Lecture 2006, The Hague 2006, 13–24.

[1] For a much fuller statement on these reasons, see my introduction to: Hans Joas/Klaus Wiegandt (eds.), Säkularisierung und die Weltreligionen, Frankfurt a.M. 2007, 9–38 (English translation forthcoming).

of their own culture. Thus questions become inevitable like those that inquire whether Europe can only define itself as Christian or rather by delimiting itself against its Christian origins, whether Christianity is only a cultural heritage or rather a constant source of inspiration, whether it is only Christianity or all Abrahamic religions with their shared view of transcendence that can be the foundation of European identity.[2]

With regard to the less obvious changes I think we first have to have the courage to declare the end of 'postmodernity'. By this I want to say that an intellectual current that has dominated intellectual and cultural life since the late 1970's has clearly exhausted itself. It may have been a good antidote to the social planning euphoria of the 1960's and the quasi-revolutionary utopias of the 1970's, but its plea for unlimited creativity and plurality could in itself not offer any strong arguments against the enemies of pluralism and for the protection and transmission to new generations of the ethos of toleration. In this changed atmosphere important scholarly works on the emergence and the history of this ethos of toleration have been produced, but again we see the whole spectrum of responses between those who believe in a 'radical enlightenment' and those who emphasize that the first institutionalisation of religious freedom in North America in the 17th century is the result of a deeply religious motivation. I am referring to the Puritan preacher Roger Williams who argued that the religiously persecuted Puritans should not try to establish a theocratic order in America, but make it possible for every human being, all Christians, but even "Turks, heathens and Jews", to develop his or her authentic relationship to God.[3]

This 'end of postmodernity' is the third context I had in mind. This is the declaration of the exhaustion of a certain form of cultural self-understanding, not of the end of all the changes that have often been adduced as typical for our time (like individualisation in the area of religion). And the fourth is now the question that will be in the focus of my presentation. There is widespread doubt today that the secularisation thesis – an assumption that has been developed out of an overgeneralisation of certain specificities of European religious history – is truly tenable. But what exactly do we mean when we speak of the connection between secularisation and modernisation?

The concept of secularisation was originally a legal term which was first used exclusively to denote the change-over from monastic orders to 'secular priests'. Studies of the history of the concept show that the term first became general

---

[2] On these questions of European identity see my introduction to: Hans Joas/Klaus Wiegandt (eds.), The Cultural Values of Europe. Liverpool 2008, 1–21.

[3] For a more detailed argument see Hans Joas, Max Weber and the 'Origins of Human Rights: A Study of Cultural Innovation', in: Charles Camic et al. (eds.), Max Weber's 'Economy and Society', A Critical Companion, Stanford, Cal. 2005, 366–382.

currency in early 19th century Europe when large amounts of church property were transferred to, or taken over by, the state.[4] Such aspects are not the province of this paper. However, in the wake of legal 'secularisation', the 19th century also saw the emergence both of a philosophical-theological and a sociological discourse on 'secularisation' – both of which, regrettably, were fraught with their own types of multiple meanings.

The philosophical and theological narrative was primarily concerned with 'genealogical' connections between hallmark features of modern society and culture on the one hand and the Christian faith on the other. In such approaches the accent could be placed on quite different places on the value scale. Thus while some viewed modern society as such a perfect embodiment of Christian ideals that they considered the separation of the church from state and society as increasingly superfluous, others were more concerned that large parts of society still showed the imprint of Christian ideas and ways of thought that had not yet been fully discarded.

The most salient attempt to untangle the complex of meanings used in sociological discourse is that undertaken by the Spanish-American sociologist of religion José Casanova.[5] He ascribes three separate meanings to the concept of secularisation as deployed in the social sciences: the decreasing significance of religion or a retreat of religion from the public sphere or the release of parts of society (such as the economy, science, the arts or politics) from direct religious control. Confusing these meanings gives rise to a great deal of misunderstanding. Obviously clarification of the conceptual terms tells us nothing of the causal relationships existing between such disparate processes. And such elucidation is by no means the last word as the concept of religion itself is fraught with ambiguity. If we speak of the decreasing significance of 'religion', for instance, this can refer to changes in attitudes to faith or in participation in religious practices and rituals or membership of churches and faith-based communities, whereby tendencies to a decreasing significance in one respect by no means imply that they hold equally true in all other respects. People can still be believers without going to church just as they can remain members of a church even after losing their faith.

Likewise the formula of a retreat of religion from the public sphere – often expressed as a modern 'privatisation' of religion – is by no means devoid of ambiguity. We need to ask where this private sphere is actually located, whether it refers to a relinquishment of close bonds with the state or with political life in general or whether it rather serves to indicate a withdrawal from open communication in families and small groups to the closed inner life of the

---

[4] See, for example, Giacomo Marramao, Die Säkularisierung der westlichen Welt, Frankfurt a.M. 1996.

[5] José Casanova, Public Religions in the Modern World, Chicago 1994.

individual. The present context does not allow proper investigation of all these complex interweavings. This paper deals solely with the first of three meanings, treating it in as much depth as constraints of space allow.

The concept of 'modernisation' too is susceptible of a wide range of interpretation. It is not taken here to indicate the transition to some period of 'modernity' in whatever form that might take, but rather as a term for the continuous process of economic growth and its consequences and that took also place before there was anything like a period of 'modernity'. The various forms these consequences might take and their interconnections are beyond the scope of the paper. Thus the question 'Does Modernisation lead to Secularisation?' should be taken solely to mean 'Does economic growth necessarily lead to a decrease in the role played by religion?' – a decrease that can lead to the vanishing point. This paper shall investigate the implied inevitability of this process and not to what exact extent any country, Germany for instance or The Netherlands, is currently 'secularised'.

Many believers shall no doubt find such a question absurd or irrelevant as their religious convictions do not allow them to see why greater economic prosperity or technological progress should have a deleterious impact on faith. Other believers will take the assertion that modernisation leads to secularisation at face value as they have developed a view of themselves as an 'endangered' species that can best serve faith by resisting modernisation in all its forms.

But who actually shares the assertion that forms the subject of this paper, when did it first come about and on what foundations does it rest?

Since the 19th century this assumption has been shared by an astonishingly broad range of proponents in the social sciences and nearly all the famous names in philosophy. Whilst this might not be surprising for Marxist philosophers and sociologists, the assumption is also shared by such thinkers as Max Weber and Émile Durkheim, Sigmund Freud and George Herbert Mead, not to mention Friedrich Nietzsche, one of the most vehement critics of Christianity. It is indeed more difficult to find those who did not share it. Leading names here are William James and Alexis de Tocqueville, Jacob Burckhardt and Ernst Troeltsch. And whether Max Weber should figure in the list is a debatable point: although his thesis of "the disenchantment of the world" can certainly be read as a contribution to the theory of secularisation, his insights into the inevitability of the personal struggle for salvation can, with equal certainty, be read in a different light.[6] Even the Protestant sociologist of religion Peter Berger predicted in 1968 that by the year 2000 there would be practically no more religious institutions, just isolated believers huddled

---

[6] For an intense plea not to see Weber as a secularisation theorist, cf. Joachim Vahland, Entzauberung. Max Weber und seine Interpreten, in: Kant-Studien 90 (1999), 410–433.

Does modernisation lead to secularisation? 29

together in an ocean of secularity.[7] To date there is no conclusive research as to the exact historical point when the assumption of the disappearance of religions first came about. What is meant here is not a history of atheism but rather the prediction that the workings of history itself, without the need for any interventions on the part of militant atheists, would lead to the disappearance of religion. According to our present state of knowledge, it would appear that this assumption can be first found in the early 18th century among the early proponents of the English enlightenment who forecast the demise of Christianity by 1900 at the latest. Certain remarks in the writings of Frederick the Great, Voltaire and Thomas Jefferson also foreshadow it. By the 19th century these various springs had come together in a mighty river.[8]

It is remarkable that proponents of the assumption found it so obvious that they were hardly bothered with its theological derivation and empirical investigation. In the light of this we can question in fact whether it is correct to speak of a theory of secularisation and ask whether it would not be more accurate to use the more lowly term secularisation thesis. If we look at the implicit assumptions in this literature we find that it is often based on overtly problematic understandings of what religious faith is. Religious faith is taken to be pseudo-knowledge or pseudo-science doomed to impotence by the progress of science, or the consequence of material and intellectual impoverishment to be rendered superfluous by the advent of greater prosperity and a more just social and political order, or products of circumstances in which questions of meaning and the choice between different meaning systems are devalued by authoritarian education and cultural uniformity so that the onset of individualism and cultural pluralism shall force religion into retreat. All such interpretations of faith are fundamentally wide off the mark. To mount a critique, we need a more appropriate definition of faith, religious experience and their interpretation.[9]

However, at this juncture we are dealing with quite a different issue, namely a view of the social reality of faith or in other words with a sociological critique of the secularisation thesis. Let us assume that this thesis applies to Europe – the most secularised part of the world – at least as a description if not as a way of analysis. This brings us a first step nearer to the advocates of the assumption under scrutiny. However, we then need to ask in four stages, (1) whether European exceptions to the secularisation rule can be adequately explained by the secularisation theory; (2) what does the major exception of the USA look like when viewed closer up; (3) what picture is given from a non-Eurocentric perspective; and (4) what forms do the older histories of religion take in the

---

[7] New York Times, February 25, 1968.
[8] Rodney Stark, 'Secularisation', r.i.p., in: Sociology of Religion 60 (1999), 249–273.
[9] For a more detailed discussion see my book „Do We Need Religion?" in the Yale Cultural Sociology series, Boulder Co., Paradigm Publications 2008.

30   Hans Joas

secularisation thesis. Answers to all these questions can obviously only be given here in a very summary way.

1. There is a general consensus that countries like Poland and Ireland, and to some extent Croatia and the old parts of Bavaria, are exceptions to the secularisation rule. Proponents of the secularisation theory explain the relative robustness of religious resistance in these countries by the fusion of religious and national identities. The Polish people have certainly always found Catholicism a decisive factor in their resistance to Protestant Prussia and Orthodox or communist Russia while a similar view can be applied to the Irish in their struggle against the Protestant British. It is not my intention to cast doubt on such a connection; what we are questioning, however, is whether religion should be understood as a relic from the past that owes its continued existence to political reasons without which it would be destined to vanish. This standpoint conceals the fact that religious identity in all its clear demarcations is first formed in the same process as that of national identity or at least receives impulses that strengthen or disseminate or perhaps even instrumentalise it from the same process. Political mobilisation of religion can lead to the re-emergence of traditional forms of religion where forms of religious practice on the verge of dying out have new life breathed into them or are reinvented as pseudotraditions. Thus new dangers of exclusion (e.g. Protestants in an independent Catholic Ireland) are also inherent in the political mobilisation of religion. If national and confessional identities are closely interwoven, it is difficult for a confessional minority not to be identified with the old repressive powers once national independence has been achieved. As the troubles in Northern Ireland show, such lines of conflict are still very much in evidence in present-day Western Europe. Even so, in global terms the political mobilisation of Islam is currently of far greater significance. Yet here too it would be missing the point to simply regard Islam as a traditional legacy of the past in the modern world. Similar considerations also apply to the political mobilisation of Hinduism in India. What is crucial in all these cases is that we need to abandon the understanding of religion as a relic.

2. Whilst the European exceptions always offer an opt-out of classifying less secularised societies as not fully modern, this option is closed when we turn to the USA. Nobody contests the 'modernity' of America just as nobody contests that according to all the indicators – no matter how controversial any particular one might be – America shows substantially and continually higher levels of religiosity than nearly all European societies: religious life in America is flourishing and even highly productive. New forms of evangelism are engendered (TV evangelism, mega churches) along with new, often highly successful, religious movements (Mormons, Pentecostalism). Leading American figures were among the pioneers of the internal reforms of the Catholic Church in the Second Vatican Council (John Courtney Murray). America now sets the tone for the reception of eastern religions by educated sections of the

population and indeed nowhere else do all the world's religions interact and mutually influence one another more intensely than they do in America.

The enduring view that like the European 'exceptions' this could be explained by a fusion of national and religious identities ('the Puritan legacy') was discredited when empirical studies showed that membership of religious communities in the USA has risen fairly steadily from 1800 to 1950 and indeed practically tripled during this period (relative to the size of the population). Thus any talk of a secularisation process that has been simply delayed can definitely be ruled out.

Another closely related explanation can also be discounted on empirical grounds: the assumption that the high level of religiosity in America, even though not a legacy of the puritanical Pilgrim Fathers, was part of the baggage brought over by later generations of immigrants. As a great number of these came over from countries like Ireland and Poland, it could be argued that America constituted a kind of geographic displacement of European backwardness or aberrance. It could be equally shown, however, that migration to the USA made migrants in general more active in their religious lives than they previously were. And the same would apply (with a few exceptions) to the waves of migration we are now experiencing.

The most plausible explanation now in circulation ascribes the vitality of religious life in America to the plurality of religions in conjunction with an early separation of state and 'church' – a separation, however, in which the state adopts a nurturing attitude to all forms of religion and not a sceptical stance as did the secular state in France. Unlike in Europe with its state-protected religious territorial monopolies, in America a person dissatisfied with the politics or theology of a religious community must never drop out into a fringe group or counter-culture, they can always find their niche in the rich and broad spectrum of religious communities. Such communities are more market-oriented and less dependent on the state; they tend to adopt an entrepreneurial not a bureaucratic stance. For instance, church congregations have no qualms about using marketing instruments like questionnaires to determine the level of satisfaction among their members and prospective members. And as the readiness of members to make donations is of vital importance for the continued existence of the community, it is fostered and promoted by professional forms of management. Market-like conditions promote endeavours to found new 'enterprises'. Religious communities do not sit back and wait for new members to join them but rather embrace a proactive stance that combines religious aspects with the daily concerns of the target group (such as migrants). This brings its own set of dangers and off-shoots which are not less important than those of the bureaucratically structured official churches. So-called church shopping is the least of them; to a large extent this is only played out in the Protestant churches and aided by the increasingly wide-spread perception that theological differences between the swath of Protestant denominations are of minimal importance. It refers to an act of free choice (for instance when moving house) to join a new religious community that offers more attractive social or spiritual assets than the old one. In my opinion certain problems arise when religious communities advertise faith or community membership particularly as means to preordained ends. Aspirations for wealth or political power but also for such ideals as a slim body or physical beauty then become endowed with a magic dimension. What we should note here is that the legal and economic conditions underpinning the actions of religious communities appear to be the decisive factors in terms of the secularisation effects of modernisation. Of equal importance, however, is the question of whether the given plurality of religious communities is perceived as a valuable asset – in other words whether there is a commitment to plurality as a value. Thus what is decisive for the USA is not the existence of a market of religious options in itself, but rather a fixed institutionalisation of religious freedom.[10]

3. The mere act of taking account of the USA can prove unsettling to the Euro-centric point of view. From the standpoint of global history, the idea of the 19th century as a time of comprehensive secularisation is completely untenable. On the contrary this period can rather be countenanced as a time of the quasi triumphalist expansion of religion.[11] A Euro-centric perspective overlooks two essential factors: the religious consequences of European expansion in the 19th century, and the impact of technological innovations on non-European religions.

Obviously, although European expansion did not begin in the 19th century, it reached its peak during that time and was frequently coupled with the efforts of missionaries. It is difficult to outline the effects of missionary work and colonialisation in such a short space but it should be immediately apparent that any other description for them is more apposite than that of 'secularisation'. In Africa and parts of Latin America the spreading of Christianity occurred (accompanied in Africa by the spreading of Islam) even though this was 'from the top downwards' so that it required a spreading of the faith across several generations before it was firmly rooted in the population. In Asia colonialisation and missionary work tended to encounter cultures and religions that saw themselves as superior to the intruders even though they felt threatened by them. Here we find a spectrum of reactions ranging from a transformation of the own religious traditions in the sense of a partial rapprochement to Christianity to forthright opposition. Especially with regard to Hinduism and Confucianism, observers have noted how these two faiths first constituted themselves as religions under the pressure of the challenges thrown up by

---

[10] On the religious situation in the US (with bibliographical references) see Hans Joas, 'Die religiöse Lage in den USA', in: Joas/Wiegandt (eds.), Säkularisierung, 312–328.

[11] C. Bayly, The Birth of the Modern World 1789–1914. Oxford 2004, 325–365.

Christianity and colonialisation. The use of printing presses by the missionaries and the building of churches revolutionised the use of media and construction technology, including those of non-Christian religions. For the understanding of the subsequent development of religion in the 20th century, two factors are of key importance: the development of the state in a post-colonial era and the respective relationships between state and religion. In Latin America we can see a transition from the mainly state-supported monopoly of Catholicism to a plurality of religions, whilst in Africa the failure of states to achieve or retain consolidation in the post-colonial era is the crucial factor.

4. Most proponents of the secularisation theory totally overestimate the actual extent of religiosity in Europe prior to the onset of the modern secularisation process. Yet for a very long time even among priests (to say nothing of the laity) knowledge of the faith was in a lamentable, not to say grotesque, state of underdevelopment. Church attendance was meagre and churches themselves were thin on the ground whilst anti-clericalism and indifference to religion was rife, particularly in rural areas. Industrialisation in its cradle country of Great Britain first brought with it a significant increase in religious practices and church membership over a long period which reached its peak at the beginning of the 20th century. Thus we cannot talk of the de-christianisation of Europe – simply because Europe was never properly 'christianised' in the first place; this is how Gabriel LeBras once put it, perhaps slightly overstating the case.[12] The 19th century saw in some newly industrialised countries (like Germany) the tragic alienation of large parts of the urban working class from the church on the one hand and intensive campaigns, often taking the form of re-traditionalised doctrine, for those sections of the population amenable to faith on the other.

None of these remarks suggests that Western Europe and a small number of ex-colonial settler-states (such as New Zealand) or a small number of post-com-munist societies are not heavily secularised. Even so, after the overview given in this paper, it should be difficult to retain a belief in the validity of the thesis that secularisation is a necessary corollary of modernisation. The reasons why Europe constitutes an 'exceptional case' certainly need closer investigation.

But for our discussion today let me draw three main conclusions from such a refutation of the secularisation thesis:

1. The assumption shared by radical secularists and anti-modern religionists that a strict separation of state and religion forces religion into the private sphere and leads in the long run not only to a privatisation of religion, but also its decline – this assumption is wrong. Radical secularists would welcome such

---

[12] Gabriel Le Bras, 'Déchristianisation': mot fallacieux, in: Social Compass 10 (1963), 447.

a development, anti-modern religionists abhor it – but the assumption is wrong. Religion can flourish under conditions of separation if, on the one hand, this separation encourages the participation of believers and of religious organisations in political life and if, on the other hand, the believers and their organisations develop their own theological reasons for such a separation.

2. To the extent that the secularisation thesis is a self-fulfilling prophecy, the destruction of this prophecy will have consequences on religious life. Although we should not speak of a 'return of religion' as if it had ever disappeared and we should not conflate an increased attention paid to religion in the media with a religious change in itself, there are indicators that indeed a changing cultural climate in Europe leads to a slight reversal of the secularizing trends since the 1960s.

3. Religions as such don't act. It is always human beings who act, i.e. believers with a certain understanding of their faith, but also with certain political goals, economic interests and social characteristics. If we bear this in mind, we can immediately recognize all talk about a possible clash of religions (or civilisations) as misguided from the outset. It is, therefore, more fruitful to interpret some of the typical bones of contention in the current political and religious landscape – like headscarves and the full-body veil – as symptoms of conflicts and not as indicators of the unassimilability of certain religions. As believers always have to ask themselves as to whether their articulation of their faith is convincing, so secularists have to be willing to see signs of religious protest as indicators for a less than convincing appearance of a political and social order.

The Author

Hans Joas is vice-president of the International Sociological Association (ISA), director of the Max Weber Center for Advanced Cultural and Social Studies in Erfurt (Germany) as well as professor of Sociology at the University of Chicago. He is a regular member of the Berlin-Brandenburg Academy of Sciences. His most recent books include „Do We Need Religion? On Experiences of Self-Transcendence" (2008); „Social Theory" (with W. Knoebl) (2009); and „Kriegsverdrängung" (2008). He has a long-standing interest in the sociology of religion, particularly with regard to the conditions for the emergence of religious and other value commitments and their dynamics under conditions of modernisation.

Jaco S. Dreyer

Do we live in a secular world?
An African perspective

1. Introduction

A practical theologian is always attuned to context. The theme of this article explicitly refers to context: the global context of the world as well as the regional context of Africa. We shall return to these contexts. I would like to start, however, with the context in which the conference of the *International Academy of Practical Theology* of 2007 took place, namely Berlin.[1] Berlin is a significant symbol for some of the key aspects of this article. Let me explain. On 25 March 2007, the members of the European Union celebrated the signing of the Treaty of Rome,[2] which eventually gave rise to the European Union with its 27 member states at present, at a special session of the European Council in Berlin. Berlin was a very suitable venue for this occasion as Berlin is the symbol of a transformed Europe that has overcome the Cold War. To mark this festive occasion, a new document was signed, namely the Berlin Declaration, that is intended to be a symbol of a new, united, but culturally diverse, socially and economically strong Europe. Berlin is thus a symbol of political, economic, social and cultural transformation for the European region in a global context.

Going back in time, Berlin is of course also important in the post World War II era, when the Cold War had so much influence, not only in Europe and America but also in Africa, as a result of the power struggle between the two superpowers. The Berlin Wall, that divided the city from 1961 to 1989, was a symbol of the Cold War, and the fall of the Berlin Wall in 1989 became a symbol of freedom in the world.

If we go even further back in time, to the late nineteenth century, we can mark another important milestone in the history of Berlin. On 26 February 1885, Berlin was the venue for the signing of another document, namely the General Act of the Conference of Berlin of 1885. Germany's Otto von Bismarck was the key architect and convenor of the Berlin-Congo Conference, which lasted from 15 November 1884 to 26 February 1885. This conference was called to try to settle the dispute about international navigation and commercial rights in the Congo basin in Central Africa. The conference also drew up some ground

---

[1] This is a revised version of a paper delivered at the International Academy of Practical Theology (IAPT) Conference "Secularization Theories, Religious Identity and Practical Theology" at the Humboldt-Universität zu Berlin, 31 March 2007.

[2] "The creation of the European Coal and Steel Community (ECSC) in 1951 laid the foundations for European unity. The Treaty of Rome, signed in 1957, established the European Economic Community (EEC) and the European Atomic Energy Community (Euratom). This marked the birth of the European Union." (www.bundesregierung.de)

rules for the "effective occupation" by the colonial powers of African territory. Although this was not intended at the start, the conference arbitrarily, and without consulting any of the indigenous people of the African continent, set the scene for the division of the African continent among the European colonial powers. This division was done without regard for the approximately two thousand ethnic groups in Africa or for the cultural and historical differences of this vast continent. It thus brought traditional enemies under the same government, and at the same time divided communities that belonged together. This has caused tensions and problems up to the present.[3]

If we put these dates in chronological order, we can see that this famous city is a symbol for the extreme insensitivity and haughtiness of the colonial era in the late nineteenth century, for the stalemate and tensions of the Cold War in the twentieth century, but also for optimism, dynamism and hope in the twenty-first century. It has been a witness to the changing political and economic landscapes of the modern era. In the history of the city of Berlin we see reflected some of the historical developments that are in the background of this article, namely the changing political landscapes: from pre-colonial to colonial and post-colonial states, and from nation-states to globally interconnected regions. Given the history of Berlin and its current status in the global world, it is a good place to consider the topic of this article: *Do we live in a secular world? An African perspective.*

Do we live in a secular world? This seemingly simple question has kept sociologists of religion and theologians very busy during the last decades. During the heyday of the grand narrative of secularization, few scholars would have answered this question in the negative. There seemed to be a consensus that we, or at least those in modernized countries, live in a secular world. This hegemony of secularization theory has, however, come to an abrupt end in the last decade or so. Religion today is still of public and political importance, despite predictions by secularization theorists in the second half of the twentieth century that religion would disappear from the public scene. After 9/11 we have even seen an increase of religious discourse in the public domain. Religious diversity, an important part of the diversity and pluralism of our times, seems to create problems in many parts of the world. The days are gone that the world religions could be related to specific geographical areas. The massive migrations of people in the twentieth century as well as the communication explosion have led to multifaith societies in many parts of the world. There are no longer oceans separating Christians from adherents of other faiths, and Christians, Muslims, Hindus, Sikhs and Buddhists rub shoulders on every street in Western countries, writes David Bosch.[4] Despite

---

[3] See http://www.thenagain.info/WebChron/Africa/BerlinConf.html.
[4] David Bosch, Transforming mission: paradigm shifts in theology of mission, Maryknoll, New York (Orbis) 1991, 475.

the processes of modernization and rationalization, religion and religious issues still seem to be part of the fabric of modern societies. There also seems to be a renewal of the traditional bond between religion and nationalism in certain societies, and an increase in the kind of religious expression associated with fundamentalist and national religious expansion and religious communities catering for racial, ethnic and social identities.[5] Even established democracies seem to struggle with religious plurality as part of their multicultural societies, as multiculturalism and religious diversity often go hand in hand. The question thus remains: Do we live in a secular world?

Religion is, however, not only attracting new attention from scholars as a result of the problems and conflicts in which it is involved. Although certain institutionalized forms of religion have declined in some parts of the world, especially Europe, we have also witnessed a rapid rise of religions in other parts of the world, especially in the Global South.[6] Carpenter writes with regard to Christianity that one of the "most important but least examined changes in the world over the past century has been the rapid rise of Christianity in non-Western societies and cultures. [...] Christian people and institutions in places such as Brazil, the Philippines, and Nigeria are engaging the personal, social, and political dimensions of life and seeking to redirect them in light of the Christian gospel."[7] Religion has not disappeared from the public scene as predicted, but seems to play an important role in modern societies. Again we can ask: Do we really live in a secular world?

We start in the next section with the first part of the topic, namely the question of whether we live in a secular world. In order to try to answer this question, I seek to develop a perspective on "the secular" from secularization theory and constitutional theory (section 2). Next we shift our attention to the second part of the title of the article, namely an African perspective. In section three we ask whether Africa is part of a secular world. In this section we explore the relation of state and religion in the African context from a historical perspective, and also consider the constitutions of African states with reference to religious freedom. This is followed by a reflection on the relation of religion and state in secular Africa (section 4). The article ends with a brief conclusion (section 5).

---

[5] Cho-Yee To/Witold Tolasiewicz, Conclusion, in: Witold Tolasiewicz/Cho-Yee To, eds., World religions and educational practice, New York (Cassell) 1993, 178; Bosch, 476.

[6] An intriguing fact of the academic debate whether we live in a secular world or not, whether modernization inevitably leads to secularization, whether Europe is the exception or whether the USA is the exception, is that the debate has centred almost exclusively on the "Western world", and more recently on the Western world in its relation to Islam and Islamic countries.

[7] Joel A. Carpenter, Preface, in: Lahmin Sanneh/Joel A. Carpenter, eds., The changing face of Christianity: Africa, the West, and the world, Oxford (Oxford University Press) 2005, vii.

38   Jaco S. Dreyer

2. A secular world? Theoretical perspectives

The answer to the question whether we live in a *secular* world is of course dependent on the meaning that we attach to the concept "secular." One way of exploring the meaning of this word is to look at the conceptual history of the term. This can be done through a study of all the meanings of the concept "secular" (a semasiological approach) or we can do a linguistic study of all the parallel or synonymous in a language for the same concept (an onomasiological approach).[8] In this article I follow another approach, namely to explore the meaning of "the secular" from two different theoretical perspectives. The main aim is not to discuss any of these perspectives or related theories in depth, but to construct a perspective on the concept "secular" that helps us to understand the continuing role of religion, both in its negative and positive forms, in a globalizing world at the beginning of the twenty-first century.

I start with the theoretical perspective implied by the theme of the IAPT's 2007 conference, *Secularization Theories, Religious Identity and Practical Theology*, namely secularization theory (section 2.1). Next we turn to a perspective that is not often discussed in practical theological research, namely a constitutional (legal) perspective (section 2.2). This section ends with a brief discussion of the main points that we distilled from these different theoretical perspectives (section 2.3).

---

[8] Melvin Richter, The history of political and social concepts: a critical introduction, New York (Oxford University Press) 1995, 47–48. Richter, 47, writes with regard to the concept secularization: "Research is necessary to determine whether a historical phenomenon such as secularization was designated by just one concept, by several concepts, or by a combination of concepts. If the investigator follows only one name for the concept, the results of such an inquiry may be incomplete of mistaken. The phenomenon of secularization may be understood in either a narrow or broad sense. Treated narrowly, it may be confined to the transfer of property from churches or church-connected orders to private individuals or the state; or it may also refer to the abolition of such orders. Treated more generally, the term 'secularization' may refer to the replacement of religious by secular motives, interests, or institutions." W. Clark Gilpin explains the use of the concept secularization as follows: "Academic employment of *secular* and related terms has gone through two phases. The first phase predominated in the middle decades of the twentieth century, and the second began in the late 1990s and gathered energy around Talal Asad's book of 2003, *Formations of the Secular: Christianity, Islam, Modernity*. In neither phase has the terminology been fully consistent – secularization, secularism, the secular – but most scholars have distinguished between secularization as a social process and secularism as a social or political philosophy." W. Clark Gilpin, Secularism: religious, irreligious, and areligious. The Religion and Culture Web Forum, March 2007, http://marty-center.uchicago.edu/webforum/032007/commentary.shtml.

2.1 Secularization theory

Browsing through the sociological literature on secularization, one is struck by the immense literature on this topic. Schultz, in a bibliographic essay on secularization, describes the history of secularization theory, from the classical theories of secularization (eg Comte, Durkheim, Weber), to second generation theoreticians (eg Berger, Cox, Dobbelaere, Luckmann), and to critics of secularization theory (eg Asad, Martin, Stark) and attempts to formulate a new theory (eg Casanova, Chaves, Norris & Inglehart, Smith, Stark & Finke).[9] Instead of such an overview of the "generations" of secularization theory, I take as starting point the syntheses of secularization theories by a leading secularization theorist, José Casanova.[10]

Casanova distinguishes three different meanings of secularization. He identifies the first, secularization as the decline of religious beliefs and practices in modern societies, as the most recent, but by now also the most widespread meaning attached to secularization. A second meaning is the privatization of religion. This privatization of religion is often seen both as an historical trend and as a normative condition for modern, liberal democratic democracies.[11] The third meaning is secularization as the differentiation of the secular spheres (state, economy, science); this is usually understood as the emancipation of these spheres from religious institutions and norms. This is, according to Casanova, the core meaning attached to secularization in the classic theory of secularization, and the one meaning that seems to be fairly widely accepted by sociologists, especially in Europe.[12]

---

[9] Kevin M. Schultz, Secularization: a bibliographic essay, in: The Hedgehog Review 8 (1–2), 2006, 170–177.

[10] José Casanova, Public religions in the modern world, Chicago (University of Chicago Press) 1994; Rethinking secularization: A global comparative perspective, in: The Hedgehog Review 8 (1–2), 2006, 7–22. Dobbelaere provides a similar synthesis. He relates the three core meanings of secularization to the macro or societal level (functional differentiation), the meso level (functional rationality and the reactions and changes in the religious system), and the micro level (the impact on the individual), and also discusses the relationship between the different levels. Karel Dobbelaere, Secularization: an analysis at three levels, Bruxelles (Peter Lang) 2004; Assessing secularization theory, in: Peter Antes/Armin W. Geertz/Randi R. Warne, eds., New approaches to the study of religion. Volume 2: Textual, comparative, sociological, and cognitive approaches, Berlin (Walter de Gruyter) 2004, 229–253.

[11] In his book *Public religions in the modern world*, Casanova (n. 10) has convincingly argued that secularization does not necessarily lead to privatization, that is, that there is no structural link between secularization and privatization of religion.

[12] Dobbelaere concludes that "secularization is only the particularization of the process of functional differentiation for the religious sub-system and a macro-level phenomenon." Dobbelaere, Assessing secularization theory (n. 10), 249.

40 Jaco S. Dreyer

Casanova identifies two key problems with regard to secularization theory.[13] The first problem is that these different analytical perspectives are not clearly distinguished. This leads to confusion, because some sociologists only work with the first meaning mentioned above, namely the decline in religious beliefs and practices, and this clearly does not fit the American scene. A second problem is that secularization theories are mainly formulated in Western societies and with reference to Christianity. The relation between modernity and secularization that became such a core assumption of secularization theory suited the European scene. However, Casanova maintains that it is the tendency to link secularization to modernization "rather than to patterns of fusion and dissolution of religious, political, and societal communities – that is, of churches, states, and nations – that is at the root of our impasse at the secularization debate".[14]

Let me elaborate a bit more on this last point. In the glory days of the "master narrative" of secularization, few questioned the core assumptions of this theory. The theory seemed to fit the European context well. From a historical perspective we can see that the process of institutional differentiation took place over a number of centuries in the European world. Of particular importance was the end of the religious wars in Europe in the seventeenth century after the signing of the Peace of Westphalia.[15] This marked the end of the Holy Roman Empire and the beginning of the modern era, characterized by a separation of church and state, the granting of religious freedom and the development of the nation-state. The secularization theories were an attempt by sociologists to explain this process and its outcome in the European context.[16] On the individual (micro) level, empirical studies confirmed that people were losing their traditional faith and beliefs, on an institutional (meso) level it became clear that religious institutions were pushed to the margins of society, and

---

[13] Casanova, Rethinking secularization, (n. 10).

[14] Casanova, Rethinking secularization (n. 10), 15. Casanova therefore prefers to follow S.N. Eisenstadt and to speak of "multiple modernities."

[15] "The Peace of Westphalia refers to the pair of treaties (the Treaty of Münster and the Treaty of Osnabrück) signed in October and May 1648 which ended both the Thirty Years' War and the Eighty Years' War. The treaties were signed on October 24 and May 15, 1648 and involved the Holy Roman Emperor Ferdinand III, the other German princes, Spain, France, Sweden and representatives from the Dutch republic. The Treaty of the Pyrenees, signed in 1659, ending the war between France and Spain, is also often considered part of the treaty" (Wikipedia).

[16] However, secularization theories were not only empirical theories, but also normative theories. In time, these theories were used by secular, liberal academics to also try and influence state policies, for example in the sphere of education. See: Christian Smith, Secularizing American higher education: the case of early American sociology, in: Christian Smith, ed., The secular revolution: power, interests, and conflict in the secularization of American public life, Berkeley (University of California Press) 2003, 97–159.

on a social (macro) level, religion was seen as no competition for the dominant systems such as the state and the economic sphere.[17]

Comparative research in the USA changed the scene. Traditional secularization theories did not fit the USA, one of the most modern and secular countries. Despite being modern and secularized, religion in America seemed to flourish and grow instead of losing ground. This started a debate among theorists of secularization as to whether the USA is the exception to the rule, or whether Europe is the exception. But people within Europe also started questioning some of the universal assumptions of secularization theory. It became clear that the different countries in Europe have institutionalized the relation between state and religion in different ways.[18] France, for example, differed very much from Germany and other European countries. Each nation-state has its particular political, social, economic, cultural and religious complexity and history. It also became clear that the particular religious tradition that dominated in a specific context (Protestant or Catholic) had a major impact on the way in which the relation between religion and state was institutionalized. Comparative research in other contexts, such as Latin America and the Islamic countries such as Turkey, also contributed to the undermining of the dominant paradigm of secularization theory. It thus became clear that classical secularization theory, as a universal theory of religious transformation, could not be maintained. A more historical and a less ideological use of secularization theory were called for.[19] Secularization must be conceived in all its variety on the local and contextual level, especially as it relates to specific nation-states.

This historical rather than ideological understanding of secularization opens up the possibility for understanding the continuing role of religion in modern societies. Secularization does not mean that religion is absent from a secularized society, but it is "the end of a certain kind of presence of religion or the divine in public space" writes Charles Taylor.[20] The historical unfolding of the nation-states indicates that God was no longer seen, at least by the elite of the

---

[17] Jos Pieper/Paul Vermeer, Religious consciousness of Dutch youth, in: Journal of Empirical Theology 14(2), 2001, 68.

[18] Matthias Koenig, Politics and religion in European nation-states: Institutional varieties and contemporary transformations, in: Bernhard Giesen/Daniel Šuber, eds., Religion and politics: cultural perspectives, Leiden (Brill) 2005, 291–315.

[19] The following statement by the well-known philosopher Paul Ricoeur echoes this sentiment: "[…] the religious as well as the political are tied to a history. Each of these histories is already complex, but their intersections make them even more so. I think that in order to examine problems tied to secularism, one must have a greater historical sense and a less ideological one." Paul Ricoeur, Critique and conviction: conversations with Francois Azouvi and Marc de Launay, Cambridge (Polity Press) 1998, 132.

[20] Charles Taylor, Modern social imaginaries, Durham (Duke University Press) 2004, 187.

42 Jaco S. Dreyer

societies, as the "action-transcendent grounding of society".[21] The idea of "higher time" disappeared, as all action is now taking place in secular time.[22] Politics was now seen as based on the common will of the people, and thus freed "from its ontic dependence on religion".[23] This opened new possibilities for religion in public life. Religion became part of the identities of people in the struggles that accompanied the intricate processes of the formation of nation-states. Taylor describes this as a shift "from the enchanted to the identity form of presence that set the stage for the secularity of the contemporary world, in which God or religion is not precisely absent from public space, but is central to the personal identities of individuals or groups, and hence always a possible defining constituent of political identities".[24]

2.2 Constitutional theory

One of the insights gained from the discussion about secularization theory is that the relation between religion and state is differently institutionalized in different political entities. We can thus gain insight in the way in which this relation is structured in a specific state by studying the constitution of that state. A constitution is a very important document for understanding the role and place of religion in a particular society because it is legally binding and it sets out the ground rules for dealing with religion in that state. Secondly, a constitution is important because it is, at least in theory, supposed to give expression to the values and sentiments, and thus also the religious values and sentiments, of the people of that state.

In this section we first look at different models of secular constitutions as discussed by Jacobsohn in *The wheel of law. India's secularism in comparative constitutional context*.[25] What does a secular state mean in terms of constitutional theory? Jacobsohn, in an insightful chapter in this book on "Nations and constitutions: dimensions of secular configuration", writes that secularization is a process "in which the various sectors of society are progressively liberated from their domination by religion; but the emphasis on separate spheres unnecessarily obscures the diversity among regimes that aspire to be constitutionally secular".[26] This implies that states can have different possible configurations of the relation between religion and politics, and still be considered as constitutionally secular. But what is a secular constitution? Jacobsohn describes a secular constitution as follows: "In reference to the secular consti-

---

[21] Taylor, Modern social imaginaries (n. 20), 186.

[22] Taylor, Modern social imaginaries (n. 20), 194.

[23] Taylor, Modern social imaginaries (n. 20), 187.

[24] Taylor, Modern social imaginaries (n. 20), 193–194.

[25] Gary J. Jacobsohn, The wheel of law: India's secularism in comparative constitutional context, Princeton (Princeton University Press) 2003.

[26] Jacobsohn, Wheel of law (n. 25), 27.

Do we live in a secular world? An African perspective 43

tution, what is meant is simply this: a polity where there exists a genuine commitment to religious freedom that is manifest in the legal and political safeguards put in place to enforce that commitment".[27] The constitutional guarantee of religious freedom thus seems to be the core of a secular constitution.

A secular constitution leaves room for different configurations of the relation of the political and the religious in different contexts. Jacobsohn argues that secular constitutions vary according to two main dimensions.[28] The first dimension is the "consequential dimension of religiosity", and this refers to the importance of religion ("thick" versus "thin") for the people and their well-being within a specific state. The second dimension is the "official cognizance of religion", that is, the extent ("partial" or "impartial") to which the State "is decisively identified with any particular religious group".[29] These two dimensions lead to four quadrants with three variations of a secular constitution (which he calls visionary, ameliorative and assimilative respectively) and one variation that is a nonsecular constitution. He describes an example of each of the secular constitution models: Israel for the visionary, the USA for the assimilative and India for the ameliorative model.[30]

Table 1: Configurations of secular constitutions[31]

	Sociocultural	consequence
Official cognizance	*Thick*	*Thin*
Partial	Nonsecular constitution (1)	Visionary constitution (2)
Impartial	Ameliorative constitution (3)	Assimilative constitution (4)

An important principle of these different models of secular constitutional design is that a constitution is not an abstract document unrelated to the society

---

[27] Jacobsohn, Wheel of law (n. 25), 28.

[28] Jacobsohn, Wheel of law (n. 25), 28-33.

[29] Jacobsohn, Wheel of law (n. 25), 29-30 states: "While government neutrality is thus key to this dimension, the formal identification of a State with a particular religion does not in itself remove the State from the category of secular regimes." He mentions Sweden as an example of a State that identifies with a particular religion (Lutheran Church), but that does not disqualify Sweden from being a secular state. However, if Sweden were to "become known as 'the Lutheran State,' and consistent with that description were it to distinguish in some of its policies and symbols between Lutherans and non-Lutherans, it would violate an essential requirement of liberal constitutionalism, but still admit of the possibility, as the Israeli example will show, of achieving a secular (albeit not unambiguously liberal) constitution."

[30] Jacobsohn mentions Iran as an example of a nonsecular constitutional model. Jacobsohn, Wheel of law (n. 25), 29.

[31] Adapted from Jacobsohn, Wheel of law (n. 25), 29.

44   Jaco S. Dreyer

for which it is formulated.[32] The "spirit of the laws" thus plays a role in constitutional design, and "expresses itself in contrasting constitutional approaches to
Church/State relations that reflect, either directly or through designed
confrontation, distinctive regime-defining attributes of nationhood [...] an
assimilative model manifests the ultimately decisive role of political principles
in the development of the American nation, a *visionary* model seeks to accommodate the particularistic aspirations of Jewish nationalism in Israel within
a constitutional framework of liberal democracy, and an *ameliorative* model
embraces the social reform impulse of Indian nationalism in the context of the
nation's deeply rooted religious diversity and stratification".[33]

For the sake of brevity we do not discuss the different models of secular constitution in more depth. The following important points can be made. Firstly,
these models are (ideally) rooted in the (religious) histories of the different contexts, and they therefore take the importance and functioning of religion in the
different contexts into account.[34] Secondly, this typology does not mean that
political assimilation, social amelioration and communal vision operate in isolation from each other, but in each case one of the characteristics is more in the
foreground in a particular secular constitution.[35] Thirdly, and most importantly,
the core of a secular constitution is a guarantee that religious freedom will be
protected.

It is this last point that has become very important in recent years, as a result of
the growing influence of human rights discourses. Human rights discourses
reflect the idea that the world is increasingly becoming a "global world" in
which the sovereignty of nation-states is relativized. An-Na'im says that
"normative propositions about human relations are now made on behalf of all

---

[32] Jacobsohn quotes Montesquieu who said that laws "should have relation to the degree of liberty which the constitution will bear; to the religion of the inhabitants, to
their inclinations, riches, numbers, commerce, manners, and customs." Jacobsohn,
Wheel of law (n. 25), 49.

[33] Jacobsohn, Wheel of law (n. 25), 50.

[34] "For the inhabitants of India, the imprint of religion is deeply etched in the patterns
of daily life, such that social structure and religious activity are indissolubly linked. For
the inhabitants of Israel, religious affiliation is imbued with a political meaning that
ultimately determines membership in the larger governing community. And for the
inhabitants of the United States, religion is an essentially voluntary activity that pervades the domain of private life, providing active as well as passive support for a
shared public theology. In all three countries, religious liberty is a principal, if heavily
contextualized, goal of constitutional interpretation, differently provided for in each
instance to mirror the socio-political conditions of the respective local setting." Jacobsohn, Wheel of law (n. 25), 50.

[35] Jacobsohn, Wheel of law (n. 25), 52.

Do we live in a secular world? An African perspective 45

human beings as such, rather than as citizens of particular states".[36] The relation between religion and politics is no longer only decided within the confines of a nation state. If human rights are violated, the international community has the right to step into the situation. This does not, however, mean that the state is not an important "actor" in this process. The state has firstly to freely ratify these international human rights treaties in order to be bound by their terms, and secondly it is the state's responsibility to implement the terms of the treaties in the area of jurisdiction.[37] To complicate matters, an individual who believes that his or her rights have been violated by the state or government officials has to take legal action against the state. This makes the legal protection of human rights dependent on factors such as access to legal services, an independent and effective judiciary, and compliance by government officials with court orders.[38] It is important, therefore, to consider the relation between religion and politics in the tension between the local and the global.

2.3 A secular world? Concluding remarks

What can we distil from these theoretical perspectives with regard to the question whether we live in a secular world? Let us start with the contribution of secularization theory. The main contribution of secularization theory, at least for the sake of this article, is the insight that it gives in the changing role and place of religion in the modern era on a macro or societal level. However, as critics of secularization theory have indicated, the theory has to be related to concrete political, economic, social and cultural processes in specific contexts. The modern state provides a starting point for such research, as this is the context on a macro level where policies are made that influence the role and place of religion in a specific context. It is here that constitutional theory helps us to understand the different ways in which the relation between religion and state

---

[36] Abdullahi Ahmed An-Na'im, Introduction: Competing claims to religious freedom and communal self-determination in Africa, in: Abdullahi Ahmed An-Na'im, ed., Proselytization and communal self-determination in Africa, Maryknoll New York (Orbis) 1999, 14.

[37] An-Na'im, Introduction (n. 36), 14–15.

[38] An-Na'im, Introduction (n. 36), 17. The focus on individual human rights is especially problematic in Africa where people do not have the resources to challenge the state in court. An-Na'im writes: "[...] this model is not only limited, exclusive, expensive, and inaccessible to most Africans whose human rights are routinely violated by officials as well as nonofficial actors, but it is also incapable of redressing the type and scope of violations most frequently suffered by Africans. Recent experiences with genocide and ethnic cleansing, massive forced population movements, increasingly unequal economic and political power relations, unpayable national debt, and coercive structural adjustment programs in Africa make an exclusive focus on individual human rights unrealistic, if not counterproductive." An-Na'im, Introduction (n. 36), 17.

46   Jaco S. Dreyer

can be structured in the modern world. But we also see today that we have to move beyond the macro level of the modern state to the level of the global village, as religion and politics are no longer confined to specific territories and states. We therefore have to see the local in relation to the global in order to understand the transformation of religion in the modern world.

3. Is Africa part of a secular world?

> We have overcome the force of darkness that was Apartheid. We now have a constitution that is one of the most forward looking and progressive constitutions in the world. The Apartheid state was a white Christian nationalist state. Our democratic state is a secular state. As citizens of the Republic of South Africa each and everyone [sic] of us has inalienable rights which no one can take away from us. Our secular state will ensure that these rights are fully protected. Included in these rights is the freedom to practise our religion, sustain and nourish our beliefs and cultural practices and revere our chosen symbols and legends of humanity.[39]

In the previous section we have taken the view that the question of whether we live in a secular world can be answered by analyzing the situation in different nation-states. We have further argued that an important criterion of a secular society is whether religion has lost its role as an umbrella system[40] and has become a subsystem in the public sphere. Another important indicator of a secular state is the constitution of a country. Although there are different types of constitutions, a state can be regarded, from a legal perspective at least, as secular if the constitution provides for freedom of religion. A state that only allows one religion as state religion, and actively discriminates against other religions, is a theocracy and not a secular state.

In this section we now turn to Africa, the vast continent that covers 20% of the land surface on earth, and which consists of 53 states with approximately 700-800 million people. It is usually divided into the following regions: North Africa, West Africa, East Africa, Central Africa, and Southern Africa. Africa is known for its great ethnic, cultural and religious diversity, with approximately two thousand ethnic groups, more than two thousand different languages[41] and

---

[39] Mr J.S. Ndebele, the MEC for transport in the province of Kwazulu-Natal and founder and chairperson of the African Renaissance Trust. Joel Sibusiso Ndebele, Keynote address at the opening of the "Durban Diwali Festival" at the Bay of Plenty, Durban, 21 October 2000, http://www.kzntransport.gov.za/speeches/2000/21-10-2000.htm.
[40] Pieper & Vermeer, Religious consciousness (n. 17), 67.
[41] About 374 different languages are spoken in Nigeria alone. See: Commission for Africa, Our common interest. Report of the Commission for Africa, 2005, source: http://www.commissionforafrica.org/english/report/thereport/english/11-03-05_cr_report.pdf, 126.

Do we live in a secular world? An African perspective

a huge variety of religions and religious movements.[42] It is clearly not possible to give any kind of representative point of view of the continent as a whole. What are presented here are only very general ideas, without sufficient regard for contextual differences.

An intriguing fact of the academic debate whether we live in a secular world or not, whether modernization inevitably leads to secularization, whether Europe or the USA is the exception, is that the debate has centred almost exclusively on the Western world, and more recently on the Western world in its relation to Islam and Islamic countries. But what is the situation in Africa, the continent that is so easily dismissed as "dark Africa"? On the basis of our theoretical deliberations in the previous section we shall try to determine whether Africa is, or more particularly whether the different states in Africa are, secular. First, we give a very brief historical sketch of Africa (section 3.1). This historical background is important for understanding the development of states in Africa, and also for understanding the role of religion in African societies that we will consider in section four of this article. In this brief overview we also consider the relation between religion and state in colonial and post-colonial Africa in order to gain some insight in the role of religion in the political history of Africa. Secondly, we briefly consider religious freedom in Africa, especially with regard to the constitutions of African states, in order to gain insight into the secular nature of Africa at the beginning of the twenty-first century (section 3.2). This section ends with a few concluding remarks (section 3.3).

3.1 From colonial to independent Africa

The history of Africa stretches back many millions of years. On the basis of paleontological and archaeological evidence, Africa is often regarded as the cradle of humankind. In this article we shall not try to give an overview of the early history of Africa. Our focus is rather on the "modern" history of Africa that started with the colonialization of Africa. This was, however, not the first challenge to the freedom of Africans. Ekeh refers to the conquering of North Africa and the Sahara by Arabs from the seventh to the eleventh centuries.[43]

---

[42] Rosalind I.J. Hackett, Prophets, "false prophets," and the African state: emergent issues of religious freedom and conflict, in: Phillip C. Lucas/Thomas Robbins, eds., New religious movements in the twenty-first century: legal, political, and social challenges in global perspective, New York (Routledge) 2004, 151–178. The Commission for Africa draws attention to this huge diversity in Africa, and warns: "At the very least, although it may occasionally be convenient to make generalised statements about 'Africa', it is essential to pay constant regard to the continent's diversity." Commission for Africa, Our common interest (n. 41), 126.

[43] Peter P. Ekeh, Keynote address. Civil society and the construction of freedom in African history, in: Ebere Onwudiwe, ed., African perspectives on civil society. A Report of the Second Wilberforce Conference on Africa held in cooperation with the Associa-

48   Jaco S. Dreyer

The Arab slave trade (950–1850) and the European slave trade (1480–1850) left severe scars on the peoples of the African continent. In these centuries of slave trade, "kinship provided its members worthy sanctuary from persecution from forces of the state," writes Ekeh. The Age of Discovery from the early fifteenth to the eighteenth century by European explorers was followed by the period of European imperialism (1880–1960). On the eve of this period that became known as the "scramble for Africa", only ten percent of Africa was under colonial control. Within a decade of the Berlin-Congo conference in 1884–1885, only a few settlements in Africa were independent from colonial masters, and in 1902 90% of the African continent was under European control, the main colonial powers being Great Britain, France, Belgium, Spain, Italy, Germany and Portugal.[44]

The European rulers set up a variety of administrations in Africa. In some parts of Africa, for example British West Africa, there was a low level of colonial control. In other colonies, Europeans came to settle temporarily or permanently. However, in most areas colonial administrations did not have the manpower or resources to fully administer the territory. They therefore had to rely on local power structures to help them. This often led to a situation whereby "factions and groups within the societies exploited this European requirement for their own purposes, attempting to gain a position of power within their own communities by cooperating with Europeans".[45]

Missions were one of the three "agencies of the colonial machinery", writes Sindima, the others being commerce and government.[46] The history of colonial Africa testifies to the often symbiotic relationship between the missionary enterprise and the governmental administration in these colonies. Missionaries were important for the government for a number of reasons, among them to legitimize the colonial rule, to educate people for service in government, and to break down the African value systems and ritual practices such as ancestor veneration.[47] In return, the government provided security for missionaries and

---

tion of Nigerian Scholars for Dialogue, New York (Tri-Atlantic Books) 1998, http://www.waado.org/nigerian_scholars/archive/pubs/triatlantic1.html.

[44] See articles on "History of Africa", "Berlin Conference", "Scramble from Africa" and "Decolonization of Africa" from Wikipedia contributors in Wikipedia, the online encyclopaedia, http://en.wikipedia.org/.

[45] See http://en.wikipedia.org/wiki/History_of_Africa.

[46] Harvey J. Sindima, Religious and political ethics in Africa: a moral enquiry, Westport Connecticut (Greenwood Press) 1998, 1. Van der Veer says that the transformation of the religious domain by the missionaries played a central role in colonialism and nationalism. Peter van der Veer, Introduction, in: Peter van der Veer, ed., Conversion to modernities: the globalization of Christianity, New York (Routledge) 1996, 7.

[47] Sindima has the following to say about the mission school: "The mission school was a critical institution for both missionaries and the government. It was through schools that missionaries and colonial administrators launched an onslaught on African value

Do we live in a secular world? An African perspective 49

missions. State and religion, or more precisely, government and church, also shared the same belief, namely that they had "to 'civilize the backward people of Africa' through true religion and principles of civilization".[48] There was thus, with some exceptions, a harmonious relationship between religious and governmental institutions in colonial Africa. Missionaries even acted as representatives of African interests in legislative councils. The colonial period was in general characterized by a lack of participation by African clergy in political life.[49] Sindima writes that churches in Africa had been slow to identify with the people's struggle for dignity and freedom.[50]

With a few exceptions, religion was also used to keep the people of Africa subservient, accepting their position and obeying the civil authorities.[51] However, the missionaries clearly acted in their own self-interest and with a view to their own future. Sindima writes that when it became clear that Africans would not be stopped from achieving independence, the missionaries turned around and were suddenly concerned about the African condition and even supported political parties.[52]

What is the legacy of the colonial era with regard to the relation between state and religion? Longman, in an article on church politics and the genocide in Rwanda, mentions three key principles that were established in Rwanda during the colonial period.[53] Firstly, missionaries became involved in the country's

---

systems and ritual practice. [...] The school was the right place to begin to instil that fear and hate for African values, customs and the past – attitudes that became characteristic of educated and alienated Africans." Sindima, Religious and political ethics (n. 46), 2.

[48] Sindima, Religious and political ethics (n. 46), 3. Smidt argues that Immanuel Kant, through his descriptions of Africa, Africans and African religions paved the way for the colonialization of Africa by providing them with an "'understanding' of Africans, which, instead of making his followers more prudent, gave them great confidence into the superiority of Europe and Europe's 'civilizing mission'." Wolbert Smidt, Fetishists and magicians – the description of African religions by Immanuel Kant (1724–1804), in: Frieder Ludwig/Afe Adogame, eds., European traditions in the study of religion in Africa, Wiesbaden (Harrassowitz Verlag) 2004, 110.

[49] Sindima mentions a few exceptions: The Malawian martyr John Chilembwe, Ndabaning Sithole, and Bishop Abel Muzorewa. Sindima, Religious and political ethics (n. 46), 6.

[50] Sindima, Religious and political ethics (n. 46), 5.

[51] Birgit Meyer, Modernity and enchantment: The image of the devil in popular African Christianity, in: Van der Veer, Conversion to modernities (n. 46), 203–207. Sindima, Religious and political ethics (n. 46), 4.

[52] Sindima, Religious and political ethics (n. 46), 5.

[53] Timothy Longman, Church politics and the genocide in Rwanda, in: Journal of Religion in Africa 31, 2, 163–186.

political struggle, and tried to make churches important actors in this struggle.[54] Secondly, churches became actively involved in ethnic politics and the establishment of fixed ethnic identities. It was part of the missionary approach to target the "elite" for conversion, and on the basis of the then current conceptions of race they divided the different groups in rigid racial categories. The missionaries thus regarded "the Twa as a 'pigmoid' group, less intelligent and more 'savage'; the Hutu as Bantu, simple, solid and hardworking; and the Tutsi as Hamitic, more closely related to Europeans and naturally more intelligent".[55] These ethnic categories became the basis for the colonial administration of Rwanda and Burundi, and continued to play an important role in the genocide in Rwanda. A third principle that was established during the colonial period was that churches provided not only spiritual resources to converts, but also economic and cultural resources.[56] Converts benefited from education and health care provided by the churches, and many of them eventually also became employed by the churches. The resources of the churches thus also created power struggles within the churches.[57] These three principles can probably also be generalized to other parts of Africa. The significance of these principles lies in the fact that they influence the politics of these African states up to today.

Although colonial Africa cannot be regarded as secular in the modern, legal sense of the word, the missionaries played an important role in the seculari-

---

[54] Longman concludes in this regard: "Christian churches were thus established during the colonial period not simply as allies of the government but as important players in contestation for state power." Longman, Church politics (n. 53), 168.

[55] Longman, Church politics (n. 53), 168. Longman writes: "Both because they saw Tutsi as the established elite who needed to be appeased and because they believed in the natural superiority of Tutsi, missionaries initially offered educational and employment opportunities overwhelmingly to Tutsi." Due to education and the opportunities presented by the church, Tutsi's entered the priesthood. After the World War II, Catholic missionaries repeated this mistake by fostering a Hutu "counter-elite" in order to address the inequalities in Rwandan society. The Hutu counter-elite came into political power after the 1959 revolution. Longman says that although the church support shifted from Tutsi to Hutu, "the churches' participation in political struggles and engagement in ethnic politics remained consistent." Longman, Church politics (n. 53), 169.

[56] Meyer, writing about the socio-economic motivations for and consequences of conversion, says: "Indeed, the Christian religion was attractive because it offered the material means to achieve a prosperous and relatively high position in colonial society." Meyer, Modernity and enchantment (n. 51), 207.

[57] "In short, churches as they developed in colonial Rwanda were centres of political contestation where people struggled for influence and access to resources. Churches had patrimonial structures and factions that competed for power, and, though church groups were often involved in struggles over state power, the status of churches as political institutions should not be understood exclusively in relation to the state, because the primary political struggles within the churches concerned the distribution of power *within* the churches themselves." Longman, Church politics (n. 53), 170.

Do we live in a secular world? An African perspective 51

zation of Africa. The establishment of government structures, of educational and health centres contributed to the differentiation of the different subsystems, including religion, in society. Samarin writes that one "should have to rank Christian missions as the greatest secularizing force in Africa" due to the role of educational institutions and medical services provided by the missionaries.[58]

The drive for independence of Africa from their colonial masters already started in the early twentieth century. Ekeh writes that by "the 1930s and 1940s, a handful of freedom fighters had arisen in Africa to question the authority of European imperialism".[59] Freedom from colonial rule became the major driving force of resistance in those decades. In the 1950s the African nations started gaining independence from their colonial masters. However, freedom from colonial masters quickly turned into oppression from the new rulers. African countries also became pawns on the chessboard of the West and the Soviet Union, and many countries experienced military *coups d'état*. However, with the fall of the Berlin Wall a new era started in Africa.

Since the 1990s we have witnessed an increasing democratization of the African continent, with elections being held and new initiatives formulated to hold governments accountable.[60] Initiatives by African people themselves, such as NEPAD and the formation of the new African Union, indicate the resolve of the people of the African continent to be part of the global political and economic world. In the Constitutive Act of the African Union of 2000, the Heads of State and Government say that they are determined "to promote and protect human and peoples' rights, consolidate democratic institutions and culture, and to ensure good governance and the rule of law" and that they are further determined "to take all necessary measures to strengthen our common

---

[58] William J. Samarin, Religion and modernization in Africa, in: Anthropological Quarterly 39, 4, 288–297; here 295.

[59] Ekeh, Keynote address (n. 43).

[60] Gifford writes: "In the late 1980s, at the time of the end of the cold war, Africa experienced the beginning of a second liberation, as the peoples of Africa tried to throw off the political systems that had increasingly oppressed and beggared them." Paul Gifford, Introduction: Democratisation and the churches, in: Paul Gifford, ed., The Christian churches and the democratisation of Africa, Leiden (Brill) 1995, 1–13; here 1.
Mule mentions a number of "successes" in Africa in recent times, and writes that "in the 1990s there has been a major expansion of political space in many African countries. Civil liberties and popular participation in political processes have improved. In 42 of 48 African countries there have been multi-party presidential and parliamentary elections. The second success therefore is the opening up of the political space and the expansion of civil and individual liberties to the majority of Africans." Harris Mule, Challenges to African governance and civil society, in: Public Administration and Development 21, 2001, 71–76; here 72f.

institutions and provide them with the necessary powers and resources to enable them discharge their respective mandates effectively".[61]

There are also a number of significant new initiatives, such as that of the Commission for Africa, the Joint EU-Africa Strategy and the UN Millennium Development Goals. The Commission for Africa reports for example on the progress that has been made by African governments in tackling the lack of effective policies, actions and systems: "They are now working more closely together, through the African Union, to tackle this. Some 24 countries, representing 75 per cent of Africa's population, have so far signed up to an initiative by the African Union's NEPAD programme to establish an African Peer Review Mechanism where a country puts itself forward for scrutiny by its peers to help identify its weaknesses and the actions needed to correct them. The aim is to foster adoption of good policies and practice by sharing information on what is working, and what is not".[62]

What can we conclude at the end of this section with regard to the first "indicator" that we formulated above, namely that a secular state is one that is characterized by the differentiation of the state (government), the legal system, civil society, educational and health systems, and so forth? I think it is clear that despite weaknesses and limitations, the states in Africa in general qualify to be called "secular" in the sense that we elaborated on in the previous section.

3.2 Secular constitutions and religious freedom in Africa

In the previous section we argued that an important indicator of the secular status of a state is whether there is a secular constitution that legally guarantees religious freedom in a country. It is possible that a country can enshrine religious freedom in a constitution without really putting it into practice.[63] We cannot therefore rely only on the constitutions of states in order to determine whether religious freedom actually exists in a country. However, referring to religious freedom in a constitution gives some weight to the importance of this freedom for a state. In the words of the constitutional expert Van der Vyver: "Although the same legal protection afforded to an aspect of religious freedom by the constitution of a particular state may also be found in legislation other

---

[61] African Union, The Constitutive Act, 2000, http://www.africa-union.org/root/au/AboutAu/Constitutive_Act_en.htm.

[62] Commission for Africa, Our common interest (n. 41), 33.

[63] "The constitution of a country does not accurately reflect the state of religious freedom in that country. Many issues pertinent to religious freedom may be regulated in other statutory enactments, and implementation of constitutional principles through extra-constitutional instruments may take a turn, or involve detail, not reflected in the constitution itself." Johan D. van der Vyver, Religious freedom in African constitutions, in: An-Na'im, Proselytization (n. 36), 109–143; here 109.

Do we live in a secular world? An African perspective 53

than the constitution of another state, having afforded constitutional protection to that aspect would indicate the special significance attached to religious freedom in the first mentioned state".[64]

Do we have African states with secular constitutions?[65] It is interesting to note that 83% of the constitutions of African states provides for freedom of religion[66] (see Table 2 below), and the rest of the states, with the exception of Somalia and Libya which have no constitutions at present, and Eritrea where the constitution has not yet been implemented,[67] make provision for freedom of religion with some reservations. Some countries, especially in North Africa, refer in their constitutions to being "Muslim states," but they guarantee religious freedom subject to certain conditions, and some explicitly proclaim the secularity of the state.[68] There seems to be in general a clear distinction between state and religion, and Van der Vyver therefore claims that, except in Muslim countries, "the notion of an established religion no longer finds favor in African states".[69]

Table 2: Freedom of religion in African constitutions and in practice

	In constitution	In practice
Yes	83% (n=44)	62% (n=33)
Partly	11% (n=6)	23% (n=12)
No	6% (n=3)	15% (n=8)

---

[64] Van der Vyver, Religious freedom (n. 63), 109.

[65] I do not use Jacobsohn's typology of different types of secular constitution in this section as this is not really the focus of this article. The main point is whether African states have secular constitutions, and not the type of these secular constitutions.

[66] This statistic is based on the 2006 report of the U.S. Department of State on the 53 African states. The report itself classifies Algeria, Egypt, Libya, Morocco and Tunisia under the category "Near East and North Africa," but I include them here under the category of African states. U.S. Department of State, Report on international religious freedom, 2006, http://www.state.gov/g/drl/rls/irf/2006/.

[67] The U.S. Department of State's report on religious freedom says with regard to Somalia that there "is no constitution and no legal provision for the protection of religious freedom". With regard to Libya it reports that the country "does not have a constitution, and there is no explicit legal provision for religious freedom. However, a basis for some degree of religious freedom is provided in the Great Green Charter on Human Rights of the Jamahiriya Era, dated December 6, 1988," and with regard to Eritrea that the "constitution, written in 1997, provides for religious freedom; however, the constitution has not been implemented." U.S. Department of State, Report (n. 66).

[68] Van der Vyver, Religious freedom (n. 63), 110–118.

[69] Van der Vyver, Religious freedom (n. 63), 118.

The promise of religious freedom in the constitutions does not necessarily imply that religious freedom is also put into practice as we indicated above.[70] That is the situation with regard to the actual practice of the freedom of religion in these African states? Table 2 gives a summary of the results based on the 2006 Report on the state of Religious Freedom by the U.S. Department of State.[71] Religious freedom seems to be generally respected by the governments of 62% of the African states.[72] In almost a quarter of the states freedom of religion is partly respected, with some restrictions on specific religious groups or specific religious practices. In eight (15%) of the African states there seems to be no or very limited respect for freedom of religion.

3.3 Is Africa part of a secular world? Concluding remarks

What can we conclude with regard to the question whether African states are secular or not? On the basis of the political and economic developments in Africa we can conclude that African states in general are characterized by differentiation of the subsystems of state, economics, law, religion, education, health care, and so forth. They thus satisfy our first criterion for status as secular states. The analysis of the situation with regard to the freedom of religion as reflected in the constitutions of the African states, as well as in practice, also supports the notion that the majority of African states are secular in nature.

4. Religion and state in secular Africa

"Hawking and Preaching Prohibited by Management"
Sticker in Kenyan municipal buses[73]

In the previous section we concluded that the majority of African states are secular states according to the "indicators" that we use in this article, namely differentiation of the public sphere, with religion as a subsystem among other subsystems, and a secular constitution that protects freedom of religion. From our deliberations in section two above it is clear, however, that the relation

---

[70] Lipton writes in the Preface of the book *Religious freedom in Africa*: "Human rights, of which the freedom of religion is a central component, are promised by most governments on planet Earth. But promises are promises, are promises. In real life, religious liberty is far from a universal fact." Edward P Lipton, Religious freedom in Africa, New York (Nova Science Publishers) 2002.

[71] U.S. Department of State, Report (n. 66).

[72] In most of these cases the report states: "The constitution provides for freedom of religion, and the government generally respected this right in practice." U.S. Department of State, Report (n. 66).

[73] Quoted in Katharina Hofer, Implications of a global religious movement for local political spheres: Evangelicalism in Kenya and Uganda, Baden-Baden (Nomos), 2003, 10.

between religion and state can be institutionalized in very different ways in secular societies. Different nation-states have different constructions of secular space and different institutional arrangements regarding politics and religion.[74] These variations can be attributed to aspects such as the type of modern polity (statist/republican, liberal, state corporatist or social corporatist), the religious demographics of a specific context (majority versus minority religions; Catholic versus Protestant; Islam versus Christianity), the composition of the population of a specific area (including different ethnicities), the history of a specific context (for example the role of missionaries in a specific context) and so forth. We also saw that constitutions are "living documents" that should in some way reflect the history, ethos and composition of a specific context.

Let me illustrate this by an example from my own context, South Africa. The history of the intersection of religion and the state in South Africa is unique. Due to the Reformed view of the state as an extension of the church, the state was seen as under God's reign during the Apartheid years. This view of the relationship between state and church changed drastically with the adoption of the new constitution of South Africa in 1996, with its Bill of Rights. South Africa became a secular state, as the quotation by Ndebele at the beginning of section three clearly states.[75]

Being a secular state did not, however, make the South African state antireligious. This is clearly demonstrated in the work of the Truth and Reconciliation Commission (TRC) during 1996–1998 and the appointment of a religious leader, Archbishop Desmond Tutu, as its chairperson. The work of the TRC was also characterized by a religious-redemptive narrative and the Commission often drew from Christian theology in formulating its moral positions.[76] The new government also turned to religions and religious leaders for assistance in rebuilding the country, specifically with regard to "moral regeneration". In June 1997 President Nelson Mandela met religious leaders to discuss a partnership in the rebuilding and social transformation of South African society and to foster tolerance. A direct consequence of this meeting was the formation of the National Religious Leaders' Forum (NRLF). This group of interfaith religious leaders usually meets the president bi-annually and has come to be the forum that the state interacts with regarding religious matters.

A further development of this partnership between the government and the religious sector was the signing of a "Memorandum of understanding" between

---

[74] König, Politics and religion (n. 18).
[75] Ndebele, Keynote address (n. 39).
[76] Richard A. Wilson, The politics of truth and reconciliation in South Africa: legitimizing the post-Apartheid state, Cambridge (Cambridge University Press) 2001, 103.

56   Jaco S. Dreyer

the NRLF and the government.[77] In the preamble of this Memorandum it is stated that the government recognizes that the challenge to eradicate poverty and underdevelopment is such that the government needs the assistance of civil society, the private sector and faith based organisations. The nature of the partnership is described as "programme-based" and each sector undertakes to take responsibility for "specific niche projects where each sector can contribute in terms of its comparative advantage".

What does this say about the relation between state and religion in South Africa? In terms of the different models for the relation between state and religion,[78] it is clear that the South African state does not identify with one particular religion (theocratic model), it does not suppress religion (repressionist model), it does not completely divorce state and religion (separationist model), but it affirms both the legal separation of religion and state and constitutional impartiality towards religion (co-operative model).[79]

What is the situation in the other African states? Although there seems to be in general a positive relation between state and religion in many African states, conflict between state and religion in some of the African states is also evident.[80] Deng, in an article "Scramble for souls: Religious intervention among

---

[77] Memorandum of Understanding between Government of the Republic of South Africa and the National Religious Leaders' Forum (NRLF), 2005. (Copy of the document provided to the author by the President's Office.)

[78] Venter writes that "being a secular state allows for various 'modalities of state conduct regarding religion' and infinite variations on these modalities." Francois Venter, Religious freedom in South Africa, Paper presented at the conference "Public law themes in South Africa and Germany," Stellenbosch, South Africa, 8–10 September 2005, http://law.sun.ac.za/publawconf/papers/FVenter/Religious_Freedom.pdf.

[79] One of the best examples of this choice of model for the relation of state and religion in the "new" South Africa is the new Policy on Religion and Education that was adopted in 1998 after extensive consultation. In the introduction to the policy on religion and education, as published in the Government Gazette of 12 September 2003, it is clearly stated that the new policy is in accordance with the values of the South African Constitution (Act 108 of 1996). A clear distinction is also made between teaching about religion and religions and religious instruction and religious nurture. Teaching about religion is an educational responsibility in public education, but religious instruction and religious nurture should be provided by the home, family and religious community. The relation between religion and the state underlying the policy is also clearly stated in the introduction to the policy. The four models mentioned above are introduced and the choice is made for a co-operative model, in which "both the principle of legal separation and the possibility of creative interaction are affirmed." This model thus combines constitutional separation and mutual recognition. Department of Education, National policy on religion and education, Pretoria (Government Printer), 2003.

[80] Mutua specifically mentions Nigeria and Sudan as two African states that "have particularly been ravaged by religious conflict between Muslims and Christians in the contexts of the struggles for group autonomy and the control of the political state." Makau

Do we live in a secular world? An African perspective 57

the Dinka in Sudan," discusses for example the divisive role of the state and the state policies of Arabization and Islamization in Sudan.[81] He describes three patterns of religious intervention in the Sudan that, although not strictly sequential, have moved from "the private and informal processes of early Islamization, through the Christian missionary activities, carried out in a context of separation of state and religion, to the postcolonial promotion of the Islamic agenda that has now culminated in the military Islamic regime of the National Islamic State, which is dedicated to the establishment of an Islamic state".[82] It is not possible to give an overview of the different histories and policies in all the African states, but it underlines the conclusion that we reached at the end of section two, namely that nation-states are important entities in our considerations about religion in a secular world, and that different contexts have very different histories regarding the relation of state and religion.

Although we cannot provide details of the "modalities of state conduct regarding religion"[83] for each African state, we can draw attention to another important aspect in the relation of religion and state in the African context: that religion becomes in a sense an extension of government by delivering services that the state cannot provide.[84] In the report of the Commission for Africa it is stated that the growth of many religious movements in Africa is directly related to this issue: "Where the state can no longer deliver, religious movements are gaining a new attractiveness".[85] The report also refers to Africa's informal networks and specifically the role of religious networks.[86] These networks provide not only spiritual support, but also economic and social support, and they therefore play a very important role in the daily struggle for survival in the harsh world of Africa.[87] The reason suggested for the growth of these religions and

---

Mutua, Returning to my roots: African "Religions" and the state, in: An-Nai'im, Proselytization (n. 36), 169–190; here 184.

[81] Francis M. Deng, Scramble for souls: Religious intervention among the Dinka in Sudan, in: Na'im, Proselytization (n. 36), 191–227.

[82] Deng, Scramble for souls (n. 81), 222.

[83] See Venter, Religious freedom (n. 78).

[84] The Commission for Africa mentions the following example of service delivery: "In the Congo, because there is no working national postal service, people leave letters in Catholic churches to be transmitted to other parts of the Congo since the Church is the only reasonably coherent nationwide infrastructure." Commission for Africa, Our common interest (n. 41), 31.

[85] Commission for Africa, Our common interest (n. 41), 31.

[86] Commission for Africa, Our common interest (n. 41), 126–129.

[87] "Religious beliefs, movements and networks cross the lines between material and spiritual experience. They affect all aspects of how people live, including the social, economic and political parts of their lives. Indeed, many Africans voluntarily associate themselves with religious networks for purposes that go beyond a strictly religious aspect. Religion provides the means by which to understand and adjust to conflict and

58 Jaco S. Dreyer

religious networks thus seems to support the thesis of Karner and Aldridge, that religions seem to respond to the "economically induced 'survival anxiety'" that characterizes the processes of globalization.[88]

The growth of religion in Africa[89] can be hypothesized to be related to social, political and economic globalization. Social globalization, for example, has facilitated large-scale migrations of people, and has increased their interaction with different religions. It is interesting to note that religion often plays an important role for migrants as part of their identities and of their adaptation to a new context. Political globalization leads, for example, to an increase in an awareness of the civil, economic, political and judicial rights of people. The right to freedom of religion, for example, creates spaces for people to practise their religions without fear of prosecution. Economic globalization causes major insecurity and anxiety on a psychological level, and a daily struggle for survival for millions of people around the world. Religion is one way, perhaps the most important way, for many people to cope with the results of economic globalization. One can also theorize that the important role of religion in an African context is the result of a combination of all the different aspects of globalization. Migrants, for example, are often desperately poor, and struggle to construct their identities in a harsh, unfriendly political, economic and social environment.[90]

---

tragedy such as AIDS. It provides language of hope and aspiration. These networks are also plugging Africa into globalisation." Commission for Africa, Our common interest (n. 41), 128.

[88] "Thus we return to a founding theme in the sociology of religion. However, the explanatory direction of the Weberian paradigm is now inverted: *In place of the economic consequences of doctrinally induced 'salvation anxiety' during early capitalism, we are now confronted with economically induced 'survival anxiety,' for which religions appear capable of offering some form of antidote.*" Christian Karner/Alan Aldridge, Theorizing religion in a globalizing world, in: International Journal of Politics, Culture and Society 18, 1, 2004, 5–32; here 11. This also lends some support to Norris and Inglehart's theory of existential security and secularization which links secularization and human development. Pippa Norris/Ronald Inglehart, Sacred and secular: religion and politics worldwide, Cambridge (Cambridge University Press) 2004.

[89] Karner and Aldridge write in this regard about the "widely documented contemporary religious revivalism" that "spans continents as much as traditions," a "de-privatization" of religion, a global "desecularization of the world", "an increase in anti-secular movements and discourses disenchanted with the project of modernity and insistent on the political potential and public role of religious beliefs and practices." Karner/Aldridge, Theorizing religion (n. 88), 11–12.

[90] Asad, writing about Muslims in Europe, says for example: "Too often in post-Enlightenment society 'to tolerate' differences simply implies not taking them seriously. This has certainly been the attitude behind religious toleration bequeathed to the modern secular state by the European Enlightenment. But it is no longer adequate to regard 'religion' simply as a type of *private belief.* In a political world where everyone

Do we live in a secular world? An African perspective

An important phenomenon is the growth and influence of religious networks in Africa. These religious networks do not only provide a response to or a way of coping with economic, political and social globalization. They are themselves part of these globalization processes. Two examples in particular stand out in this context. The first example is the proliferation of Non-Governmental Organizations (NGOs) and Faith-Based Organizations (FBOs) on the African continent. A second example is the remarkable growth of Evangelical (Pentecostal) Christianity in Africa.[91] These transnational movements not only offer "new ways of being modern in a religious idiom,"[92] but they also become part of transnational political processes. Despite their remarkable adaptation to local contexts, they are also embedded in larger, transnational economic, political and social globalization processes. The ingenious use of the modern electronic mass media by these groups also increases the potential for conflict.[93]

How do we evaluate the above from the perspective of the relation between state and religion? On the positive side, one can appreciate the growth of religion and religious networks and of the opportunities for religion and religious institutions to become involved in the daily struggle for survival of the people of Africa and the human development of these people.[94] The African Religious Health Assets Programme (ARHAP) network[95] provides an excellent example of the positive role that religion and religious institutions can play in dealing with the scourge of HIV/Aids on the African continent. These initiatives are therefore certainly to be applauded.

There seems to be, unfortunately, also a negative side to these developments from the perspective of the relation between state and religion. These initiatives are not politically neutral, and thus often provide opportunities for becoming part of a struggle for political power. Norris and Inglehart write, for example, that in "many poor societies, where religion is central to society, authoritarian rulers have a direct interest in promoting or controlling religious institutions in

---

is said to have the right to construct himself or herself, 'religion' is now also a base *for publicly contested identities*. As such it is at the very center of democratic politics, from which only the most determined anti-democratic power can keep it out." Talal Asad, Europe against Islam: Islam in Europe, in: Ibrahim M. Abu-Rabi', ed., The Blackwell companion to contemporary Islamic thought, Malden (Blackwell Publishing) 2006, 302–312; here 311.

[91] Alan Anderson, New African Initiated Pentecostalism and Charismatics in South Africa, in: Journal of Religion in Africa 35, 1, 2005, 66–92.

[92] Brian Larkin/Birgit Meyer, Pentecostalism, Islam & culture: new religious movements in West Africa, in: Emmanuel Kwaku Akyeampong, ed., Themes in West Africa's history, Athens (Ohio University Press) 2006, 286–312; here 308.

[93] Larkin/Meyer, Pentecostalism (n. 92), 310.

[94] Ignatius Swart, The churches and the development debate: perspectives on a fourth generation approach, Stellenbosch (SUN Press), 2006.

[95] See http://www.arhap.uct.ac.za/.

60 Jaco S. Dreyer

order to maintain their power and legitimacy".[96] Hackett also refers to the growing potential for conflict due to, among other things, the increasing religious pluralisation in Africa, the increase in religious revivalism and militancy, and the "growing tendency to frame socio-political insecurities and economic failures in terms of satanic and occult forces".[97] It is in particular the minority religious groups and the New Religious Movements (NRMs) in Africa that are at risk.[98] Ironically, democracy and the global emphasis on human rights and religious freedom are among the factors that create space for the "new phase of inter-religious and religion-state tensions taking shape across Africa".[99]

Religion has not disappeared from public life in secular Africa. This is evident on both the "grassroots level," where religion plays an important role in the lives of millions of Africans on a daily basis, and the global level, where African religion has become part of global networks. However, the new space taken up by religion in modern, secular societies as theorized by Taylor[100] and referred to above, namely that of providing identity in a modern and global world, is certainly also true for Africa. This new space of religion in a modern, secular Africa provides many opportunities for religion to play a positive role. The downside is that this new space for religion in a modern, secular Africa also provides opportunities for religion to be exploited in power struggles based on religion, class, race, gender and all the other boundaries that are continually being revived by those in power or those seeking power.

5. Conclusion

We started with the context of the 2007 IAPT conference, namely Berlin, and we conclude with Berlin. Berlin is not only famous for political reasons. Berlin is important for practical theologians for another reason. It was the place where the great theologian Friedrich Schleiermacher worked as pastor and academic at the beginning of the eighteenth century. Schleiermacher was such an influential pastor, theologian and leader in the cause of social and political reform that his death did not go unnoticed in Berlin. Brandt describes the funeral procession as follows:

---

[96] Norris/Inglehart, Sacred and secular (n. 88), 230.
[97] Hackett, Prophets (n. 42), 151–152.
[98] Hackett, Prophets (n. 42), 170. Hackett also refers to the importance of power relations within the different nation-states, especially with regard to the NRMs: "Treatment of and attitudes towards these groups serve as important pointers to the differential power relations within each nation-state and reflect popular cultural attitudes of religious tolerance and intolerance." Hackett, Prophets (n. 42), 170–171.
[99] Hackett, Prophets (n. 42), 169.
[100] Taylor, Modern social imaginaries (n. 20).

> The funeral procession for pastor and theologian Friedrich Schleiermacher included a line of mourners on foot, stretching over a mile in length. Behind these mourners on a cold February day in 1834 came some 100 horse-drawn coaches; in the first of these rode Friedrich Wilhelm III (1770–1840), King of Prussia, along with his son, the crown prince, six years later to be Wilhelm IV (1795–1861). And lining the streets were additional masses of people, conservatively estimated at 20,000 to 30,000. Clearly, some organization had gone into this event, but according to contemporary witnesses, it was even more – a spontaneous expression on the part of the people of Berlin, meant to honor the one who had died.[101]

In this quotation we see represented both the religious and the political. Schleiermacher was known not only for his contribution to the establishment of theology and practical theology as academic disciplines,[102] but also for his social engagement. His view of the task of practical theology, namely to reflect on the rules of Christian leadership, was not only concerned with practical theology as an academic discipline; it was also concerned with society and societal issues. In short, his theory of Christianity focused not only on the church, but on the church within modern society.

The work and ideas of Schleiermacher could thus inspire us to reflect on the implications of our research for religion, and more particular for churches and church leadership, in our global and secular societies. More specifically, we have to consider what the implications are for churches in secular African contexts. I only mention a few pointers.[103] We can start with the enormous challenges presented by the inadequate functioning of civil society in many African states, with states that are not functioning and that only provide for the elite of the countries, with poor governmental policies, and so forth. But we should not stop there. I think one of the major challenges for churches is to function as an example in secular society of how power could be used in a responsible way, how to deal with plurality, and how the divisions that still cause so much disruption in the lives of the majority of Africans could be overcome. The role of church leaders in this regard is of particular importance. Another very important challenge for churches is to take part in the grassroots

---

[101] James M. Brandt, Schleiermacher's social witness, in: Currents in Theology and Mission, 2003, http://www.thefreelibrary.com/Schleiermacher's+social+witness-a099699732.

[102] For an exposition of Schleiermacher's understanding of practical theology as a discipline, see Wilhelm Gräb, Practical theology as theology of religion. Schleiermacher's understanding of practical theology as a discipline, International Journal of Practical Theology 9, 2, 2005, 181–196. Gräb writes: "Friedrich Schleiermacher is the founding father of practical theology as one of the disciplines of theological studies." Gräb, Practical theology, 181.

[103] Casanova provides an excellent overview of the challenges that face religions and religious institutions in a modern, secular world. Casanova, Public religions (n. 10), 211–234.

development of the societies in which they are located. This is a massive challenge for churches in Africa as a result of the general lack of human development. Churches can play an important role in two areas where they have always played an important role in Africa, namely education and healthcare. However, the way in which churches become involved is crucial.[104] Only a participatory approach, that treats all human beings with respect, must be followed. In all of this we must not forget to attend to the vitality of our congregations.[105] All these aspects pose enormous challenges for practical theological education and training in Africa, not only with regard to the content of these educational programmes, but also the infrastructure, as many of the pastors and leaders of the churches in Africa are inadequately trained.

Do we live in a secular world? I think most of us do, at least in the sense that I outline "the secular" in this article. Instead of lamenting the fact that we live in a secular world, I think we should be grateful for the space that a secular world provides for the continuation and transformation of religion in public life.

The Author

Jaco S. Dreyer, Dr. theol., born 1961, is an Associate Professor in the Department of Practical Theology of the University of South Africa. His current research examines religion and modernisation in sub-Saharan Africa. He is a co-author of "Is there a God of human rights? The complex relationship between human rights and religion: A South African case" (2004).

---

[104] Fergusson says churches have to develop a differentiated approach for its contribution to public life "which leads no neither domination, nor cultural captivity, nor isolation." David Fergusson, Church, state and civil society, Cambridge (Cambridge University Press) 2004, 164.

[105] Casanova maintains that the ability of religion to contribute to civil society depends on the vitality of its congregational life. Casanova, Public religions (n. 10), 224. Fergusson says that religions have to combine public effectiveness with private appeal. Fergusson, Church (n. 104), 162.

Grace Davie

Why is Europe the most secularized continent?[1]

A number of factors must be taken into account if we are to understand the place of religion in twenty-first-century Europe.[2] These include the legacies of the past, more particularly the role of the historic churches in shaping European culture; an awareness that these churches still have a place at particular moments in the lives of modern Europeans, even though they are no longer able to discipline the beliefs and behavior of the great majority of the population; an observable change in the churchgoing constituencies of the continent, which operate increasingly on a model of choice, rather than a model of obligation or duty; and the arrival in Europe of groups of people from many different parts of the world, notably the global South, with very different religious aspirations from those seen in the host societies.

Each of these factors will be taken in turn in order to answer the question set out in the title: is Europe an exceptional case in terms of its patterns of religious life? The answer leads in turn to more questions. If we conclude that Europe is indeed "exceptional," why is this so? Or, conversely, why not? And what can we say about the future? Will Europe continue within the trajectory set by its past or will it become more like the patterns found elsewhere? Or – it must be asked – will the rest of the world become more like Europe?

Cultural Heritage

Two points are important in relation to the role of the historic churches in shaping European culture; the Christian tradition is indeed a crucial element in

---

[1] This essay first appeared in The Hedgehog Review's double issue "After Secularization," vol. 8, no. 1–2 (Spring/Summer 2006): 23–34. Its original title was: "Is Europe an Exceptional Case?" The editors are grateful to the review for their generosity.

[2] Overviews of the place of religion in European societies can be found in Gerhard Robbers, ed., State and Church in the European Union (Baden-Baden: Nomos Verlagsgesellschaft, 1996); René Rémond, Religion and Society in Modern Europe (Oxford: Oxford University Press, 1999); Andrew M. Greeley, Religion in Europe at the End of the Second Millennium: A Sociological Profile (London: Transaction, 2003); John Madeley and Zsolt Enyedi, eds., Church and State in Contemporary Europe: The Chimera of Neutrality (London: Frank Cass, 2003); Hugh McLeod and Werner Ustorf, eds., The Decline of Christendom in Western Europe (Cambridge: Cambridge University Press, 2003); and in the publications emerging from the European Values Study, listed on the frequently updated EVS website www.europeanvalues.nl/index2/htm. Alongside these overviews, there is a rapidly growing literature on the presence of Islam in Europe; see Jorgen Nielsen, Muslims in Western Europe (Edinburgh: University of Edinburgh Press, 2004) for a useful summary of this material.

64   Grace Davie

the evolution of Europe, but it is by no means the only one. O'Connell identifies three formative factors or themes in the creation and re-creation of the unity that we call Europe: Judeo-Christian monotheism, Greek rationalism, and Roman organization.[3] These factors shift and evolve over time, but their combinations can be seen in forming and reforming a way of life that we have come to recognize as European. The religious strand within such combinations is self-evident.

One example will suffice: the Christian tradition has had an irreversible effect on the shaping of time and space in this part of the world. Both week and year, for instance, follow the Christian cycle, even if the major festivals are beginning to lose their resonance for large sections of the population. Or to put the same point in a different way, we have had heated debates in parts of Europe about whether or not to shop on Sundays. We do not, for the most part, consider Friday an issue in this respect—though this may change. The same is true of space. Wherever you look in Europe, there is a predominance of Christian churches, some of which retain huge symbolic value. This is not to deny that in some parts of Europe (notably the larger cities) the skyline is becoming an indicator of growing religious diversity. Europe is changing, but the legacies of the past remain deeply embedded in both the physical and cultural environment.

Vicarious Religion

Physical and cultural presence is one thing; a "hands-on" role in the everyday lives of European people quite another. Commentators of all kinds agree that the latter is no longer a realistic aspiration for the historic churches of Europe. That does not mean, however, that the churches have entirely lost their significance as markers of religious identity. In my own work, I have explored this continuing ambiguity through the concept of "vicarious religion."[4]

By vicarious, I mean *the notion of religion performed by an active minority but on behalf of a much larger number, who (implicitly at least) not only understand, but, quite clearly, approve of what the minority is doing.* The first half of the definition is relatively straightforward and reflects the everyday meaning of the term – that is, to do something on behalf of someone else (hence the word "vicar"). The second half is more controversial and is best explored by means of examples. Religion, it seems, can operate vicariously in a wide variety of ways: churches and church leaders perform ritual on behalf of others; church

---

[3] James O'Connell, The Making of Modern Europe: Strengths, Constraints and Resolutions, University of Bradford Peace Research Report no. 26 (Bradford: University of Bradford, 1991).
[4] Grace Davie, Religion in Modern Europe: A Memory Mutates (Oxford: Oxford University Press, 2000).

Why is Europe the most secularized continent? 65

leaders and churchgoers believe on behalf of others; church leaders and church-goers embody moral codes on behalf of others; churches, finally, can offer space for the vicarious debate of unresolved issues in modern societies. Each of these propositions will be taken in turn in order to demonstrate the fruitfulness of looking at European religion from this point of view.

The least controversial of the above list concerns the role of both churches and church leaders in conducting ritual on behalf of a wide variety of individuals and communities at critical points in their lives. The most obvious examples can be found in the continuing requests, even in a moderately secular society, for some sort of religious ritual at the time of a birth, a marriage, and, most of all, a death. In many parts of Europe, though not in all, the demand for the first two of these diminished sharply in the later decades of the twentieth century. The same is not true with respect to churches' services at the time of a death. It is at this point, if no other, that most Europeans come into direct contact with their churches and would be deeply offended if their requests for a funeral were met with a rejection. A refusal to offer either a funeral liturgy or appropriate pastoral care would violate deeply held assumptions.

Exactly the same point can be made the other way round. It is perfectly pos-sible to have a secular ceremony at the time of a death; de facto, however, rela-tively few people do this. Much more common is what might be termed a "mixed economy" funeral—that is, a liturgy in which the religious professional is present and the Christian structure maintained but filled with a variety of ex-traneous elements, including secular music or readings and, with increasing fre-quency, a eulogy rather than a homily. Princess Diana's funeral in September 1997 offers an excellent example. Churches, moreover, maintain vicariously the rituals from which a larger population can draw when the occasion de-mands it, and whilst that population anticipates a certain freedom in ritual ex-pression, they also expect the institutional structures to be kept firmly in place.

But churches and church leaders do more than conduct ritual: they also believe on behalf of others. And the more senior or visible the role of the church leader, the more important it becomes that this is done properly. English bishops, to give but one example, are rebuked (not least by the tabloid press) if they doubt in public; it is, after all, their "job" to believe. The most celebrated, and not entirely justified, case of a "doubting bishop" in the Church of England was that of David Jenkins, Bishop of Durham from 1984 to 1994.[5] To a large extent the controversy turned on a frequently misquoted statement concerning the Resurrection. The phrase "not just a conjuring trick with bones" quickly

---

[5] Shortly after David Jenkins' consecration in York Minster, the building was struck by lightning, an event that was seen by some as a sign of divine displeasure. This episode was given extensive press coverage at the time (July 1984). See also David Jenkins' own account in The Calling of a Cuckoo (London: Continuum, 2002).

turned into the opposite, for which the Bishop was widely pilloried. The cultural expectation, in other words, is that bishops believe. When they doubt, something quite clearly has gone amiss.

Similar pressures emerge with respect to behavioral codes: religious professionals (both local and national) are expected to uphold certain standards of behaviour – not least, more rather than less traditional representations of family life – and incur criticism when they fail, from outside churches as well as within. It is almost as if people who are not themselves participants in church life want the church's representatives to embody a certain social and moral order, thereby maintaining a way of living that has long since ceased to be the norm in the population as a whole. Failure leads to accusations of hypocrisy but also to expressions of disappointment (interestingly, royal divorces provoke a similar reaction). Such expectations become at times unreasonable, particularly in relation to the partners and children of religious personnel; it is hardly surprising that clergy families come under strain. The pressures on the Catholic priest are somewhat different, given the requirement of celibacy, but in their own way they are equally demanding.

A final possibility with respect to vicariousness develops this point further, and more provocatively. Could it be that churches offer space for debate regarding particular, and often controversial, topics that are difficult to address elsewhere in society? The current debate about homosexuality in the Church of England offers a possible example, an interpretation encouraged by the intense media attention directed at this issue – and not only in Britain. Is this simply an internal debate about senior clergy appointments in which different lobbies within the church are exerting pressure? Or is this one way in which society as a whole comes to terms with profound shifts in the moral climate? If the latter is not true, it is hard to understand why so much attention is being paid to the churches in this respect. If it is true, sociological thinking must take this factor into account. Either way, large sections of the European media are, it seems, wanting to have their cake and eat it too, pointing the spotlight at controversies within the church whilst maintaining that religious institutions must, by their very nature, be marginal to modern society.

Social scientific observers of the scene cannot afford to make a similar mistake. The public attention displayed in the examples set out above demands that we understand how religious institutions matter even to those who are not "participants" in them (in the conventional sense of the term). That, moreover, is the norm in European societies – a situation rather different from that found in the United States. Indeed, in a decade of lecturing across both Europe and the U.S., I have seldom met an audience in the former who do not immediately grasp the notion of vicariousness and its implications for the European scene. This is much less the case in the United States, where the connections between the population and their religious organizations are very differently understood. There

Why is Europe the most secularized continent? 67

are exceptions, but to act vicariously is not part of American self-understanding.[6]

Herein, moreover, lies an important explanation for the "exceptional" nature of Europe's religion. It derives from a particular history of state-church relationships, out of which grows the notion of a state church (or its successor) as a public utility rather than a private organization. A public utility is available to the population as a whole at the point of need and is funded through the tax system. Precisely that combination remains in place in the Lutheran countries of Europe. Elsewhere both constitutional and financial arrangements have been modified (sometimes radically), but the associated mentalities are, it seems, more difficult to shift.

From Obligation to Consumption

The changing nature of churchgoing in modern Europe is important to understand, and to do so, one must clarify the constituency: here are Europe's diminishing, but still significant churchgoers – those who maintain the tradition on behalf of the people described in the previous section. And here an observable change is taking place: from a culture of obligation or duty to a culture of consumption or choice. What until somewhat recently was simply imposed (with all the negative connotations of this word), or inherited (a rather more positive spin), becomes instead a matter of personal choice: "I go to church (or to another religious organization) because I want to, maybe for a short period or maybe for longer, to fulfill a particular rather than a general need in my life and where I will continue my attachment so long as it provides what I want, but I have no obligation either to attend in the first place or to continue if I don't want to."

As such, this pattern is entirely compatible with vicariousness: "the churches need to be there in order that I may attend them if I so choose." The "chemistry," however, gradually changes, a shift that is discernible in both practice and belief, not to mention the connections between them. There is, for example, an easily documentable change in the patterns of confirmation in the Church of England. The overall number of confirmations has dropped dramatically in the post-war period, evidence once again of institutional decline. In England, though not yet in the Nordic countries, confirmation is no longer a teenage rite of passage, but a relatively rare event undertaken as a matter of personal choice by people of all ages. Indeed, there is a very marked rise in the proportion of adult confirmations among the candidates overall – up to 40 percent by the mid-1990s (by no means enough, however, to offset the fall among teenagers). Confirmation becomes, therefore, a very significant event for those individuals

---

[6] Grace Davie, "Vicarious Religion: A Methodological Challenge," Religion in Modern Lives, ed. Nancy Ammerman (New York: Oxford University Press, 2006).

who choose this option, an attitude that is bound to affect the rite itself – which now includes the space for a public declaration of faith. Confirmation becomes an opportunity to make public what has often been an entirely private activity. It is increasingly common, moreover, to baptize an adult candidate immediately before the confirmation, a gesture which is evidence in itself of the fall in infant baptism some twenty to thirty years earlier. Taken together, these events indicate a marked change in the nature of membership in the historic churches, which become, in some senses, much more like their non-established counterparts. Voluntarism (a market) is beginning to establish itself de facto, regardless of the constitutional position of the churches. Or to continue the "chemical" analogy a little further, a whole set of new reactions are set off that in the longer term (the stress is important) may have a profound effect on the understanding of vicariousness.

The trends are considerably more visible in some parts of Europe than in others. There is, for instance, a marked parallel between the Anglicans and the Catholic Church in France in this respect: adult baptisms in the Church of England match very closely those in France – indeed, the similarity in the statistics is almost uncanny, given the very different ecclesiologies embodied in the two churches (one Catholic and one Protestant).[7] But it is precisely this shift across very different denominations that encourages the notion that something profound is taking place. Lutheran nations, however – despite their reputation for being the most secular countries in Europe – still stick to a more traditional pattern as far as confirmation is concerned, though the manner in which they do this is changing. Large numbers of young people now choose the option of a confirmation camp rather than a series of weekly meetings.[8] In making this choice, confirmation becomes an "experience" in addition to a rite of passage, implying a better fit with other aspects of youth culture.

The stress on experience is important in other ways as well. It can be seen in the choices that the religiously active appear to be making, at least in the British case. Here, within a constituency that is evidently reduced, two options stand out as disproportionately popular. The first is the conservative evangelical church – the success story of late twentieth-century churchgoing, both inside and outside the mainstream. These are churches that draw their members from a relatively wide geographical area and work on a congregational, rather than parish, model. Individuals are invited to opt in rather than opt out, and membership implies commitment to a set of specified beliefs and behavioral codes. For significant numbers of people, these churches offer firm boundaries, clear guidance, and considerable support – effective protection from the vicissitudes of life. Interestingly, however, it is the softer charismatic forms of

---

[7] Davie, Religion in Modern Europe, 71–2.
[8] The figures for confirmation stay particularly high in Finland.

Why is Europe the most secularized continent? 69

evangelicalism that are doing particularly well; old-fashioned Biblicism, relatively speaking, is losing its appeal.

Very different and less frequently recognized in the writing about religion in modern Britain (as indeed in Europe) is the evident popularity of cathedrals and city-center churches. Cathedrals and their equivalents deal with diverse constituencies. Working from the inside out, they are frequented by regular and irregular worshippers, pilgrims, visitors, and tourists, though the lines between these groups frequently blur. The numbers, moreover, are considerable – the more so on special occasions, both civic and religious. Hence, concerns about upkeep and facilities lead to difficult debates about finance. Looked at from the point of view of consumption, however, cathedrals are places that offer a distinctive product: traditional liturgy, top-class music, and excellence in preaching, all of which take place in a historic and often very beautiful building. A visit to a cathedral is an aesthetic experience, sought after by a wide variety of people, including those for whom membership or commitment presents difficulties. They are places where there is no obligation to opt in or to participate in communal activities beyond the service itself. In this respect, they become almost the mirror image of the evangelical churches already described.[9]

What then is the common feature in these very different stories? It is the experiential or "feel-good" factor, whether this be expressed in charismatic worship, in the tranquility of cathedral evensong, or in a special cathedral occasion (a candlelit carol service or a major civic event). The point is that we feel something; we experience the sacred, the set apart. The purely cerebral is less appealing. Durkheim was entirely correct in this respect: it is the taking part that matters for late modern populations and the feelings so engendered.[10] If we feel nothing, we are much less likely either to take part in the first place or to continue thereafter.

New Arrivals

The final factor in this complicated mosaic is somewhat different: the growing number of incomers in almost all European societies. There have been two stages in this process. The first was closely linked to the need for labour in the expanding economies of post-war Europe – notably in Britain, France, Germany, and the Netherlands. Wherever possible, each of these countries looked to its former empire to expand its workforce: Britain to the West Indies and the Indian sub-continent, France to the Mahgreb, Germany (with no empire) to

---

[9] The attraction of cathedrals and city-center churches is closely related to the growth in pilgrimage across Europe; see Davie, Religion in Modern Europe, 156–62.
[10] See in particular Emile Durkheim, The Elementary Forms of Religious Life (1912; London: Harper Collins, 1976).

Turkey and the former Yugoslavia, and the Netherlands to its overseas connections (Indonesia and Surinam), but also to Morocco. The second wave of immigration occurred in the 1990s and included, in addition to the places listed above, both the Nordic countries and the countries of Mediterranean Europe (Greece, Italy, Spain, and Portugal) – bearing in mind that the latter, until very recently, have been countries of emigration rather than immigration. The turnaround has been truly remarkable – the sharpest illustration of all being the transformation in the 1990s of Dublin, Ireland, from a relatively poor city to a thriving, expensive, and increasingly diverse place to live.[11]

Different host societies and different countries of provenance have led to a complex picture – generalization is dangerous. Some points are, however, common to most, if not all, cases. It is important to remember that those who are arriving in Europe are coming primarily for economic reasons – they are coming to work. If the first wave provided labour for expanding industrial economies, the second filled a rather different gap. As the twentieth century drew to a close, Europeans were becoming increasingly aware that there were insufficient numbers to employ in Europe to support the rising proportion of dependent people – notably the growing number of retired. The pull factor in this case is the shifting demographic profile in Europe. A second point follows from this: all is well, or relatively well, as long as there is sufficient work for everyone in an economy able to maintain the services necessary for incoming populations. All is less well when there is a downturn in the economy (as happened in the late 70s and 80s) or when those who work to support dependent Europeans become dependent themselves. Hence the unrest in France in the autumn of 2005: a population excluded both from the economy itself, and from its concomitant benefits, expressed its frustration on the streets.

What, though, are the implications for the religious life of Europe? The short answer is that they vary from place to place depending on both host society and new arrivals. Britain and France offer an interesting comparison. In Britain immigration has been much more varied than in France, both in terms of provenance and in terms of faith communities. West Indians, for example, are Christians – and much more formed in their Christianity than their British equivalents. One result of this is the vibrant Afro-Caribbean churches of Britain's larger cities – some of the most active Christian communities in the country.[12] From the sub-continent, moreover, come Sikhs and Hindus as well as a sizeable number of Muslims (1.5 million). Britain is also a country where

---

[11] In terms of its religious life, Ireland is in many respects a "Mediterranean" country. It is also very like Poland, insofar as Catholicism has become a marker of national identity.

[12] There is a negative side to this story. For a variety of reasons, among them racism, Afro-Caribbeans were largely excluded from mainstream churches when they first arrived in Britain, an episode that the historic churches have come to regret bitterly.

Why is Europe the most secularized continent?

ethnicity and religion criss-cross each other in a bewildering variety of ways (only Sikhs and Jews claim ethno-religious identities). The situation in France is very different: here immigration has been largely from the Maghreb, as a result of which France has by far the largest Muslim community in Europe (between 5 and 6 million) – an almost entirely Arab population. Rightly or wrongly, "Arab" and "Muslim" have become interchangeable terms in popular parlance in France.

Britain and France can be compared in other ways as well – an exercise that provokes some interesting questions, among them the tensions between democracy and tolerance. France, for example, is markedly more democratic than Britain on almost all institutional or constitutional measures. France is a Republic, with a secular state, two elected chambers, and no privileged church (in the sense of connections to the state). There is a correspondingly strong stress on the equality of all citizens whatever their ethnic or religious identity. Hence, France holds a strongly assimilationist policy towards incomers, with the express intention of eradicating difference – individuals who arrive in France are welcome to maintain their religious belief and practices, provided these are relegated to the private sphere. They are actively discouraged from developing any kind of group identity. Exactly the same point can be put as follows: any loyalty (religious or otherwise) that comes between the citizen and the state in France is regarded in negative terms. The result, whether intended or not, is a relative lack of tolerance, if by tolerance is meant the freedom to promote collective as well as individual expressions of religious identity – that is, those expressions that impact the public as well as the private sphere.

Britain is very different. On a strict measure of democracy, Britain fares less well than France – with no written constitution, a monarchy, a half-reformed and so far unelected House of Lords, and an established church. More positively, Britain has a more developed tradition of accommodating group identities (including religious identities) within the framework of British society, a feature that owes a good deal to the relatively greater degree of religious pluralism that has existed in Britain for centuries rather than decades. Hence a markedly different policy towards newcomers: the goal becomes the accommodation of difference rather than its eradication. Rather more provocative, however, are the conclusions that emerge if you look carefully at who, precisely, in British society is advocating religious as opposed to ethnic toleration. Very frequently it turns out to be those in society who do not depend on an electoral mandate: the royal family, significant spokespersons in the House of Lords (where other faith communities are well represented by appointment, not by election), and prominent members of the established Church. The latter, in

72   Grace Davie

fact, become the protectors of "faith" in general rather than the protectors of specifically English expressions of Christianity.[13]

One further point is significant and reflects a shift that is taking place right across Europe. The growing presence of other faith communities in general, and of the Muslim population in particular, is challenging some deeply held European assumptions. The notion that faith is a private matter and should, therefore, be proscribed from public life – notably from the state and from the education system – is widespread in Europe (not only in France). Conversely, many of those who are currently arriving in this part of the world have markedly different convictions, and offer – simply by their presence – a challenge to the European way of doing things. Reactions to this challenge vary from place to place, but at the very least, European societies have been obliged to reopen debates about the place of religion in public as well as private life – hence the heated controversies about the wearing of the veil in the school system and about the rights or wrongs of publishing material that one faith community in particular finds offensive. The repercussions of the now famous (or infamous) Danish cartoons are a case in point.[14] The lack of comprehension on both sides of this affair, together with an unwillingness to compromise, led alarmingly fast to dangerous confrontations, both in Europe and beyond.

Such episodes raise a further point which, if developed, could become an article in its own right. That is the extent to which the secular elites of Europe use these events in order to articulate an ideological alternative to religion. The point to grasp in the space that remains in this paper is that such elites – just like their religious alter-egos – vary markedly from place to place. The fact that the cartoons were first published in Denmark was not simply a coincidence; nor was the insistence on the part of the media in some countries rather than others (most notably France) that the cartoons should be repeatedly republished in order to affirm the freedom of speech. Such attitudes have historical roots. France, for example, is the European society where the Enlightenment has been most obviously configured as a freedom from belief, an attitude which finds expression in the democratic, though not always very tolerant, institutions already described. In the United States, the Enlightenment becomes something very different: a freedom to believe. A developed treatment of this theme would reveal, however, that other European societies (much of Northern

---

[13] For a more detailed presentation of this argument, including the discussion of specific examples, see Grace Davie, "Pluralism, Tolerance and Democracy: Theory and Practice in Europe," The New Religious Pluralism and Democracy, ed. Thomas Banchoff (New York: Oxford University Press, 2007).

[14] The cartoons were first published in the autumn of 2005 and reprinted in many parts of Europe in the early months of 2006. The depictions of Mohammed were considered derogatory by many sections of the Muslim community; for most Europeans, they were simply "cartoons."

Europe, Germany, and Italy) fall somewhere between the two. Europe as ever is far from homogeneous.

Concluding Remarks

Several things are happening simultaneously in the religious life of Europe. The fact that they are occurring at the same time is partly a coincidence – each, however, encourages the other. The historic churches, despite their continuing presence, are losing their capacity to discipline the religious thinking of large sections of the population (especially the young). Simultaneously, the range of religious choice is widening all the time both inside and outside the historic churches. New forms of religion are coming into Europe from outside, largely as the result of the movement of people. Finally, at least some of the people arriving from outside are offering a significant challenge to the widely held assumptions about the place of religion in European societies.

It is equally clear that at least some aspects of exceptionality can be pursued by framing these statements in the form of questions, and by looking carefully at their implications for the religious life of Europe. For example: is Europe likely to produce a religious market like that found in the United States? The turn from obligation to consumption could be seen in this light. Conversely: is the residue of the state church sufficiently strong to resist this – maintaining thereby the notion of religion as a public utility rather than a freely chosen voluntary activity? And where in these complex equations do we place the newly arrived populations, whether Christian or not?

The answers must be tentative, but I will offer three; the last takes the form of a cautious prediction about the future of religion in Europe.

There are effectively two religious economies in Europe, which run alongside each other. The first is an incipient market, which is emerging among the churchgoing minorities of most, if not all, European societies, and in which voluntary membership is becoming the norm, de facto if not de jure. The second economy resists this tendency and continues to work on the idea of a public utility, in which membership remains ascribed rather than chosen. In this economy opting out, rather than opting in, remains the norm and is most visible at the time of a death. Interestingly, the two economies are in partial tension, but also depend upon each other – each fills the gaps exposed by the other. Exploring these tensions offers a constructive route into the complexities of European religion in the twenty-first century.

Religion will increasingly penetrate the public sphere, a tendency driven largely by the presence of Islam in different parts of Europe. Paradoxically, in many ways this is easier for the active, increasingly voluntarist, Christian minorities to understand than those who remain passively attached to their (public) historic churches. For the former, seriously held belief leads to public implications; for the latter, seriously held belief is seen as a threat rather than an opportunity.

The religious situation in Europe is and will remain distinctive (if not exceptional), given the legacies of the past. It is not, however, static. Clearly things are changing, and in some places very fast. Exactly how they will evolve is not easy to say, but I will conclude by making a cautious and three-fold prediction – the first part is tentative, the second more certain, and the third increasingly evident. First – I think that vicarious religion will endure at least until the mid-century, but maybe not for much longer. It follows that the actively religious in Europe will increasingly work on a market model, but the fact that their choices will include the historic churches complicates the issue (the alternatives are not as mutually exclusive as they first appear). Second – I know that the presence of Islam is a crucial factor that we ignore at our peril. Not only does it offer an additional choice, but it has become a catalyst of a much more profound change in the religious landscape of Europe. Finally, the combination of all these factors will increase rather than decrease the salience of religion in public, as well as private, debate – a tendency encouraged by the ever more obvious presence of religion in the modern world order. In this respect, the world is more likely to influence the religious life of Europe than the other way round.

The Author

Grace Davie has a personal Chair in the Sociology of Religion in the University of Exeter. In addition to numerous chapters and articles, she is the author of Religion in Britain since 1945 (Blackwell 1994), Religion in Modern Europe (OUP 2000), Europe: the Exceptional Case (DLT 2002) and The Sociology of Religion (Sage 2007); she is co-editor of Predicting Religion (Ashgate 2003) and co-author of Religious America, Secular Europe (Ashgate 2008).

Secularization Theories, Religious Identities, and Practical Theology:
Practical Theology and Secularization

Riet Bons-Storm

**Beyond the obsession with guilt and atonement.
Towards a theology of blessing and its implications for our practices**

Re-sacralization and the empty churches

We hear it everywhere: we live in a secularized world. Nevertheless P.L. Berger speaks of the "de-secularization of the world" (Berger, 1999). Paul Avis speaks of "the re-sacralization of life, the persistence of religion and the re-surgence of theological issues in public debate" (Avis, 2003, 51). Indeed, even in the Netherlands, where religion was very much absent in public debate, national politics nowadays explicitly give room to religion. We see it on tele-vision screens: after events of violence on the street people come together, light candles, make altars with flowers and meaningful objects. We witness a need, greater than some years ago to construct or revive rituals on important days like a wedding, a funeral. But organized religion and the role of the (main) churches are still diminishing. An intriguing question is: if the need to be religious and act in a religious way is alive in our societies, why do many people leave the churches? This question is a challenge for every practical theologian who is concerned about the faith people live by – or don't live by – in their contexts.

Seen in the broadest sense secularization is a product of the interaction between Christianity and modernity (Avis, 2003, 52). Society and culture are nowadays balancing on the border between late modernity and post modernity. The Dutch theologian André Lascaris states: "Postmodernism stimulates Christians to lib-erate themselves from the coercion to adapt themselves to an as unchangeable presented tradition and identity." (Lascaris, 1995, 67). I think the key to answer the intriguing question I posed lies in the words *coercion* and *presented as unchangeable*.

Modernity: a changed attitude towards authority and coercion

In pre-modern times it was clear who had authority and why. The ideology of patriarchy granted authority to males, the more when they could be seen as fathers and were endowed with properties and knowledge. In tune with this ideology it is self-evident that God has to be father, king of all and all-knowing: 'the almighty'.

Modernity gave people the new idea that authority could be earned by every-body. A new social system: a meritocracy evolved. Basic to this development was the idea, earlier seen as outrageous and impossible, that a human being as such has the possibility to think, to choose, to form an opinion on her/his own, in its own context, and can be held accountable for it. More and more people,

The allegedly unchangeable core ideas of mainstream theologies

non-male, non-fathers, non-rich and not with superior education took the freedom to be independent in their acts, thoughts, feelings and commitments. Many modern persons are allergic to authority from above.

The allegedly unchangeable core ideas of mainstream theologies

Since St. Paul and St. Augustine (to name some main thinkers) personal guilt, original sin and the drama of Cross and Blood became the backbone of mainstream Christian theology. This theology is based on a patriarchal bias, where God is a powerful father – without a mother next to him – who loves conditionally: he wants people to do his will. The reconciliation between God and humankind is reached by a lot of pain and blood. Grace – mirabile dictu – is not given freely. Especially women ask themselves: what kind of a father is God, who tortures his son to get satisfaction? Furthermore, people are given little self-regard by this dominant Christian theory, for this theology is tainted by St. Augustine's idea of original sin. This means that whatever a person does, s/he is thoroughly sinful. Even newborn babies. Next to that, St. Anselm's image of God as the Medieval Lord who has to have satisfaction if his honour is hurt still pops up in current theological thinking.

Of course people suffer from guilt feelings, and pastoral care has to deal with that fact. Humankind is fundamentally torn by its possibility to choose between good and evil, as is pictured in the Garden story in Genesis: Adam and Eve ate the fruit of the Tree of Knowledge of Good and Evil. They transgressed the boundary between divinity and humanity, as God is depicted saying in Genesis 3:22: "Here, the groundling has become as one of us, knowing good and bad" (translation by Mary Phil Korzak, 1992). In the next verse God keeps life eternal – the fruits of the Tree of Life – for himself. The 'knowing of good and bad' is our condition humaine. To derive from these texts a theology of original sin is not right, as the South African/Dutch Old Testament scholar C.J. Labuschagne writes. "In the biblical doctrine of sin the central idea is that the human being does not sin by virtue of what he is through his birth, but by what he does during his life, by the wrong choices he makes". This means that the Garden story of Genesis does not tell us of the fall of humanity, but of its transformation (Labuschagne, 1994, 129). We humans are capable of wrong choices and thus of doing evil things. But we can choose also the right things: it is possible for human beings to be a just person, through and through, whole, in Hebrew: a tzadiq, tamim, although this is not easy. To become whole means: to become a person that is transparent in her/his pursuit of a good, a just life, not based on fear for punishment, but trusting the gracious love of God. Repentance is important: a human act of shame and sorrow about evil behaviour. Repentance and if possible reparation make reconciliation possible. The image that Jesus gave us is that of the prodigal son, taken to his parents' bosom.

Although we are now far advanced in modernity, the old attitudes of the pre-modern and patriarchal era do still linger in the minds and hearts of many, especially of those who were understood and understood themselves as intrinsically dependent: many women for instance. But while education reaches still greater groups of formerly dependent people, the attitudes of modernity spread in wider and wider circles. The churches, with their core-theology of a loving but stern father-God and people as dependent children, can not any longer appeal to the majority of women and men in this late-modern, even post-modern age. The problem is that this core-theology, depicting the relationship between God and humankind as based on sin-cross-redemption, is understood as orthodoxy. Well known scholars and church authorities have declared this theology as the right one. Hence the feeling of coercion that gives many persons, born and bred in modernity, a feeling of aversion towards the churches.

Underlying research

In my researches, resulting in the books *Kracht en Kruis. Pastoraat met Oudere Vrouwen* (2000) and *Met één been in de kerk* (2004), many of the people who told me the story of their life and faith – women and men, the youngest 35, the oldest 90 years old, living in big cities, little towns or villages, some university-educated, some with only a basic formal education – found themselves in the margins of the churches: "With one foot in the church". But all of them said that they still believed in God. But not in the God of orthodoxy. They told me that in their personal faith, what I called their '*survival faith*' – which lay *under* the top layer of their faith, which was more according to the 'official' doctrines they had heard in their church – Jesus' death was not all-important for them. Faith in an unconditionally loving God who was with them in their daily lives gave them strength and courage in their often so difficult lives. What they need in pastoral care is an affirmation of this trust in God's presence in their lives: they long to be blessed. I therefore think it is appropriate to design a theory and a practice of pastoral work based on this contextual faith of people in this time, not based on the paradigm of sin, cross, redemption, but on the God who blesses.

The possibility of other images of the relationship between God and humankind

The German scholar of the Old Testament E.S. Gerstenberger shows that the Old Testament contains many contextual theologies. The images given of God and God's relationship to people change all the time, depending on social and political circumstances. It is therefore difficult to choose one opinion about God that can be understood as the timeless canon of Christian faith. In the periods of exile and afterwards the identity of Israel as one nation with one God had to be maintained at all costs. God, before the exile-period a god of (groups

80   Riet Bons-Storm

of) families, sharing his power with others, for instance with the Queen of Heaven (see Jeremiah 44:15 ff.) evolved towards the fatherly and almighty monarch, maintaining his law nationally and thus maintaining the welfare of his state, land and people (Gerstenberger, 2002).

We usually read the New Testament through the eyes of St. Paul, a man, torn by guilt feelings because he persecuted Jesus' followers. He was influenced by Hellenistic thinking, putting the soul and the body apart and he was susceptible to ideas of a world of purity and disembodiment above this world: heaven. For Paul, being-in-the-flesh means being tainted by earthly desires, keeping humanity far from heaven, where God is supposed to be. God is the monarch, who maintains his laws, powerful in his punishments. Jesus' terrible death became understood as the price that necessarily had to be paid to the Father/ Monarch-God above, in order to clean human beings from being tainted by earthly desires. Salvation became dependent – not only on repentance and a desire to go back to God's way – on a personal confession of faith in the sacrifice Jesus made, taking on himself the punishment meant for all humankind. However, it is not self-evident that Jesus' ideas were the same as St. Paul's (see for instance Johnson 1997, Dunn, 1997, Den Heyer, 1998, 2003, Hermes, 2002, Luttikhuizen 2005). In the gospels of St. Matthew and St. Luke Jesus shows that he is a tzadiq, tamim, by not giving in to the temptations of the devil. In the four gospels Jesus is recognizable as being close to God – resembling God as only a son/daughter can resemble her/his parent – by doing just deeds, being close to all kinds of people. The concept of God recognizable in human beings is incarnation, an ongoing phenomenon, because God is a God of love and can be imaged as longing to be near Her/His people. "The gospels present Jesus as the by God accepted direction indicator, who not only directs people to the way with God, but also walks that way himself and calls others, to go that way with him" (Gerstenberger, 2002, 173). By being this just person, through and through, Jesus was recognized as Messiah, who will bring about liberation and the situation, where God will be all in everything and everybody, and life will be abundant for everybody. Using the old monarchic metaphors this situation is commonly called: the Kingdom of God.

From the God of guilt and sacrifice to a God of blessings

The idea of an unconditionally loving God and Jesus as the inspiring prototype of just humanity makes it possible to think about the relationship of God and humanity as developing under the blessing of God. Our life can be imaged as a day-by-day walk with God. The path is directed by God to a situation of life abundant for all. Jesus as the direction indicator is an invaluable help. Nevertheless: the way through life together with God is a hectic one, full of conflicts, but one never needs to be alone. Magdalene Frettlöh states that the idea of blessing draws God into everyday life (Frettlöh, 1998, 19. See also Greiner 1999).

Beyond the obsession with guilt and atonement

The archetype of blessing could be the Aäronitic blessing of Numbers 6:24–26. It starts with: "May the Eternal One bless you and protect you". In Hebrew poetic language the same meaning of one line is repeated in other words or other images in the following line. We may assume that the second line: "May the Eternal One let the light of his Face shine over you and be gracious to you" can be understood as an explanation of the first line. The third line: "May the Eternal One lift his Face towards you and give you peace" elaborates further on what being blessed means.

In this imagery *God's face* plays a significant role. The face expresses the character of a person. The core of this imagery is: God does not turn his/her back towards the one who is blessed. God turns towards the person, looks at her/him and shines over her/him. God's face illuminates all it is turned to. A blessed person experiences God's presence and warm attention. The light radiating from God's face is benevolent, it is supposed to keep, to protect a person. God's face radiates light on our path, so we can see more clearly who we are and what our task and destination are. The nearness of God's face reminds us of the creation narrative, in which the Eternal One creates the world and blesses it. Adam, the human being–in–the-making, part of the material world, only becomes a real living human being when God's face becomes that near that God's breath can reach Adam's nostrils.

> "YHWH Elohim formed the groundling, soil of the ground
> He blew into its nostrils the blast of life
> And the groundling became a living soul."
> (Genesis 2, verse 7, translated by Mary Phil Korzak, 1992).

According to Hebrew imagery to be created human means: to be an embodied material being that is inspired, literally, by the nearness of God's benevolent face. When a person becomes conscious of this 'condition humaine' s/he is endowed with an enormous dignity. S/he may not be hurt or destroyed by others. S/he is not without her/his own will and purposes. As God's 'mate' (Gen. 1 verse 26) a human being can choose, makes her/his own decisions, is responsible and accountable.

And that's the trouble. That's why living as a blessed person, walking in God's benevolent presence, is not always peaceful, nor immune for disaster with a human or non-human origin. God is willing to give peace, that is: a just situation of equal prosperity for parties, who most of the time do not have shared interests. Peace is, in the language and imagery of the Bible and elsewhere, always a situation that can only be brought into being by negotiation about conflicting interests. Peace can never be cheap in this world. Being blessed takes its own ethics with it: living with the benevolent presence of God, who loves not only us but also the rest of humankind, means: to protect and to inspire, to give courage to survive with dignity till death does us part, to be empowered and to empower to walk and work together with God on the way to justice and peace. Being blessed gives us the possibility of seeing ourselves as God's be-loved ones, as God's friends, inspired to become human beings according to God's longing, like Jesus was: tzadiq, tamim: just through and through. To live as a blessed person means aiming at integrity. As in this theory the body be-comes as important as the soul, sin can be defined as hurting or destruction of God's good creation and everything in it. But sin is never a condition, it is always an act. Repentance – and often reparation – can open the way back to God's way.

The formative theological ideas of our practices need not be any longer: sin-cross-redemption, but can be creation-blessing-recreation.

The blessing God and our practices

In our secularized world the traditional pre-modern and patriarchal imagery of the gospel of the Eternal One lost credibility. Many cannot look at themselves any longer as 'children' of God, unable to choose for themselves. In our time, with its emphasis on self-awareness and experience, people, living in a world full of threats of terrorism, new incurable illnesses and innumerable changes, want to experience the benevolent and inspiring nearness of God in everyday life. They can experience this support if concrete persons, as places of incar-nation, embody and enact the loving and inspiring support of the Eternal One. This is the core of all our practices as people of God, lay persons or pro-fessional pastors. God, the Eternal One, is not more and not less than a Point of Reference, supposed in our longing, which can give us a promise that we are not lonely in this world, that things do not happen at random, that to despair is not the only logical thing to do. This Image of Hope can be communicated in imagery, stories and enactments, by persons who try to live as blessed by the unconditional love of the Eternal One, as such seeing others as valuable. As blessed people they bless others: inspire them and protect their integrity body and soul. Being blessed means also: acknowledge the power of Evil that is still in this world and tries to destroy God's blessed creation. It means: to name it and look for ways and means to overcome it.

In my argument being or giving a blessing means more that the concrete act of blessing: the laying on of hands for instance. It means: living and acting as direction indicator to the *experience of the God who is a benevolent, inspiring presence in the everyday life of a person*. This blessing can only be experienced in a community that makes the blessing effective. Orthopraxy becomes more important than orthodoxy. A theory of pastoral work in the broadest sense, based on a theology of blessing, asks for the presence of pastors (professional ones or lay women and men) who have themselves a healthy idea of their self-worth and of the dignity of the women and men they meet: the old and the young, healthy or dying. Work as a faithful person – for instance in pastoral care – is aimed at comfort and empowerment, to live life and make peace. Special attention has to be given to feelings of guilt induced by traditional imagery of the gospel. In a practical theology of blessing the worth and integrity of the body is as important as the worth and integrity of the soul. Pastoral work cannot only consist of pastoral counselling. Working towards the integrity of all human beings, in the Spirit of the Eternal One as known to us by the life of Jesus and others like him, must include social work, even political activity. This does not mean that a blessing-formula may not be spoken at the proper moment.

A blessing-formula is like an invocation, but not by magic. In a magical invocation the effect is dependent on the right wording and the spiritual power of the invocator. In a blessing the right wording is not important, but the wording need to be explicit, contextual. Important is the longing of the person who is blessed to be comforted by God's presence and be empowered, just, whole. De effectiveness of the blessing is dependent on faith in God, who is willing to be with Her/His friends.

In Celtic spirituality faith was based on blessings. There were blessings for every situation. This spirituality is more based on a creation-theology than on a traditional soteriology of cross and blood. In a world not manipulated and made easy by technology, where dependency on the forces of nature prevailed, one knew that one needed God's blessing. This God was male, but Celtic women trusted also in Brigit, a Celtic deity, who was made a Christian saint. In this respect they were like the Jewish women who persisted in baking cookies for the Queen of Heaven (Jer. 44).

> "Brigit is my companion
> Brigit makes my song;
> Brigit will help me
> The best of the women, the woman who leads me"
> (De Waal, 2000, 20).

The Celts used the word 'caim': a circle of trust around a person, where s/he is safe and can become whole. A pastoral encounter can be an 'enactment', or at least a reminder of this 'caim' by the hands of God.

References

Avis, Paul, 2003. Church Drawing Near. Spirituality and Mission in a Post-Christian Culture. London/New York: T&T Clark Ltd.

Berger, P.L. ed. (1999). The Desecularization of the World: Resurgent Religion and World Politics Grand Rapids: Eerdmans.

Bons-Storm, Riet (2000). Pastoraat met oudere vrouwen. Kampen: Kok.

Bons-Storm, Riet (2004). Met één been in de kerk. Gorinchem: Narratio.

Bons-Storm, Riet (2007). Gezegend Leven. Op weg naar een pastorale gemeente in een verbrokkelende wereld. Gorinchem: Narratio.

Dunn, James D.G. (1997). Unity and Diversity in the New Testament. London: SCM Press.

Frettlöh, Magdalene (1998). Theologie des Segens. Biblische und dogmatische Wahrnehmungen. Güterloh: Chr. Kaiser/Güterloher Verlaghaus.

Gerstenberger, Erhard S. (2002). Theologies in the Old Testament. London: T & T Clark.

Greiner, Dorothea (1999). Segen und Segnen. Eine systematisch-theologische Grundlegung. Stuttgart: Verlag W. Kohlhammer.

Heyer, C.J. den. (1998). De Messiaanse Weg. Van Jesjoea van Nazaret tot de Christus der Kerken. Kampen: Kok.

Heyer, C.J. den (2003). Van Jezus naar Christendom. De ontwikkeling van tekst tot dogma. Zoetermeer: Meinema.

Hermes, Geza (2002). The Changing Faces of Jesus. London: Penguin.

Johnson, Elisabeth A. (1997). Consider Jesus. New York: Crossroad Publishing Company.

Korzak, Mary Phil (1992). At the start… Genesis made new. Louvain: European Series, Louvain Cahiers, number 124.

Labuschagne, C.J. (1994). Zin en onzin over God. Zoetermeer: Boekencentrum.

Lascaris, André, 1995. "Mag ik 'wij' zeggen?" in Herfsttij van de moderne cultuur. Theologische visies op het postmoderne. Manuela Kalsky, Erik Borgman and Marianne Merkx, red. Nijmegen/Zoetermeer: DSTS/De Horstink.

Luttikhuizen, G. (2005). De Veelvormigheid van het Vroegste Christendom. Budel: Uitgeverij DAMON.

Waal, Esther de (2000). Het Keltische Visioen. Zoetermeer: Meinema. Dutch translation of The Celtic Vision. London: Darton, Longman and Todd, 1988.

The Author

Riet Bons-Storm, Prof. Dr., emerita Professor of Practical Theology and Womenstudies at Groningen University, the Netherlands. Research interests: religious faith, or the lack of it, in our time and situations; the position of women and men in society and churches; peacemaking, especially in the Middle East. Recent publications: Gezegend leven, Op weg naar een pastorale gemeente in een verbrokkelende wereld (2007); Met één been in de kerk (2004).

Thomas Groome

Educating for Religious Identity in a Secularizing World

"May God Be With the Days"

I grew up in a small village about forty miles west of Dublin, Ireland, where it was impossible to become anything other than a Catholic, and a very Irish one at that. Every aspect of family and communal life was permeated by a deeply enculturated version of this "faith," its sacraments and rituals, its outlook on life, its values, virtues, and vices. That Irish village Catholicism was like a powerful marinade which steeped to "the marrow bone" (Yeats), shaping our "being" both as noun and verb – who we were and how we lived – our whole identity.

Everyone went to Mass on Sunday and to a full church. If someone should miss, neighbors would visit that afternoon to wish a speedy recovery – they must be sick. Greetings and partings and the conversation in between were laced with God-talk; the anticipated was with "God willing" and the realized with "thanks be to God." Faith could explain the most immediate of things like the weather ("'tis a grand day, thank God"), and the ultimate mysteries, like birth and death, joy and suffering. The Angelus bell at noon and 6 pm reminded all to turn their minds and hearts toward God.

Even as I reminisce, I must add "may God be with those days"; for my Irish village, they are well gone. It is a very different place than the one I left almost 40 years ago. Though still a "life-style enclave" of sorts, its ethos is much more of a post-modern eclectic suburb than of an Irish Catholic village. With a six-lane motorway connecting it to Dublin – itself now a diverse metropolis – that village enjoys the economic boom of the "Celtic tiger" and thousands of "new people" have flocked into the area. Its once common language world laced with God-talk is more a tower of Babel today. What was once approached by faith is now explained more *reasonably*, if addressed at all. And this past summer, I found its Sunday mass three-quarters empty. In sum, my old Irish village is now *secularizing* – with religion and its influence in precipitous decline.

I use the adverb seculari*zing* for two reasons: a) though its public effects are receding, there are still traces of a Catholic culture in that village; and b) its ethos is having a secularizing effect upon its inhabitants – it is now more countercultural to go to Mass on Sunday than to stay away. This leads me to wonder whether and how the children growing up there – like my nieces and nephews – will become Catholic Christians? For I understand Christian faith as, at bedrock, a mode of human identity. It is to engage all of "heart and soul, mind and strength" (Mk 12:30), providing the Christian person and community the foundation for their whole way of being in the world. Meanwhile, I accept from the social sciences that such identity formation is primarily by socialization and enculturation.

My proposal here is that in secularizing contexts, faith communities must be all the more intentional to socialize/enculturate people into religious identity; what my old Irish village once did by osmosis now requires deliberate crafting and planning. However, the traditional mode of non-reflective religious socialization, what I call "naïve socialization," is both inadequate and hazardous in post-modern contexts. It is not adequate to the challenges of secularization and post-modernity, and its favor for "the same" can encourage exclusion and violence toward "the other." The world is desperately in need of religious identity that is well grounded in the particular and yet open to the universal. Indeed, the very future of our world may depend on whether or not the great religions can promote both faith identity and inter-faith understanding.

I further suggest that there are assets to "educating for religious identity in a secularizing world." Such socio-cultural contexts may encourage, for example: a faith marked by *personal conviction* – less likely to be achieved through naïve socialization; a religious identity *devoid of sectarianism*, inviting people beyond the village to recognize the universality of God's love and saving intent; an identity in faith disposed to *engage the public realm*, able to devise strategies for effective social participation and credible public witness; a religious identity that *enriches and is enriched by its culture*, embracing the "living exchange" between the two[1]; a faith conviction that is *open to learn from the other* – naïve socialization favors only "the same." So, rather than rejecting or despairing of our secularizing context, or wallowing in nostalgia for the old village, we have opportunities now to promote a more life-giving sense of religious identity.

It Still Takes a Village

Becoming a Polish person requires the socialization and enculturation of a Polish community, becoming a Hispanic person requires a Hispanic community, and a Christian person requires a Christian community. Regardless of the culture, it still "takes a village" to raise a Christian person, even while she/he must also be disposed to reach beyond the village. So, what could be taken for granted in villages like my original one, must now be crafted intentionally. It requires each Christian family, parish, and program/school to be proactive in molding its milieu to socialize and sustain people in Christian identity.

---

[1] A phrase and concept taken from Vatican II's, "Constitution on the Church in the Modern World," #44, in Walter Abbott, ed., *Documents of Vatican II*, (New York: America Press, 1966), 246.

Here the challenge is not only from secularizing cultures but from the hegemony of the schooling paradigm. At least in the West, the "school" has triumphed as the sole mediator of education of any kind, including religious education. The Church has even encouraged parents in the absurd assumption that a one-hour once a week "Sunday school" (for about 30 weeks a year) can make Christians out of their children. Meanwhile we leave parents without the training, resources, networking, and practices they need to intentionally fulfill their role as the primary religious educators of their children. To "de-school" the Church's approach to religious education will not be easy, yet we need to move beyond schooling (without leaving it behind) to a paradigm of faith community that is capable of socializing Christian identity, even in secularizing contexts.

One term for this new paradigm is "total community catechesis" (TCC). It amounts to *a coalition of parish, family, and programs/school, engaging every member and all aspects of each, by and for people of all ages, teaching and learning together, ever fostering Christian identity that is realized in lived faith*. Such intentional socialization requires that every Christian family, parish, and school/program take on a "catechetical consciousness" whereby its members constantly review each aspect of their shared life to make it effective in fostering Christian identity.

One schema for implementing such total community catechesis (TCC) is to imagine how all Christian ministries can be suffused with a catechetical consciousness. In addition to catechesis as a ministry of the word, we must engage the catechetical potential of the other ministries of the Church as well, and of the family as domestic church. Since the first Christian communities, the Church has described its core ministries as: *koinonia*, to be a community of living *witness* to Christian faith; *leitourgia,* to offer public *worship* to God together; *kerygma* to evangelize, preach, and teach God's *word* of revelation that comes through scripture and tradition; and *diakonia*, to care for personal and public *welfare*. So, we can summarize the Church's core ministries as *witness*, *worship*, *word*, and *welfare*.

Because of exigency of space, I will elaborate my proposal only around the family; however, the reader can readily imagine how it would pertain to the parish and the formal program/school of religious education.[2] So, let's imagine how families might fulfill each of the four essential functions of Christian ministry – as appropriate to their context – and do so *with a catechetical consciousness*.

---

[2] See my "Total Catechetical Education," in *Religious Education of Boys and Girls,* Lisa Cahill and Werner Jenrond, eds, London: SCM Press, *Concilium,* Vol 4, 2002.

The Total "Family" as Catechist

Beyond the two parent ideal, here "family" includes extended and blended families, single, double, and triple parent families; any *bonded network of domestic life* can function as a family for socialization in faith. The Second Vatican Council stated that "parents must be acknowledged as the first and foremost educators of their children."[3] Vatican II also reclaimed an ancient image of the family as "the domestic church."[4] Putting these two insights together, we can begin to imagine how the family, in its own way, can carry out all of the Church's ministries, and do so with a catechetical consciousness.

Family as community of Christian **witness** requires that the ethos of the home be suffused with the values and perspectives of Christian faith. This calls for constant attention by the family to its environment, lifestyle and priorities, relationships and gender roles, modes of discipline and accountability, language patterns and conversation themes, work and recreation – every aspect – to monitor how well it reflects the convictions and commitments of Christian faith. Everything about the Christian family can be made to *witness* to its faith, thus socializing its members in Christian identity.

Family as community of **worship** calls it to integrate shared prayer and sacred ritual into its patterns of daily life, and to have religious symbols and practices within the home. Every Christian family needs such "home liturgy" to symbolize and celebrate, nurture and sustain its faith. Surely every family can create or rediscover (old Christian cultures had lots of them) sacred rituals and symbols to encourage Christian nurture.

Family as community of God's **Word** calls members to share their faith around scripture and tradition, among themselves and in the broader faith community. Parishes must help parents with the resources and training needed to integrate faith themes into daily conversation, to be able to take advantage of the teachable moments that arise inevitably. Modern parents are admirably intent to teach even the youngest children their numbers, alphabet, days of the week, and so on. Why not be equally proactive in handing on the language and stories of Christian faith.

Family as community of human **welfare** requires it to put its Christian faith to work in caring for the spiritual and physical, emotional and moral well-being of its own members, rippling outward toward others in need and serving the common good of society. Christian family life must reflect love and compassion toward all, and promote justice both within and without. This is how it is likely to form and sustain its members in the social responsibilities of Christian faith.

---

[3] "Decree on Education" #3, in *Documents*, Abbott, 641.
[4] "Constitution on the Church" #11, in *Documents,* Abbott, 29.

Educating for Religious Identity in a Secularizing World 89

To conclude this section, the socialization that was once ready at hand in the villages of another era must now be crafted intentionally by every Christian family, parish, and school/program. But then, while such socialization is essential to nurturing Christian identity, it is not sufficient to sponsor people beyond a conventional faith and one that endures in secularizing cultures. To push beyond the limitations of naïve socialization, we need a critically discerning and consciousness raising mode of pedagogy that promotes the dialectic between the person and her/his Christian community, between the Christian community and its secularizing culture.

A Shared Praxis Approach

For many years I have attempted to articulate and use a pedagogy that brings people to name and reflect critically upon their lives in the world, to have access to Christian faith with hermeneutics of retrieval, discernment, and creativity, and to integrate these sources – life and faith – into lived Christian faith that is "for the life of the world" (John 6:51). I've called it a "shared praxis approach." Reflecting my context, I will write about it here as a "shared *Christian* praxis approach" but it could well be a shared Jewish or Muslim or Buddhist or Hindu or world religions praxis approach. It can access spiritual wisdom from any religious tradition or draw from various traditions.

In sum, a shared *Christian* praxis approach to religious education entails creating a community of conversation and active participation in which people critically reflect together on their own historical agency in time and place and on their socio-cultural realities, have access together to the spiritual wisdom of Christian Story and Vision, and are encouraged to appropriate this wisdom with the intent of renewed praxis of Christian faith. I summarize its dynamics simply as "bringing life to faith and faith to life"; I elaborate its pedagogy into a focusing activity and five "movements."

The Focusing Activity: Here the educator's intent is twofold: a) to engage people as active participants in the teaching-learning event, and b) to focus a curriculum topic as something of real interest to the lives and/or faith of participants. Thus, it should dispose people to actively participate by turning them to look at their own lives in the world, and begin to engage them with a "generative theme" (Freire), symbol or text that is of real import to their present praxis of life, of faith, or of both.

Movement One: Expressing the Theme as in Present Praxis: The educator's intent here is to encourage participants to express themselves around the generative theme, symbol, or text from the perspective of their present praxis. They can express what they do or see others doing, their own feelings or thoughts or life-centered interpretations, or their perception of what is going on around them in their socio-cultural context. The key is that people "pay attention" and name what emerges as their encounter with the theme, symbol or text – how they see it, engage it, interpret it, or whatever. Their expressions can be spoken, written, drawn, constructed or mediated by any means of human communication.

Movement Two: Reflecting on the Theme of Life/Faith: The intent here is to encourage participants to reflect critically on what they expressed in M1. Critical reflection can engage reason, memory, imagination or a combination of them; such reflection can be both personal and socio-cultural. Reason questions or questioning activities can ask why things are the way they are, what causes them to be this way, what their significance might be, why participants' own perceptions or interpretations are as they are, and so on. Memory questions or activities might ask participants about the origins of their own present praxis, their recall of past experiences regarding it, to uncover how the social or cultural history is shaping present praxis, to recognize how their own biography or context influences how they respond to the theme, symbol, or text, etc. Imagination type questions or activities invite people to imagine beyond present praxis for its likely consequences, its potential and desired outcomes.

Movement Three: Christian Story and Vision: Here the pedagogical task is to teach clearly the Christian Story and Vision around the particular theme, symbol or text, and to do so with integrity and persuasion. The key is that people have ready access to the spiritual wisdom of Christian faith regarding the particular life/faith focus. Likewise, it is important to intentionally raise up the Vision out of the Story, what Christian faith teaches and means for lives now around the topic and how to respond.

Movement Four: Appropriating the Wisdom of Christian Faith: M. 4 begins the dynamic of moving back to life again with renewed Christian commitment (M. 5). The pedagogy here encourages people to come to see for themselves what the wisdom of Christian faith might mean for their everyday lives, to personally appropriate this wisdom and to "take it to heart" in who they are and how they live. So the educator might inquire what participants are intuiting in response to the Story/Vision, what they are coming to recognize for themselves, what they agree with or disagree with or might add to what has been presented in M 3, and so on.

Movement Five: Making Decisions about Christian Faith: Here the intent is to give participants an opportunity to choose how to respond to the spiritual wisdom of Christian faith. Decisions can be cognitive, affective, or behavioral – what people believe, how they might relate with God or others, or the ethics and values by which to live their lives.

Though I lay out these movements sequentially, they have great flexibility and many possible combinations. And more important by far than the movements are their under girding commitments. The focusing act reflects commitment *to engage* participants in the teaching/learning dynamic and with something generative for their lives. M 1 reflects commitment to have people *pay attention* to their own lives in the world and *to express* their present praxis. M 2 reflects commitment to *critical reflection*, encouraging people to think for themselves, personally and socially, to question and probe, to reason, remember and imagine around the life/faith theme, symbol or text. M 3 reflects the commitment to give people ready *access* to faith Story and Vision, enabling participants to encounter spiritual wisdom for their lives. M 4 reflects commitment to *appropriation*, encouraging participants to integrate their lives and faith tradition, to make its spiritual wisdom their own. And M 5 invites people to *decision*, choosing a response to the spiritual wisdom they have encountered.

These commitments to *participation* and *conversation*, to *engaging* and *attending*, to *expressing* and *reflecting*, to *accessing* and *appropriating*, and to *decision-making* should run throughout the process. In other words, engagement does not end with the focusing activity but must be maintained throughout; likewise expression is not limited to M 1, nor reflection to M 2, nor decision-making to M 5, and so on. Rather, the religious educator should promote these activities throughout the whole event, and not in lock-step sequence.

So, to summarize my essay, intentional socialization/enculturation, and then some critical approach to religious education like shared praxis, is what is needed in order to "educate for religious identity in a secularizing world."

The Author

Thomas Groome is a Senior Professor of Theology and Religious Education at Boston College, and Director of BC's Institute of Religious Education and Pastoral Ministry. His most recent book is *What Makes us Catholic: Eight Gifts for Life*, (San Francisco: HarperCollins, 2004).

Lewis S. Mudge

Jose Casanova on Public Religions and Modernity:
The Basis for a Practical Theological Agenda?

At the close of his book *Public Religions in the Modern World* the sociologist José Casanova makes the following extraordinary statement:

> Religious traditions are now confronting the differentiated secular spheres, challenging them to face their own obscurantist, ideological and inauthentic claims. In many of these confrontations it is religion which, as often as not, appears to be on the side of human enlightenment. It would be profoundly ironic if, after all the beatings it has received from modernity, religion could somehow unintentionally help modernity save itself.[1]

Reading these words, one's first impulse is to ask what world we are talking about. Religious communities might, even unintentionally, help modernity save itself? What religious communities? In what sense "save"? Casanova's assertion sums up a book-length demolition of the once widespread consensus among sociologists and others that, in the "modern" world, religious organizations, activities and beliefs would become ever weaker, more marginalized, and publicly ineffective. Casanova has produced here a denial of crucial parts[2] of the so-called "secularization hypothesis," the *grand récit* (to use a term of Fernand Braudel) or "story" of modernity favored in the last century by a seeming majority of secular scholars. At mid-twentieth-century these observers believed, and many of their successors still do believe, that religion, faced by modernity, would inevitably decline in public influence, become increasingly marginalized and privatized, and eventually disappear from the public sphere altogether.

For theologians this outlook has been, to say the least, challenging. We have wondered whether to dispute the secularization hypothesis altogether, to look for chinks in its armor, or to find ways of accommodating our strategies to it. Was "the modern world" what sociologists said it was, and, if so, what were the implications for religious communities trying to live faithfully within it? Little agreement emerged. But then, in the late eighties and early nineties of the

---

[1] José Casanova, *Public Religions in the Modern World* (Chicago: University of Chicago Press, 1994), 234.

[2] Casanova understands the "secularization hypothesis" to involve three quite different understandings: (1) secularization as the decline in religious beliefs and practices; (2) secularization as the privatization of religion; and (3) secularization as the differentiation of different secular spheres (e.g. state, economy, science) so as to "emancipate" the latter from religious institutions and norms. These distinctions allow examination of the validity of each proposition independently, making possible the description of different patterns of secularization in different cultural situations.

last century, things began to change. Along came the young American sociologist Jose Casanova at the New School in New York with case studies purporting to show new vitality and influence on the part of religious communities in the public world, and with the stunning hypothesis that these communities might turn out to help save modernity from its betrayals of the promise of the Enlightenment. Could that insight, whether or not intended by Casanova for such a purpose, be made the basis for a practical theological agenda?

In his 1994 book, Casanova demonstrates that religious bodies, since the early 1980's if not before, began to play totally unexpected and remarkably potent political and social roles. The sociologist cites a series of developments involving Roman Catholicism in Spain, Poland, Brazil, and the United States, along with signs of a then-newly potentiated American protestant evangelicalism.

Such groups, Casanova argues, not only began in this period to be newly effective participants in debates over public issues. They often found themselves, sometimes inadvertently; it seems, on the side of values such as democracy and human rights. The Roman Catholic Church in Poland, for example, fought for its own survival against Communism, but – partly through its connection with the "Solidarity" movement – became a powerful democratizing influence in Polish society. In other places as well, religious institutions – often in spite of themselves – turned out to be carriers, in some sense, of "human enlightenment." Secular institutions, even those with roots in *the* Enlightenment, often did not.

In the light of these historical case studies, and in the face of a "modernity" struggling with deteriorating political institutions and now increasingly given over to the destructive logics of rivalries for global dominance and the ideology of the global market, religious communities might now, in Casanova's view, turn out to be significant contributors to restoring the Enlightenment's promise of values such as freedom, human rights, and democracy to the human race. Casanova explains what lies behind this hypothesis. He writes:

> [...] normative traditions constitute the very condition of possibility for ethical discourse, and [...] fictional 'ideal speech situations' and 'original positions' notwithstanding, without normative traditions neither rational public debate nor discourse ethics is likely to take place. [...] One after another, all the modern public institutions which at first tended to exercise some of the public functions traditionally performed by religious institutions abandoned their public normative roles: academic philosophy, the specialized social sciences, the universities, the press, politicians, intellectuals. Under such circumstances one cannot but welcome the return of religion to the public square.[3]

---

[3] Casanova, *Public Religions*, 205f.

94   Lewis S. Mudge

But obviously Casanova is not thinking of the kind of "return to the public square" we have recently been witnessing across the globe, i.e. fundamentalist or very conservative groups seeking to dominate the politics of their nations or regions: evangelical extremists (not all evangelicals) in America, Wahabist Muslims in Saudi Arabia exporting their ideologies to Afghanistan, Pakistan and Iraq, absolutist Israeli groups opposing serious peace talks with Palestinians. The list could go on. Instead, Casanova is thinking of religious groups that have imbibed enough of the Enlightenment critique of religion to be able constructively to enter the public dialogue about modernity's own self-contradictions. Here is how he puts it:

> [...] only a religion which has incorporated as its own the central aspects of the Enlightenment critique of religion is in a position today to play a positive role in furthering processes of practical rationalization.[4]

This sounds at first like a circular argument. Religious groups should accept the Enlightenment's criticisms in order to be able to help modernity save itself from the Enlightenment's consequences? This is certainly not a formula that comports with Casanova's case studies of Roman Catholicism in Poland or Spain, or Brazil, or even the United States. But note that there is a second clause. Casanova says that absorbing Enlightenment critique is for the purpose of "furthering processes of practical rationalization." These words seem not to refer to the Philosophers' anti-religious epistemology but to another aspect of Enlightenment thought: a practical interest in the way things, including society, work. They refer to the introduction of a kind of practical theology or *phronesis* in which believers take responsibility for dealing with the conditions of their lives together rather than depending only on traditional, authoritative, probably world-alienating religious teaching.

I find in Casanova, then, a platform for practical theology. Absorbing the Enlightenment critique means for him uncovering those strands in religious traditions that support, and give direction to, such human responsibility-taking. Instead of staging a hostile take-over of worldly responsibility from religious authorities, the Enlightenment critique of religion permits us to see that the Abrahamic scriptures, they at least, teach in the stories of creation and covenant-making that such responsibility already belongs to human beings as a divine gift. To put this in (no doubt controversial) Christian terms, the kingdom comes when believers have by their own practices made the world ready for it.

In short, Casanova's "practical rationalization" could mean, in H. Richard Niebuhr's words, to grasp "what is going on" and to take action to try to bend events in a certain direction. Casanova seems to be saying that religious groups that have accepted an Enlightenment critique of themselves can find better warrants in their sources for such historically conscious responsibility-taking

---

[4] Casanova, *Public Religions*, 233.

than can "secular" institutions that uncritically assume themselves to be heirs of the Enlightenment promise, yet fail to deliver its promised blessings.

If so, it follows that helping modernity "save itself" is for religious communities not a matter of succumbing to some thin theological gruel in order to sound almost like everybody else. It is rather a matter of enlightened social positioning and responsibility-taking for congregations living in the fullness of faith. But grasping opportunities to do the sorts of humanizing things described in Casanova's late 1980's cases was often the by-product of institutional self-interest.

To base a self-conscious theological strategy on the Casanova analysis it is necessary to move the democratizing, humanizing, intention from inadvertence to intentionality. Now that we see what happened in Poland, Spain, Brazil and the United States we need to ask where similar opportunities may exist in the early 21st-century world. Casanova's cases offer a kind of template for the search that, in summary, goes like this. Religious communities, having internalized Enlightenment critiques of their former self-understandings to the extent of seeing their traditions as validating responsible social action, may now be able to help modernity transcend the distortions of Enlightenment values that threaten it.

But this will not happen unless traditions, such as the Abrahamic ones, can act together. Only so can they overcome the suspicion of sectarian special pleading. The practice of parallel and interactive hermeneutics, i.e. reading scriptures together in relation to commonly experienced situations, can help with this. It can produce unprecedented mutual enlightenment (small "e") about one another as co-actors in a uniquely shared space-time world. *The* Enlightenment generated cultural assumptions that have made such encounters possible. But taking advantage of this does not mean *substituting* Enlightenment perspectives for the religious traditions in order to make them more compatible. Rather, this activity produces enlightened attitudes *within* religious traditions as they recognize relationships within differences and differences within relationships. Such dialogue enacts a relativety-in-practice that superficially resembles the academic style of "comparative religions" but is not at all the same thing. Here actual identities are engaged, yet remain distinct. Neither conversion nor syncretism is in view. The Other becomes more deeply known, *but remains Other.* Such dialogue-in-situation generates a sense of mutual responsibility for the interpretations offered and for the public consequences of these interpretations. Fundamentalisms can some-times be pragmatically dissolved in such situations without direct confrontation. Shared ethical perspectives can be made available to the surrounding world free of debilitating sectarian labels. Today such interfaith sharing is foundational to seeing and acting on the sorts of opportunities about to be discussed. Our early-21st-century world seems to offer opportunities of at least three kinds.

96   Lewis S. Mudge

First, religious communities, acting together, can help modernity "save" itself by bringing to light its forgotten moral and religious sources. Most, if not all, programs of secular moral reasoning depend for their persuasiveness on implicit metaphors that go back to hidden religious assumptions. Without such sources, standing *incognito* behind our modern notions of the good, our glittering contemporary capabilities have little directional control. An early Enlightenment figure like John Locke depended on religious warrants for the maintenance of social cohesion, even building Calvinist assumptions into his system, while he and others simultaneously strove, in the name of autonomy, to reinvent the very idea of the human and of human society. Adam Smith later straddled the two worlds, moving from his *Theory of Moral Sentiments* to *The Wealth of Nations*. The "invisible hand" in the latter book may refer back to moral factors developed in the former. One can read an interpretation of these phenomena in Carl Becker's *Heavenly City of the Eighteenth-Century Philosophers*. Our contemporary Charles Taylor carries the argument forward. He claims in *Sources of the Self*[5] that modern life is full of assumptions about human rights, human dignity and so forth, but that we are incapable of articulating the origins and root meanings of such "frameworks." It is not autonomous reasoning that leads us to such assumptions. Rather we come by them as unwitting beneficiaries of the historical and literary transmission of certain root metaphors. Many (of course not all) such sources of our ideas about our selves and our societies are found in religious traditions. To save the very fabric of our modern morality, Taylor claims, to be able to talk intelligibly about it, to be able to defend it, to be able to apply it, we need to become aware of these sources. Taylor on this point is well worth quoting.

> [Our] identity is much richer in moral sources than its condemners allow, but [...] this richness is rendered invisible by the impoverished philosophical language of its most zealous defenders. Modernity urgently needs to be saved from its most unconditional supporters – a predicament perhaps not without precedent in the history of culture.[6]

Religious communities that self-consciously preserve such sources by living in accord with them may in some circumstances be the only institutions around capable of reminding us who we really are.

Second, the public presence of religious communities working together, especially the Abrahamic ones, may help modernity better understand its enemies. Our culture is threatened by its ignorance of religion. The past year has seen a spate of books in England and America that identify religion as such, whether at home or in the Middle East, as the enemy of rational, "reality-based," civilization. The authors put forward arguments that they confidently

---

[5] Charles Taylor, *Sources of the Self,* (Cambridge, MA: Harvard University Press, 1989).
[6] Ibid., xi.

believe will undermine all religious faith and destroy it. In short, they take the superiority of Enlightenment values of a certain kind as self-evident, and assume that people, once they understand, will flock to them. In fact, such attitudes only oppose fundamentalism of the religious kind with fundamentalism of the positivist scientific kind. Such naïve attitudes leave modernity exposed to its fundamentalist enemies because such a construal of the struggle fails to grasp what is really going on. It fails to grasp why the West is morally reviled by so many around the world and why the opposition is so lethally passionate. To answer such threats, modernity needs not to answer one fundamentalism with another but to reach an open, dialogical, pluralistically expressed, religious consciousness that puts foundations under its values. For this it needs knowledge of its moral and metaphorical sources. It cannot have such so long as its leading thinkers assume that fundamentalism – Jewish, or Christian, or Islamic – is the only form that religion can legitimately take. This is why a religious vision generated out of "parallel and interactive hermeneutics" is potentially so important. Such relationships overcome religious isolation and undermine doctrinal exclusivisms, allowing a religious or theological form of humanism to appear that can exist in many traditional expressions: Jewish, Christian, Islamic, or otherwise.[7]

And third, the gathering of religious groups into communities of constructive dialogue can, in some times and places, generate cells of "civil society" where no such thing otherwise effectively exists. Civil society, often defined as a region of public interlocution distinct from established economic and political spheres, has often proved itself to be a seed-bed for the sorts of democratic assumptions needed to undergird free elections, effective parliaments and the like. Attempts to impose these things where the cultural ground is not prepared for them have proved unsuccessful again and again. In Western Europe and North America civil society has grown organically, only to be undermined of late by manipulative party politics and the power of giant corporations. In Eastern Europe and the Middle East, it has scarcely existed. Whether waning or struggling to be born, civil society needs the right social conditions and institutions such as coffee houses where talk can be passionate and free. Where such conditions do not exist, religious communities acting together can now, as seldom before, begin to play this role: precisely because, in Casanova's words, they uniquely bring "normative traditions" that "constitute the very condition of possibility for ethical discourse." Knowing that they have been sources of so much sectarian violence and seeking to renounce that way of life, such groups may be particularly motivated today to form such discourse communities. In some situations these can be the only points of sustained contact among otherwise mutually alienated segments of society. Such interfaith discussions

---

[7] For a different view, see the book by Lee Harris, *The Suicide of Reason: Radical Islam's Threat to the West,* New York: Basic Books, 2007.

98   Lewis S. Mudge

can "stand in for" otherwise missing settings for civic discourse, while contributing needed moral sources to the mix. Such relationships can then prepare the ground and plant seeds for wider public involvement. They can help create conditions for the birth of democratic institutions. Such units of civil society can also become social spaces in which organized resistance to injustice and oppression can grow. Such spaces can nurture alternatives to political and economic tendencies from which modernity needs to be saved.

All these are ways in which we may imagine Casanova's thesis working itself out in the early 21st century. Yet there is always the problem of recognizing such models even when they are present amid the complexity of actual events. And actual events are bound to generate models not thought of in this paper or any other. To paraphrase a military maxim, few strategic ideas survive their first contact with the actual data. That could be the fate of these attempts to learn from Casanova's cases for our own time.

Yet is the thought that any of this might happen wholly visionary? It is too early to tell. In any case, visionary narratives have their uses. They can motivate close attention to the reality of one's situation as containing the rudiments of promise when that is not obvious to most. They can help counteract despair. It is better to approach a situation with *some* idea of what one is looking for, rather than with no hypothesis at all. Better even if one's starting hypothesis is later modified, as it will be, by unexpected events.

Thinking retrospectively, the French historian Fernand Braudel identified historical processes of "long duration," e.g. characteristics of "the Mediterranean world in the age of Philip II" and other similar phenomena. Here it is as if something equally portentous were being projected in advance, before the fact, as a kind of principle of orientation for future struggles. We can wrestle together as Abrahamic communities with the specific conditions of our situation and thereby generate case-study material for historians and sociologists of a future generation. Those coming after us might, or might not, conclude that our efforts were indeed part of a world-historical process in which modernity turned out to be "saved," i.e. delivered from its present travail to something like the "sunlit uplands" of which Churchill spoke at the outset of World War II. Some future writer might indeed say, "here, at just this moment in world history, modernity began to turn the corner, above all because of what religious communities did, even if no one could have known this at the time." So we conclude for Casanova's case studies, whose future implications are yet to unfold. And so we must also think about our own.

The Author

Lewis S. Mudge is Robert Leighton Stuart Professor of Theology, Emeritus, at San Francisco Theological Seminary and the Graduate Theological Union, Berkeley, CA.

Hans-Georg Ziebertz

The Impact of Culture on Religiosity
An empirical study among youth in Germany and the Netherlands

This short research report will answer the questions: does a transnational structure (Germany and the Netherlands) of individual religiosity exist and which role does the national context play in the forming of this structure? Both questions are answered on the basis of the survey among German (N=729) and Dutch young people (N=552) who filled in a questionnaire with approx. 300 items on individual religiosity (cf. Ziebertz/Kalbheim/Riegel 2003). The German group consists of 309 (42%) female and 420 (58%) male young people and is on average 16.2 years old. Over two thirds are Roman Catholic (71%) and a quarter is Protestant (24%). In the Dutch group there are slightly more females (55%) than males (45%). There is an average age of 16.5 years, of which 42% are Roman Catholic and 7% Protestant. As both groups are not representative of their country of origin the resulting analyses have an explorative character.

In the first step we develop a typology of individual religiosity. This is the basis on which we will answer the question of the existence and the characteristics of a transnational structure. Next we will investigate the influence of origin from Germany and the Netherlands on the types found in order to answer the question of national context. Finally we will discuss the findings with regard to the structural characteristics, according to which a transnational structure of individual Religiosity can be researched.

Types of individual Religiosity

In the analysis we have used a cluster analysis. As the cluster analysis generates homogenous groups the results reflect the structure of individual religiosity. We can talk about a transnational structure when German and Dutch young people are found in each of the types.

Ascertainment of the definers and implementation of the cluster analysis

The cluster analysis is based on definers, which have been chosen according to theoretical and statistical criteria. As regards theory the cluster analysis should reveal structures of religious individualisation. The latter penetrates the entire society, i.e. it works on a social (macro-level), institutional (meso-level) and individual level (micro-level). All three levels should thus be represented through the definers of the cluster analysis. As individualisation is most effective in the setting free of the individual from traditional contexts we have chosen three definers from the micro level and always one from the meso and macro-level. As regards statistics the definers should include a maximal distribution of individual religiosity. As a yardstick of individual religiosity the item "do you perceive yourself as religious?" (yes – don't know – no) was chosen because it contains the autonomy that is characteristic for religious individualisation. Therefore all scales of the investigation were related to the said item and on individual levels those were chosen which revealed a maximal scattering of means. In addition the definers had to be mutually independent so that there would be no cross-correlations. With this process the following definers were ascertained for the cluster analysis (cf. fig. 1): religion and the modern (negative), self-construction of faith, orientation guide, world orientation and image of God.

Fig. 1: Predictors to define Religiosity

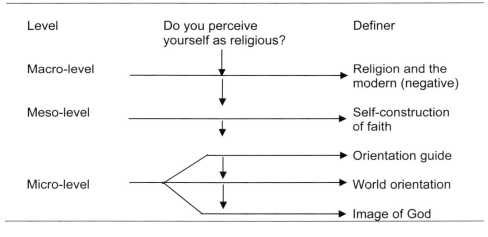

The chosen definers stand for the following attitudes: Firstly *religion and the modern (negative)* refers to the attitude that religious beliefs do not fit into a modern society and is situated on the macro-level. Secondly *self-construction of faith* represents the attitude that personal faith has to be build up by the individual and cannot be guaranteed by the institutions. It is situated on the meso-level. Thirdly *orientation guide* deals with the fact that religion gives orientation to someone's life. Fourthly *world orientation* contains the agreement with religious values. Fifthly *image of God* is about God as a being that can be experienced in oneself and other people. The last three scales are situated on the micro-level. The five chosen sets of statements cover themes in which differences in religious self-understanding can be seen. They are therefore suitable as a base for defining an empirical typology of the religious orientation among young people. The predictors have sufficient inter-item correlation (see fig. 2).

The Impact of Culture on Religiosity

Fig. 2: Items and psychometric properties of the scales that are used for the cluster analysis

Religion and the modern: α = .82 (6 Items)
Self-construction of faith: α = .71 (3 Items)
Orientation guide: α = .70 (5 Items)
World orientation: α = .89 (4 Items)
Image of God: α = .77 (5 Items)
Further information: Ziebertz/Kalbheim/Riegel 2003

To ascertain the number of clusters a hierarchical cluster analysis was carried out with a random selection of approx. 100 cases from the random sample (cf. about the method: see Ziebertz et.al. 2001). In addition it was ascertained that approximately half of the cases of this reduced random sample always came from the German and from the Dutch random samples. This analysis showed that five clusters result in a theoretically sound and statistically satisfactory result of the typology. Above the whole random sample the cluster analysis generates a typology that lies on average 1.3 from the cluster centres. Thus, the result of the analysis is acceptable.

Types of individual Religiosity

The single types of individual religiosity are characterised by the modelling of the five definers (cf. fig. 3). They are described in the following way:

Fig. 3: Empirical Typology of individual Religiosity

	Religion and the modern (neg.)	Self-construction of faith	Orientation guide	World orientation	Image of God
Churchly Christian	2.4	3.0	3.7	4.1	3.4
Autonomously Christian	2.9	4.3	3.7	3.7	3.9
Conventionally religious	3.3	3.8	2.8	2.7	3.2
Autonomously religious	3.0	4.6	3.4	1.8	3.3
Non-religious	3.6	4.3	2.3	1.4	2.0

1 = disagree strongly; 5 = agree strongly

The first group of young people is characterised by its nearness to the Christian faith as it is represented by the Church. These young people see no contradiction between religion and modern society; they recognise the Church as a religious community that lives the meaning of faith. Religion is to them an orientation guide for their own life and values like trust in God and being a believer are very important to them. In total churchly-Christian young people show a religious orientation that strongly agrees with the convictions of churchly Christianity. In their parish they have found a community that supports their faith socially. We therefore call these young people "churchly Christian". 18.3% of the young people in the entire random sample belongs to this group.

The second group of young people have several things in common with the first group. These young people also regard religion and the modern as compatible, orientate their life on religion and consider religious values as important. However, these young people are convinced that each one must find out for himself what he wants to and can believe. In this issue they do not prescribe any religious institution authority. In the image of God there are strong immanent characteristics, i.e., they imagine God as a power that moves human beings inside. We call this method "autonomously Christian." Approx. one quarter of the young people (24.6%) form this group.

The third type of religiosity is to be found in the evaluation of criteria in the mainstream. The young people of this type answer the question whether religion and modern society go together ambivalently. This also applies to religious values like faith in God or the desire that God will accompany them through their life. The fact that these young people recognise religion as an orientation and life guide shows that it is not a matter of religious indifference. For young people of this type religion is not a predominant theme and their relationship to religious attitudes and religious groups is not binding. Thus we call this type "conventionally religious". From the entire random sample 22.2% of the young people are conventionally religious.

The characteristic feature of the fourth type of religiosity is the desire for religious self-ascertainment and the strong distancing from Christianity as defined by the Church. Thus they reject values such as faith in God or being a believer. Religion and the modern do not fit together in their eyes, although religion is strongly connected to church-orientated Christianity. Religious autonomy is, however, not identifiable with an unreligious outlook for these young people. They accept religion as an orientation guide for their own life and represent an immanent conception of God. They contradict the different spiritual opportunities and "paint" their own personal beliefs by referring to different religious traditions. We call this type "autonomously religious". It represents 18.9% of the random sample.

The Impact of Culture on Religiosity   103

"Non-religious" young people could be identified as the fifth group. They are convinced that religion and the modern are not compatible; they cannot imagine that religion orientates their life and reject religious values. They are of the opinion that faith is something that a human being creates for himself, thus they reject the concept of God as an immanent power. Roughly a sixth of the young people (16%) are non-religious.

The existence of the typology confirms the conclusion of this investigation, according to which processes of religious individualisation lead to a differentiated field that does not consist of isolated peculiarities but is characterised by differentiable models. With regard to the first research issue it is decisive that young people from both countries belong to each of the types. That is the case (cf. fig. 4).

Fig. 4: Religious Types (in percent)

	Germany	Netherlands
Churchly Christian	25.0	9.7
Autonomously Christian	31.1	15.2
Conventionally religious	25.1	23.1
Autonomously religious	11.1	29.4
Non religious	11.4	22.6

Thus the first question can be answered as follows: although Germany and the Netherlands are clearly different in their religious life and in their access to cultural plurality the processes of religious individualisation follow a common model. There is thus a transnational structure to this individualisation.

The influence of nationality on the types of individual Religiosity

Alongside the fact that youth from both countries are to be found in each of the five types table 4 also shows that the five types in both countries are distributed differently. If Germany and the Netherlands agree on the proportion of conventionally religious youths in the German sample there are mostly autonomously Christian and churchly Christian youths, whereas in the Netherlands there are mostly autonomously religious and non-religious youths. These differences are highly significant (Cramers-V: .35***). German young people orientate themselves more in their individual Religiosity on the Christian symbolic system, whereas the Dutch young people have more religious variety.

These findings show that the cultural context influences the processes of religious individualisation. This influence is not principal as religious individualisation follows the same structures in both countries. As these structures are modelled differently, however, the modelling influence seems to be predominant. In order to confirm this suspicion we have investigated the distribution of the types in a tree analysis of the influence of the variables age, gender, religious conviction and nationality. The tree analysis produces the following results (cf. fig. 5).

Fig. 5: The impact of denomination and nationality on the frequency of individual religiosity (Answer Tree)

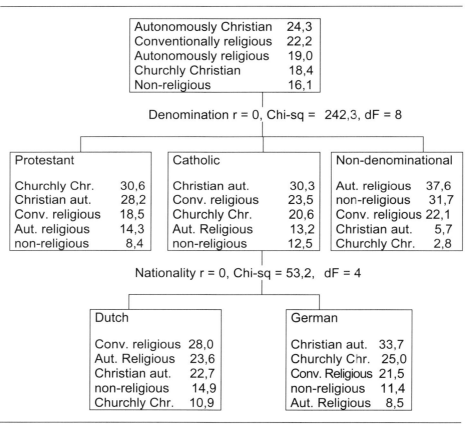

Legend: in %, d.F.: degrees of freedom; Chi.-sq.: Chi-square; r: correlation

The variables age and gender do not influence the distribution of the types of individual religiosity. For the answer to the second question this means that the two variables, which do not have any cultural connection, are not important.

The first difference appears with regard to the confession of the young people. The Catholics are one third autonomously Christian, almost one quarter are conventionally religious, a fifth churchly Christian and around an eighth autonomously religious or non-religious. The Protestant young people are mostly

The Impact of Culture on Religiosity

churchly Christian or autonomously Christian, almost a fifth are conventionally religious, followed by the autonomously religious youths (14.3%) and finally the non-religious young people with less than ten percent. In the group of the non-confessionals there are the most non-religious young people (31.7%), but this is also not the largest group. The autonomously religious type (37.6%) is predominant. More than a fifth of the young people are conventionally religious, autonomously Christian and churchly Christian youths together make up less than ten percent of the confessionals.

Nationality only plays an important role in the Catholic group. Here the distribution of religious types among the German Catholics corresponds to the distribution of the Catholic group in both countries. The Dutch Catholics reveal a clearly changed distribution in types: here scarcely 30% of conventionally religious youths can be found, followed by 23.6% autonomously religious young people and 27.7% autonomously Christian young people. Approximately one seventh of the Dutch Catholic youths are non-religious, a good tenth churchly Christian.

If we take these findings together the influence of religious traditions i.e. the confessional culture is more significant for the distribution of the types of individual Religiosity than the national culture. The latter only appears in the group of Catholic youths. This means simultaneously that the differing Protestant traditions in Germany (Lutheran) and the Netherlands (Calvinist) do not effect religious individualisation. The second research question can be answered as follows: The processes of religious individualisation are influenced by the cultural context, although the confessional inside culture has more of an effect than national differences.

Discussion

First of all the results confirm the assumption that in Germany and the Netherlands there is a transnational structure of religious individualisation. The setting loose of religious traditions is not different from country to country but reveals certain models that remain stabile across national borders. Furthermore religious individualisation is not a one-dimensional process away from the Church. If the churchly Christian and non-religious types are seen as the two end-poles of such a dimension the remaining three types cannot be conclusively found in them. If we placed the autonomously Christian type in this one-dimensional continuum we would have to explain why it was less religious than the churchly Christian type. There is thus a genuine differentiation in the field, not only an orientation more or less modelled on the religious institutions. The fact that we find common dimensions of religiosity in Germany and the Netherlands leads us to suspect that the religiosity in other European countries is dependent on similar dimensions. A further investigation into religiosity in Europe can be implemented on the basis of the selection made here; the three dimensions of Religiosity (macro-, meso- and micro-levels) could be used as a formal criterion for further empirical investigations in Europe. The modelling of the transnational culture remains linked to the cultural contexts of Germany and the Netherlands. The cultural climate of both states contributes to the concrete formation of the religious self-positioning of young people. According to the above findings both national and confessional aspects play a role. Culture proves itself as a complex concept that cannot be completely explained by nationality. Again it is suggested that these findings do not just deal with German-Dutch peculiarities. The precise influence of the cultural context and national peculiarities could be investigated in further representative, cross-cultural studies.

References

Campiche, R.J. (2001), Croire: le paradigme de L'individualisation? In: Ziebertz, H.-G. (ed.), Imagining God: Empirical Explorations from an International Perspective, Münster, 55–71.

Dubach, A., Campiche, R.J. (1993), Jede(r) ein Sonderfall? Religion in der Schweiz, Zürich.

Francis, L. (2001), The social Significance of religious Affiliation among Adolescents in England and Wales, in: Ziebertz H.-G. (ed.), Religious Individualization and Christian Religious Semantics, Münster, 115–138.

Krüggeler, M. (2001), Religious Individualization in Switzerland: Christian and Neo-religious Semantics, in: Ziebertz H.-G. (ed.), Religious Individualization and Christian Religious Semantics, Münster, 49–62.

Tomka, M. (2001), Persistence and Change or Religiosity and of Stereotypes of God in Eastern Central Europe, In: Ziebertz, H.-G. (ed.), Imagining God: Empirical Explorations from an International Perspective, Münster, 81–108.

Wippermann, C. (1998), Religion, Identität und Lebensführung. Typische Konfigurationen in der fortgeschrittenen Moderne, Opladen.

Ziebertz, H.-G., Kalbheim, B., Riegel, U. (2003), Religiöse Signaturen heute. Ein religionspädagogischer Beitrag zur empirischen Jugendforschung, Freiburg/Gütersloh.

Ziebertz, H.-G., Schlöder, B., Kalbheim, B., Feeser-Lichterfeld, U. (2001), Theologiestudierende im religiösen Suchprozess, in: Fürst, W. et al. (eds.), Theologiestudierende im Berufswahlprozess, Münster, 97–118.

The Author

Dr. *Hans-Georg Ziebertz* is Professor of Practical Theology and Religious Education, Faculty of Theology, University of Würzburg, Germany. His main research interests: religious socialization, comparative empirical research, religion and modernity. Latest publications: Hans-Georg Ziebertz and Ulrich Riegel (eds.), Europe: secular or post-secular? LIT: Münster/Hamburg/London 2008; Hans-Georg Ziebertz and Ulrich Riegel, Letzte Sicherheiten. Eine empirische Untersuchung zu Weltbildern Jugendlicher. Gütersloher Verlagshaus (Gütersloh)/Herder (Freiburg) 2008; Hans-Georg Ziebertz, William K. Kay (eds.), Youth in Europe II. An international empirical Study about Religiosity, LIT: Münster/Hamburg/London 2006.

Eberhard Hauschildt

The Factor Religion from the Perspective of the Third Sector Comparative Studies: Where Practical Theology needs to speak out against methodological secularisation

The following study on secularisation is about the secularisation of theory. In this case it is through methodological design that religion as an object of research evaporates. I want to show a) how it comes that religion is excluded from a whole field of study, b) that it is necessary for theology to engage in this field of interdisciplinary debate, and c) I also want to give one example of the contribution theology can make to this field of study. If theologians or other experts of religion had been included in the third sector comparative research or had shown more interest in this project and accompanied it with their critical remarks, it may have taken another route. But so far this is something that still has to be done, and my remarks are meant as preparatory to such an endeavour.

I. The pragmatic argument

The "Comparative Nonprofit Sector Project" studies (cf.: http://www. jhu.edu/ ~cnp/) form a cluster of renowned research, based in the Johns Hopkins University at Baltimore, Maryland. They aim to clarifying the scope and amount of a phenomenon in modern societies commonly called the "third sector". The metaphor of the third sector is derived from presenting modern society as being formed by two organisational forces: state and business organisations. Both, politics and economy, have a distinct logic, the former of hierarchical power, and the latter of the market effectivity. However, against the background of state failure as well as market failure, private initiative arose to meet certain human needs. Above all it is the social challenge of the poor and the suffering which asks for a solution that can neither be given through profitable business nor can it be effectively solved by a state bureaucracy. In practically all modern societies, whatever the very diverse traditions and – also very significant – tax laws might be, there is a third sector of non-profit organisations to be found.

It is one of the achievements of these comparative studies that the size of this sector, its weight in regards to employment figures and rates of financial growth have now been widely recognised.

The project starts out from a definition of the organisations of the field to be studied. Third sector organisations have a number of characters in common. They are "organised" (not just informal), "private" (separate from government), "non-profit distributing", "self-governing" and "voluntary" (with a significant amount of voluntary work) (cf. Salomon/Anheier 1997). Thus, religious organisations in principal qualify as organisations of the third sector.

The Factor Religion from the Perspective of Third Sector Comparative Studies   109

Nevertheless: "Religious organisations are excluded [...] for reasons of data availability and cross-national comparability" (Anheier/Seibel 2001: 26; cf. Anheier et al. 1997: 154). The reasons given for the exclusion of religion are solely pragmatic ones: it is simpler to do so. It makes the tasks easier; otherwise the data collection could not conveniently be based on existing statistics.

Such a rationale would be justified if the religious factor were negligible for the field to be studied. However, such a claim is obviously absolutely unfounded in regards to history (cf. Kaiser 1998) and at least very debatable for the description of the situation today. To make this point one needs not even go to other authors than those of the Johns Hopkins Project or to such theories of the third sector which are in contrast to the theories employed by these authors.[1] It is quite clearly stated that the relations between this sector and the churches are "especially close and manifold" (Anheier et al. 1997: 226). Anheier suggests for the future of the third sector, that it should "keep its core of charitable activities – here, the value orientation of the third sectors promises an advantage in competition for such groups of society, which are cherishing a Christian, humanitarian or other value-oriented mission." (Anheier 2001:71).

II. Other facets of methodological secularisation

The picture of methodological oversimplification of a complex scientific task needs to be completed.

Facet 1: Since for practical reasons churches are excluded, the effect is that also an analysis of the field of religious organisations seems to be not necessary for the project. When the different types of third sector organisations are categorised in the project, religious organisations which work in certain fields of the society such as social services, health care or education, are registered as third sector organisations of the subtype social services, health care etc. And thus, the fact that they are religion-based and religion-related is, to a lesser or stronger extent, now invisible. As "religious organisations" as such are excluded from research, only such organisations count which have the organised

---

[1] Also the theories about the rise of the third sector, which the authors have in mind, all do have to say something about religion (I follow the discussion in Anheier et al. 1997): The theory of *heterogeneity* states that religious organisational pluralism creates a large non-profit sector. The theory of *supply* (Angebot) points to religiously motivated entrepreneurs in a situation of competition. According to the theory of *contract failure* people seek for the credibility of non-egoistic suppliers. The theory of *welfare states* replacing pre-modern religious activity, however, has been proved false (236). The theory of *interdependence* rather concludes that there was a co-evolution of the third sector and the welfare state. *Institutional theories* distinguish between corporatistic, liberal, etatistic and social democratic models of society. In the first two cases religions do play an important role, in the second they have been rather marginalised.

110 Eberhard Hauschildt

liturgical or verbal expression of faith as their main task. Thus here is an implicit reductionist definition of religion at work: religion is a matter of preaching and praying. Only explicit religion is counted, the fact is not taken into account that for many religious bodies it is a core activity of faith to show also religiously motivated action in which religion is not explicit but implicit.

Facet 2: About the thus reduced core organisations of religion it can be stated that they account for a not so large part of the third sector. A study including data from 27 countries (Salamon et al. 2003: 25) concludes that only 8 % of the non-profit workforce (5 % of paid, 13 % of unpaid) belongs to religious bodies. Such findings then could serve as a legitimation in retrospect for the pragmatic exclusion at the start of the project. If, however, one takes the religiously motivated and related organisations into account, the figures, I suggest, will be significantly different. Then we will have cases like Germany where in a number of activities in the important areas of health care and social services around 30% of the work have clear institutional ties with one of the two large church bodies (Wissenschaftliches Institut 1998: 9). I find it safe to assume that in quite a number of countries the figures for the actual religious participation in the third sector should at least double the figures given by Salomon et al.

Facet 3: There are hints in the literature that the authors finally simply follow the classical theory of secularisation which states that religion has significantly lost its weight for society and therefore will lose even more in the future. For the case of Germany, Anheier quotes figures of members leaving the church and of a decline in church service attendance and in the numbers of priests and nuns/deaconesses in order to support the thesis that "in the future, the church [...] will lose ground and therefore will be no more a politically effective force" (Anheier 2001: 60). Meanwhile simplistic secularisation theories have been challenged. Theories of transformation rather than simply a reduction of religion would lead exactly to the question as to in what way more privatised religious motives are present in all kinds of third sector idealism. Theories which say that secularisation is a special case of Western Europe, rather than of all industrial societies, would make it feasible that the influence of religion in the third sector might just as well grow as decline. Thus in regard to the theory of religion in society these studies rely on a somewhat outdated state of the discussion on secularisation.

Facet 4: The authors do not take into account the distinctions between different religious affiliations. An important theory for the rise of the third sector in Germany states that its size is the result of a historical compromise between state and church, a weak state and a strong church, whereby the Catholic Church is implied. For the beginning of the social legislation in the early 1920s following the model of subsidiarity which was the idea of a catholic party to be included in the government coalition this is correct. However, in the 19th century we have a predominance of protestant activities closely linked to the protestant political establishment – not at all in conflict with the state. The incorrectness to present only the catholic Church and the workers movement as the decisive forces (Anheier et al. 1997: 81) is of significance, because the logic of religious institution is not the same as in Protestantism. In catholic institutional understanding social activities are ideally an integral part of the hierarchic ordered Church, in protestant reasoning they are the enterprise of individual Christians or local churches. So it is typical at least in Protestantism, though a similar environment also leads to similar trends in Catholicism, for Christian individuals to form organisations in the third sector which are not so much directly (through organisation), but rather indirectly (through Christian ideals) linked with the field of religion. Protestant organisations of health care and social services may appear secularised and are to a stronger degree exposed to the trends of loosening the ties with the church. This, however, does not mean that these ties can be neglected completely. The development of a strong sector is not simply a case of strong organisations competing with the state; it is also a matter of a culture of idealistic entrepreneurism and a delicate relationship between the organisational independence of "Diakonie", i.e. protestant social service organisations, and the churches and congregations. These observations do not simply apply to Germany, but also to other countries (cf. Lienhard/ Schmidt 2006).

Methodological secularisation does not only consist of a pragmatic exclusion of religion, but also leads to the uncritical use of a reductionist definition of religion and of outdated secularisation theories; it results in the invisibility of the real impact of religion.

III. Values in third sector organisations

Beyond complaining about the fact that its expertise about religion is overlooked, theology should actively participate in the constructive interdisciplinary discourse. One way would be to discuss another question in the third sector debate which baffles the discussion: what is it that makes third sector organisations special? (Birkhölzer et al. 2005) Do they have a logic which is unique to them or is there rather simply an area of mixed logics of state and business? Anheier talks at one point of "value boundedness" (Anheier 2001, 70) as a characteristic of the third sector. And indeed, if we actually want to name a distinct characteristic of third sector organisations it seems to be this value orientation. (Birkhölzer et al. 2005) The literature in the project is very vague about this, as are the sociological and political concepts (cf. Wex 2004). In theology however (as well as in philosophy), there is a thorough debate about what values are and what they can do, also a critical debate about what values are not and what their dangers are. It seems to me that a theory of the third sector can profit considerably from these discussions. I will not go into this in more detail, but rather outline the scope of discussion as providing an

112 Eberhard Hauschildt

interesting interdisciplinary field between third sector research and theology (cf. Körtner 2003; Wegner 2005):

1. Values make interest relative. Third sector work is driven not simply by the criteria of effectiveness or meeting the demands of stakeholders, but also by the question: what is right to do? What is the truth about what it means to be human and what can be concluded for necessary action? This has consequences for the culture of the third sector organisations.

2. Talking and reasoning about values combines individual experience of what is right and wrong (e.g. in the context of religious experience and matters of conscience) with an intersubjective debate of what in a group and in a society should be considered as intersubjective values, and thus can be used for an ethical debate about which goods in a certain situation are preferable.

3. This discourse on values enhances awareness and responsibility and thus differs from a culture of obedience by the threat of sanctions.

4. Values are helpful for reducing a complex situation to a limited number of options in positioning the conflicting values concerned. However, the discourse on values can be abused to produce never ending discussions rather than reaching decisions.

5. Certain values are particularly cherished in the different sectors. Third sector organisations are an embodiment of the value of solidarity, whereas the value of freedom forms the foundation for business, and equality the foundation for the state with its lawgiving power. Values must be seen in a historical context. The value of solidarity is rooted in the different traditions (humanism, workers movement, Jewish/Christian tradition) with distinct interpretations.

6. The third sector in a way guarantees the liberality of society, for it states that there are limits to the logics of the political and also the economical system. The discourse on values in the third sector is an occurrence of *civil* religion – a way to point to transcendence in such a way that all members of society can be included in this discourse.

7. Value discourse as civil *religion* points to transcendence of values being connected with transcendence in the religious sense: God in his actions of love and justice stands for values and demands that values be respected.

8. Religion is also critical about values. The Jewish/Christian tradition at least has a vision that humans do *not* in fact meet the demands the values proclaimed (in religious language this is called "sin"). They also say that a distinction must be made between the value of every human being

(“created in the image of God”) and the consequences of deeds (“the justice according to one's deeds”). And they say that this discrepancy is bridged by God himself (“salvation”, “justification of the sinner”). Thus value orientation and albeit religiously legitimised values are contrasted with a religious experience of truth that is critical of a “tyranny of values” (Jüngel: 1979) and a “moral overkill” in third sector organisations.

I thus conclude: a theologically informed discussion of values offers three contributions to the third sector debate: 1. It increases the awareness of the implications of the value discourse in the third sector. 2. It points to special benefits of the third sector for the presence of values in society at large. 3. It points to specific benefits from religious organisations in the third sector for restricting the value orientation to a humane degree.

Religious identities in the third sector as fractured and multifold as they are should be taken into account. If one does so the results become simply more accurate compared to simplifying methodological secularisation.

References

Anheier, Helmut K. (2001) Der Dritte Sektor in Europa: Wachstum und Strukturwandel, in: Eckhard Priller and Anette Zimmer (eds), *Der Dritte Sektor International. Mehr Markt – weniger Staat?*, Berlin: sigma, 57–74.

Anheier, Helmut K. and Seibel, Wolfgang (2001) *The nonprofit sector in Germany: Between state, economy and society.* Manchester /New York: Manchester University Press.

Anheier, Helmut K., Priller, Eckhard, Seibel, Wolfgang and Zimmer, Anette (1997) (eds) *Der Dritte Sektor in Deutschland: Organisationen zwischen Staat und Markt im gesellschaftlichen Wandel*, Berlin: sigma.

Birkhölzer, Karl, Klein, Ansgar, Priller, Eckhard and Zimmer, Anette (2005) (eds) *Dritter Sektor / Drittes System: Theorie, Funktionswandel und zivilgesellschaftliche Perspektiven*, Wiesbaden: Verlag für Sozialwissenschaften.

Jüngel, Eberhard (1979) Wertlose Wahrheit. Christliche Wahrheitserfahrung im Streit gegen die ‚Tyrannei der Werte‘, in: Carl Schmidt, Eberhard Jüngel and Sepp Schelz, *Die Tyrannei der Werte*, Hamburg: Lutherisches Verlagshaus, 45–109.

Kaiser, Jochen-Christoph (1998) Die Bedeutung des religiösen Faktors für die soziale Arbeit im 19. und 20. Jahrhundert in Deutschland: Bilanz der Forschung, in: Arnd Götzelmann, Volker Hermann and Jürgen Stein (eds), *Diakonie der Versöhnung: Ethische Reflexion und soziale Arbeit in ökumenischer Verantwortung*, Stuttgart: Quell, 116–131.

Körtner, Ulrich H.J. (2003) Wirken mit Werten. Theologische Erwägungen zum Jahresthema der Diakonie 2003, in: *Danken und Dienen 88,* 26–32.

114 Eberhard Hauschildt

Lienhard, Fritz and Schmidt, Heinz (2006) *Das Geschenk der Solidarität. Chancen und Herausforderungen der Diakonie in Frankreich und Deutschland*, Heidelberg: Winter.

Priller, Eckhard and Zimmer, Anette (2001) *Der Dritte Sektor: Wachstum und Wandel. Konzepte Stiftungen 2. Aktuelle deutsche Trends. The Johns Hopkins Comparative Nonprofit Sector Project, Phase II*, Gütersloh: Bertelsmann Stiftung.

Salamon, Lester M. and Anheier, Heltmut K. (1997) (eds) *Defining the Non-Profit Sector: A Cross-National Analysis*, Manchester: Manchester University Press.

Salamon, Lester, Sokolowsky, Woijcech and List, Regina (2003) *Global Civil Society: An Overview*, Baltimore: Johns Hoskins University.

Wegner, Gerhard (2006) *Wirtschafts-Werte. Wertschöpfung oder Begeisterung?*, Berlin: Lit.

Wissenschaftliches Institut der AOK (1998) *Der Pflegemarkt in Deutschland: Ein statistischer Überblick*, Bonn: AOK.

Wex, Thomas (2004) *Der Non-Profit-Sektor der Organisationsgesellschaft*, Wiesbaden: DUV, Gabler.

The Author

Eberhard Hauschildt, Prof. Dr. theol., born 1958, is Professor for Praktische Theologie at the Evangelisch-theologische Fakultät of the Rheinische Friedrich-Wilhelms-Universität Bonn. Recent publications: Claudia Schulz/Eberhard Hauschildt/Eike Kohler. Milieus praktisch. Analyse- und Planungshilfen für Kirche und Gemeinde, Vandenhoeck&Ruprecht, Göttingen 2008; Klaus-Dieter Kottnik/Eberhard Hauschildt (Hg): Diakoniefibel. Grundwissen für alle, die mit Diakonie zu tun haben, CMZ-Verlag/Gütersloher Verlagshaus Rheinbach/Gütersloh 2008; Public Theology in the Market of Academic Education. Reflections on the Involvement of Practical Theology in the Master of Arts in Social Services Administration Programme at the University of Bonn, in: Elaine Graham/Anna Rowlands (eds.), Pathways to the Public Square. Practical Theology in an Age of Pluralism. International Academy of Practical Theology, Manchester 2003 (International Practical Theology, vol. 1), Münster 2005, 295–302.

Terence Kennedy

Natural Law in a Time of Secularization

The category of natural law seems to have disappeared from ethics and social theory, not so much pushed out of consciousness as simply forgotten. Three centuries ago it was the mainstay of these disciplines. Since it identified what was common to all humanity it was employed to provide the language needed for communication between cultures. Its demise is associated with secularization understood either as the disappearance of religion altogether or as its ever diminishing influence on society due to the processes of modernization. The impact of this process recently became apparent in the debate over the Christian roots of Europe in the proposed Constitution. This essay does not pretend to examine natural law as such but to look briefly at this phenomenon. It does not sketch a comprehensive account of its evolution but only indicates some important changes in the history of ideas that helped bring it about.

The Predicament of the Natural Law Today

The moment of truth arrived with the French Revolution. By 1820 natural law as a point of reference for ethics and the social sciences was invisible except in a few enclaves of Catholic theology. The age of revolution was hailed to mark the victory of secularism over superstition.[1] The Revolution itself was based on a version of natural law or natural rights which is why it declared the Rights of Man. Of course society in the age of reason willingly ascribed to the Ten Commandments as encapsulating what reason required in morality. Although the Church was widely appreciated as a moral instructor she was just as thoroughly rejected as a teacher of dogma. Philosophers believed that en-lightened reason could give a better rendition of moral rules than faith which consequently became unnecessary in morality.

Except for a few isolated attempts to update natural law thinking in terms of contemporary ideology, as in Ernst Bloch's *Natural Law and Human Dignity*,[2] it seems to have exhausted its history in a secular society.

Bloch's title is significant since it reveals that the focus has shifted, the dignity of the person replacing natural law as the source of human rights. Attempts to codify the Rights of Man into constitutions and civil codes in the nineteenth century ran strongly in this direction. The United Nations' Declaration on

---

[1] See J. B. Schneewind, *The Invention of Autonomy*, Cambridge University Press, Cambridge 1998, 457–8 for its influence on ethics.

[2] MIT Press, Cambridge MA 1986.

116 Terence Kennedy

Human Rights in 1948 and the Covenants that give birth to the new generations of human rights completed the cycle.

Various reasons are given for the collapse of natural law – the Enlightenment's invention of autonomy, Newton's physics that refuted the hierarchical structure of the universe into which natural law was inserted, the relativizing and historicizing effects of the theory of evolution, not to mention nihilism and the wave of relativism we are currently experiencing. In short, enlightened reason was held to have overcome the obscurantism of medieval Christendom.

Another Way of Telling the Story: Sociology and History

But there is another way of recounting natural law's fortunes. This will be done first from the point of view of sociology and history, then in philosophy and theology.

F.X. Kaufmann, the sociologist, is convinced that the roots of secularization go back much further than the standard account.[3] He traces it to the separation of the Eastern and Western Churches, to the conflict between Pope and Emperor in the Middle Ages and to an original way of distinguishing the secular and sacred orders in society. This released resources of reason that brought about a liberation of the secular sphere from ecclesiastical hegemony at the Reformation. The wars of religion occasioned a new theory, Grotius's *etiamsi Deus non daretur,* a formulation that effectively rendered God redundant. This in turn led to the ideas that inspired the Revolution and its attempt to apply natural human rights to remodel the political community.

The historian Ernesto Galli della Loggia can affirm this account but, as is usually in countries with a Catholic culture, views it in terms of Church-State relations. For him secularization has arrived in two waves.[4] First, the liberation of social institutions from ecclesiastical hegemony since the time of the Revolution, and second, the psychological process that has become predominant in the last 30 years whereby people's way of life, mentality and mental framework are no longer influenced in depth by the Church as formerly. Natural law fell out of sight in the middle in this upheaval.

---

[3] See his argument in "Religion and Modernization in Europe," in *Journal of Institutional and Theoretic Economics,* 153 (1997) 1, 80–96.

[4] Points taken from a talk, "Fondamenti del pensiero cristiano e sfida della cultura laica: Chiesa al bivio?" at the *Istituto S. Tommaso*, Pontifical Angelicum University, Rome, March 3, 2007.

The Philosophers' and Theologians' Story

Philosophers and theologians see secularization as a phenomenon that happens within the Judeo-Christian tradition. This touches the question of the rationality of ethics and social theory in this tradition directly.

Patristic scholars emphasize that natural law entered this tradition when the Fathers in a rather catechetical way assimilated the Stoic conception into their narration of the history of salvation. We might ask what gave natural law such a sacred awe that it became a fit candidate for secularization. First of all the Stoic sources are both utterly rational and profoundly religious, but in a confused pantheistic way. In a certain sense the Fathers invoked the Christian doctrine of creation to demythologize the Stoics' philosophy so that reason emerged in its own right as open to revelation and capable of welcoming it by grace. In turn this made a revealed vision of God's action in human history possible. This interpretation contradicts E. Troeltsch's version[5] of a hellenizing of the Scriptures, taming them to meet the demands of the Greek *logos*. Medieval theologians continued this line of argumentation, treating natural law as a species of *lex divina,* that is, the rationality of ethics and social institutions have their origin in God. This is no divine command theory in the modern sense, but the autonomy of ethics and the social order rather finds its ultimate fount and justification in God.

In this faith vision the rationality of natural law was instilled interiorly in creation. But when it became obscured by evil it had to be restored externally by the written revelation of Sinai. The Ten Commandments promulgated to Moses on stone tablets but served to manifest the profundity of human nature, the law inscribed on the human heart. The same natural law was reproclaimed and redisvcovered in Christ through what we call the New Law of the grace of the Holy Spirit. The natural law as seen through the eyes of faith provided the rational criteria the Fathers needed to engage in public discourse on issues of religion and morality in the Roman Empire.

A. Passerin d'Entrèves[6] was a professor of jurisprudence at Oxford who set out to explain how natural law functioned in various legal systems. For example, in Justinian's Code natural law was sacralised to legitimate the Caesaropapist conception of state power in the Byzantine Empire. But, precisely because it was embedded into the legal system as a whole, it became so extremely effective in moulding social mores. Natural law here represents not just transcendent values but acts as an imminent force for their realization. In the Middle Ages natural law was used to give proper weight to the secular in theology so that marriage, family, education, trade and commerce were recognized as truly

---

[5] *Die Soziallehren der christlichen Kirchen und Gruppen,* Mohr, Tübingen 1912.
[6] *Natural Law,* Hutchinson's University Library, London 1951.

secular institutions willed by God. A. Passerin d'Entrèves also highlights how the revolutionary ideal of the Rights of Man derive from a rationalist secularized conception of natural law. He concluded that that natural law had been the motor behind both sacralizing and secularizing thought according to the worldview under whose spell it fell or which was predominant at that moment. But his approach was not historicist. We might well also inquire: whether natural law was more the cause or the victim of secularization, or both?

Voluntarism and Intellectualism

Harold Berman in his study of the origins of the Western legal tradition, *Law and Revolution*[7] sees secularization as being a long-term outgrowth of the Gregorian reform that put the dialectic between secular and sacred in motion. Both civil and canon lawyers could dynamically integrate and elaborate natural law as part of their comprehensive visions of society but in different manners. This had the results already noted so that Berman believes that our situation is a result of that dialectic.

The balance that had thus been set up shifted at the Reformation which treated natural law not so much in terms of a natural deliverance of reason but on the basis of God's will revealed in Scripture. This stance was inherited from the voluntarist current in medieval philosophy that set itself steadfastly in opposition to the intellectualism of a theologian like Thomas Aquinas.

Baroque Catholic scholasticism in the person of Francisco Suarez tried to harmonize the voluntarist and intellectualist streams by writing them both into his theory of natural law. He explained natural law as both descriptive, that is, its norms represent intrinsic goods or evils on the hypothesis of their belonging to an order of pure nature, and as imperative, that is, it becomes binding by adding an obligation imposed by God's will. It now became possible to separate or split off the rational content of natural law, expressed as intrinsic goods and evils, from its obligatory force deriving from the divine will. Suarez's version of natural law dominated in manuals of Catholic moral theology up till Vatican II. But could natural law be legitimated without reference to the divine will so that religion no longer played an essential role in constituting it?

The ground was now ready for Hugo Grotius to declare that when he practiced the law he found no need of referring continually to God. Although a deeply religious scholar he introduced the conception that switched the fundamental direction in which theories about natural law moved and developed thereafter. He wanted to bring the wars of religion to an end by proceeding on the nominalist hypothesis of *etsiamsi Deus non daretur*. That would remove the denominational divisions that were sadly destroying the political community from

---

[7] Harvard University Press, Cambridge MA 1983.

Natural Law in a Time of Secularization

the public square. He was determined to discover a minimum standard on which the parties in conflict would be compelled to agree. This he found in the demands of reason as founding natural rights in law.

The process reached a natural climax when Immanuel Kant realized that reason conceived in this way had to find a new basis for its operation. It was a fact that since Grotius it had been swirling around a vacuum at its centre. It was Kant's genius to perceive that the concept of the dignity of the human person should fill this vacuum. Such a person has to be treated always as an end in itself and never merely as a means. Its dignity derived from the autonomy of practical reason which imposed the moral law on the human subject. Human rights were then to be founded on the dignity of the human person acting autonomously according to this law. That this was a radical secularization of thought with distant consequences not clearly foreseen at that time was something its authors did not appear to fully appreciate.

Person and Natural Law

The person in Christian and in Jewish theology is defined as the image of God, the *imago Dei* given in creation. In the Judeo-Christian tradition natural law was impressed with the *imago Dei* at creation as the person's inclination to realize itself precisely in God's likeness.[8] This inclination was toward the absolute good, God, for whom it had a natural desire. Faith like reason then shared or participated in the divine reason. It was therefore fundamentally rational even if it does not clearly see the evidence of that for which it yearns. The task of reason was to guide our actions as they actualized our inclinations in search of fulfillment in God. The conception of reason at the base of natural law in this tradition is that it is a participation in the divine creative reason. Further, if reason is a participation in the divine wisdom then the diametrical opposition of faith and reason that characterized the Enlightenment is not possible in this tradition. Here, however, is a very different concept of reason from that which has held sway for the last few centuries since the age of rationalism.

The Christian idea of the person was fixed in the tradition by the early Ecumenical Councils of the Christian Church at Nicea and particularly Calcedon, in the dogmas on the Incarnation of the Word and of the Trinity.[9] Kant and with him the tradition of the Enlightenment by excluding dogma as completely beyond the range of philosophical concern[10] thus in fact saw the person as self-

---

[8] The ideas and those that follow are best expounded in St. Thomas Aquinas's *Summa Theologiae.* As regards the *imago Dei* consult *S.T.,* I, 93. For Aquinas's ideas on law and its types see his law tract in *S.T.* I-II, 90–105.

[9] See Johannes A. van der Ven, Jaco S. Dreyer, and Henrich J. C. Pieterse, *Is there a God of Human Rights?,* Brill, Leiden 2004, 428.

[10] See J. Werbick, *Soteriologia*, Queriniana, Brescia 1993, charter 1.

120 Terence Kennedy

founding and so in no rational need of God. Still the Ten Commandments remained valid on the basis of pure reason alone, that is, as extraneous to the history of salvation.

Habermas's Contribution

Jürgen Habermas seems to be the author most insightfully and acutely aware of how the conflict between faith and reason impinged on the image of God as a faith dependent concept, something reprehensible to modern criteria of reason. He notes that the *imago Dei* was the ideal that enabled the modern democratic state to treat all citizens as equal and as enjoying the same rights. This was made available by a religious conception of morality that helped contribute this mainstay of democracy, a mainstay that democracy depends on in its workings but which it does not provide just of itself as Böckenförde has so powerfully argued. Habermas has changed his previous opinion and is now convinced that believers must engage from their particular point of view in public discussions on bioethics or the environment. Nevertheless, the traditional conception of natural law remains problematic[11]. He also has pointed out that secular humanistic thought has been unable to distance itself from the Judeo-Christian schema of sin and redemption even though it does not share the faith that makes it intelligible. He acknowledges therefore that secularized conceptions of both salvation and the moral law have permeated contemporary culture as tacit premises for both personal and social conduct. In his own theory Habermas assigns natural law what he calls discourse-theory meaning which provides an answer to the following question: "what rights must citizens [...] mutually grant one another if they decide to constitute themselves as a voluntary association of legal consociates and legitimately to regulate their living together by means of positive law."[12]

The Contemporary Catholic Problematic

Johannes van der Ven insists that the notion of natural law has become ambiguous and fears that it may be employed by religious bodies as a pretext for hegemonic universalism.[13] The Catholic Church has consistently used natural law as the reference point for what reason requires in morality and in her social doctrine. Since Pope Leo XIII this doctrine has often been under-stood both as a response to and on the same level as secular autonomous reason. When Vatican II came to consider "The Church and Man's Vocation," Part I of *Gaudium et Spes,* it based its teaching on human dignity and human rights on

---

[11] See J. Habermas and J. Ratzinger, *Dialektik der Säkularisierung*, Herder, Freiburg 2005, 32.
[12] See van der Ven et al. 2004, 252.
[13] Van der Ven et al., 213–216.

the Church's understanding of Scripture and tradition without making any explicit mention of natural law. It seems that the Council Fathers were not persuaded that natural law was an apt and suitable means of communication in a document that aimed at dialogue with the contemporary world.[14] This seems strange since natural law might be considered as a sort of depth grammar for human rights, ensuring that what is common to all humanity be respected. And so it guarantees communication between diverse cultures and societies. The Council did, of course, invoke natural law as a foundation for religious liberty and it has returned strongly in Pope John Paul's encyclical *Veritatis Splendor* in 1993 as an fundamental constitutive of moral theology.

J.B. Schneewind in his history of "the rise and fall of modern natural law" places the turning-point at the moment when Grotius remodeled the tradition, making it discontinuous, so that it assumed a completely different profile. His intention, like most of the new natural lawyers, was not anti-religious, nor did they have any plan to secularize society. Nevertheless the tectonic plates underlying Western culture shifted in a seemingly irreversible way. Schneewind sums it up this way, "Grotius removed natural law from the jurisdiction of the moral theologian, to whom Suarez assigned it, and made its theory the responsibility of lawyers and philosophers. Numerous Protestant writers on ethics and the foundations of politics followed him in using the language of natural law while detaching it from the specific doctrines of any particular religious profession, whether Protestant or Catholic."[15]

We might conclude that the Catholic Church is confident that human reason can account for of its autonomy but that natural law has become problematic to a society that denies the theological and philosophical conceptions that support it.[16] She remains convinced that she should use natural law to communicate with the wider society and with other cultures. But there remains a tension between her conception of natural law, the person and human rights and the modern presuppositions of autonomous reason. For this reason Pope John Paul II in January 2004 called on Catholic scholars to rethink natural law in the conditions of contemporary culture. This is a tremendous challenge.

The Author

Terence Kennedy, C.Ss.R., born 1942, ordained a Catholic priest in the Redemptorist Order in 1969, professor ordinarius of systematic moral theology in the Alphonsian Academy, Rome, and visiting professor at the Gregorian University. Research interests in the philosophy of science, rhetoric, and the pastoral practices of the Catholic Church.

---

[14] See Philippe Bordeyne, *L'Homme et son angoisse: la théologie morale de »Gaudium et Spes«*, du Cerf, Paris 2004, 236–244.

[15] J. B. Schneewind, 82.

[16] Habermas and Ratzinger, 18–21.

Recent publications have been on the theology of the virtues, grace, and human dignity and natural law. He has published a two volume manual of moral theology "Doers of the Word" (St Pauls, London 1996), translated into Italian as "Praticare la Parola" (Dehoniane, Bologna 2007).

Annemie Dillen

Highlighting children's spirituality in a de-traditionalised society: The challenge of theologising with others for religious education and pastoral care

Religion in society: an ambiguous situation

The phenomenon of secularisation causes much concern in many involved with Christian education and pastoral care. In Belgium, teachers are confronted with children for whom Christian concepts are totally strange. It is obvious today that many 17-year-old adolescents could not tell you what is Lent or the name of the Pope, even after following 12 years of obligatory religious education. On the other hand, we still find many references to Christian elements in Belgian society, for instance in advertisements or holidays, which take into account Christian days such as Ash Wednesday or Pentecost. At the same time, teachers also notice an increased openness of their pupils to learn about the significance of religion because they continue to be confronted with it, but do not really know what it means. People engaged in the church are confronted with a similar phenomenon. In crisis situations or at important life events, people often expect the church to offer a ritual or even a sacrament. Simultaneously, pastoral workers notice that many people do not have any feeling of connection with the church and often do not want to be engaged in it.

Secularisation, pluralisation, de-traditionalisation

This exemplary description reveals a lot of ambiguity concerning religion. 'Secularisation' processes explain much about this situation in the twentieth century[1], but the religious reality today can be even better grasped via the concept 'de-traditionalisation'[2] (in combination with pluralisation). It is not that religion is totally absent from people's lives or the public arena; parts of religious traditions are still present. What happens is that traditions as such are experienced in a fragmented way. We find also the rise of different forms of religiosity, as, for example, the phenomena of new age religion and even the

---

[1] H. COX, *The Myth of the Twentieth Century. The Rise and Fall of 'Secularisation'*, in G. BAUM (ed.), *The Twentieth Century. A Theological Overview*, New York, Orbis, 1999, 135–143, p. 135.

[2] L. BOEVE, *Beyond Correlation Strategies. Teaching Religion in a De-traditionalised and Pluralised Context. A Playground for Socio-Cultural and Theological Renewal*, in H. LOMBAERTS & D. POLLEFEYT (ed.), *Hermeneutics and Religious Education* (BETL, 180), Leuven, Peeters, 2004, 233–254; See also: L. BOEVE & H. GEYBELS, *Catholic Theology in Europe*, http://www.uni-tuebingen.de/INSeCT/cd/europe-boeve-geybels.html#_ftnref18 (access 12.03.2007).

124 Annemie Dillen

rather vague faith in 'something'[3] ascribed by many. In any case, the present 'pluralisation' means that people are confronted with a kind of 'heretical imperative'[4], the obligation to choose one of the many religions available in our society.

De-traditionalisation and two general reactions

This de-traditionalisation confronts people with ambiguity. Human experiences are not easily interpreted as either positive or negative in light of a larger tradition. This awareness of ambiguity should not be neglected by trying to add new certainties and securities. To recognise the ambiguity of reality means to be willing to think critically. It means, for instance, that in an apparently dysfunctional family situation, one can seek and stimulate elements of hope and positive interactions. It also means that in apparently healthy family situations, one can also look for hidden injustices; it is clear that being a 'model family' is vital to some families, whereas this does not always mean every family member is happy. Another example of this ambiguity is the wonder of nature. Whereas the awesome beauty of nature can be interpreted as a sign of God, nature can be equally dangerous and destructive, making the reference to God more difficult.

Together with a general awareness of ambiguity in society, ambiguous attitudes towards religion due to de-traditionalisation lead to various responses[5]. Some people try to minimalise religious ambiguity by prioritising secularisation. This attitude leads to an easy acceptance of current developments, such as banning Christmas figures from public, or replacing religious education in schools with philosophy. Louvain theologian Lieven Boeve's description of the model of 'institutional secularisation' similarly: "result[s] in a neutral or neutral-pluralistic institution, an institution in which Christians are present although not necessarily so. Explicit reference to the Christian tradition out of which a particular institution has evolved (for example in the name it adopts) is then abandoned"[6].

---

[3] See for instance: G.D.J. DINGEMANS, *Ietsisme. Een basis voor christelijke spiritualiteit?*, Kampen, Kok, 2005; K.E. BIEZEVELD *et al.*, *In iets geloven : ietsisme en het christelijk geloof*, Kampen, Kok, 2006.

[4] P.L. BERGER, *The Heretical Imperative. Contemporary Possibilities of Religious Affirmation*, Garden City, Anchor, 1980.

[5] For theological reflections on ambiguity, see for instance R. PAGE, *Ambiguity and the Presence of God*, London, SCM, 1985; S. ROSS, *Extravagant Affections. A Feminist Sacramental Theology*, New York-London, Continuum, 2001, p. 65ff.

[6] L. BOEVE, *Giving a Soul to Education in Europe: A Challenge for Catholic Schools*, http://www.kpszti.hu/magyar/kulugy/AGBudaEN.rtf (access: 09.03.2007).

Another reaction is the search for security in order to overcome the ambiguity. Due to a lack of safety and unchangeable truths in a de-traditionalised society, we notice a movement that aims to create more secure places for children. I will focus on children as this highlights general characteristics of our society and church.

Searching for security for children

Children are today often perceived as very vulnerable. Many parents are afraid of the various dangers threatening their children, such as the internet, sexual abuse or traffic accidents. This general fear that is characteristic of our 'risk society' (Beck)[7] accompanies a romantic image of children: children are seen as very precious, needing protection against these and other threats.

Historians speak of a beginning, or at least an intensification, of this image of children as vulnerable with social acts to protect them in the romantic period. Although the thesis of Philippe Aries[8] – that childhood was only discovered after the Middle Ages – is controversial, the tendency of 'pedagogisation' is clear[9]. This is the movement towards an increasingly pedagogical treatment of children and 'setting children apart' in pedagogical islands such as schools, youth movements and playgrounds. A protective attitude often complements a focus on children's socialisation: their need to learn what is necessary to live in society and develop themselves. Socialisation is often directed towards the future and the way in which children can become performing adults. From the perspective of childhood studies, one hears the critique that children are often presented as not-yet-adults, those who are not yet competent.

Searching for personal happiness

This aim of securing children, in reaction to the modern ambiguity that characterises our post-modern, de-traditionalised society, is not only influenced by the rather romantic idea about vulnerable and incompetent children, but also by the search for personal happiness and wellbeing. The idea that children should be protected and socialised is typical for the contemporary period and refers to the adult authority and even the power to create a better world by, among other things, educating children. The search for personal happiness, however, is something typically post-modern and can be seen as a response to the end of

---

[7] U. Beck, *Risikogesellschaft. Auf dem Weg in eine andere Moderne*, Frankfurt a.M., Suhrkamp, 1986.

[8] Cf. P. Aries, *L'enfant et la vie familiale sous l'Ancien Régime* (Civilisations d'hier et d'aujourd'hui), Paris, Plon, 1960.

[9] M. Depaepe, *De pedagogisering achterna. Aanzet tot een genealogie van de pedagogische mentaliteit in de voorbije 250 jaar*, Leuven-Amersfoort, Acco, 1998, ²1999.

126 Annemie Dillen

the big stories: people like to find their own, unique personal stories that lead them to wellbeing. The search for personal happiness and wellbeing is meant to give sense to life in a confusing world. This striving for personal happiness can change the aim of pedagogisation in the way that socialising and protecting children is not necessarily a means for creating a better world, but it is at least a means to help children live in the world. The combination of the socialising and protecting attitude with the goal of guaranteeing personal wellbeing leads to a form of security that helps people to deal with the ambiguity of the de-tra-ditionalised society.

Value education as an expression of the search for security and happiness

Within this general movement to give children a safe and clear education, I distinguish between two common reactions. The first reaction can be characterised by striving for 'value education'[10]. Christian institutions, schools, and pastoral care services are wrestling with the question of what Christian identity means in a secularised and pluralistic context. When asked about their Christian identity, schools often refer to Christian values. Belgian parents also, when asked why they want their child to receive first communion, for instance, or to go to a Catholic school, often answer that the child they care so much about will receive a good value education in this Christian context.

The term 'moralistic therapeutic deism', used by the American researcher Christian Smith[11] to describe the American situation, can also be applied. Many schools, teachers and parents want children to learn how to be good citizens, how to behave in a morally acceptable way, how to be able to have a productive life and fulfil social norms. Religion is used as a 'moralising' tool in many situations. Additionally, Catholic care services or Catholic youth movements often define their Catholic identity in terms of values or value education. In this context, God is often used as a principle (deism) legitimising an education in values. In this discourse one sometimes hears about following Jesus and being his disciple. However, the God of Abraham, Isaac and Jacob who challenges people and who is not easily grasped, only seldom appears in this kind of discourse. Nevertheless, many questions about the meaning of life, suffering and death, the presence or the absence of God, could occur in these settings. There is a danger that these existential questions be answered too

---

[10] L. BOEVE, *Katholieke universiteit: vier denkpistes*, in *Ethische perspectieven* 10 (2000) nr. 4, 250–258.
[11] C. SMITH et al., *Soul Searching: The Religious and Spiritual Lives of American Teenagers*, Oxford, Oxford University Press, 2005. For a comment, see also: K.M. YUST, *God is Not your Divine Butler and Therapist! Countering 'Moralistic Therapeutic Deism' by Teaching Children the Art of Theological Reflection*, in A. DILLEN & D. POLLEFEYT (ed.), *Children's Voices. Children's Perspectives in Ethics, Theology and Religious Education*, Leuven, Peeters, 2009 (forthcoming).

simply and easily. This is what is meant by 'therapeutic deism': religion is presented as a therapeutic tool, rather than a way to live with the insecurities of life[12].

'Reconfessionalisation' as an expression of the search for security and happiness

Whereas this first reaction reduces faith to values, others try to find safety in a strong and neo-orthodox focus on Christian identity. Boeve describes the 're-confessionalisation' of Christian institutions, where "Catholic education aims at the explicit expression of its Catholic identity and organises its educational system for Catholics and by Catholics."[13] This model of thought may focus on Christians alone to the negligence of the public secular debate. The Catholic World Youth Days are an expression of this choice: although they are highly public, they intend to be an activity of Catholics for Catholics (or 'not-yet-Catholics'), to help young people build stronger Catholic identity by meeting each other. The (Youth) Alpha course is another example of this second reaction, which focuses on the Bible, faith and liturgy as well as building strong communities by bringing people together and giving them a sense of belonging to a group, a particular identity and an unambiguous religion. The course – approximately ten meetings centring on the gospel and the spirit – is meant to help people seeking sense in our de-traditionalised world[14] by giving clear religious answers to existential questions or assisting with personal healing along the lines of Smith's 'moralistic therapeutic deism'.

We also find this reaction in pedagogical theories that focus on a strong initiation of children in Christian faith, without space for discussing other religions or perspectives. Some people would say that children are not able to deal with many different perspectives, and thereby espouse a not-yet vision of children, as explained above. In the call to give children and adults more initiation into the essence and truth of Christian faith, and in the common opinion that children cannot deal with different perspectives, this rather dogmatic reaction is

---

[12] See also: M. WOHLRAB-SAHR, *Zwischen Unsicherheitstoleranz und rigider Sicherung. Biographien Jugendlicher in der sich modernisierenden Moderne*, in G. HILGER & G. REILLY (ed.), *Religionsunterricht im Abseits. Das Spannungsfeld Jugend-Schule-Religion*, Munich, Kösel, 1993, 171–181, p. 179–180.

[13] L. BOEVE, *Giving a Soul to Education in Europe*.

[14] See A. VAN HARSKAMP, *Religieuze ruis. Over de wedergeboorte van het religieuze*, in A. DILLEN & D. POLLEFEYT (ed.), *God overal en nergens. Theologie, pastoraal en onderwijs uitgedaagd door een 'sacraal reveil'*, Leuven, Acco, 2006, 25–50, p. 43. See also S. HUNT, *Anyone for Alpha? Evangelism in a Post-Christian Society*, London, Darton, Longman and Todd, 2001 and T. WATLING, *'Experiencing Alpha'. Finding and Embodying the Spirit and Being Transformed. Empowerment and Control in a 'Charismatic' Christian Worldview*, in *Journal of Contemporary Religion* 20 (2005) nr. 1, 91–108.

128 Annemie Dillen

similar to the model of values education, as it seeks to exclude insecurity and ambiguity while providing emotional and intellectual safety and comfort.

Knowing children and their spirituality

From the literature on children's spirituality we learn however that there are alternatives to these reactions – alternatives that are based on different concepts of the child and theology. Children are vulnerable, and in need of protection and socialisation. These images need not blind us to the competences of children and their capability to give. If children are seen as 'active agents', if they are described as 'knowing children'[15], it is possible to theologise with children and to take seriously their own spirituality and their own search for sense and faith.

Childhood studies and the children's rights movement advance the idea of children as 'competent subjects' with a certain degree of autonomy, as a complement to the idea of children who are vulnerable and need to be socialised and protected. Children are not only passive receivers and objects of care and protection by adults, but they have an 'agency' and are able to act in a significant way[16]. This also means they can have ethical and religious insights which are, although influenced by parents, teachers and other significant others, not only a copy of what others say, but a testimony of a personal, autonomous view of the world.

Research on the spirituality of children, as well as reflections on children's characteristics, show us that the classical paradigms of developmental psychology (Piaget, Kohlberg and others) should not form the only or absolute foundation[17]. Classical developmental psychology sees children in terms of 'not-yet', whereas both theological and empirical research teaches us that children are able to reflect upon and to experience religious elements, although this is not an automatic process.

---

[15] A. HIGONNET, *Pictures of Innocence. The History and Crisis of Ideal Childhood*, New York, Thames and Hudson, 1998; See also B. MILLER-MCLEMORE, *In the Midst of Chaos. Caring for Children as Spiritual Practice*, San Francisco, Jossey-Bass, 2007, p. 64–66.

[16] P.B. PUFALL & R.P. UNSWORTH (ed.), *Rethinking Childhood*, Camden, NJ, Rutgers University Press, 2004.

[17] E. MARTENS, *Kinderphilosophie und Kindertheologie – Familienähnlichkeiten*, in A.A. BUCHER et al. (ed.), *'Kirchen sind ziemlich christlich'. Erlebnisse und Deutungen von Kindern (Jahrbuch für Kindertheologie, 4)*, Stuttgart, Calwer, 2005, 12–28, p. 19.

Theologising with children

If children are also seen as active subjects, theologising with children is relevant as a way of integrating their own ideas and questions into the process of religious education. Theologising with children is an approach similar to philosophising with children, an increasingly popular activity today[18], with the basic assumption that philosophical questions can be discussed with children, rather than reserved for academics alone. Questions like 'is this shoe real?' and 'what does "real" mean?', or 'can you classify people?' can be discussed with children and usually leads to deep insights that even surprise and teach adults. Doing philosophy with children does not mean that the classical philosophical theories are explained to children in an easy way. It is a method of stimulating children to be astonished about the world, to think for themselves, to search for answers and new questions. Philosophical thinking with children is a way to help children experience themselves as 'spiritual beings', if we use 'spirituality' in a broad sense[19].

Theologising with children differs in content: religious themes, such as biblical stories or rituals, are dealt with explicitly and elements of religious traditions are discussed. Theologising with children is aimed at stimulating children's Christian spirituality. 'Theologising with children' offers children religious tradition not as something to be easily accepted, but rather as a valuable legacy that can be explored in different ways. This 'open' way of speaking about religion is not self-evident. In comparison to philosophising, certain issues, like awareness of children's competences and keeping the tradition's 'orthodoxy', may prevent people from accepting the value of theologising with children. The teacher can use religious elements as starters for 'theologising with children'; for instance a painting of Christ, a movie with religious elements or the sign of the cross. 'Theologising with children' presupposes that one does not see the tradition as 'fixed' or 'closed', but as open to change.

This model is relevant also in other contexts than just the classroom. For instance in a hospital, a pastoral worker may have the opportunity to touch upon a religious theme, which can lead to a 'theological talk' where the patient is taken seriously, where there is mutual exchange and learning between the pastor and the patient, and where elements from the tradition are not taken for granted. 'Theologising with children and others' acknowledges that adults and

---

[18] G. MATTHEWS, *Philosophy and the Young Child.* Cambridge, MA, Harvard University Press, 1980; ID., *Dialogues With Children.* Cambridge, MA, Harvard University Press, 1984.

[19] D. RATCLIFF & S. MAY, *Identifying Children's Spirituality, Walter Wangerin's Perspectives, and an Overview of This Book*, in D. RATCLIFF (ed.), *Children's Spirituality. Christian Perspectives, Research and Applications.* Eugene, OR, Cascade Books, 2004, 7–21, p. 9.

130 Annemie Dillen

children are not completely different but can learn from each other in a common, complex world that challenges them and their religious understandings.

Theologising with children, as a model for conversations about religious themes, implies resisting the two reactions towards social ambiguity and uncertainty that give people a feeling of belonging and certainty, namely the reduction of religion to value education or secure truths. Theologising with children, but also with others, takes seriously the ambiguity of life – teaching a certain 'tolerance of uncertainty' – without adopting a relativistic mentality of 'anything goes'. This does not mean that a secure foundation (e.g. the Christian tradition) is placed against the insecurities of life, but that people are able to deal with insecurity as a necessity in life. It requires abstinence from "moral rigor that makes a clear distinction between good and bad or between friend and enemy"[20] as well as necessitating strong basic trust. Therefore, religious education and pastoral care that includes 'theologising' must be grounded in non-intellectual values, such as trust, awe, mutual recognition and appreciation and communal belonging.

The Author

Annemie Dillen, Prof. Dr., born 1978, Assistant Professor of Pastoral Theology at the Faculty of Theology, K.U.Leuven, Belgium; Chair of the Academic Centre for Practical Theology, K.U.Leuven. Research interests: family ethics, children and theology, pastoral care, religious education. Recent publications: A. Dillen, *Children Between Liberation and Care: Ethical Perspectives on the Rights of Children and Parent-Child-Relationships*, in *International Journal of Child Spirituality* 11 (2006) nr. 2, 237–250; A. Dillen, *Encourager la spiritualité chez les enfants: à la recherche du don mutuel entre parents et enfants*, in *Counseling et spiritualité/Counselling and spirituality* 26 (2007) nr. 1, 125–142; A. Dillen (ed.), *When 'Love' Strikes. Social Sciences, Ethics and Theology on Family Violence*, Leuven, Peeters, 2008 (in press).

---

[20] M. WOHLRAB-SAAR, *a.c.*, p. 180.

Solange Lefebvre

Secularization and Disestablishment of the Church: Theoretical and empirical discussion around the case of French Roman Catholics in Quebec

This paper reflects on the relationship between religions and civil society, with special attention to the Francophone Roman Catholics in Quebec. The Francophones are a special case in English-speaking North America, and exploration of that matrix of communities opens to more detailed analysis of Canadian religious and social structures in relation to the global secularization discussion, both in sociology and theology. In particular, it illustrates positive and negative functions that the Catholic Church can play in history and the multiple consequences of the current secularization process. In this paper, I focus on the Francophones in Quebec.

Theoretically, this paper considers theological resources needed to face a religious institutional decline and to cope with diverse forms of disestablishment in western countries. The work of two authors will be particularly helpful, the theologian David Fergusson and the sociologist Jose Casanova.[1] The simple question of the relation among church, state, and civil society is sociological. Therefore, is it outside of a theological scope? In many ways, it is. But today, if theologians are involved in public debates regarding religion in the public arena, they inevitably address issues of disestablishment. The question of how to address these questions is complex, and is not fully evident. To reflect adequately on the theological dimensions, we need to do so in relation to sociological elements that compose the so called "secular societies."

Fergusson, inspired by Casanova, elaborates a combined theological and sociological approach, taking into account the differentiation among diverse social spheres and paying particular attention to *civil society*. His project, contextualized in England and Scotland, is quite similar to my project in Quebec, even if the state-religion relationship is quite different. At the end of his book he argues in favour of disestablishment in the two countries. Casanova also helps to understand the conditions of a "relevant" disestablishment.

Theology in Canada does not take an active part in discussing this framework, but practical theology is on the front line of the concrete issues related to it. The paper focuses on the province of Quebec as a case study, seeking to understand the secularization and disestablishment processes. Through these

---

[1] David Fergusson, Church, State and Civil Society, Cambridge (Cambridge University Press) 2004; Jose Casanova, Public Religions in the Modern World, Chicago (The University of Chicago Press) 1994.

132 Solange Lefebvre

developments, the paper shows some of the main issues addressed by practical theology.

The Quebec Roman Catholicism

Within the larger Canadian context, Quebec offers an interesting case study to illumine the processes of secularization and disestablishment and to identify challenges for practical theology. We analyse the province of Quebec as a case study in dialogue with theories and theological reflections on secularization and disestablishment, especially those proffered by Casanova and Fergusson. Table 1 reveals the patterns of religious affiliation in Quebec. Quebec is still the province with the highest proportion of Roman Catholics, mostly from French origins, even if the percentage is diminishing (2001, 83%; 1991, 86%). The other world religions are mostly concentrated in the area of the city of Montreal.

Table 1: Major religious denominations, Quebec, 1991 and 2001[2]

	2001		1991		Percentage change 1991 – 2001
	Number	%	Number	%	
Roman Catholic	5,930,385	83.2	5,855,980	86.0	1.3
Protestant	335,595	4.7	359,750	5.3	-6.7
Christian Orthodox	100,370	1.4	89,285	1.3	12.4
Christian, not included elsewhere[3]	56,750	0.8	38,975	0.6	45.6
Muslim	108,620	1.5	44,930	0.7	141.8
Jewish	89,915	1.3	97,730	1.4	-8.0
Buddhist	41,380	0.6	31,640	0.5	30.8
Hindu	24,530	0.3	14,120	0.2	73.7
Sikh	8,220	0.1	4,525	0.1	81.7
No religion	400,325	5.6	257,270	3.8	55.6

1. For comparability purposes, 1991 data are presented according to 2001 boundaries.

2. Includes persons who report "Christian", as well as those who report "Apostolic," "Born-again Christian," and "Evangelical."

---

[2] Statistics Canada, 2001.

[3] See http://www12.statcan.ca/english/census01/Products/Analytic/companion/rel/tables/provs/qcmajor.cfm#ftnt2.

As far back as 1986, Montreal's estimated 1,500,000 Catholics already included more than 20% (350,000) people whose mother tongue was not French; of these, 225,000 were of Italian origin.[4] Each Sunday, mass is celebrated in more than 25 languages. In 2005, the diocese of Montreal had a list of forty cultural and worshiping communities in its territory: Italian, Cambodian, Congolese, Laotian, Latvian, Latin American, Copt, Haitian, Lithuanian, Spanish, Vietnamese, Portuguese, Hungarian, Polish, Croatian, Japanese, Korean, Chaldean, Tamil, Philippine, Slovak, and Czech Missions. The question is: will these ethnic communities compensate for the decline of the Catholic Church? Maybe partly, but we do not know much about this impact yet.

In his comparative studies, Reginald Bibby mentions the 'magnitude' of the drop-off in church attendance in Quebec from the 1970s on. In the first "severe crash," attendance dropped from 88% in the mid-1950s to 42% by 1975 and it then fell further to 28% by 1990, around 20% more recently. He observes a similar "measure of disenchantment with the Catholic Church" in the other provinces, but the decline has been less dramatic and attendance still remained at 37% in 1990, partly due to Catholic immigration.[5] Ferretti (1999) agrees that Roman Catholicism has been particularly marginalized in the province of Quebec. However, all the authors agree that there exists certain dynamism on the issues of social justice and political transformation in all of Canada's French-speaking Catholic communities[6].

Nevertheless, we certainly need to conduct a specific reflection on the complex reasons for institutional decline. Because of the complexity, theoretical analysis is vital for full understanding. Thus, we now turn to a theoretical discussion on secularization.

Casanova's thesis

Jose Casanova's famous contribution has been to clarify the concept of secularization and its three meanings: differentiation, decline of religious beliefs and practices, and marginalization and privatization. Beyond this contribution, he has also described religion's departure from the private sphere to get into the public arena, which Casanova calls "deprivatization."[7] All of the cases he studies are characterized by a dynamic civic movement, which is supported by the

---

[4] Mario Paquette, Les Communautés Ethniques et Rituelles dans le Diocèse de Montréal [Ethnic and Ritual Communities in the Diocese of Montreal], in: L'Église de Montréal 1836–1986, Montréal (Fides) 1986, 342–365.
[5] Reginald Bibby Restless Gods. The Renaissance of Religion in Canada. Toronto (Studdart) 2002, 17–18.
[6] Lucia Ferretti Brève histoire de l'Église catholique au Québec. Montréal (Boréal) 1999.
[7] Casanova, Public Religions in the Modern World.

churches. Casanova values the churches' contribution to civil society, even suggesting that the way to succeed in the modern or postmodern world is to accept disestablishment, and give support to the differentiation of the spheres. Indeed, this is one meaning of the secularization concept: "secularization as differentiation remains the valid core of the theory of secularization" as well as the modern principle of citizenship.[8] Looking at the United States example and a few European countries, Casanova writes, after Tocqueville and Marx:

> [I]t was the caesaropapist embrace of throne and altar under absolutism that perhaps more than anything else determined the decline of church (the second meaning of secularization – religious decline of religious practice and beliefs) religion in Europe (exceptions being in this regard France, Spain, Ireland, Poland). … One may say that it was the very attempt to preserve and prolong Christendom in every nation-state and thus to resist modern differentiation that nearly destroyed the churches in Europe[9].

I would add that it was also some negative public functions that people perceived the churches playing in some national histories, in Quebec and Ireland for instance. Casanova presents five case studies, five different patterns of separation of church and state: Poland, Spain (which resisted tragically to the modern trend of differentiation), Brazil, and the United States (Catholicism and Evangelicals). Three of these are national churches with quasi-monopolistic control over the religious market in their countries, and two are inserted in a highly pluralistic religious market, the United States.

I will give attention to what seems to me to be one key idea of Casanova, around the denomination as a voluntary and dynamic religious group. He writes: "[W]hen a religion becomes disestablished … it becomes a voluntary religious association, either a sect or a free church (and) and turns into denomination(s): 'a general modern structural trend' similar to Tocqueville's democratization, Marx's proletarianization, and Weber's bureaucratization."[10] If Casanova's study says very little about the types and nature of modern private religions, or about the character and modes of self-reproduction of the modern differentiated religious sphere, he tentatively suggests that those religions that accept and embrace the modern principle of differentiation will usually accept the modern denominational principle of voluntarism. Further, they will be in a better position to survive modern process of differentiation and adopt a form of evangelical revivalism as a successful method of religious self-reproduction in a free religious market.[11]

---

[8] Casanova, 212–13.
[9] Casanova, 29.
[10] Casanova, 212.
[11] Casanova, 214.

Casanova lists three conditions that justify the deprivatization of religion: (1) when religion contributes to public debates to improve modern freedoms, rights, and democracy against an authoritarian state; (2) when it struggles against the pretension of the secular spheres to be independent from external ethical considerations or principles; and (3) "when religion enters the public sphere to protect the traditional life-world from administrative or juridical state penetration."[12] The first way for religion to enter the public sphere serves "in the very constitution of a liberal political and social order." In the second and third ways, religion serves "to show, question, and contest the very 'limits' of the liberal political and social order."[13] This brief resumé of Casanova's thesis opens the way to reflect on the challenge of voluntary culture for Christianity, especially for Francophone Roman Catholics in Canada.

Voluntary Culture as a Theological Challenge

The "voluntary religious culture," as well as the civil society, is central to the Quebec case, which is itself in a process of secularization at all of Casanova's three levels: differentiation, decline, and privatization. The process is stronger in some areas, weaker in others, but is, overall, an ongoing process. Statistical data on certain forms of civic voluntary culture are important at this point, so we turn to a governmental study called "Formal and Informal Volunteering and Giving in Different Regions of Canada."[14]

In 2000, the lowest rates of voluntary giving were found in Quebec and British Columbia (74%), with the lowest average annual donation in Quebec ($117). Quebec also had the lowest rate of volunteering (19%) and, along with the Prairies, the lowest median hours volunteered (69 and 68 hours, respectively).[15] Paul Reed and Kevin Selbee explain this trend in terms of the disaffinity of Quebecers for formal organizations, both in their contributory behaviour and in their participation in community organizations.

---

[12] Casanova, 57–8.

[13] Casanova, 58.

[14] Paul B. Reed/L. Kevin Selbee, Formal and Informal Volunteering and Giving. Regional and Community Patterns in Canada, Statistics Canada, 2000, Catalogue No 75F0048MIE – No. 05.

[15] While public commentators have been noting these differences for years, particularly the low levels of contributory behaviour in Quebec, no explanations have been advanced so far, to account for them. In their paper, Reed and Selbee suggest that any analysis of variations across Canada in the patterns of contributory behaviour is incomplete if it focuses solely on the formal modes of contributing. When informal modes of contributing – those ways of giving and helping that are not mediated by formal organizations – are also considered, the pattern of regional variations changes significantly.

136 Solange Lefebvre

> One perspective [...] suggests the aversion to formal organizations in Quebec may be symptomatic of the weaker development of civic culture among Francophones.[16] Alternatively, aversion to organizations may be an adjunct of Quebecois culture.[17] Simply put, one consequence of the traditional dominance of the Catholic Church and the English economic elite in Quebec society is that Quebecers place less trust in formal organizations than is the case elsewhere in Canada. As a result Quebecers place more emphasis on informal as opposed to formal means of helping than other Canadians do.[18]

We should add that Quebec Francophones were more involved in the reform movement following Vatican II, influenced by a strong movement of lay participation. This was somewhat broken by the project of re-centralization and re-clericalization under the pontificate of John Paul II.[19] To understand the dynamics, however, we need to inquire into the qualities and power of voluntary culture: for what kind of organization do people get involved, and why do they put their confidence in such an organisation? The data collected by Statistics Canada helps to reflect on some links between this weak civic culture and Catholicism. Whether we agree or not with Casanova's thesis, it is true that civic culture, or voluntary culture, is a key to the churches' survival. In theological terms, the church relies on the capacity of people to stand up for their faith, regardless of the relevance of the hierarchy.

Disestablishment

But what does disestablishment mean? The prior question is to define an "established church." Fergusson offers a few perspectives. One perspective emerged in the time of Thomas Erastus; "Erastianism" means that the State controls the Church. More generally, however, establishment means a partnership:

> a partnership between church and state that recognises the integration of civil and church life. This can be marked in a variety of ways [...] establishment is not a univocal concept. It has different meanings across space and time. The same applies to 'disestablishment.'[20]

In this regard, establishment can include:

---

[16] John Goyder/ Timothy I. McCutcheon, Francophone Life Satisfaction and Civic Culture. A Meta-analysis of the Canadian Case, in: Social Indicators Research 34, 1995, 377–394.

[17] The authors refer to a similar aversion to organizations in the Italian-American community of Boston, in: Herbert J. Gans, The Urban Villagers. Group and Class in the Life of Italian-Americans, NewYork (Free Press of Glencoe) 1962.

[18] Reed/Selbee.

[19] The last news concerning this re-clericalization comes from Quebec City, where a conservative bishop was nominated: very soon, lay people have found themselves restricted in their roles.

[20] Fergusson, 168–169.

Secularization and Disestablishment of the Church

- Privileges in return for services rendered (church taxes, financial privileges), ministry for rites of passage, chaplaincy in civic bodies;

- Ratification of some church decisions by the state, or approval in making pastors' appointments; head of state in a ceremonial relationship with the church;

- Civil citizenship and religious baptism interrelated (complete distinction between the two occurred in Quebec only a few years ago, in Sweden in 1996);

- Monarch as the Church Head or special member (as in England);

- Privileges for church regarding careers in Parliament, municipal office, etc.

In Quebec, there were certainly social established Churches. Even if the Protestant and Catholic Churches did not have an official status in the Canadian constitution, they had lots of privileges, and they still have some. The Supreme Court of Canada declared in 1955 that "in our country, there is no state religion."[21] Indeed, the Canadian constitution does not attribute privileged status to any religion; nevertheless, the constitutional and legislative texts do *not* treat all religions equally.[22]

Let us look at a few examples of the integration of civil and church life, past or present, in Quebec:

- In 2000, the government decided to secularize the public school system which provided denominational religious education for Catholics and Protestants; each Canadian province can decide whether or not they maintain this privilege, established in the 1867 Canadian Constitution;

- Until the 1960's, religious communities often gave public services to the State (health and social services, education), a practice that continued in many cases until recently, but has declined rapidly since then; a Christian-labelled organization can hardly be financed by the state since the 1980's;

- Some religious symbols and practices have been present in the political arena, such as: prayer in political assemblies, oaths on the Bible, Christian symbols in government buildings (like the crucifix). To eliminate these symbols and practices, some groups have gone to court, and some have won, appealing to the religious freedom embedded in the Canadian (1982) and Quebec Charter of rights.

---

[21] Legal reference, Chaput c. Romain, [1955] R.C.S. 834, 840 (M. le juge Taschereau).

[22] See for example: Pierre Bosset/Paul Eid, Droit et religion. De l'Accommodement Raisonnable à un Dialogue Internormatif [Law and Religion. From Reasonable Accommodation to Internormative Dialogue], in: Actes de la XVIIe Conférence des Juristes de l'État, Cowansville (Éditions Yvon Blais) 2006, 63–95.

138 Solange Lefebvre

Let us look a little bit more carefully at the secularization of the public school system. In Quebec, until recently, Catholic and Protestant churches enjoyed the privilege of offering denominational instruction within their separate public systems. Then, adoption of the 1977 French Language Charter ushered in a period of growing diversity in Quebec's French-language schools, especially in greater Montreal. With the charters of rights and freedoms (Quebec in 1975 and Canada in 1982), respect for freedom of conscience and religion became a matter of greater concern. After several years of debate,[23] the government succeeded in redefining the schools along linguistic lines (French and English) rather than religious lines (Catholic and Protestant). By 2008, religious education will take the form of a series of courses entitled "Ethics and Religious Culture." As for now, each school should already be offering a neutral "Spiritual Care and Guidance and Community Involvement Service" addressed to the various groups of religious and non-religious students; which means that there is no more denominational chaplaincy allowed. This reform has huge consequences on practical theology in Quebec, since many practical theology graduates have been working in the public denominational school system. Practical theology now has to deal with new professions: teachers of religious culture and spiritual care, which will be interreligious and neutral at the same time. The field is now under redefinition.

This example shows that the Charters of rights have major consequences in the process of disestablishment. Furthermore, a thin frontier exists between the cultural and religious meanings of any symbol or expression. For example, after the secularization of the public school system, the remaining religious symbols in the schools are to be considered carefully with respect to their historical and cultural meaning. At the same time, these symbols should not impair the religious freedom of any student or teacher. How do we keep the balance between history and the growing pluralism of our society? How do we balance between the majority and minority? These are common issues in all Western countries. Some say that Canada is ahead of the movement. Certainly, Christianity still

---

[23] Ministère de l'Éducation [Ministry of Education], Laicité et Religions. Perspective Nouvelle pour l'École Québécoise [Laity and Religions. New Perspective for the Quebec School], Research Report from the Groupe de Travail sur la Place de la Religion à l'École [Working Group on the Place of Religion in Schools], Quebec (Government of Quebec) 1999; Ministry of Education, Dans les Écoles Publiques du Québec. Une Réponse à la Diversité des Attentes Morales et Religieuses [Public Schools in Quebec. A Response to the Diversity of Moral and Religious Expectations], Quebec (Government of Quebec) 2000. Concerning the practical theology debate on religion in Quebec's schools, see, for instance: André Charron (ed.), École et Religion [School and Religion], Montreal (Fides) 1995; Solange Lefebvre (ed.), Religion et Identités dans l'École Québécoise [Religion and Identities in Quebec Schools], Montreal (Fides) 2000; Raymond Brodeur/ Gilles Routhier/Brigitte Caulier (eds.), L'Enseignement Religieux. Questions Actuelles [Religious Education: Current Issues], Quebec/Paris/Brussels (Novalis/Cerf/Lumen Vitae) 1996.

Secularization and Disestablishment of the Church   139

has an influence but its privileges are disappearing more quickly than else-where. Moreover, many recent institutional and juridical decisions enhance people's rights to express minority religious faith publicly, as in wearing a religious symbol or respecting religious holidays in the workplace or at school.

The Disestablishment Religious Option

We must consider a counter hypothesis. Could establishment be a protection against secularism? This counter argument is quite important, even if Fergusson sees it as "residual support." A pluralistic social vision, with strong argument in favour of equality, may promote, in reality:

> [a] new form of establishment, the establishment of the secular which prohibits the intrusion of religious convictions in public debate. It is partly on account of this fear, that leaders of other churches and faith communities express a preference for something like current forms of establishment.[24]

In England, for instance, some would prefer an inclusive Anglicanism to an intolerant secularism. In Canada, and especially in Quebec, the same attitude is present. Groups and individuals who plead for the recognition of pluralism (consequently secularizing the public school system and religious education, removing prayers from the public sphere, and so on) are often implicitly or explicitly secularist, in the name of religious pluralism. There are also believers who think that the secularity of the state and the public sphere is fundamental. Many religious people, however, would prefer to keep religious traditions in the public sphere.

The anthropologist Talal Asad takes Casanova's thesis seriously, but he criticizes it, arguing that the separation between the secular and religion is not so clear, between the rational state and the irrational religion. He is making an anthropological reading of the secular, asking for instance the following question: "secularists accept that in modern society the political increasingly penetrates the personal. At any rate, they accept that politics, through the law, has profound consequences for life in the private sphere. So why fear of religious intrusion into private life?" Recalling the debates in France on "laïcité," he argues that secularism attempts to redefine the "practices of the self that are articulated through class, gender, and religion, in order to create in people an identity that transcends local identities."[25] To the view of Asad, secularism was

---

[24] Fergusson, 187–188.

[25] Talal Asad, Formations of the Secular. Christianity, Islam, Modernity, Stanford (Stanford University Press) 2003, 181–6, 5. See similar arguments in my article: Solange Lefebvre, Origines et Actualité de la Laïcité. Lecture Socio-Théologique [Origins and Actuality of Laity. A Socio-Theological Reading], in: Théologiques, ed. Solange Lefebvre, 6, no 1, March 1998, 63–79. See also: Richard Figuier, Dieux en Sociétés. Le Religieux et le Politique, Paris (Autrement) 1992.

140 Solange Lefebvre

defined in light of a particular conception of the world and its problems. In a certain way, the clear separation of religion and the state is a myth. Casanova replied to Asad in a recent text, saying mainly that he did not intend to examine all forms of religions, Islam for instance, but "those modern forms of public religion that are not intrinsically incompatible with differentiated modern structures"[26].

The Canadian theologian Douglas Farrow also critiques Casanova's view:

> Christianity understands the concept of secularity precisely as a principle of modesty, even if it hasn't always lived by that modesty itself. The present age, it insists, contains nothing final or ultimate except the promise of the gospel itself. Politicians and judges, and clerics too, must not imagine that they are competent to introduce true freedom and peace on earth. That is sheer hubris and self-deception [...] Casanova, however, appears content to ignore most of this, since it does not conform to Enlightenment canons.[27]

I question whether Casanova endorses the Enlightenment so extensively. The diverse forms of deprivatization he points out are precisely ways to challenge Enlightenment, without threatening the necessary separation of powers between the State and religion (the remaining valid core of the secularization thesis). I do think, as Fergusson does, that Casanova's central hypothesis is insightful: that the civil society constitutes the most relevant theological and ecclesiological locus of the churches.[28] Fergusson gives three reasons for new interest in this concept:

1. the necessity in a post-communist and post-totalitarian era to recreate the semi-autonomous institutions of civil society: diverse community groups, unions, and religious organizations;

2. the state's need to act "in partnership with the private sector" to provide welfare and to support living communities (in which churches have long experience);

3. the social crisis in western societies due to fragmentation, individualism, and consumerism, which causes a crisis in all institutions, especially in churches (and the diverse religious groups of Canada). "These require the

---

[26] J. Casanova, "Secularization Revisited: A Reply to Talal Asad", in D. Scott & C. Hirschkind eds. Powers of the Secular Modern. Talal Asad and His Interlocutors (Stanford University Press) 2006, 12–30, 13.

[27] Douglas Farrow, Quel Sécularisme? [Which Secularism?], in: La Religion dans la Sphère Publique [Religion in the Public Sphere], ed. Solange Lefebvre, Montreal (Les Presses de l'Université de Montréal) 2005, 344–345.

[28] Fergusson, 158–165.

health of households and civic groups organized on a non-market, non contractual basis."[29]

The concept of secularization underscores the importance of a transnational civil society for dealing with global problems (economic, rights abuses, and so forth). In this regard, religions "occupy social spaces that are protected."[30] Fergusson notes Casanova's contribution on secularization and describes ways in which churches can make a public contribution in secularized contexts. Public effectiveness and private appeal will require the distancing of the church from the state. In a more pluralist setting, citizens wish to choose their political, moral, and spiritual identity rather than have this imposed. One extensive study was conducted in Quebec around the public contribution of the Catholic Church, between the 1960's and the 1990's, regarding nationalist aspirations and struggle against economic injustices[31].

If I consider the history of the various Canadian French Roman Catholic minorities, I tend to agree with Fergusson and Casanova. One consequence of the past dominance of the Catholic Church and the English economic elite in Quebec society is that Quebecers are defiant of formal organizations. Elsewhere in Canada, Catholicism was less a power and more of an ally in the French minorities' struggle to survive[32]. The latter show more religious dynamism than the Quebec Catholicism. Still, how can a process of disestablishment succeed in such conditions?

Practical Theology and Disestablishment

After disestablishment, what is left? According to Buchanan, several functions and resources persist: nationwide organization, standing of the episcopate, the church's material resources, custodianship of churches buildings, and concerns for life in society.[33] Earlier, we gave the example of the involvement of the Catholic Church in some political debates and its acceptance of the secularization of certain dimensions of the collective life of Quebecers. What else can we say about the new roles a Church can play in the civil society?

---

[29] Ibid.

[30] Fergusson, 144–147.

[31] See David Seljak, Why the Quiet Revolution Was 'Quiet': The Catholic Church's Reaction to the Secularization of Nationalism in Quebec after 1960, in Canadian Catholic Historical Association, *Historical Studies* 62, 109–124.

[32] I refer to my comparative study of Roman French Catholics in Canada. See S. Lefebvre, The Francophone Roman Catholic Church, in P. Bramadat & D. Seljak, Christianity and Ethnicity in Canada, Toronto: Toronto University Press 2008, 179–235.

[33] Colin Buchanan, Cut the Connexion. Disestablishment and the Church of England, London (Darton, Longman & Todd) 1994. Quoted by Fergusson, 169.

142 Solange Lefebvre

Significant sectors of the population need some spiritual facility. If just a few people identify themselves with traditional churches through membership and attendance, others might connect with Christian churches through public funerals as civic events. The church is also present in hospitals and armed forces (chaplaincy services) and educational institutions (private ones). Practical theology, reflecting on the process of secularization and on the continuing and changing roles of religious communities, responds to society's need for deeper understanding of these trends and for discernment of new directions. As seen earlier in this paper, practical theologians do this by reflecting on ministries in the new pluralistic context.

A few temptations exist in a post-Christian era, however: diluting the faith in adapting too much to society (to maintain national significance); diluting religious education in the pluralistic school system; maintaining religious rites of passage, despite the non religious significance it has for numerous people; and quieting political critique to keep harmonious relations with political and social authorities. Debates of the last thirty years in Christian communities and practical theology are related to these matters, notably in religious education. Especially around the rites of passage, theologians are divided between those who think we should restrict access to the sacraments to people ready to live a full Christian life and those who interpret positively the basic anthropological need for rituals and thus recognize the social function of the Church.

In 1989, the Catholic Bishops of Quebec decided to organize an action research project among Quebec Catholic communities to define future directions for the Church. In the final document, they offered the following diagnosis: "Too many Catholics are acting in the Church as simple consumers of the services a particular religious institution can offer to them, without feeling themselves as full members of a communion, a family, one people."[34] They recommended that Christian communities impose more demanding criteria for access to the sacraments, predicting that this change would provoke conflicts and tensions for Catholics accustomed to having easy access to any church service.[35] The spirit of this proposal was well expressed in the report's title: *Risking the Future*. Another action research was conducted by a team from my faculty, and it actually took a different direction, saying that pastoral ministers needed

---

[34] Comité de Recherche de l'Assemblée des Evêques du Québec sur les Communautés Chrétiennes Locales [Research Committee of the Quebec Assembly of Bishops on Local Christian Communities], Risquer l'Avenir. Bilan d'Enquête et Prospective [Risking the Future. Assessment and Prospective], Montreal (Fides) 1992, 9. See also: Quebec Assembly of Bishops, La Concertation des Eglises Diocésaines. Visite ad Limina [The Diocesan Churches' Concertation. An Ad Limina Visit], Montreal (Fides) 1988, 64. In French, the documents read: "Trop de catholiques se situent encore dans l'Église comme de simples consommateurs des services d'une institution religieuse particulière, sans se sentir membres à part entière d'une communion, d'une famille, d'un peuple."
[35] Risking the Future, 171.

Secularization and Disestablishment of the Church 143

anthropological and sociological tools to understand the meaning of rites of passage and consequently to infuse Christian meaning into the process of Christian initiation.[36]

Many theological issues are raised regarding the new functions and resources of the Churches in the context of disestablishment. Some of these are current or new:

1. The meaning of custodianship of religious buildings versus a critical theology of the temple, a strong issue in ecclesiological reflection in Quebec;[37]

2. Theological interpretation of the chaplaincy in a religiously pluralistic context and in a society that often considers itself as "not religious but spiritual";[38]

3. New forms of engagement in public theology: conflict resolution and public support of diverse faiths, notably in the ways they deal with symbolic expressions against secularist ideology;

---

[36] Jacques Grand'Maison/Lise Baroni/Jean-Marc Gauthier (eds.), Le Défi des Générations [The Challenge of Generations], Montreal (Fides) 1995. See a resume and other references in: Solange Lefebvre, Socio-Religious Evolution and Practical Theology in Quebec, Canada, in: International Journal of Practical Theology 4, 2000, 284–303.
[37] My Chair on Religion, Culture and Society organized a conference on the religious and theological challenges of Quebec's religious heritage (proceedings to be published in 2008: Solange Lefebvre (ed.), Le Patrimoine Religieux du Québec. Éducation et Transmission du Sens [Quebec's Religious Heritage. Education and Transmission of Meaning], Montreal (Presses de l'Université de Montréal). This took place after a governmental commission published a final report on the subject. See Assemblée Nationale du Québec [National Assembly of Quebec], Croire au Patrimoine Religieux du Québec. Mandat d'Initiative Entrepris par la Commission de la Culture [Believing in Quebec's Religious Heritage. Initiative Mandate Undertaken by the Commission on Culture], Quebec (Government of Quebec) June 2006 report.
[38] In this regard, some practical theologians made significant contributions, especially on spirituality in the health care and public school systems. For instance, Jean-Pierre Proulx, the president of the committee that suggested secularizing the public school system, a professor in education and a former journalist, did his Ph.D. in practical theology (1979). See: Ministère de l'Education [Ministry of Education], Laïcité et Religions; Guy Lapointe (ed.), La Pastorale en Milieu de Santé: Une Question de Crédibilité?, [Pastoral Care in the Health Care System. A Question of Credibility?], Montreal (Fides) 1991; Comité sur les Affaires Religieuses [Committee on Religious Affairs], Le Développement Spirituel en Education [Spiritual Development in the Educational System], Quebec (Government of Quebec) 2004. See also Fides publications in the "Collection de Théologie Pratique" by theologians from the University of Montreal; publications by professors in spiritual anthropology at the University of Sherbrooke; publications on pastoral dimensions of health care, by University of Laval's Editor, "Les Presses de l'Université Laval."

144 Solange Lefebvre

4. The theological signification of "Catholicism," beyond national citizenship, as a transnational network that is not compromised by political power and is a leader in contemporary visions of civil society (Liberation and Contextual Theologies);[39]

5. The crisis in the Catholic Church around ministry and leadership. The organization of the Catholic Church is more than ever centered on catholic priests. Without them, there is no real community life, only a community life "while waiting" for the priest. In South America, for instance, one of the main reasons the faithful have changed the church is a lack of real leadership.

6. Tensions between the innerwordly vocation ("to seek the welfare of the city") and the spiritual mission of Christians.[40] A tension exists regarding fundamental vocation. In the Bible and Christian history, we find similar tensions between the sacred functions and worldly vocation of Christianity. In Quebec, for example, where Catholic Action has been strong, few sociologists think that it has devalued liturgy, prayer, or spiritual expressions.[41] At the same time, younger generations do not integrate the traditional Christian practices and movements.

Conclusion: a theology of civil society

The theological significance of civil society can be found in the concepts of solidarity and subsidiarity. In ecclesiology, one can say that local congregations are the primary form of the body of Christ. One of David Fergusson's primary arguments is that diverse examples of local communities' dynamism show that a significant contribution to society does not depend upon national status or the model of Christendom. Christian dynamism is linked to voluntary societies. Indeed, the United States of America gives a powerful example of this dynamism.

Other societies are still seeking the way to constitute a voluntary culture, especially in the face of decreasing membership and decreasing resources. This is the case for Canada, and especially for French Catholics in the province of Quebec. The remaining question is critical: since a voluntary culture, like the one in the United States, results from a long tradition and a history of funda-

---

[39] See the works of Michel Beaudin and Denise Couture, members of the Institute of Contextual Theology, University of Montreal.

[40] See Robert Mager (ed.), Dieu Agit-il dans l'Histoire? [Does God Intervene in History?], Montreal (Fides) 2006.

[41] I reported this debate in: Solange Lefebvre, Théologie Pratique et Questions de Transmission [Practical Theology and Issues Regarding Transmission], in: Laval Théologique et Philosophique 60, no 2, June 2004, 251–268.

mental choices over centuries, can any society dream to build such a culture in just a few decades?

Even more crucial is a counter argument revaluating this meaning and sources of the civic dynamism. In Canada, the decline of the Christian churches in general could also be related to the secularization of the social and education services. Once the state assumes most of the social and educational functions, there is not much left to the churches, except respond to the strictly religious needs of the population. Beyer is stressing the point very clearly: "If Canadians are to return to denominational religion in the numbers that they did in the past, then the religious suppliers will have to offer more than good and pure religious product lines. They will have to find a replacement for the social projects of the past, for re-entry into the secularized structures of power and influence"[42].

In this regard, the religious denominational strength of the United States could also be related to the fact that these functions are entrusted for a large part to the private sector, much more than in Canada and even more than it is the case in Quebec. A theory of civil society needs to take into account this major factor.

The Author

Solange Lefebvre, born 1959, is full Professor of Theology and Religious Studies at the University of Montreal, where she is the Chair, Chair religion, culture and society, and where she founded and directed the Center for studies of religion from 2000 to 2008. She has edited several books on ages and generations and published numerous articles and book chapters on secularity, religious diversity and Christianity in the public sphere. In 2008 she published Cultures and spiritualities of youth and young adults (Cultures et spiritualités des jeunes Montreal, Bellarmin); and edited Reasons to Be. A Dialog between Sciences and Religion (Raisons d'être. Le sens à l'épreuve de la science et de la religion, Presses de l'Université de Montréal); and for instance, the paper "International Report: Disestablishment of the Church: Discussion with Jose Casanova from a Canadian Point of View", in International Journal of Practical Theology 11, 2007, 285–309.

---

[42] Peter Beyer, «Religious Vitality in Canada: The Complementarity of Religious Market and Secularization Perspectives», in Lori Beaman eds. *Religion and Canadian Society. Traditions, Transitions, and Innovations*, Toronto: Canadian Scholar's Press, 2006, 71–90.

Robert Mager

Secularization in Quebec: Phenomenon, Expression and Theory

For some years now, along with many others, I have been trying to understand the evolution of Quebec society with regard to its religious heritage. In Quebec, this recent history is commonly referred to as a secularization process, or modernization. But a society's evolution is never simply recorded as is: it is always given a certain interpretation, with elaborate terms that immediately function as symbols. Hence most educated people in Quebec would easily agree that they live in a secular, pluralistic, modern or postmodern, industrialized, consumeristic, information oriented, mass-media, individualistic and market-minded society. And they would subscribe to all these terms without professing any particular theory. As they enter the realm of commonly accepted ideas, these descriptive terms become, in turn, powerful elements that shape society's evolution.

The same reciprocal relationship can be perceived at the level of scientific study. As interpreters, we listen to the expressions of reality in discourse, we try to discern the meanings involved in those words, and strive to build an interpretation that makes sense, that is that understands the central issues of reality. But such interpretation does not simply stem from practice, as we would often like; theoretical views and preconceived ideas determine the type of attention we give to actions or phenomena. Theoretical views make it possible to make sense of reality, though they inevitably risk acting as filters undermining proper perception of reality's original aspects.

In other words, the task of understanding the evolution of any society has to address a key factor: *language*. Reflecting on the necessary mediation of language, I came to the following conclusions: if I wished to understand the evolution of Quebec society with regard to religion, 1) I had to pay attention to a carefully chosen set of discourses; 2) I needed to sift through theoretical material about secularization, postmodernity, and the like; 3) I had to engage in conversation with these two levels of language.

1. Religion in Public Schools: a Debate

I decided to focus on the deconfessionalization of Quebec's public school system, an issue tightly woven into the evolution of modern Quebec over the past forty-five years. This ongoing debate has been periodically revived by parliamentary committees, government commissions and the like, until very recently, when the decision was made to deconfessionalize the whole education system and to maintain a comparatively lean program of ethics and religious culture.

Secularization in Quebec: Phenomenon, Expression and Theory 147

My purpose is not to present the details of this debate[1], but rather to examine the variety of briefs presented by social organizations throughout this period: unions, associations, coalitions, and the like, both religious and secular. The idea was to analyse the arguments put forward in those briefs, to see *how* each one of them argued either for or against religion in the school system, and specifically how they envisioned the relationship between religion and society. My assumption was that beyond the pros and cons, and the specific arguments, there had to be some kind of common horizon of thought, and that we might be able to perceive an evolution of this horizon throughout the period, corresponding to the depth of the observed changes.

Such an evolution can indeed be demonstrated. In the 1960s, almost everyone argued in favour of, or against, a vision of man and the world pertaining to run-of-the-mill scholastic philosophy. Let me just quote this brief from a cultural association:

> [In education], we deal with two realms of realities that are nonetheless closely interrelated. [...] Spiritual aspirations are, by their nature and their object, incomparably superior to the material demands, but these two levels cannot be separated. On the contrary, these preoccupations are to be maintained in a hierarchy. Here, as in everything that has to do with man, what is important is to know the order and to comply with its requirements[2].

The opponents of such a view battle on the same grounds, but they suggest a new direction (I quote here another cultural association):

> Many fine minds wish to demonstrate that only the catholic school system can fulfill the requirements of holistic education. But we believe that on this [philosophical and religious] ground, the discussion leads nowhere. The issue no longer rests on the search for a common agreement as to what constitutes holistic education, but rather to find a way for everyone to continue living together as a society, while they no longer agree on such matters. A productive solution to this issue should thus place the focus at the level of the institutions, that is, within the political sphere, and not at the religious or metaphysical level[3].

---

[1] Cf. Task Force on the Place of Religion in Schools in Québec, *Religion in Secular Schools*, Québec, Government of Québec, 1999 (www.mels.gouv.qc.ca/REFORME/religion/inter.htm; consulted in Oct. 2007); Rectorat de l'Université du Québec à Montréal [ed.], *40 ans après le Rapport Parent*, Sainte-Foy, Presses de l'Université du Québec, 2006.

[2] Fédération des Sociétés Saint-Jean-Baptiste du Québec, [Mémoire à la Commission royale d'enquête sur l'enseignement dans la Province de Québec], 1962, par. 25. (This brief, and others, can be found at the documentation center of the Ministère de l'Éducation, du Loisir et du Sport, Government of Québec.)

[3] Mouvement laïc de langue française, [Mémoire à la Commission royale d'enquête sur l'enseignement dans la Province de Québec], 1962, p. 17–18. See *supra*, note #2.

148 Robert Mager

Thus, in those years, we can witness a clear shift from a philosophical and religious horizon to a political horizon, where the State emerges as the main actor which can keep society together, and help their members make independent decisions concerning their society's future.

I cannot go into details here[4]. Let me just point out two of the main characteristics of the debate during the following decades.

At the end of the 1970s, all the participants, regardless of their position, begin to argue in terms of *human rights*: the right of parents to educate their children according to their religious values, rights of religious freedom, of liberty of conscience, of equality for all, so on. This corresponds to important events: in 1975, the Quebec National Assembly adopts an almost constitutional Charter of Rights; the Parliament of Canada does the same in 1982. In my analysis of this debate, both sides use human rights, understood primarily as individual rights, as the basis for the discussion.

Another theme increasingly pervades the whole debate from 1980 on: *pluralism*. Quebec society had always known and acknowledged a certain level of plurality, but this was mainly understood as the coexistence of a majority and minorities, each group defending its institutions and privileges. Something else is happening now. In the collective conscience, individuals matter more than groups, and demand recognition and equal treatment by society, whatever their particularities might be. *Plurality* thus becomes *pluralism*, that is, a state of affairs by which plurality is valued as such and defended in such a way that the will of the majority can hardly be invoked any longer to impose a common view or measure. Moreover, each individual demands that his or her particularity be recognized as such in the public sphere. Paradoxically, pluralism gets to be presented as the cement of Quebec society, as a crucial element of its new self-image.

Many other elements of the debate should be pointed out. These three (that is, the shift from religion to the political sphere, the rise of human rights, and the appeal to pluralism) are sufficient to move to the next question: what do secularization, individualization, and modernization mean? How could I develop an interpretation which made sense and was consistent with my observations?

---

[4] Cf. R. Mager, "Religion in the Public Realm in Québec": *British Journal of Religious Education* 24/3 (2002), p. 183–195; R. Mager and P. Bergeron, "Sortir la religion de l'école, ou l'école de la religion?", in F. Nault [ed.], *Religion, modernité et démocratie*, Québec, Presses de l'Université Laval, 2008.

2. A Political Exit from Religion

During my research, I began to pay close attention to the work of French historian and political philosopher Marcel Gauchet. Gauchet's main work, *The Disenchantment of the World*, was originally published in French in 1985, and in English twelve years later[5]. Gauchet was prompted to study religion by the torments and deadlocks of contemporary democracy[6]. He thus writes:

> It might not be obvious, but the place and status of religion are at the heart of the present transformations of democracy [...]. To fully understand the considerable transformations that are affecting the intimate substance of democracies and their self-understanding [...], it is necessary to take into account the religious dimension. Conversely, religion is undergoing very profound changes [...] that cannot be fully understood unless they are related to the social and political dimension[7].

Gauchet suggests that the history of the Western world, all the way from the emergence of the State some 3000 years BCE to the establishment of modern individualistic democracy, has demonstrated a long and decisive shift from heteronomy to autonomy. In his view, religion is essentially heteronomy, that is, not so much a matter of belief as "an organization of the social human world, generating an order that holds people together from the outside, as an exterior and anterior order, superior to their will[8]". The radical change brought about by the appearance of the State, and boosted by the advent of Christianity, has consisted in the progressive dissociation of the divine and the human realms, to the point that Western societies, from the Reformation on, began to consider and realize the possibility of developing foundations on their own rather than under a divine sky. Which does not mean that they got rid of religion altogether: "God does not die, He simply ceases to mingle with human political affairs. This is the great split that separates past from present. Religion has become primarily an issue for individuals, while it had previously been first and foremost a matter for communities[9]."

Gauchet insists: the desacralization of the political organization of human societies means an exit *from* religion as organizing sphere, but not the exit *of* religion as experience. Religion remains but is transformed; it shifts from a foundational common horizon to a matter of individual beliefs and commitments, however commonly held and vocally expressed they might be. This translation has allowed our societies to become autonomistic, radically individualistic, market-based and open to ongoing change and development. In this

---

[5] *The Disenchantment of the World*, Princeton, Princeton University Press, 1997.
[6] *La démocratie contre elle-même*, Paris, Gallimard, 2002, p. XV–XVI.
[7] *Un monde désenchanté?*, Paris, Éd. de l'Atelier / Éd. Ouvrières, 2004, p. 182.
[8] *Ibid.*, p. 183.
[9] *Ibid.*, p. 140.

perspective, this has meant both opportunity and loss: an opportunity to face and take on the adventure of freedom, but also a radical loss of meaning, which our democracies try to compensate through all possible means, including by appealing to the wisdom of religions and other sources of values. Thus the so-called "reenchantment of the world[10]"consists of different phenomena that are either reacting to, or compensating for, the departure of our societies from their religious foundations.

This theory of Gauchet is much more complex and subtle than what I can report here. It can be considered a secularization theory, though Gauchet himself considers the term "secularization" as simply descriptive and not going to the heart of the matter. His theory is intensely debated in France, and has been fiercely critiqued in English-speaking countries. It remains very thought-provoking, and has proven to be very illuminating for my research.

3. A Difficult Process of Refoundation

Indeed, let me briefly recall the three characteristics of the deconfessionalization debate I pointed out earlier. First of all, the shift from a religious horizon of thought to a political one corresponds exactly to Gauchet's "exit from religion" theory. It is not simply that religion has lost its hold and spell on Quebec's institutions and culture; Quebec society literally went through a process of refoundation, though it could be argued that it has not fully completed this process.

Secondly, Gauchet has written extensively on the rise of what he calls the ideology of human rights[11]. Not that he opposes human rights *per se*, of course; his argument is that the intense appeal to human rights which has spread throughout the Western world in the last decades is an attempt to find a new transcendent foundation for human affairs, and that this process basically fails because human rights, as they are conceived and promoted, are inescapably tied to individualism and provide neither keys nor means for political action.

Thirdly, Gauchet's theory helps to understand the key role pluralism plays in our societies. Pluralism is not simply a "value" that happened to arise, but the way our societies restructure themselves in absence of any transcendent horizon. In our societies which have departed from religion, the State cannot claim any transcendent stance: it is led to accept public expression of all the different identities and positions within society, religious and others, in an equal manner. "*Pluralism*, here, is the key word pointing to the self-understanding of civil

---

[10] P.L. Berger [ed.], *Le Réenchantement du monde*, Paris, Bayard, 2001.
[11] Cf. M. Gauchet, *La révolution des droits de l'homme*, Paris, Gallimard, 1989, 341 p., and two important articles in *La démocratie contre elle-même*.

society in its relationship to the state, a relationship made of representation and recognition[12]."

Quebec's situation features characteristics that deviate from Gauchet's description. Mainly, Gauchet argues that the wall-to-wall prevalence of the human rights ideology tames the problem of social cohesion. In Quebec's debate, the call to human rights coexists with a profound disquiet regarding this issue of social cohesion. But this might be explained by contextual history. France, as many countries, can count on a clear political foundation; however shaken it might be by the contemporary transformations of society. In comparison, Quebec appears like a sailboat on the sea, with no anchor, shaken by wind and waves, too ambivalent about its past to rely upon it, and with no common project to guide its future.

This research has convinced me of three main things. First, the analysis of language is indeed an extremely important way of understanding the evolution of a person, group or society. Second, this type of analysis benefits greatly from the interaction between social discourse and theory. Third, it is crucial for practical theology to try to understand reality as it is, before it undertakes to imagine the world as it would like it to be, or sizes it up according to what it considers to be God's will. In particular, it should keep in mind that it is not about saving religion, but about a gracious God that saves the world.

The Author

Robert Mager, Prof. Dr., born 1960; professor of Practical Theology and Systematic Theology at Université Laval (Quebec, Canada). Research interests: theoretical and methodological issues in practical theology, theology of action, religion and public sphere. Recent publications: (ed.), Dieu agit-il dans l'histoire? (2006); (with E.-M. Meunier [ed.]), Globe. Revue internationale en études québécoises, vol. 10, no 2: «La religion au Québec» (fall 2007); « Sortir la religion de l'école, ou l'école de la religion?», in F. Nault (ed.), Religion, modernité et démocratie (2008).

---

[12] *Un monde désenchanté?*, p. 186. Cf. C. Taylor, *Multiculturalism and The Politics of Recognition*, Princeton, Princeton University Press, 1992; J. Beauchemin, *La Société des identités*, Montréal, Athéna, 2004.

Lies Brussee – van der Zee[1]

Postmodernism and Mennonites in the Netherlands

A few years ago, the Mennonite congregation of the city of Leyden in the Netherlands made the following announcement on the occasion of the opening of the winter season, following the summer break.[2]

> On September 23 at 9:30, the church doors of the Congregation will again stand wide open. On this Sunday, we hope to start the new season in a contemporary manner for young and old. The service will be contemporary because we plan to make this Sunday morning service interactive." [...] "This does not suggest a smoothly conducted service. On the contrary, it means that we will have to make great efforts together to try to understand each other for the purpose of deepening our faith, even though one of the deepest convictions of our faith actually is that no one can express it for us...

Now why do I quote today these lines from this announcement? Because it reflects, in my view, how postmodernism and the postmodern way of living have shaped church life in the Netherlands. Postmodern people are seekers, and they reach their goal in the process of seeking. Indeed, the seeking itself becomes their goal, not the certainty of a settled outcome. Apparently, the Leyden congregation considered it outdated to regard the service a priori as a service for all present, based on the faith of all believers. And also to assume that the language used by the pastor, the hymns sung, and the faith addressed to the members will touch the people and set them in motion. Instead, the stated goal of the service is to seek, to seek together words in an effort to understand each other's faith... The service is an event focused on horizontal communication about our faith.

How do we interpret this in the light of our understanding of postmodern culture?

Postmodern culture in the Netherlands

It was not until the 1980s that the term *postmodernism* came into common use in the Netherlands. The concepts of the *condition postmoderne* developed by the French philosopher Jean-Francois Lyotard have had perhaps the greatest influence in the Netherlands in shaping philosophies of life. Lyotard's often-quoted assertion is "The time of the Great Stories is over." With this statement, he disavows the notion that one human system has the privilege of dominating

---

[1] All translations of quoted material within this chapter are by the author of the chapter.

[2] "Gemeente in Lokhorst," *Periodiek van de Doopsgezind-Remonstrantse gemeente te Leiden*, Sept., 2001.

Postmodernism and Mennonites in the Netherlands 153

other such systems. In Christian terms, this means that the dominance of Christian ideology has ended and is no longer justifiable. The concepts of Lyotard and other postmodern thinkers such as Derrida, Foucault, Baudrillard, Jameson, and Rorty[3] have been amplified by Dutch theologians. For instance, Ilse N. Bulhof, a Dutch philosopher who became a professor in Leyden based her inaugural speech, "Towards a postmodern spirituality?" on Derrida's concept of void.[4]

Cornelis van Peursen provides a good summary of the main elements of the forenamed philosophers' thoughts that are important for theology and pastoral care.[5] He adopts Lyotard's statement that the days of the Great Stories are over. It is no longer possible to hold reality within one system. Drawing on Derrida's concept of deconstruction, he asserts that by deconstructing a text, one can search for the hidden and suppressed meanings. One of the means for this deconstruction is the concept *différance*, introduced by Derrida. In contrast to *différence* (difference), *différance* refers to a method that breaks through common meanings, so that one word can have multiple meanings. In other words, a text (a pastoral conversation, for example) is uncontrollable and not fully comprehensible, because there are always factors contributing to new points of significance concerning our micro-, meso- or macro-world.

Another element of postmodernism to which Van Peursen points is the perspective on the importance of "the I, the subject" (Rorty) or the denial of "the I" as autonomous acting subject (Derrida). The question, which arises in a philosophical sense in the absence of an autonomous acting Self is, what is left over of reality? That is, what is a realistic world without acting subjects?

I also want to call attention to another philosophical concept of the postmodern thinker Derrida, namely the concept of void. Bulhof refers to this notion by asking if it creates the possibility of a postmodern answer to nihilism. She compares Derrida's view of void with varied interpretations of a musical score.

---

[3] Jean Baudrillard, *Simulations* (New York: Semiotext(e), Inc., 1983); Baudrillard, *In the shadow of the silent majorities and other essays* (New York: Semiotext(e), 1983); Jacques Derrida, Margins of Philosophy (Chicago: University of Chicago Press, 1982); Derrida, *God en godsdienst: Gesprekken op Capri* (Kampen: publisher, 1997); Derrida, *Hoe niet te spreken* (Kampen: publisher, 1992); Jean-François Lyotard, *Het postmoderne weten* (Kampen: publisher, 1994); Lyotard, *Le différend* (Paris: Editions de Minuit, 1983); Richard Rorty, *Contingency, Irony and Solidarity* (Cambridge and New York: Cambridge University Press, 1989).

[4] Ilse N. Bulhof, *Naar een postmoderne spiritualiteit?* (Leyden: Rijks Universiteit, 1992).

[5] Cornelis van Peursen, "'Postmodern,' Een nieuwe context voor beleid?" [Postmodernism: A New Context for Policy?], *Praktische Theologie* 23.3 (1996), 243–254.

Philosophy as music takes some getting used to. Yet, in this sense, void is "motherly and nourishing," according to Bulhof.[6] Void is a manner of being.

Lindijer, in his book *Postmodern Existence: To Exist and Believe in an After-Modern Culture,* devotes a chapter to the postmodern way of living.[7] He concludes that postmodernism does express itself in a recognizable way of living. He says that postmodern people are often ambivalent, rarely choosing a single path. They are, one could say, satisfied, for the time being, to live in bits and pieces.[8]

Postmodern people do not wish to commit themselves for the long term; they do not want to become institutionalized. They are averse to ideologies, including aspects of Christianity that have been made into ideology. In contrast to the 1960s, when the capacity of society and humanity for unlimited psychic growth was still believable, postmodern people today see that much of life is more complicated than that. This realization causes postmodern people to be pragmatic. They are not attracted by fancy principles, but rather look to what is realistic and act accordingly. They no longer believe in the collective. The feeling of "we" has been traded in for the feeling of "I," and for personal freedom.

A concept of postmodern thought that finds expression in postmodern experience is deconstruction. The postmodern person has a tendency to unravel programs – political and religious programs and ideologies – and subsequently not to know what to choose. Each argument in favor of a choice evokes an argument against it. Unlike in the 1960s and 1970s, people today do not have a blueprint in mind of what to do. For example, what policy should be followed with respect to asylum seekers? What do I think of euthanasia these days? Postmodern people live with, "on the one hand … and on the other hand," and are generally content with this.

The postmodern outlook also knows irony, which is a sense of relativism. Besides this, there is also gloominess. Faith in progressive thinking has vanished; not much remains of great ideals. One does not expect much of humanity anymore. Postmodern human beings definitely hold ethical concepts, but ethics does not express itself in the applying of rules. The moral consciousness of postmodernism is situational.

Lindijer detects a sense of contingency towards religion and faith in those expressing the postmodern way of living. Not everything is determined beforehand from above and not everything serves a purpose. Postmodern people

---

[6] Ibid., 15.

[7] Coert H. Lindijer, *Postmodern bestaan: Mens zijn en geloven in een na-moderne cultuur*, (Zoetermeer: Boekencentrum, 1998).

[8] See I.N. Bulhof en J.M.M. de Valk, eds., *Postmodernisme als uitdaging* [Postmodernism as a Challenge] (Baarn: Ambo 1990), 9.

express a definite openness towards transcendental experiences, the "encounter with something else,"[9] but this does not necessarily lead to commitment to a certain church. Postmodern people are eclectically religious and often "religion shoppers."

When Lindijer speaks of the congregation "colored" by postmodernism, he states first that it offers room. Postmodernism means valuing differences, honoring the reality of people who are different, having an eye for diversity. The Great Story of the Bible is no longer understood as a whole. People live fragmentarily as they experience their own small stories.

How do Mennonites view the postmodern era?

In the interest of examining how postmodern perspectives have entered the consciousness of Dutch Mennonites, I will consider postmodern ideas as they are evidenced in two recent Mennonite publications.

The first document I will consider is "The Story, the Place and the People," a policy paper of the General Mennonite Council from October of 2000, which states as its purpose to define a "comprehensive policy, to open constructive dialogue," and to invite others to contribute.[10] The other publication I will analyze is a Mennonite handbook for believers, "Touched by the Eternal."[11] I base my method of investigation on the concept of deconstruction as we met it with the philosopher Derrida.

Analysis of the policy paper

My searching for signs of postmodern ideas in the policy paper is an example of reading against the text, because this manner is contrary to the paper's stated intent, that is, to define policy, open dialogue, and invite contributions.

The first section of this paper is titled "The World Around Us". It sketches a picture of the world that Dutch Mennonites have encountered since World War II. The sketch identifies two movements: "On one side there is the movement from public to private [...] On the other side we see forerunners of new structures in which universal [...] humanity stands central."

---

[9] Lindijer, 72.

[10] Het Verhaal, de Plek, en de Mensen, *Contourennota van de Broederschapsraad van de Algemene Doopsgezinde Sociëteit: Een aanzet tot integraal beleid, de opening van een constructieve dialoog, een uitnodiging aan u om bij te dragen* (Amsterdam: Algemene Doopsgezinde Sociëteit, 2000).

[11] Gerke. van Hiele, ed., *Aangeraakt door de Eeuwige: Geloofsboek ten behoeve van doopsgezinde gemeenten* (Zoetermeer: Boekencentrum, 2001).

When I look for the postmodern themes that I outlined earlier in this chapter, I find no traces of them in this section of the policy paper. This is because the section deals with the "modern person in our society," that is, an individualistic person who, without much hampering by doubts and uncertainty, rationally tries to achieve his or her own purposes. This person in the community of faith is encouraged to strike his own individual "Dutch Mennonite" note, which is called "modern." The policy paper does not define the term modern further, but suggests that readers have a unique opportunity and enormous potential for reaching other "modern people". This section of the policy paper exhibits an optimistic outlook on the future that is unshared by many postmodern thinkers. The word postmodern is not used. Nor does the policy paper suggest the postmodern perception that the era of the Great Stories – including the Christian Story – seems to have passed.

But I detected a certain postmodern attitude to life in another part of the policy paper. I found the following question: "Are we able to bring people with existential questions together and include them in our combined efforts in search of new forms for the community of believers?"[12] The document provides no blueprints for suggested new forms. The paper does state that the "congregation of the future" will have forms and characteristics that are not yet present,[13] yet the paper omits any consideration of the nature of those forms. The writers leave much open in this regard, whereas in other matters they point the way. This coincides with the image of the postmodern person who lives fragmentarily, deconstructs programs, and lives by "either/or", but does not choose. For such people, seeking is more important than finding.

Analysis of Touched by the Eternal

In a similar manner as above, I have analyzed the Mennonite handbook for believers entitled *Touched by the Eternal*, which was published in October of 2001. The preface of the book states that Mennonites in recent years have experienced increasing separation between "a personally experienced faith and the community of faith [...] since that which we hold in common is not recognized and experienced [as much as before]." This book aims to "bring these two great and important experiences together again: experiencing one's own faith and experiencing the community of the congregation."[14] Definite emphasis is placed on "experiencing."

Here I think there is a clear influence from postmodern thought. As we saw, postmodernism places great emphasis on experiencing and searching. People

---

[12] Verhaal, de Plek, en de Mensen, 10–11.
[13] Ibid., 3.
[14] Hiele, 7.

want to share their subjective experiences, but their intention is not that this sharing should lead to a common goal.

The first three parts of this 120-page handbook are entitled: (1) Personally Addressed, (2) Continuing Together, and (3) Becoming Involved. The fourth part is concerned with five common confessions of faith. In the preface, we read that the book is based on a dialogical frame of "learning from one another." The dialogical framework tries to walk the middle ground between "disastrous individualism" and "unattainable collectivism." It refers to diversity as a neutral fact. Placing the accent upon diversity as a method "to make [diversity] fruitful" calls to mind Derrida's concept *différance* as a tool to break through understood meanings.

The book contains many illustrative quotations from personal statements of faith. In most of these, I note that the words *seeking* or *search* stand out. One person wrote, "Sometimes I think that He [God] exists only in the yearning, the search." The confession of faith is presented as participation in the process of believing, "which probably never ends."[15] It appears that for many, the meaning of faith lies in the search itself.

The chapters address many open questions to the reader. Each reader can answer according to his or her own experiences. The reader is invited to find her or his own place. It is not astonishing, then, to find the term of *seeking* (or *search*) almost sixty times in these chapters. The words of *differences* (or *diversity*) appear nearly fifty times. Another word that that is used frequently is *space*. In contrast, expressions like *unity* or *eternity* appear twice only. The accent on dialogue stands out through the frequent appearance of the phrase *each other*. *Diversity*, *search*, *space*, and the need to *learn from one another* in experiences of faith, are key ideas that characterize this book.

My conclusion is as follows: The first three parts of the book is in keeping with the postmodern attitude toward life, which holds a positive appreciation for searching, and finds diversity a goal in itself. It is also in keeping with the fragmentary character of postmodern people who can only identify with certain ideas of the Christian faith. The book is in line with the importance that postmodernism attaches to one's own religious experiences as a musical interpretation of the void. The fourth part, however, in my opinion shows that the authors think that sharing subjective experiences does not lead to a common goal. Part 4 thus affirms the thesis that if the Mennonite Fellowship has to base its right to existence on common experiences, it no longer has grounds for existence.

---

[15] Ibid., 26, 39.

Part 4 reveals no postmodern traits and does not keep with the formulated purpose of the book. So there is an inconsistency here. My pastoral conversations confirm that Mennonites in the Netherlands recognize this inconsistency.

The Author

Lies Brussee – van der Zee, Drs., born 1948; assistant professor emeritus of Practical Theology at the Mennonite Seminary and the Faculty of Theology at the Free University of Amsterdam. Research interests: pastoral counseling and clinical supervision, Mennonite history. Recent publication: Postmodernism, Mennonites and Pastoral Care in the Netherlands, in: Daniel S. Schipani (ed.), Mennonite Perspectives on Pastoral Counseling, Elkhart (IN) and Scottdale (PE), USA (2007).

Practical Theology and Empirical Research

Friedrich Schweitzer

Empirical Research in the Service of the Church?
The Evaluation of Ecclesial Praxis as a Task of Practical Theology

On the background of recent empirical work carried out by the author and his team at the University of Tübingen, the paper describes examples of evaluative empirical research in the fields of religious education. Based on these examples, an analysis of the different motives and reasons for such studies is presented. Special attention is given to the specific difficulties in the cooperation between academic research on the one hand and political decision making on the other. Finally the author addresses the question what role evaluative research in the service of the church should play for practical theology in the future. Should practical theology strive for becoming something like a professional partner and authority for political decision making within the church? What chances and potentials would this possibility hold for this discipline? What limitations will follow from having to adapt research to the needs of an institution?

I have chosen this topic because of my own experiences during the last few years. Doing research on the basis of special contracts most of all with the church has come to play a major role in my academic life. In the following, I will make my experiences the starting point for some more general observations about practical theology.

1. Examples from my Present Work

Let me start by telling you about some examples from my present work at the University of Tübingen. At this point, I am involved in a number of research projects that are carried out either directly for the church or, in the case of religious education in state schools, with a more indirect relationship to the church. (You have to keep in mind that the German constitution establishes religious education as a subject taught at state schools in agreement with the teachings of the Christian or other religious denominations.)

The first project concerns research on confirmation work in Württemberg, the area of the regional church to which Tübingen belongs. More specifically, the church has asked me to find out about two questions: a) if the innovations introduced by the church ten years ago have actually been taken up and put into practise, and b) if the new model of dividing up confirmation classes into two parts – one during childhood and one in adolescence – really works. Consequently, we are doing interview studies with children and adolescents, with pastors and volunteers, with parents and others. Moreover, we are using the method of participant observation. Our results will be used by the synod for future decision making. In addition to this, there will be scholarly publications as well as publications for practitioners. It should be noted that this is the first major project on confirmation work that includes children as adolescents and does not limit itself to interviewing the pastors. In the meantime, the project has taken on a nationwide scope. In addition to this, an international consortium of researchers has started a comparative study in a number of European countries.

The second project is about so-called cooperative or dialogical religious education. In this case, both, the church – or rather the churches because the Catholic church is involved as well – and the state ministry of education want to know if a particular model of religious education really has beneficial effects on the students. The model is based on having Protestant and Catholic students together in the same class in order to learn about the other denomination. Our approach entails classroom observations as well as interviews mostly with students, teachers, and parents. We are also using some kind of test based on the curriculum of the schools. The results will be used as a basis for further decision making most of all by the churches but, indirectly, also by the state.

The third project has its focus on intercultural and interreligious learning in preschool institutions, mostly the German kindergarten. We want to find out how the teachers are dealing with the different religious backgrounds of the children, whether they feel that they are able to support children with non-Christian backgrounds in their religious development and what kind of support they would like to have themselves. In terms of numbers, the major non-Christian group in German kindergartens is made up by Muslims but many other religions are present as well. This project has no direct connection to political decision making. It is sponsored by a private foundation related to a publishing house (the Stiftung Ravensburger Verlag). Indirectly, however, it is also related to the new German preschool curriculum that, at least in a number of the states, includes religious education as a task for all kindergartens independently of their religious or non-religious affiliation. Our results will most likely play a role in how this task will be treated in the future.

Although I cannot go into the details of these projects here, my brief descriptions should indicate that all three projects have strong roots outside the academic world. Explicitly and implicitly, they are carried out in the service of the church or in the service of the state cooperating with the church in matters of religious education in state schools. Moreover, the research is funded by sources that are not part of the academic world – by the church, by the state, or by private foundations. This is another reason why we have to ask about the motives and reasons for this kind of research.

2. Motives and Reasons

In my understanding, three reasons play a major role in the context described above:

First, there are financial reasons. Churches in Germany are going through a very difficult period of time financially. Due to a number of factors, there is less money available to them, and the long-term financial expectations are also low compared to today. Consequently, the churches have to make severe cuts in their spending. In this situation, research projects can be of help for devising new effective programs and for making sure that the funds available will be spent in a most helpful manner. Moreover, research can be used for evaluating existing programs that might be expensive but do not really yield the results expected from them. It may sound paradoxical but is still true: Financial constraints may be a good reason for the churches to spend extra money on research because of the long-term beneficial effects of this research.

A second reason plays an important role in the background, even where it is not explicitly addressed. There is a growing concern with the educational quality of programs for children and youth. Most of all parents express this concern but it also plays a role within the church itself. In my understanding, the critical question about educational quality is related to the changing position of the church in society. In earlier times, the authority of the church was sufficient for answering all possible questions about quality and legitimacy of church-related programs. It was enough to know that it was the church or the pastor who is responsible for the program. Opposed to this, the present situation is much more open and programs have become subject to critical questions. One way of responding to this situation is the attempt to explicitly guarantee educational quality through empirical research. In this case, the research has to identify strengths and weaknesses of respective programs, for example, of confirmation classes. Moreover, the academic analysis should point out possible procedures for solving the problems identified and for improving the overall quality of the programs under study.

The third reason that I want to take up here, is of a more internal nature. Religious education and practical theology have themselves developed in such a way that they are interested in professional quality. To the degree that they are in a position to not only offer very general analyses but also – to borough Don Browning's term – strategic proposals that can be used in praxis, these disciplines must include an interest of their own in evaluating programs and procedures. In any case, the object of research in these disciplines is not limited to the more general questions of, for example, religious attitudes or interests but it clearly should include practical procedures and their effects.

3. Difficulties

If there are good reasons for establishing research in the service of the church, there also are clear difficulties. These difficulties have serious implications for research and should not be overlooked.

Again I start with finances. In my experience, research funded by the church goes along with special financial restraints. The funds that are made available are often not defined by the research needs in the first place. Instead, it is the budget plans of the church that define the possible leeway for funding. The church offers a certain amount of money, more or less independently of what is needed in order to find out about a particular question. There may be some space for negotiations but the situation remains very different from the ideal procedure of designing a research budget by starting out with a research question and then spelling out the financial consequences. Even if I do not want to be idealistic about academic funding that, quite independently from its source, is never available without limits, a church-defined budget can jeopardize the academic quality and credibility of a research project.

Another difficulty concerns the issue of time and timing. Decision making processes in church or state tend to follow a set agenda. They are based, among others, on election dates, on the beginning of the school year or on similar agendas external to research. Such agendas are not very sensitive to the needs of research. People expect research results when they are needed for decision making and not when the researchers have come to the conclusion that they have finally reached the point of responsibly making their results public.

Even if researchers comply with the timing of the political decision making processes, there is no guarantee that they will be heard. Since church or state have invested financial resources into the research projects, some interest and openness can certainly be expected. Yet how far this openness will go is a difficult question. Experience (including my own) indicates that this openness certainly is not unlimited, especially in the case that the research results are in tension with the expectations of church leaders. Researchers may easily feel disappointed and possibly even abused.

Taken together these difficulties can be seen as a clear jeopardy for the integrity of academic research. This is why I consider it important to be clear about such difficulties from the beginning. Some of the difficulties are built into the situation and cannot be solved. Others can at least be addressed and compromises can be found, for example, between the different agendas of politics and research. Beyond this, I am convinced that it would be a mistake for practical theology to refuse this kind of research in order to maintain its academic integrity. We have much more to win from working for the church than we might lose, especially in terms of how practical theology is perceived by the church and by the wider public!

4. Long-term Aims

What does the kind of research described in this paper mean for practical theology in the longer run? Should we try to do more work of this kind and possibly approach the church with research proposals in an active manner? What are the implications for the role of practical theology as a discipline?

In a recent review of the research available in Germany, I have come to the conclusion that, in the past, religious educators have not produced a major body of research that could count into the category developed in the present paper. In other fields of practical theology in Germany, a limited number of studies have been carried out. Yet the general picture is roughly the same. Either practical theologians have not been sufficiently interested in doing this kind of work or, maybe even more likely, the church has not been prepared to contract researchers for such projects. Given the reasons for this kind of research mentioned above, this is an unfortunate situation for both, for the church and for religious education and practical theology. Moreover, it raises the question of who sets the standards for quality in this field. Should practical theology not strive for a major say in such matters? If practical theology is interested in being or becoming a serious partner in ecclesial praxis, it should clearly attempt to take on more research tasks related to political decision making. In other fields of research like medical science, the role of academic research seems to be more defined and more established. In my understanding it would make sense to work towards establishing practical theology in a similar way – as an authority that is in the position of defining and maintaining standards for the praxis of the church.

This does not mean, however, that the evaluation of ecclesial praxis should become the only field of research for practical theology. Given the difficulties and constraints of this kind of research, this would not be commendable. It would also deprive the church of the independent voice of practical theology that presupposes research based on purely academic interests. Otherwise practical theology might return to the status of applied theology, this time not in terms of a sequential order of theological subdisciplines but in relationship to the theological interests of the church. Yet as long as we keep this in mind and as long as we continue our independent research agendas (if today's universities still allow for such independence), I see no reason why practical theology should not become more active in acquiring research tasks in the evaluation of ecclesial praxis.

166 Friedrich Schweitzer

References

Biesinger, A., Kerner, K.-J., Klosinski, G., Schweitzer, F. (2005) (eds.), Brauchen Kinder Religion? Neue Erkenntnisse – Praktische Perspektiven (Weinheim, Beltz).

Schweitzer, F., Biesinger, A. with R. Boschki, C. Schlenker, A. Edelbrock, O. Kliss, M. Scheidler (2002), Gemeinsamkeiten stärken – Unterschieden gerecht werden. Erfahrungen und Perspektiven zum konfessionell-kooperativen Religionsunterricht (Freiburg/Gütersloh, Herder/Gütersloher).

Schweitzer, F. (2007), Religious individualization: new challenges to education for tolerance, British Journal of Religious Education 29 (1), 89–100.

Schweitzer, F., Boschki, R. (2004), What children need: co-operative religious education in German schools: results from an empirical study, British Journal of Religious Education 26 (1), 33–44.

Schweitzer, F., Biesinger, A., Conrad, J., Gronover, M. (2006), Dialogischer Religionsunterricht. Analyse und Praxis konfessionell-kooperativen Religionsunterrichts im Jugendalter (Freiburg, Herder).

The Author

Friedrich Schweitzer, Prof. Dr., born 1954; Professor of Practical Theology/Religious Education at the Protestant Faculty of Theology of the Eberhard-Karls-University Tuebingen/Germany. Research interests: methodology and foundations of practical theology; religious and moral education; international comparative research. Recent publications: Religious Education between modernization and Globalization: New Perspectives on the United States and Germany (with R.R. Osmer, 2003); The Post-modern Life Cycle: Challenges for Church and Theology (2004); Religionspädagogik (2006).

Hans-Günter Heimbrock

**The Gestalt of the Cross –
phenomenological and theological remarks**

1. Beyond Secularisation: Religious praxis between tradition and everyday culture

This conference focuses on secularisation theories and their impact on Practical Theology. In my presentation, I will address a central objective of Christian faith, the cross. Based on this issue I try to give an indirect contribution to the conference theme.

For Christians and especially for Christian theologians the sign of the cross is of crucial significance, because it represents the centre of the gospel, Christ's death and resurrection. Every Christian theologian is familiar with the basic interpretations, to pass down the message of Christ's passion as revelation of God as well as a new beginning of human life against the power of death and sin. From the reformation theology (Luther; Kolb 2002) up to recent biblical research there is a broad convergence about the understanding of this topic. The theology of the cross as form and as basis of theology in general is crucial to the appropriate interpretation of Christian faith (Luz 1974; Zumsteeg 2002). Essential issues of this interpretation of the cross are:

- the paradoxical structure of the central notion of God: the almighty in his most estranged incarnate gestalt, in the passion of Golgatha,

- the reverse structure of the theological epistemology: Christ's cross is no longer an object of theological interest, rather the subject.

And the order of the traditional liturgical calendar especially these times gives space to the *memoria passionis* in our services and celebrations. Also in this respect this conference is theologically exactly on time.

As to the cultural context of most western societies, you do not need extended empirical research to realise that this central element of Christian faith in terms of doctrinal knowledge does not belong to every Christian's basic set of belief, not to talk about the knowledge of the broader public concerning only basic elements of the Christian confession regarding the cross and the crucified.

The interesting point and challenge for Practical Theology which is aware of cultural contexts, however, is not this deficiency of knowledge, is not simply disbelief or hostile unbelief, rather something else. Despite the decline of churches' influence even in a „post-Christian"area crosses did not entirely disappear from personal and public life. Not only within church life paintings and sculptures of the cross made of wood, metal or glass are still to be found in prominent places. In the midst of the everyday life of societies that are being regarded as highly secularized they are still to be found, may it occur as element of jewellery, as pop cultural emblem like Madonna's outfit, as icon in the symbolic codes of advertisement, or even as a confusing arrangement of most instrumental everyday culture and religiously loaded pieces of veneration like the arrangement of pieces on this wall, which I discovered in a Cafe somewhere in Crete. To reflect on the theological relevance of these phenomena is the interest of my paper. These phenomena however, are rather poorly grasped, if one fails to realize the embodiment of everyday aesthetic praxis, the collective form of the matter. The doctrinal knowledge of individuals is not wrong, but simply not the exhaustive theoretical category to deal with such phenomena both candidly and fruitfully.

2. Encountering a Cross

In the aftermath of iconoclasm for a long time protestant theology hardly reflected on the relation between the "preaching of the cross" (1Cor 1,18) and the message of perceptive images and the material gestalt of various crosses both in pieces of art as in popular culture. Exactly here I take my point of departure. Narrowing the focus of my attention, I now turn to some more concrete phenomena highlighting the aesthetic praxis of a cross sculpture. Let me briefly indicate my focus introducing some steps of a class with my students during the last winter term on the theme "The gestalt of the cross".

After doing some basics with biblical and dogmatic texts introducing the structure and substance of the "theology of the cross" in a conventional approach it was my intention to relate this body of knowledge to the aesthetic praxis, to perceptions and interactions of learning students. In order to do so we made a trip to encounter a concrete piece of art. In the vicinity of Frankfurt, at 20 minutes distance in the St. Paul's congregation of Kelkheim, there is a very specific sculpture of the cross to be found, made by a female German artist, Madeleine Dietz in 1997. During the last decades she has been working especially with elements like stone and metal, doing among other things sculptures within church rooms. However, browsing her website you will quickly recognize that she is not devoted particularly to something like "sacred art".

The Gestalt of the Cross – phenomenological and theological remarks

(Photography by Hans-Günter Heimbrock)

Our whole group spent several hours in order to encounter physically and extensively the cross in the sanctuary. The morning session included orientation within the whole room in silence and without any photo shooting, open as well as more directed practice to sharpen one's own senses. The intention was not to study a piece of art or the artist's intentions. It was rather to become aware of the subjective resonance to the perceived elements of the sculpture within the context of light, architecture, the walls, glasses, floor, roof etc. through the different sensory channels of seeing, smelling, touching and feeling. The session also included conversation about the dynamics of "eye-catching" and other affections of our senses which were consciously or unconsciously at stake, when we encountered as mind-body units the cross sculpture, and tried to uncover their particular theological perspectives on the cross. Finally I invited the group to some guided imaginations. For the students as well as for me this morning session turned out to be a real journey of discovery. And following the perceptions with theological reflections it became another discovery, in order to conceive a theology of gestalt.

Just to indicate in a rather crude and de-contextualised way some outstanding elements of what the group responded to, some poor notes. As to the particular sculptural object at Kelkheim, most significant is the combination of materials, its particular gestalt, which shows in condensed way the process of its making. In the centre on the wall right behind the altar you see a compact dark steel blue or grey piece of metal, sized one square meter. When you step closer towards it, you will realise that it is not a flat plate but rather a case. In the middle of this case there is a cross to be seen, made by loam or clay. Out of the metal case the form of a Greek cross has been cut out and the whole case is filled with the earthen material. During the years it has dried and many lines and fissures are to be seen. Depending on the lighting resp. the time of the day the whole site is rather dark. Only if you switch on a spot light the brown centre is shining and catches your attention.

(Photography by Hans-Günter Heimbrock)

After the several hours' visit and mutual exchange within the church building, I asked the students to note their perceptions accurately and to elaborate them in a theological way. Many of them did most creative essays. Let me present now only two commentaries:

> *Lisa: The dualism of the two materials is essential. The cross does not exist separately; it is loosely connected with its frame/foreground. Thus, it is in interplay with its surrounding world. The world around is shaped by darkness, the cross in itself is light. Thus it is shining due to this choice of colours towards the perceiver. Its effect is lighting and inviting – as if you as human being only had to grab it and God would be closer.*

> *Stefan: To me it was obvious why this congregation had decided not to have a cross but rather an image of the cross. To me the message is clear: the cross has to do with perception. On this piece is appears as part or clip of perception, as something which came by supplementary. To me it seems as if it means to express: Our aspects or perceptions of God are only a clip, a limited glimpse through a window.*

3. Phenomenology and Theology of the Gestalt

What might be the general relevance of my little exploration concerning a particular cross sculpture at a particular congregational surrounding? And how to understand the underlying logic of this praxis? Of course, the participants of the class didn't start at zero, with their way of doing theology of the cross.

The Gestalt of the Cross – phenomenological and theological remarks 171

There is a cognitive frame in place. Focussing this particular cross at Kelkheim church took place within a seminar, in which the group had dealt with biblical texts and dogmatic conceptual language about the Christian cross. A conventional hermeneutical approach would tend to encounter the concrete cross as an instance to apply the contextual cognitive frame of doctrinal knowledge, at best as an impulse to reframe or adjust it. The necessary condition for this venue is, of course, the primordial transfer of the subject's impact into merely cognitive spheres of meaning. But how to grasp the productive theological elements of the students reactions, including pre-reflexive elements?

The conventional hermeneutical model is less capable to pick this up but also tends to omit other important phenomena at stake. A more intense theoretical reconstruction of the ongoing process is able to identify structural anthropological conditions which frame the perceptive processes as steps of meaning making. Based on phenomenological theory as well as gestalt theory (Perls 1973), the very process of sensual perception gets transparent in its intentionality, as active-re-active mind-body interplay of the human subject with the given reality (Waldenfels 2002). The human body-subject with its emotions, desires and sensations might well be mediated by physical and social conditions. However specifically *human* perception does not take place in an abstract or intellectualistic way, nor in a causal-mechanistic way, but rather in a situated connection to a finite bodily subject of perception which is living and perceiving the world in a specific spatial situation. The everyday encounter with reality includes a layer of pre-conceptual bodily rooted experience. Through one's body one understands the other and becomes aware of things. Hence, this behavior is not the result of previously and consciously taken decisions to act. Theoretical reconstruction self-evidently describes them in conceptual language, however this description should reflect upon the illusory character of "lived experience" (Meland 1969; Heimbrock 2007b).

This general approach to human perception helps to understand the experiences in my class. More intense perception of the piece of art does not start with abstract notions behind the visual phenomena, rather through the particular way the phenomenon of the cross appears to one's senses, within that which is given to the senses: the particular quadratic extension, its geometrical characteristics and proportions, the size of one square-meter and the volume of the case related to my own body, the touchable smoothness of the metal surface, and the roughened clay. Immediate sensual perceptions lead people to distinguish a Maltese cross from a mathematical sign indicating "plus", prior to any knowledge about these two verbal labels for the two gestalts.

As to the Kelkheim cross, the sensual impression of the main materials steel and clay being in tension which each other was influencing many students' commentaries. The specific gestalt of this cross created by Madeleine Dietz, so to speak a negative cross, did not put a corps on the background, but rather left a space out. And this sight does not only evoke the thoughts of people who have gone through St. Paul's commentaries in advance. The particular artistic variation, the creative act to shape the sign of the cross by using dried ground with all these lines and wrinkles inspires people not only to talk but to see and to imagine visual metaphors about Jesus and their own lives.

Thus, it is never just the idea of a cross to be perceived and encountered but always a particular concrete gestalt, which appears to our senses and gives way to make sense of. And it is never an isolated or unconditioned mental human subject which naively opens his or her eyes, looking at a cross and starting to interpret it. For a theology which is in contact with the cultural context it is important to identify these meaning-making processes as part of human theological activity.

4. The objective of Practical Theology as Empirical Theology

What does this all lead to for a reality oriented model of Practical Theology? And what could be the benefit for discussing secularisation theories? In my final part I would like to indicate some general conclusions.

Central to my reflection so far was the theological issue of the cross. Coming back to my biblical starting point: The basic message of the Christ's cross is twofold:

- *First:* Christ's cross is not about an objective in human life, not a separate something, but rather describing the structure of Christian theology in general.

- *Second*: This includes a fundamental insight of theological epistemology, a form to conceive reality in a reversed mode, expressed in the classical way by St. Paul in 1Cor 13,12 "but then shall I know even as also I am known."

Within theology, our discipline of Practical Theology from its very beginning on is the advocate of reality. The theoretical challenge implicit in my little class example and explicitly unfolded in the theology of the cross is how to understand reality and human behaviour within Practical Theology. Theology, based on the cross, comprehends and discloses reality as praxis of life between lived experience and pathos. This includes a pathic element within the process of knowing. This is most relevant for a methodology of Empirical Theology (Heimbrock 2007a). Theology might be called a 'science of reality' only if it follows this insight. Because "suffering is the reality, to which the gospel is relating [...]. Loss of reality does occur, whenever we withdraw ourselves from the truth of suffering and thus ground hope in an unrealistic way [...]. Practical Theology might escape the very and decisive loss of reality only if it conceives itself as scientia praxeos crucis" (Schröer 1974, 224; translation HGH).

The Gestalt of the Cross – phenomenological and theological remarks 173

Thus, the object of Practical Theology is Christian praxis within the life world as action and as aesthetic praxis, seen with a specific, pathic mode of perception, that opens up for the breadth of fruitful phenomena. After almost half a century of carrying out 'hard' empirical research in theology, phenomenology might become a helpful partner by opening a new interdisciplinary discourse on the basic concepts of reality and life. Its epistemological reasoning provides secular arguments to challenge an understanding of reality that is restricted to ideals of conceiving reality in terms of cause and effect, quantitative or even determinative correlations only. The awareness of a human being interwoven with the active and pathic structure of life, with otherness, could serve as an understanding of reality in accordance with the dynamic and mysterious structure of life in theological interpretation inspired by the theology of Christ's cross.

Based upon the enlarged analysis of human subjectivity and intentionality, it is possible, to revise the categorical framework of empirical approaches to life in general and to religion in particular. To identify the objective of Practical Theology in this way sheds new light on the discussion of secularization, because it asks for reevaluating the very parameters of social scientific theory. The general anthropological basis used in my analysis above does not only provide enlarged heuristic tools for clarifying explicit human religious activity. It also allows reconstructing from a theological point of view the empirical side of human behavior in general in a renewed perspective. It broadens the scope of theological interest beyond a narrow segment of "religious life". The really interesting point of difference is not a core "religious behavior" to be distinguished from less or non-religious behavior. This distinction already would be irrelevant to artists like Madeleine Dietz, likewise irrelevant to the general public interest in her works. The theological interest is rather to identify within contemporary culture a qualified renewed perspective on life and world, might it be appearing even within the most profane praxis of life. This perspective is about the pathic element in the encounter of reality, to put it in P. Tillich's words: "The presupposition of theology is that there is a special way in which reality imposes itself on us." (Tillich 1946, 17). And this mode of reality is not restricted to any segment of culture labelled by this culture as "religious" or Christian".

References

A. Dinter/H.-G.Heimbrock/K. Söderblom (Hg.) (2007), Einführung in die Empirische Theologie (UTB), Göttingen

H.-G. Heimbrock (2004), Gestalten Bilden. In: Th. Schreijäck (Hg.), Werkstatt Zukunft. Bildung und Theologie im Horizont eschatologisch bestimmter Wirklichkeit, Freiburg, 104–124

174 Hans-Günter Heimbrock

Ders. (2006), „Evangelisch aus gutem Grund". Facetten zur Phänomenologie und Theologie einer Werbeaktion, in: G. Linde u.a. (Hg.), Theologie zwischen Pragmatismus und Existenzdenken. FS Hermann Deuser zum 60.Geburtstag, Marburg, 361–376

Ders. (2007a), From Action to Lived Experience. Considering Methodological Problems of Modern Practical Theology, in: H. Streib (Ed.), Religious Praxis and De-Institutionalized Religion. Leiden, 43–59

Ders. (2007b), Reconstructing Lived Religion, in: Heimbrock/Scholtz Religion: Immediate Experience and the Mediacy of Research, Göttingen

R. Kolb (2002), Luther on the theology of the cross, in: Lutheran quarterly 16 (2002) 443–466

U. Lutz (1974), Theologia Crucis als Mitte der Theologie im NT, in: Evangelische Theologie 34, 116–141

B.E. Meland (1969), Can Empirical Theology Learn Something from Phenomenology? in: B.E. Meland (Ed.) The Future of Empirical Theology, Chicago, 283–305

F. Perls (1973), The Gestalt Approach, and Eye Witness to Therapy

H. Schröer (1974), Forschungsmethoden in der Praktischen Theologie, in: F. Klostermann/R.Zerfaß (Hg.), Praktische Theologie heute, München Mainz , 206–224

P. Tillich (1946), The Problem of Theological Method: II, in: The Journal of Religion Vol 27

B. Waldenfels (2002), Bodily Experience between Selfhood and Otherness (Lecture given on September 12, 2002 at the official opening of the Danish National Research Foundation: Center for Subjectivity Research (http://www.cfs.ku.dk/Waldenfels-opening-lecture.pdf (download 09/06/2005)

J. Zumstein (2002), Das Wort vom Kreuz als Mitte der paulinischen Theologie, in: A. Dettwiler (Hg.), Kreuzestheologie im Neuen Testament, Tübingen, 27–41

About the artist Madeleine Dietz: http://www.madeleinedietz.de/Kirchen.htm; www.kunstportal-bw.de/madeleinedietz1.html.

The Author

Hans-Günter Heimbrock, Prof. Dr., born 1948, is Professor of Practical Theology and Religious Education at Goethe-University, Frankfurt/Main, Germany. His main research issues are contextual and empirical theology. His most recent publications include an introduction into Empirical Theology, Einführung in die Empirische Theologie (2007, co-edited with A. Dinter/K. Söderblom), and Religion: Immediate Experience and the Mediacy of Research. Interdisciplinary Studies in the Objectives, Concepts and Methodology of Empirical Research in Religion (RCR 1) (2007, co-edited with C.P. Scholtz).

Raymond J. Webb

Agency, Religion, and Hope: Palestinian Young Women Reflect

I have been observing the Arab and Muslim worlds for the past 35 years, principally as an adjunct faculty member of Bethlehem University. I have noted the changing situation of women, including the fact that the percentage of women attending Bethlehem University has risen to 70%. (44 of 123 academic faculty members are women.) An earlier study involving young women raised under military occupation pointed to areas inviting further investigation, including agency, religious sensitivity and observance, and hope (Webb, 2005).

Method

Taking up from the earlier paper, this research looks at two questions: Is a significant level of agency present, despite structural and cultural factors? Is religion related to one's dreams about the future and to present and future agency? For the present project I interviewed 12 Christian and 12 Muslim women between the ages of 15 and 25. The average age was 20.3. Twenty were attending or had attended Bethlehem University. I let the women develop my initial questions in their own ways. In this paper I report some converging notions from the data, as well as selected and, I hope, representative excerpts from individual protocols. (All names are changed.)

Margaret S. Archer

I believe Margaret S. Archer's work is a resource for understanding the data from the present study. A social theorist, she has been considering structure, culture, and agency and their interrelationship from a critical realist perspective for more than two decades, arguing that society and culture influence individual persons but do not determine their behavior. In addition, persons and socio-cultural activities can change society and culture. She cautions against conflation in these relationships.

Society and Culture

Society has its social structures of material interests, power, group alliances, and antagonisms, which are in place and influence the actions of individual human agents (Archer 1996, 281). Individuals can act collectively and modify structures, organizing and articulating interests leading to "negotiated societal transformations" (Archer 1995, 185). Archer calls the process of change "morphogenesis" (1995, 75). Social interaction is "structurally conditioned but never is structurally determined since agents possess their own irreducible emergent powers" (1995, 90).

Parallel to society and individuals are culture and socio-cultural activity. Culture exerts influence on socio-cultural activity. "As an emergent entity, the cultural system has an objective existence and autonomous relations among its components (theories, beliefs, values or, more strictly, between the propositional formulations of them)" (1995, 180). But socio-cultural activity, over time, can modify culture.

For Archer, the theoretical unification of structural and cultural analysis requires the application of the morphogenetic perspective to the field of ideas – to culture (1996, 275).

The structural and cultural domains are interrelated but do not determine each other (1996, 282). But cultural factors can suppress conflict even when the structural conditions seem ready (1996, 282–283). Social groups also have cultures (ideas). "By adopting a set of ideas the structural interest group enmeshes itself in a particular form of cultural discourse and its associated problems [...] it now has to get busy correcting, protecting, competing or diversifying because these tasks are intrinsic to upholding ideas" (1996, 284). "If opposition or differentiation are already rife there, then structural opponents find ready-made cultural weapons against the material interest group [...] which is attempting to generalize and naturalize those ideas it has adopted for its own advancement" (1996, 285). But sometimes the cultural costs are too great (1996, 285).

Agency

People are born into groups which "[...] have vested interests in maintaining their advantages or improving their lot" (1995, 185), but they "[...] are capable of resisting, repudiating, suspending or circumventing structural and cultural tendencies in ways that are unpredictable because of their creative powers as human beings" (1995, 195). Archer asserts that cultural systems define "the doctrines, theories, beliefs, etc. in existence" and limit the idea worlds of agents (1995, 196-197). The institutional structures of complex societies have second order relationships, some of which are emergent properties (1995, 188). Both structure and culture can guide agency (1995, 229). Our reflexive deliberations [internal conversations] are the processes which mediate between structure and agency (Archer 2003, 132). Since there is leeway of interpretation, agents are not determined. They weigh costs and benefits (1995, 209). Agency emerges as the result of "double morphogenesis" (1995, 255). Humans "are grouped and regrouped as they contribute to the process of reproducing or changing the structure or culture of society," all the while maintaining or changing their collective identities and "maintaining or transforming the socio-cultural structures which they inherited at birth" (1995, 255).

Present Agency

In regard to agency (personal control of one's life) at the present time, most respondents in my interviews felt they had some control of their lives (cf. Table at the end of this paper), although there were external factors (family and society) which affected that personal control.

Ramia (22, Muslim): "Circumstances can limit my control. Society has rules and instructions for me to be a member of society. Politically, the occupation control me in travel and work. It limits my ambition. I can't do my dreams. The economy limits my chance for higher education. Religion controls every step in my life – clothes, study, job, relationship to society, family, friends. This is a good thing. There is to be harmony between my life and my religion. Religion doesn't oppress me. I choose to be whoever I want by my religion. Men still think they are superior, but it's changing. Men can't prevent us anymore from getting an education because of the new global situation, technology, satellite, even marriage decisions."

Manal (19, Muslim): "I had the chance to go to the States, and I took it. My parents said that it was my choice. I go around and give talks and sometimes people give me money, which helps pay for my education. Sometimes I lose confidence and feel really weak and alone there and people talk about me. But I'm doing something for myself. I feel really lucky. I'm too free for my culture. I'm controlling my life. Sometimes I feel like I don't want to have all this responsibility, but then I say I must go on."

Rose (22, Christian): "I control everything. If I don't get a scholarship, I'll save and pay for a Masters. I want to be a university teacher. I know how to teach and get kids to like math, 20 shekels an hour for non-relatives. I train folk dancers. I used to make some radio commercials. I sold pool tickets. I wanted many different things in my life. I hate routine. I've gone camping, been in a youth group. I worked in a shop selling. I have said 'no' to men I didn't want to marry."

Maysa (20, Christian): "I don't think I control a thing. Society plays a role."

Future Agency

In regard to personal agency in the future, five Christians expected to have very strong agency, three strong agency, and four some agency. Six Muslims expected to have very strong control in the future, five strong control, and one some agency. Interestingly, both groups predicted more agency ("strong" versus "some" in my coding) for themselves in the future than at the time of the interviews, with Muslims forecasting a slightly stronger personal agency than Christians. Older subjects had lower expectations of future agency than younger subjects. Cultural controls do exercise societal influence on both groups.

Noor (21, Muslim): "I will finish the university for sure. I told my husband I would not agree to leave it. He said, 'I am your husband.' I said, 'You would need a strong reason.' I said I would divorce him. With a university degree I can get work and have freedom for a job, even remarriage. I would have freedom to get away from him and his controlling family and be independent if needed."

Manal (19, Muslim): "Education would be a weapon for me. I want to help the women and children. I can do it; God gave me opportunity. I want to study international relations, be in the government. My dreams are connected to the reality I'm living. Since I was growing up we've been occupied and didn't have our childhood. I want to be a mother, like any woman, small family, teach them well."

Raida (22, Christian): "I plan to continue for a Masters or apply for lab assistant or teacher. I'm not going to stay at home. I will try to go to the U.S. and live with my brothers. I would help them while I studied. I'm convinced that education is more important than marriage. My parents aren't educated and they don't know the value of being educated. I would suffer, away from my family, but this is my only opportunity."

Dreams

It is not surprising that persons with a relationship to a university would have dreams about their future. All of the interviewees did. Among the Christians, the dreams of nine concerned husband and family, eight further education or teaching, six travel, and three bettering society in some way. Among the Muslims, eight dreamed of having a husband and family, four of education, four of travel, and nine of working to better society. Three Christians mentioned wanting understanding husbands, one a "special guy." One Muslim mentioned marrying "the man I love."

Christians reported somewhat more dreaming of travel than Muslims. This could be because of more opportunity to travel, more relatives outside of Palestine, more thought of emigration, or less constraint from families due to cultural norms. Muslims reported significantly more dreams of improving society (nine versus three). This may be due to having more influence as Muslims in Palestine, greater hope for the future. The more frequent Christian mention of education (eight versus four) might indicate perception of an area of societal contribution that appears accessible to them in the largely Muslim context.

Hala (18, Christian): "I may be a teacher. I'm not looking forward to it, but it's the reality. I will study something after university. I'd prefer to teach little children. My real dream is to be a photographer, but I let that dream go because I can't study it here. The future wouldn't be exciting if I knew what would happen. I think of names for my kids and what my husband will look like. I am active, crazy; I sing. I want him to be like me – successful, full of life."

Aya (22, Muslim): "As an old woman, I want to have had work, to have studied, to have helped my sister and mother and changed my brother's life. Maybe I'll be a journalist. I won't live with a husband who kills my ambition. Not like my sister who married at 15 and was controlled by her husband until she decided to go back to school. My dream is not determined by religious rules. I have mixed ideas. Once I said, 'Leave religion out of my life,' but then God comes back when I think about what I should do. Homeland and dreams go together. Maybe this situation creates my dreams."

Suhair (19, Muslim): "I dream of living peacefully, maybe with occupation, but we must live peacefully, if the Israelis don't use weapons and Palestinians don't use weapons. I'm a human being without categories. I love everyone who loves and respects me. I dream of traveling to Somalia to help people, to help with food and medicine and health instruction so they can live as human beings."

Religious Practice and Relationship

Ten of the Muslims reported praying five times per day (prescribed religious practice; cf. Table). Five Christians attended church every Sunday or more. Four went sometimes, three almost never. Muslim women in the Palestinian culture usually practice religion at home, while Christians attend church. Even the "low practice" subjects reported a personal relationship of some kind to God (Allah). All of the Muslims described a personal relationship with God and additional attention to religion (praying on their own, reading Qur'an regularly, etc.). Ten Christians also had "personal relationships," (private prayer, talking to God, etc.). Interestingly, the three Christians and one Muslim who did not engage in much formal religious practice all reported a personal relationship to God. Both Muslims who did not wear the Muslim head covering (*hejab*) reported having a personal relationship to God (Allah); one prayed Muslim prayers daily, the other did not.

Rula (21, Muslim): "I respect our Muslim religion. It is what I start with when I think about doing something. I pray five times a day. If I don't pray, I feel bad things will come to me. I always talk with my God from my heart. Sometimes I talk with him to keep me, family and friends and everything I love in a good way and protect us from bad. I think he does. God is with me always; I feel him with me, many times a day."

Vanessa (16, Christian): "Religion is necessary for me. Without it I can't live. When you read the Bible it makes you happier. The right way to live, not to commit sins. I will live happily – which is doing what Jesus taught – love one another – I try to live according to it. I pray at home in the morning, at meals, going to school, going to bed. I did this since being a little girl. I read saints stories and I wanted to be like them. I go to church several times a week, even if my family doesn't go. When I pray, I begin talking with God and have a conversation with Jesus. It is a personal relationship, stronger than with my sister. I say I love you and feel I'm going to explode with love for Jesus."

Reflection

Archer's schema, in which persons as agents, society, culture, and socio-cultural activities are distinct but mutually influential, is a helpful framework for understanding this research. In the midst of an Islamic revival, whose context affects majority Muslims and minority Christians alike, some women are both part of a trend of increasing religious practice and, at the same time, part of another movement of increased agency in their personal lives. In the past, women have exercised agency in the context of home and children. This research points to a more public expansion of agency. Increased education and employment outside of the home will certainly have an effect of structures, which arguably have been home-centered in the past. The change is not without tension, as seen in the excerpts above.

Religion, understood as a cultural factor, was an active and nurturing part of life for most respondents. The personal relationship to God (Allah) is a kind of "spiritual and religious" way of living. Muslim hopes for the future were not limited by a religious overlay of what would be "suitable." Religious guidance was seen as a generally positive factor. Freedom in the ultimate choice of a marriage partner was important and seemed to be the norm: one could say "no."

Muslim women in Palestine faithfully practice their religion and appropriate a religious relationship internally, while manifesting an increasing sense of agency. Will their aspirations and activity be largely in civil society? How will Islam, a religion with a significant cultural influence, relate to this increasing agency of women?

The Christian Arab culture, somewhat influenced by the West, is certainly influenced by Islam. The Christians I interviewed claimed present and future agency equal to that of Muslims, with less overall certainty about their futures in Palestine. One can wonder about structures that would help the dwindling Christian communities to endure in the Middle East, even as its members grow in agency. Will the Church as a structure, and Christianity, perhaps as a culture, be able to make a difference in the survival and prosperity of the individual Christians?

In a cultural setting that cannot be called "secular" and in a societal structure in which women have been "home-focused," these Muslim Arab and Christian Arab women have plans for their futures, are not simply the pawns of culture and structure, and work against restrictions from structure and culture, of which they are very aware. These data may provide footnotes to the broader movements in society. In Archer's terms, the increasing strongly educational, economic, and aspirational activity of women may lead to an emerging reshaping of societal structures and culture in regard to the place and influence of women, Christian and Muslim.

Table

Present Agency	Significant	Above average	Some	Little
Muslim	3	2	6	1
Christian	1	4	6	1

Future Agency	Significant	Above average	Some	Little
Muslim	6	5	1	0
Christian	5	3	4	0

Dreams (n ≠12)	Husband/Family	Education	Travel	Society
Muslim	8	4	4	9
Christian	9	8	6	3

Religious Practice	Very Strong	Some	Occasional	Almost Never
Muslim	10	1	0	1
Christian	5	4	0	3

"Relationship with God"	Intense	Strong	Some	None
Muslim	0	12	0	0
Christian	2	8	0	2

References

Archer, Margaret S. (1995). *Realist social theory: the morphogenetic approach*, Cambridge, UK: Cambridge University Press.

Archer, Margaret S. (1996). *Culture and agency: the place of culture in social agency*, rev. ed., Cambridge, UK: Cambridge University Press.

Archer, Margaret S. (2003). *Structure, agency, and the internal conversation*, Cambridge, UK: Cambridge University Press.

Webb, Raymond J. (2005). "*Living and Partly Living: Childhood under Occupation*," American Academy of Religion Annual Meeting, Childhood Studies and Religion Consultation and Women and Religion Section.

The Author

Raymond J. Webb, Prof. Dr., born 1942; Professor of Pastoral Life at the Faculty of Theology at the University of Saint Mary of the Lake, Mundelein, Illinois, U.S.A., academic dean, chair, Pastoral Life Department. Interests: Theological Method, Christian-Muslim Dialogue, transition into ministry. Recent publications: "The Development of a Catholic Practical Theology" (2006); "Christians, Muslims, Dreaming" (2006); "Solidarity: A Dialogical Path toward Roman Catholic-Muslim Reconciliation" (2007).

Research Group on Post-Traumatic Spirituality

R. Ruard Ganzevoort

'All things work together for good'?
Theodicy and post-traumatic spirituality

Religion and suffering have a long, intimate, and paradoxical relation with each other. It has been said that suffering is the strongest impetus for religious questions, thoughts, and behaviors, but also its largest stumbling block. It is in times of crisis that individuals and societies turn to religion to fulfill their existential needs and answer their existential questions, even though these existential needs and questions can never be resolved. Religion does not remove the causes or consequences of our suffering. It cannot change the human condition of vulnerability and hence of suffering. What religion may do is offer a frame of reference from which we can construe a meaningful narrative about our suffering, for example in a promise of eternal life or a kingdom of God in which there shall be no more tears, or in seeing suffering as divine punishment that we may avoid by living obediently. It cannot provide a conclusive explanation because every answer evokes only more questions and – taken to its extremes – carries unacceptable conclusions.

Even when religion cannot resolve suffering or adequately explain it, experiences of suffering can evoke deep and meaningful questions and longings and challenge the individual to consider his or her situation in the perspective of the relation with the divine. In suffering, our lives edge on the transcendent in that they reach and transcend the boundaries of their ordinary existence. This experience beyond the ordinary, more specifically this encounter with evil in its contingent or malicious shapes, invites us to see our experiences as related with the ultimate, the numinous, the divine and the demonic. For our ordinary existence we do not necessarily need a religious interpretation, except perhaps for the preservation of our mental and/or social structure, that is for our daily guidance. This need is magnified when we touch upon the extreme.

When we focus on traumatization, we are dealing with extreme suffering. It therefore can be expected that this dialectic relation of suffering and religion will be even more present. That expectation is the starting point for this paper. I will explore the positive and negative effects of traumatization on religion, with a special interest in posttraumatic spirituality. In return, I will discuss theodicy-models as religious responses to traumatization and their positive and negative impact.

If we want to study the relation between traumatization and religion, we have to be aware that both concepts apply to a range of phenomena, differing widely in both intensity and content. Religion as such does not exist, only the particular religious traditions and the myriads of individual religious constructions. Every individual life story offers a unique posture toward the divine and an evenly unique constellation of possible meanings of suffering, embedded in this person's biographical details. For some this religious dimension is central to the story, enacted in traditional or idiosyncratic religious behavior, for someone else it is equally central but left implicit, and for still another it is but a marginal part of the person's history. The interference with traumatization will not be the same for these different roles religion plays in the various life stories. Even the different religious traditions cannot be compared along the lines of formal dimensions, because these dimensions may be structured differently in the different religions. The Bible and the Koran, for example, have a different place in the configuration of the religious traditions. Religion then is a family resemblance concept that circles around the relation people construe with the divine.

A similar caveat should be made for the concept of trauma. Far from being a unified phenomenon, it stands for all those experiences that threaten our existence or integrity on a fundamental level. Again there are differences of intensity, but there is also a wide variety in the nature of traumatization. Natural disasters that disrupt entire communities are different from societies overthrown by wars and genocide, different again from acts of evil like terrorism or mass killings in schools. All these events are on the collective plane, which distinguishes them from individual experiences like sexual and domestic violence, traffic accidents, exposure to criminal acts, or extreme bullying. According to some, medical issues like being diagnosed with cancer or HIV/ Aids or the death of one's child could also qualify as traumatizing experiences. These different manifestations of traumatization differ not only in intensity, but also in the kind of damage that they do to the individual's life. And finally it matters whether traumatization occurred in childhood or adulthood, because the interference with a developing identity makes it structurally different. Some researchers distinguish between two types of trauma. The first type can be characterized as incidental traumatization. The second type is structural traumatization, occurring within and through structures of domination and oppression, and possibly resulting in more complex forms of post-traumatic disorders (Herman 1993). It is therefore problematic to arrive at a strict definition of trauma, and we will rest with a more general understanding of trauma as the overwhelming psychosocial injuries resulting from the confrontation with devastating events.

Effects of traumatization

If we try to review the effects of traumatization on religion, we easily embark on commonsensical distinctions between different kinds of trauma. This common sense has been influenced successfully by advocacy movements that claimed for example that victims of sexual abuse will endure life-lasting con-sequences, whereas even convicted perpetrators walk free after a relatively limited punishment. Something similar is assumed for parents mourning the loss of a child, a loss that is sometimes thought to be a pain that never subsides. Veterans on the other hand, suffering from their military experiences, are usually expected to recover from their traumatization within reasonable time. Perhaps this is overstated, and it may certainly be perceived differently in other contexts, but it may serve at least to caution against common presuppositions. In reality the severity, content, and consequences of traumatizing experiences will be different for every two cases, and our generalized remarks cannot be transposed automatically to the individual level. People with extreme experiences can certainly develop serious problems, but that depends on more than the severity of the violence. Among other variables, social support, style of attribution, and coping mediate the effects of violent experiences on trauma-symptoms (Gold, et al. 1994). Cultural and religious influences may also in-fluence resilience to the effects of trauma (Doxley, et al. 1997, Maercker & Herrle 2003).

That being said, the negative effects of traumatization have been well documented. Some of the most common effects feature in the description of posttraumatic stress disorder. They fall into three groups of symptoms. The first group includes of re-experiencing the traumatic event through intrusive memories, flashbacks, nightmares and the like. The second group regards persistent avoidance of stimuli associated with the trauma and numbing of general responsiveness. The third group contains persistent symptoms of increased arousal. Re-experiencing and avoidance can be seen as complementary and mutually enforcing processes. The alternation of the two probably has a clear neurological basis, based in instinctual responses triggered by elements that remind of the traumatizing experience itself. This alternation makes it difficult for the person to move beyond the experience and meanings and keeps the traumatizing memory present. It can even be as if the person returns mentally to the moment of traumatization.

Research into the effects on religion have yielded ambiguous results. One study showed subjects diagnosed with PTSD to be more likely to report changes in religious beliefs, generally becoming less religious (Falsetti, et al. 2003). Traumatization was also found to decrease affect representations of God as loving, and strengthen representations as absent, or wrathful, but only in cases of severe traumatization or complex PTSD (Doehring 1993). A gender factor appears in the finding that sexual abuse is predictive for non-religiosity, but only in men (Finkelhor, et al. 1989). Within the specific group of victims of clergy sexual abuse, other researchers found distinct effects on spirituality and church attendance (McLaughlin 1994, Rosetti 1995).

These findings are put into perspective by other studies showing less or contrasting effects. Some researchers found only limited changes in religious convictions following traumatic events. Instead, the metaphysical religious assumptions seemed to have provided a framework for understanding and coping with trauma (Overcash, et al. 1996). Among Holocaust survivors and their offspring belief in God and in a better future was found to be stronger than in a control group (Carmil & Breznitz 1991). In the case of sexual abuse, a relation was found with transcendent religious experiences as well as with feelings of alienation from God, but not with conventional religious behaviour like church attendance (Kennedy & Drebing 2002). Religious practice decreased for conservative Christian women following sexual abuse (especially inside the immediate family), but increased for agnostics, atheists, and adherents of other religious faiths (Elliott 1994). This may be caused by the different role of the father-image: problematic for conservative Christians and a viable alternative for others. The analysis of the narrative construction of male victims of sexual abuse supports this hypothesis in that these men sought to construe religious counterstories that might offer meaningful alternatives (Ganzevoort 2002). Based on findings of an increase of post-trauma spirituality for a majority of a sample of sexually assaulted women, strongly correlated with well-being, it was hypothesized that traumatic events reduce well-being, invoking an increase in spirituality to restore well-being (Kennedy, et al. 1998). Obviously, these studies are too diverse in types and severity of traumatization, measures of religion, and outcomes to provide a meaningful synthesis. We are clearly only beginning to understand the different effects victimization may have on religion for different persons in different situations.

This brings us to the growing number of studies that focus on possible positive effects of traumatizing experiences. This occurs more often than has been acknowledged in the past decades, perhaps due to a dominant clinical psychological interest in pathology rather than health. Whereas in exposed groups levels of posttraumatic stress disorder usually stay well below 25 % (Kleber & Brom 1992), posttraumatic growth may be more common than that. According to some, growth instead of pathology is in fact the normal outcome of traumatic stress (Christopher 2004). Congenial to 'positive psychology', researchers into post-traumatic growth are interested in the health promoting factors that may be called upon in coping with traumatizing events, in order to support coping efforts and resilience (Wilson 2006). Mental health research into trauma and related fields would benefit from the complementary approaches of stress-related growth, positive psychology, and the recognition of the role of spirituality and religion (Ai & Park 2005). The emerging concept of posttraumatic growth includes five dimensions: relating to others, openness for new possibilities, personal strength, spiritual change, and appreciation of life (Calhoun & Tedeschi 2006). Researchers note that the most significant growth may be experienced in the spiritual realm, although they tend to use rather simple measures for this dimension.

'All things work together for good'? Theodicy and post-traumatic spirituality   187

That posttraumatic growth and spirituality can be so closely related, should not come as a surprise. Religious traditions commonly share stories of suffering transformed into new life and wisdom. Thus in conversion narratives we usually find a transformation that is preceded by crisis experiences. Wisdom, however is not only a possible outcome, but also a possible source. It can guide believers in dealing with their suffering. Religious wisdom may therefore be an important factor in dealing with suffering and contribute to posttraumatic growth. It invites the person to acknowledge and manage the uncertainty of life and the human limitations (Linley 2003).

Theodicy and the response to trauma

This brings us to the other side of the dialectical process, the religious response to trauma. This dimension is addressed in the psychological study of religious coping (Pargament 1997). Out of the many factors that may be involved, in this paper I will focus on the role theodicy plays in responding to suffering and here my primary frame of reference will be the Christian tradition. Theodicy may bridge the gap between psychology of religion and theology. The first usually neglects such issues of content (Furnham & Brown 1992), whereas the latter investigates theodicy with limited connection to the coping process. Obviously real life experiences, both individual and collective, are at the background of theodicy-studies, but the actual research does not connect theodicy empirically with the process of suffering and coping. Even the groundbreaking empirical theodicy-project of Hans van der Ven and his colleagues does not deal with actual suffering but only with attitudes toward different theodicy-models (Van der Ven & Vossen 1995).

Although the subject matter is probably as old as humanity, the discussion of the modern concept of theodicy is usually traced back to Leibnitz. It has been popularized in the eighties by rabbi Harold Kushner (1981) in his book *When bad things happen to good people*. Theodicies can be seen as attempts to reconcile three fundamental notions: God is omnipotent, God is all good, the world is a good place. The last one may be phrased more personally: my life is a good life and I am a worthy person. These three are in contradiction with one another in the face of suffering. Put differently: when suffering from trauma, people are confronted with the need to interpret the situation in such a way that these three notions are sustained. Because that is generally a rather complex task, people may choose instead to deny one of the three in order to construe a consistent narrative. They loose faith in either God's power or God's love, or in themselves and the value of their life.

A telling parallel for these three positions can be found in Ronnie Janoff-Bulman's (1992) psychology of trauma. She claims that in traumatization, three fundamental assumptions are shattered that ordinarily guide our life and our life story. The three are the meaningfulness of the world, the benevolence of the world and the personal value. In trauma the world is experienced as collapsing or disintegrating, people around are met with suspicion and fear, and the self is distrusted or even rejected. The many symptoms of traumatization can be interpreted from this framework: hyperalertness and avoidance signal that the world is not a meaningful coherent whole on which we can build. Distrust, fear, and isolation point to the experience that others may not be benevolent toward us. Shame and guilt focus on the contested or rejected value of the person.

The first assumption regards the meaningfulness of the world. The world we entered as a child is not a coincidental hotchpotch of people, events, and things, it is coherent and therefore solid ground. Things happen for a reason and can be understood if we try hard enough. This assumption is the basis for scientific knowledge, but is present everywhere. When we go to bed at night, we know that the sun will rise the next day. That is the reason we can understand, manage, and sometimes even change the world we live in. When this assumption is shattered in traumatization, the person gets lost in the world and looses control. Disorientation and dissociation may occur. The religious shape of this assumption is the notion of divine power. Every religion proclaims that life is not a random collection of moments and experiences. There is a larger story, a pattern of meanings that encompasses our life. This larger story, religion tells us, is created and sustained by God. 'He's got the whole world in his hand.' The meaningful coherence of the world is thus symbolized in divine sovereignty and providence. When this notion is shattered by traumatization, the trust in God's power becomes contested and we lose confidence that God preserves this world.

The second assumption deals with the benevolence of the people around us. What is at stake here is the interpersonal relations that are challenged in traumatization. In a positive context, the child learns to trust others, not without limitations, but as a fundamental stance toward others. Whenever we meet people, we ordinarily believe that they carry no negative intentions toward us, or we would not dare to buy bread or ask for directions. When this assumption is threatened by traumatization we see an increase of distrust or even paranoia that comes from the perceived need to protect one's own life and from a loss of faith in the benevolence of others. The religious shape of this is the notion of divine love. Even when we experience that the world itself has negative elements, we cling to the belief that at least God is benevolent toward us. Fundamental assumptions, and especially religion, usually have a distinct resilience to contrasting experiences. Instead of being overthrown immediately by traumatic events, they can also function as a counterstory that helps us keep our heads above water. When traumatizing experiences are too overwhelming, the religious dimension may be afflicted as well and the person may loose faith in the benevolence of God.

'All things work together for good'? Theodicy and post-traumatic spirituality 189

The third assumption concerns the value of the person and is of course directly related to the other two assumptions. A person's self-affirming identity is shaped particularly by the tangible experiences of being known, carried, and loved. These experiences have their natural starting point when the newborn child is nurtured and nourished. Where these experiences are missing or conflated with experiences of neglect, abandonment, or abuse, identity development may be disturbed or arrested. The religious shape is the notion that God has an interest in this one particular person and not only in the larger universe. It may be actualized in prayer and in the expectation or experience that God responds to these prayers. In traumatization this notion can become questionable. The shame and powerlessness that are part of the traumatizing experience indicate that the person is incapable and unsupported. In cases of man-made traumatization, like violence, this is reinforced by the fact that the perpetrator and bystanders apparently find the victim unworthy of respect or protection. For the religious person, this may evoke the existential experience that God has abandoned him or her.

There are vast differences between people, between their religious backgrounds and the stories of God that inhabit their world of meanings, and between different shapes and contents of traumatization. Because of that, in every situation the three fundamental assumptions and their religious shapes are at stake in a unique way. The God-images can be seen as a symbolization of the fundamental assumptions (Doka 2002). In natural disasters the focus may be on coherence of the world and divine power and less on benevolence and divine love. In acts of violence benevolence and divine love may be pivotal and coherence and power may be less central. In orthodox-reformed churches the issues will be dealt with more under the heading of power than of love, whereas in liberal circles the dignity and responsibility of the person may be focal. All this shows that these three assumptions (and the theodicy-attempts derived from them) offer a useful matrix for pastoral-theological interpretation.

References

Ai, A.L. & Park, C.L. (2005) 'Possibilities of the positive following violence and trauma: informing the coming decade of research', *Journal of Interpersonal Violence. 20/2*, 242–250.

Astley, J. (2002) *Ordinary Theology. Looking, listening and learning in theology.* Aldershot (GB): Ashgate.

Calhoun, L.G. & Tedeschi, J.T. (2006) 'The foundations of posttraumatic growth. An expanded framework'. In: Calhoun, L.G. en Tedeschi, J.T. (ed.) *Handbook of post-traumatic growth.* Mahwah (NJ): Lawrence Erlbaum, 1–23.

Carmil, D. & Breznitz, S. (1991) 'Personal trauma and world view. Are extremely stressful experiences related to political attitudes, religious beliefs, and future orientation?' *Journal of Traumatic Stress. 4/3*, 393–405.

Christopher, M. (2004) 'A broader view of trauma: a biopsychosocial-evolutionary view of the role of the traumatic stress response in the emergence of pathology and/or growth.' *Clinical Psychology Review. 24/1*, 75–98.

Doehring, C. (1993) *Internal desecration. Traumatization and representations of God.* Lanham: University Press of America.

Doka, K. (2002) 'How Could God? Loss and the Spiritual Assumptive World'. In: Kauffman, J. (ed.) *Loss of the Assumptive World. A theory of Traumatic Loss.* New York: Brunner-Routledge, 49–54.

Doxley, C., Jensen, L. & Jensen, J. (1997) 'The influence of religion on victims of childhood sexual abuse', *The International Journal for psychology of Religion. 7/3*, 179–186.

Elliott, D.M. (1994) 'The impact of christian faith on the prevalence and sequelae of sexual abuse', *Journal of interpersonal violence. 9/1*, 95–108.

Falsetti, S.A., Resick, P.A. & Davis, J.L. (2003) 'Changes in religious beliefs following trauma.' *Journal of Traumatic Stress. 16/4*, 391–398.

Finkelhor, D., Hotaling, G.T., Lewis, I.A. & Smith, C. (1989) 'Sexual abuse and its relationship to later sexual satisfaction, marital status, religion and attitudes', *Journal of Interpersonal Violence. 4/4*, 379–399.

Furnham, A. & Brown, L.B. (1992) 'Theodicy. A neglected aspect of the psychology of religion', *International Journal for the Psychology of Religion. 2/1*, 37–45.

Ganzevoort, R.R. (1998) 'Religious Coping reconsidered. A narrative reformulation', *Journal of Psychology and Theology. 26/3*, 276–286.

Ganzevoort, R.R. (2002) 'Common themes and structures in male victims' stories of religion and sexual abuse', *Mental Health, Religion & Culture. 5/3*, 313–325.

Gold, S.R., Milan, L.D., Mayall, A. & Johnson, A.E. (1994) 'A cross-validation study of the trauma symptom checklist. The role of mediating variables', *Journal of Interpersonal Violence. 9/1*, 12–26.

Herman, J.L. (1993) *Trauma and recovery. The aftermath of violence – from domestic abuse to political terror.* New York: Basic Books.

Janoff-Bulman, R. (1992) *Shattered assumptions. Towards a new psychology of trauma.* New York: Free Press.

Kennedy, J.E., Davis, R.C. & Taylor, B.G. (1998) 'Changes in spirituality and well-being among victims of sexual assault', *Journal for the Scientific Study of Religion. 37/2*, 322–328.

'All things work together for good'? Theodicy and post-traumatic spirituality   191

Kennedy, P. & Drebing, C.E. (2002) 'Abuse and religious experience. A study of religiously committed evangelical adults', *Mental Health, Religion & Culture. 5/3*, 225–237.

Kleber, R.J. & Brom, D. (1992) *Coping with trauma*. Amsterdam: Swets & Zeitlinger.

Kushner, H.S. (1981) *When bad things happen to good people*. New York: Schocken.

Linley, P.A. (2003) 'Positive adaptation to trauma: wisdom as both process and outcome', *Journal of Traumatic Stress. 16/6*, 601–610.

Maercker, A. & Herrle, J. (2003) 'Long-term effects of the Dresden bombing. Relationships to control beliefs, religious belief, and personal growth.' *Journal of Traumatic Stress. 16/6*, 579–587.

McLaughlin, B.R. (1994) 'Devastated spirituality: the impact of clergy sexual abuse on the survivor's relationship with God and the church", *Sexual Addiction & Compulsivity. 1/2*, 145–158.

Overcash, W.S., Calhoun, L.G., Cann, A. & Tedeschi, R.G. (1996) 'Coping with crises; an examination of the impact of traumatic events on religious beliefs', *The Journal of Genetic Psychology. 157/4*, 455–464.

Pargament, K.I. (1997) *The psychology of religion and coping. Theory, research, practice*. New York: The Guilford Press.

Rosetti, S.J. (1995) 'The impact of child abuse on attitudes toward God and the Catholic church', *Child Abuse and Neglect. 19/12*, 1469–1481.

Van der Ven, J.A. & Vossen, H.J.M. (1995 ed.) *Suffering: why for God's sake? Pastoral research in theodicy*. Kampen: Kok Pharos.

Wilson, J.P. (2006 ed.) *The Posttraumatic Self. Restoring Meaning and Wholeness to Personality*. London: Routledge.

The Author

R. Ruard Ganzevoort, born 1965, is Professor of Practical Theology at VU University Amsterdam and Windesheim University of Applied Sciences Zwolle (NL). He served on the board of the International Academy since 2003 and as president from 2007 to 2009. His publications focus on pastoral care, narratives, religious pluralism and conflict, trauma, and popular culture. Further information: www.ruardganzevoort.nl.

Research Group on Post-Traumatic Spirituality

Julian C. Müller

Spiritual narratives of adolescent orphans affected by HIV and Aids and poverty

Introduction

This article took a close look at specific children within the environment of HIV and Aids. Clearly aware of the devastating environment surrounding HIV and Aids we went on a search of orphans affected by HIV and Aids and their "God-given potential" amidst their despair. In our search we found multiple and diverse narratives. Surprisingly though not all of these narratives were about pain and sorrow. Some of these narratives contained aspects of courage; of falling but standing up from the dust. It even contained lessons which can empower others in the same situation. Therefore the focus of the study shifted to the factors which contributed to these strange, but truly amazing alternative narratives of hope and love.

We were in search of the factors, which frees us from the psychological burden of trauma. We were interested in the narratives which could tell us something about the role the idea of God plays in empowering these children to create hope for the future – a future which will create opportunities to develop this God-given potential. Narrative speaking we were in search of the "Unique Outcomes" – the factors that lay outside the problem which contributed in the creation of hope! Therefore this article strives to reveal the underlying discourses, which help to write our stories in life as we pursue a better understanding of the meaning of various traumatic experiences, and which empowers us to face the unforeseen difficulties that lie ahead.

We invite the reader to take a glimpse in the world of these children. By voicing some of the findings we hope to open a keyhole that allows others to peer in at a world, which they might otherwise have missed.

The ultimate goal of the broader study is to voice these children's capacity of creating a form of liberation which has never been thought of as capable by children, so that they will no longer be viewed as "victims", but as "survivors". Eventually the message being emancipated to our children will be that we as a society, sharing their pain, have not and will not forget them.

1. Motivation for the study

> Wendy (13) is painting a picture of how children are forced to witness the slow and painful death of their parents from HIV/AIDS. She says: "The picture is of my home. The ambulance is fetching my mother. The flower is me. I have to stand tall, protect my mother and my home. My mother had another baby. I looked after her until she died and then I looked after the baby. He also died." Wendy told her story at the opening of the national conference on Children affected by HIV/AIDS in Johannesburg on Sunday night.
>
> (The Sowetan, June 6, 2002)

The above story is one of thousands that are told daily by our African children. South Africa can no longer ignore the devastating effects the epidemic of HIV and Aids has on our social systems. This effect does not only pertain to the physical breakdown of HIV and Aids victims, but is also the main cause of breaking the spirit of thousands of people living in the environment of HIV and Aids. "The lack of social security and high levels of unemployment in South Africa means that poor households and communities slip further and further into poverty and deprivation. Invariably the burden of coping falls on women, particularly girls and grandmothers" (AIDS foundation South-Africa 2005).

Kilbourn adds further detail to this disastrous situation and by doing this she helps us to place emphasis on how HIV and Aids is affecting our children:

> The adult-sized role thrust upon children leaves them with no time or energy for play, school, friends or development of relationships. Instead of a safe, healthy home and community environment, millions of children are forced to live in an environment of fear, insecurity, suffering, poverty and trauma. Their physical, mental, spiritual and emotional needs are ignored.
>
> (Kilbourn 1996:13)

2. Relevance of the study

> The children of the world are innocent, vulnerable, and dependent. They are also curious, active and full of hope. Their time should be one of joy and peace, of playing, learning and growing. Their future should be shaped in harmony and cooperation. Their lives should mature as they broaden their perspectives and gain new experiences.
>
> (UNICEF 1991:53)

In reality though, more than 336 300 children under 18 were orphans as a result of AIDS. (cf. Centre for the study of Aids 2004). The reality is that our children live in traumatic situations where their hope is replaced by despair. They live in paralysing fear, mistrust and deep grief and they carry burdens and responsibilities far too heavy for any child to bear. Deep in their spirits an overwhelming sense of hopelessness springs up; they see no opportunities to develop their God-given potential (cf. Kilbourn 1996:13).

3. Research gap

The problem is that in these desperate circumstances, children are often overlooked in terms of their spiritual needs. The family members and others taking care of them are in a race with survival and tend to concentrate on the most basic and immediate needs. The churches lost contact with the children after the death of their parents and the dismantling of the household. The children are shifted to other households and the existing support systems diminish.

The question which is not yet addressed adequately (research gap) is the following: What are the context and need of children severely affected by HIV and Aids and what are possibilities for the creation of better support systems that will also take care of their spiritual needs?

4. Research Approach

The narrative approach to qualitative research is used and is conducted according to the Seven Movements, developed by Müller on the basis of Post foundational Practical Theology.

The first phase of the research has started and is nearing completion. Data collection was done by means of interviews.[1] Interviews were first done with the caregivers and through them with teenaged children in different HIV environments. We worked with established NGO's in Gauteng (Heartbeat, PEN, and Hospivision) and trained their professional workers and volunteers to do the interviews with the children. This was the first step in getting to grips with the reality in which the children and caregivers find themselves. Open-ended questions have been used within these interviews, as they provide space for the caregivers and children to voice their exact experiences of the situation, as they feel fit.

5. A river of despair

All the caregivers were in agreement that the worst effect of losing one's parents was the economical poverty in which these children find themselves in. They report that it is difficult to tend to the emotional and spiritual needs of the children, while they long for the basic needs of food and education. As Nomusa[2] (17 years) describes their situation after the death of her parents: "We were nine (people) at home we had a car and chickens and goats and a garden. We planted the garden to get maize and spinach and sorghum. When it was ripe

---

[1] Interviews with caregivers were held on July 7, 2006, Mamelodi, Health clinic.
[2] Pseudonyms have been used except where the children preferred that their own names be used.

Spiritual narratives of adolescent orphans affected by HIV and Aids and poverty   195

we ate and fed the goats maize. When mother has harvested, father went with the vehicle to sell (the vegetables). When it is sold, he came back from there bringing clothes and school books and something nice. But now we are a small family because both (my) parents have died. We now live alone at home the three of us... When we need something – anything – it is not easy to get it."

Lebo (16 years) talks about the need for education as she says her father told her school is very important, made her go to school and bought her a school uniform, but now she can't attend anymore because her mother is very ill from HIV and AIDS and isn't working anymore.

This corresponds to various studies which show that the traditional social structures, like the extended family, are under enormous pressure: A UNAIDS report states that "need for support is desperate in the worst-hit regions where the capacities of families are eroded by economic decline and deepening poverty" (Report on the Global HIV and Aids epidemic 2002). This in turn results in family structures changing and households fragmenting, becoming poorer and facing destitution (cf. Facing Aids 2002: 98).

Frank (16years) who also lost both his parents to HIV and AIDS now lives with his grandmother and grandfather, together with his two cousins. He states that his grandmother takes good care of him and his cousins, yet admits to the fact that this new living arrangements put an economical strain on his grandmother's pension when he says that "(My grandmother tries to buy me clothes, but she can only buy (a) few clothes as she (also) has to buy for my aunt's children." Lebo (16 years) also talks about the changing family structures after her father's death and as she calls it "(poverty in my family, there is no food, my mother doesn't work, we depend on our granny only." Children in such circumstances are therefore particularly "vulnerable to exploitation" as they sometimes need to become the breadwinners for others (cf. Facing Aids 2002: 98).

The literature shows that the impact of the epidemic on significant others, causes them to suffer various psychological trauma. Studies report, "psychosocial effects will be worsened by accompanying threats to the basic survival (food, housing, education, healthcare) and security (protection from exploitation and abuse) frequently experienced by orphans" (cf. The Sunday Independent, 6 Oct 2002).

Lerato (16 years) adds to this when she says that "[t]hings are different, it's tough now, I can't demand things from people because they get irritated and angry. I don't want to be a burden […]". Lerato (19 years) even expressed suicide ideation when admitting to the fact that when she thinks about her deceased father, she feels sad and "[…] think to kill myself because there is no help".

It seems that significant others themselves need help to come to terms with their own fears and prejudices and the implications and consequences of their loved ones (cf. Van Dyk 2005:218). It is reported that significant others also experience feelings of depression, loneliness, fear, uncertainty, anxiety, anger and emotional numbness (cf. Van Dyk 2005:218). Mostly, though, they often feel unable to cope with new demands that the infection places on them. They feel incompetent, unqualified and powerless in their interaction with the HIV-positive parent (cf. Van Dyk 2005:218), and when the parent dies, they are unable to deal with the demands of life in general. Lerato (19 years) stated that she ignored her father once he fell ill from HIV and AIDS and now feels that maybe God wouldn't forgive her because she didn't show respect towards her dying father.

Children suffer tremendously when their parents are infected, and the needs of children with infected parents are often neglected. "In many African societies there is no tradition of talking to children as equals and on an intimate basis, caregivers often report seeing 'the suffering of children who are too often hovering in the shadows of a sick room, seeing and hearing everything but never addressed directly' (UNAIDS 2000a:33)". Lebogang (15 years) tells of the terrible ordeal of seeing his parents on their deathbeds, as he recalls his parents last days as "they were only drinking water and looking at us, they couldn't swallow the medication anymore."

Children are largely excluded form the counselling process because caregivers often don't know how to talk to the children. The children in this study, however, had been given an opportunity to be part of a support group.[3] This, they reported, helps them tremendously, as they get time to debrief and discuss things which they find especially difficult to handle.

The struggle of poverty reinforces malevolent people to use this already disastrous situation as bait to exploit especially the young girl sexually. Sometimes dire poverty and need drive women from such communities to prostitution because this is the only way they feel they can survive. Their low self- image and lack of personal authority also make such women particularly vulnerable to rape. Young girls are often coerced, raped or enticed into sex by someone older, stronger or richer than themselves. It is well known that older 'sugar daddies' often offer schoolgirls gifts or money in return for sex (cf. Van Dyk 2005:25). Faced with overwhelming poverty, a woman who works in a brothel may reason: "If I work here I may die in ten years. If I don't, I will die of starvation tomorrow" (Facing Aids 2002:15–16).

Many girls in the study also reported that the household duties and the expectations to perform on an academic level became a burden sometimes too heavy

---

[3] Interviews held with children in August, 2006.

Spiritual narratives of adolescent orphans affected by HIV and Aids and poverty   197

to bear. Zanele (16 years) talks of how her life changed after her mother's death by telling about "(w)orking hard at school and helping out at home. [I have] more responsibilities now." Lerato (16 years) says that her life before her parents' deaths was wonderful, "[…] I was happy, got everything I wanted, when I wanted it. I was spoiled.", but that now she sometimes get angry with God because he took her parents "[…] when I am still so young, now I am struggling."

Most girls experienced the death of their mothers as a great loss, as they did not feel comfortable to confide in their grandmothers. Some expressed this loss as "the loss of their greatest confidant"[4]. As Lerato (16 years) puts it: "She [mother] used to love me and spoil me. She was very accommodating and I felt safe and knew that I could rely on her for anything." Another girl burst into tears as she states that she misses her mother very much and still found it difficult to deal with the loss. She added: "I always talked to my mother and she always gave me advice. Now I have no one to talk to". Most girls said that their mothers were the sole motivation behind their efforts to succeed in school. They remember very clearly, the words and advice from their mothers, which guides them through life. They stated: "I want to make my mother proud".

In our study one girl found it very difficult to cope with her mother's death. She lives with her grandmother while her older sister lives in the Free State and takes care of her younger sister. This girl stated that her mom died of 'stress' and her biggest fear is that her sister, who took over the responsibilities of caring for the family, may also die of too much stress. In her story and accompanying fears it is evident how she used her experiences to construe her own conclusions. As the African culture usually excludes children in the explanation of a death (cf. Van Dyk 2005) it seems only natural that she will come to her own understanding. This explanation is the "lens" she uses to look at her current world and contributes to her accompanying fears of the future. These children seem very aware of the dangers of HIV and Aids, but most stated that they did not know the reason for their parents' deaths. They all construe their own alternative explanatory story which guides their lives in various ways.

It was very apparent how responsible and "grown up" these adolescents were. Some of them even attended special schools/courses during school holidays as a way to better their futures. Other children got temporary jobs in the holidays to help them with the care of their family. They stated that they want to have "a good job one day" which will make it easier for them to tend (financially) to their siblings' needs and to help others in need in their communities.

Refilwe (19 years) greatest wish is to be able to complete her tertiary education in order for her to help her younger brother to also complete school, she wants

---

[4] Personal interviews held in August, 2006, Nelmapius, Heartbeat centre.

to become a chartered accountant because "my subjects are related to it, and it is a permanent job." Lerato (19 years) wants to become a teacher because "I want our children to know about life and to be educated.", while her sister Lebo (16 years) wants to become a police officer to "help and reduce crime in the community." Frank (16 years) also wants to go into the helping professions by becoming a social worker as the co-researcher who interviewed him, because "I want to help other children as you are helping us."

In conclusion it is evident that HIV and Aids is indeed a "disease in motion". Apparently Aids has thus far reached a stage where it flows like a river: into every crack, into every hole, around every corner, until it fills our souls with enough despair, so that all that is left of our bodies and souls is a wreck on the bank of the river.

6. Africa, praying to God and dancing for the ancestors

This step involves the description of experiences as it is continually informed by traditions of interpretations. "The metaphor of social construction leads us to consider the ways in which every person's social, interpersonal reality has been constructed through interaction with other human beings and human institutions and to focus on the influence of social realities on the meaning of people's lives" (Freedman & Combs 1996:1). Therefore we must acknowledge the influence of the wider macro system on the experiences and interpretations of the individual. According to social Constructionism, there are specific traditions/discourses in certain communities which inform perceptions and behaviour.

In the various meetings with the co-researchers it became evident that they find themselves in an environment which is intermeshed with the various values and traditions of the African culture, and one which struggles to integrate the meaning of HIV and Aids in this world-view.

In reflection of the literature it became evident that the African cultural perception of it is directed by intention and specific cause. They search for identifying the cause or the intention behind the cause and neutralise or eliminate it. They also belief that mental as well as physical illness can be caused by disharmony between a person and the spiritual world. This is done by natural causes, or by a breakdown in human relationships. Sometimes however, it is believed that ancestors do not actually send illness themselves but merely allow it to happen by withdrawing their protection (cf. Van Dyk 2005:116).

Furthermore there is a close connection between the ancestors and God as causal agents of illnesses. Most Africans, especially in Western society do in fact believe in the existence of God; though God is seen as too important to be bothered with everyday problems (cf. Van Dyk 2005:116). Therefore they

Spiritual narratives of adolescent orphans affected by HIV and Aids and poverty 199

incorporate their ancestors in guiding them with everyday issues. "The living spirits of the deceased ancestors are the 'mediators' between the people and God" (Mbiti 1969; McCall 1995; Sow 1980).

The untimely death of innumerable young people and the unprecedented lowering of life expectancy among all groups and classes of people reinforces the idea of punishment from the ancestors, as death in African societies is accepted as natural only when elderly people die, in most other cases death is seen as a punishment or as the work of evil spirits and witches (cf. Van Dyk 2005:118).

The question arises why this grand narrative of believing in ancestors and witches still prevails in the midst of a well westernised society, as is the case in South-Africa. Van Dyk (2005:118) explains that there are some psychological benefits enmeshed in this belief.

> If extended factors such as witches and sorcerers are blamed for Aids, this projection of responsibility consoles the family, victims and society as a whole. It also helps to alleviate feelings of guilt and anxiety [...] Attributing HIV infection to witchcraft may also help the bereaved family to avoid feeling stigmatised by their community (Campbell and Kelly, 1995).
>
> (Van Dyk 2005:118)

A widespread misperception exists that children do not understand God and religion. This is also apparent in the African tradition where the issue of death is not discussed with children. The fact that ancestors act as mediators between God and his children (Meiring 1996:13) implies that direct contact between God and his children is impossible. Where do our co-researchers go for guidance then?

In asking this very question to the co-researchers in a group[5] meeting the girls made their religious affiliation very clear. Most girls describe themselves as "born again Christians" following the deaths of their parents. Some continue their mother's affiliation towards ancestor-guidance and others are set against ancestry. Whatever their viewpoint is, all of them find their power and courage in prayer and church meetings. It seems that the church community also plays its part in encouraging these children. Some children reported that they do not attend church as they feel they can pray and sing at home or even because they can't afford transport money to the church anymore. Tebogo (15years) states this problem clearly when he says: "My church is the NICC, National Independent Christian Church. I am a churchgoer but I don't go there regularly because there is no money to go to Soshanguve."

---

[5] Group interviews conducted September, 2006, Heartbeat centre, Nelmapius.

Others think it is very important to go to church as they see it as their duty as members of the church community. All of them though reported that they have a new-found relationship with God as "He is the only one that comforts me and the only One I could rely on". They also report that they believe that their mothers are with God and this comforts them. For Zanele (16 years) it helps her to cope by knowing that her mother is with God and that once she will be with her. Another girl who relies very much on God's comfort and guidance states that she experiences her mother's presence through her relationship with God.

Two girls actively took part in ancestry evoking activities, but both of them stated that this is a tradition they set forth from their mothers as their mothers were seen as "Sangoma's" in their community. They stated that they also found connection with their mothers by this religious activity. It seems that the community surrounding ancestry also provides these girls with comfort and support.

It is clear that these children do not experience contact with God as impossible. This may be a result of Western Christian influence, as many girls said that Christianity doesn't allow the worshipping of ancestors, which is a central idea of Western Christianity (cf. Van Dyk 2005:119).

Nomusa (17 years) describes her relationship to God as one where she can talk to Him, although she sometimes gets upset with Him for allowing her parents to die and sees the death of her parents as "[…] a punishment, maybe because I didn't serve God while I was still small; or maybe it is to teach me to stand on my own feet and trust in God alone, not leaning on people."

This study thus concludes that faith, for these children, indeed plays a vital role in construction of their narratives and has an underlying meaning which in turn influences their paradigm of the world. This correlates with studies of faith, as Fowler (1986:25) explains "Faith is the process of constitutive-knowing' which underlies 'a person's composition and maintenance of a comprehensive frame (or frames) of meaning". He further states that faith "gives coherence and direction to persons' lives, links them in shared trusts and loyalties with others, grounds their personal stance and communal loyalties in a sense of relatedness to a larger frame of reference, and enables them to face and deal with the limited conditions of human life, relying upon that which has the quality of intimacy in their lives" (Fowler 1996:56).

Our interests were further stimulated by the curiosity of the difference in religious experiences between males and females. Carol Gilligan (1987) found "that women's moral thinking is characteristically relational and contextual in a way which is not true of men" and that the women in her study "appealed to the needs and demands of a relationship and to an ethic of responsibility and care, in their attempts to resolve moral dilemmas" (Slee 2004:23). Surrey (1991:52–53) states that the self is organised and developed in the context of important relationships', as well as relationship 'being seen as the basic goal of development."

These relational psychodynamic theories make us aware of the impact of the early years of childcare on an individual's later relationships, of which the relationship to God may be one. We have seen that the relationship the girls had with their mother inevitable influenced their religious affiliation. These theories also suggest that religious symbols, narratives and practices will be interpreted and internalised by the individual not only through the cognitive structures available to that individual, but also through the dynamics of their attachments, both present and past, to significant others. This is apparent where the girls feel a connection with their mothers through their relationship with God. Therefore they also highlight the strongly relational orientation of women's thinking and identity, which is likely to have a profound influence on women's appropriation of faith" (cf. Slee 2004:24).

In one group[6] meeting specific questions arose in the spiritual narratives of these and we had a controversial discussion concerning these questions. Some children wonder why God allows/causes Aids. [7]They also wanted to know "if Aids is a punishment from God?" (cf. Facing AIDS 2002:27) as Nomusa (17 years) also stated. One girl specifically asked: "Does God forgive people with Aids?" Therefore the influence of Christianity can be seen in the beliefs of some African Christians who believe that Aids is God's punishment for immorality and sins" (Van Dyk 2005:116).

As narrative therapists we are not interested in the answers of these questions, but in the meaning behind these questions. In these children's reasoning there exists a mystic relation between everything and everyone in the world, alive and dead. Everything is seen as part of each other, and as having an influence on one another (cf. Meiring 1996:3–4). This correlates with the African perception of illness and their need to know "Why?" or "Who?" (cf. Van Dyk 2005: 116).

During the conversations[8] with the co-researchers we frequently engaged in conversational questions with the aim to thicken their narratives. In the discussing of their feelings and struggles we aimed at *externalising* those factors which proved to be challenges. It soon became clear that the main struggle for

---

[6] Group meeting conducted in September, 2006, Heartbeat centre, Nelmapius.
[7] Due to the restrictions of this article no attempt will be made in answering these questions.
[8] Personal interviews conducted from June to September, 2006, Heartbeat centre, Nelmapius.

202 Julian C. Müller

these Aids orphans was the 'missing of their mothers' and doubt in knowing if they could deal with life alone.

Instead of naming the problem we collectively decided to exchange these stories of 'sadness' and 'loneliness' into narratives, which provided space for the idea that it "is okay to miss my mother". Therefore we discovered the *unique outcome*. We then thickened this unique outcome by means of deconstructive questioning. These positive memories were then used constructively to create material, which reminded them of their mothers. They collected material things of their mothers and they made notes of things their mothers said which they would like to remember. Thus by using *imagination* as a tool, we 'reconstructed' their mothers 'presence'.

We then thickened this alternative possibility by creating memory boxes which they could fill with all these concrete created memories of their mothers. The children decided that this could help them to always keep their mother's loving memories close. They decided that whenever they needed courage or words of inspiration, they would return to this 'box' to recreate proximity of their mothers. They also stated that they want to save the memory box in order to show it to their children in the future. This way they could show their mothers to their children, extending the memory of their mothers. In reflecting on this progress we returned to the co-researchers in asking how and if this memory box benefits their lives. They replied that they comforted and motivated in holding the memories of their mothers' nearby.

In explanation of why they found the idea of a memory box so appealing we can return the African idea of 'personal immortality through children': "After physical death, people continue to exist in the *Sasa* period as the 'living dead' for as long as they are personally remembered by name by relatives and the friends who knew them during their life and who have survived them" (Van Dyk 2005:121). This stresses the importance of discovering the grand narratives that underlie people's narratives, which directly also influence their language. It is imperative then to speak in the children's language to connect with what is most important to them.

7. Reflection on the process

In reflection of the process it is imperative that we should keep in mind that "For Practical Theology to reflect in a meaningful way on the experiences of the presence of God, it needs to be locally contextual, socially constructed, directed by tradition, exploring interdisciplinary meaning and it needs to point beyond the local" (Muller 2005:78). This is a circular process which continues until satisfactory interpretations have been made. This article has shown how interpretations are grounded in experience and how it may differ from one person to the other.

By placing this framework within the Cultural-Linguistic Model for Pastoral care, the dynamics of language, culture and subsequent interpretations become evident. Gerkin (1997:111) explains that this model's "structure emphasizes both the human penchant for structuring life according to stories, and the power of interpretation to shape life and express care". It facilitates an open dialogue between the Christian story and the particular life story of the Christian. "This is a dialogue that will include the sharing of feelings, stories of past experiences, mutual questioning and search for authentic connections between the two poles" (Gerkin 1997:112).

8. Conclusion

This article has showed how adolescents orphaned by Aids come to an interpretation of their situation by incorporating the situational and cultural cues in the environment in their story. It also showed how they experience the presence of God within their context and how this experience re-writes stories of hopelessness into stories of hope. Thus the tension between the story of their tradition, both African and Christian, and between their specific life situations is evident. The writing of alternative stories has equipped them efficiently to obtain a connection between the two poles, which need not be in opposition. Therefore the narratives amidst despair do not always need to be ones of hopelessness. It can be transformed into ones of hope and strength. The fact that these children have survived to tell their story is an amazing phenomenon in itself.

In reflection on how the churches can aid these children affected by HIV and Aids and their role in these orphans' lives, it can be recommended that the churches should increase their level of awareness about HIV and Aids and its impact on the lives of the children left behind. By assisting these children in finding a connection between the reality of their life stories and the message of God's story, the churches can fulfil their role as pastoral caregivers in helping them to create a future narrative of hope. If the churches can find a way to decrease the tension between the children's current story of despair and God's message of salvation more children will turn to their spirituality to guide them through life. This way God's story can become the lens through which every other experience in life is interpreted.

References

AIDS foundation South-Africa. 2005. Retrieved July 17, 2006 from http://www.aidsfoundationsouth AfricaHIV-AIDS in South Africa.htm.

204 Julian C. Müller

Aids in South Africa. MRC Technical Report. Pretoria: Medical Research Council.

Centre for the study of Aids. 2004. Basic Aids stats for South Africa. Retrieved 21 August, 2006 from http://www.csa.co.za.htm.

Erikson, M. 1998. *Postmodernizing the Faith: Evangelical responses to the challenge of postmodernism.* Grand Rapids, Michigan, USA: Baker Books.

Facing AIDS: The challenge, the churches' response 2002. Geneva: WCC Publications (a WCC study).

Kilbourn, P (ed) 1996. *Children in Crisis: A new Commitment.* California, USA, Monrovia: MARC.

Freedman, J & Combs, G 1996. *Narrative Therapy: The social construction of preferred realities.* New York: W.W. Norton & Company.

Freedman, J & Combs, G 2002. *Narrative Therapy with couples and a whole lot more: A collection of papers, essays and exercises.* Adelaide, South Australia: Dulwich Centre Publications.

Medical Research Council 2001. *The Impact of HIV and AIDS on Adult Mortality.*

Meiring, P (ed) 1996. *Suid-Afrika, land van baie godsienste.* Pretoria: Kagiso Uitgewers.

Müller, J.C 2005. *A Post-Foundationalist, HIV-Positive Practical Theology*: Practical Theology in South-Africa 20(2), 72–88.

Müller, J.C 1999. *Reis-geselskap.* Wellington, South-Africa: Lux Verbi. BM.

Slee, N 2004. *Women's Faith Development: Patterns & Process.* Hants, England: Ashgate Publishing.

Stainton Rogers, W. & Stainton Rogers, R 2000. *The psychology of gender and sexuality: an Introduction.* Buckingham, England: Open University Press.

The Sowetan, June 6, 2002.

United Nations Programme on HIV/Aids. 2000c, June. *Report on the global HIV/Aids epidemic.* Geneva: Joint United Nations Programme on HIV/Aids.

Van Dyk, A ³2005. *HIV/AIDS Care & Counseling.* Cape Town S.A: Pearsons Education.

Van Huysteen, W 2000. *Postfoundationalism and Interdisciplinary: A Response to Jerome Stone* : Zygon 35(2), 427–439.

The Author

Julian C. Müller is Professor for Practical Theology and head of the Department of Practical Theology at the Faculty of Theology/University of Pretoria (SA).

Research Group on Post-Traumatic Spirituality

Karlijn Demasure

Pastoral care and the meaning of touch in sexual abuse

1. Introduction

Although the element of power is of great importance with sexual abuse,[1] one can however notice a reduction of sexual abuse to the abuse of power in scientific literature. Over the past 15 years, the physical aspect is allotted a somewhat bigger place in psychological research, but this is often limited to the study of the relation of body and mind in the dissociation, one of the consequences of sexual abuse.

From the stories of victims, the crucial question to me is the following one: why do illicit touches exert a negative influence for a time so much longer than e.g. certain images or certain words? In what sense does the touch differ from other senses?

2. Methodological justification

I situate my contribution within the hermeneutical model based on P. Ricœur.

1. Hermeneutics have placed narrativity in a central position. It is from my experience with working with victims of child sexual abuse, from listening to their life stories that I am making this reflection.

2. My exposition is more specifically located in the second phase of the model of Ricœur, viz. the configuration. In this phase, we make an appeal to human sciences in order to achieve a 'thick description'. The sciences mainly used by practical theologians are psychology/psychiatry and sociology. My line of approach is deviant. Indeed, I want to investigate the philosophical domain. I am justifying this detour from the previously mentioned hermeneutics viz.

    *   Every detour constitutes the base of a corresponding 'disclosure' leading to a new perspective on reality and on a different manner of acting in the world. The more detours, the more explanations, the more

---

[1] We define child sex abuse as sexual violence in a relation of dependence. The adult uses the predominance he or she possesses in order to persuade the child to perform or endure sexual activities in words, gestures or acts. The threat to pass to sexual activities also qualifies as abuse. It becomes clear from the definition that sexual abuse is not limited to penetration but that every touch with sexual connotation is also abuse.

206 Karlijn Demasure

erudite and richer the comprehension. Searching for the meaning of the touch on a philosophical level leads to a better understanding of the victim's perception, and by consequence to a better pastoral care.

- Hermeneutics have focused on meaning. Next to theology, the science that works most on the giving of meaning is philosophy.

3. Philosophical reflection

3.1 The hierarchy of the senses

The philosophical reflection on touch has to be placed in the larger framework of the discussion on the hierarchy of the senses. In the largest part of our Western philosophy it is assumed that there are five senses: sight, touch, hearing, smell and taste[2]. Smell and taste end up on the fourth and fifth place. Hearing was attributed the third place. Usually sight was given the most important position in Western thinking, followed by touch.

There is little discussion about the fact that the Western culture considered sight as the main and most noble sense. It almost goes without saying that the Greek culture was visually oriented[3]. The gods were visible to man; the terms theory and theatre are related to each other; there is an idealisation of the naked body and one has the Greek philosophy postulating that knowledge (*eidenai*)is the state of having seen and *'nous'* is the mind in its capacity as an absorber of images. Truth is an idea (*Eidos*) considered to be a visual form blanched of its colour. Although the intellect does not immediately refer to the sensory perception of seeing, but to seeing with the eye of the mind, it is nevertheless a specific form of 'seeing' and not of feeling or touching. In Timaeus, Plato made a distinction between sight and the other senses. The creation of sight, of human intelligence and of the soul was placed against the other senses representing the material being.

Sight is the sense that at one moment allows to simultaneously perceiving things. Watching allows the observation of a wide visual field. In this sense, sight is considered to be less temporal than hearing or touching or feeling. Sight is the apprehension of great distances. Therefore in opposition to touch, it allows (wo)man not to have to engage him/herself immediately towards the object that

---

[2] See e.g. Kant, I. KANT, *Anthropologie in pragmatischer Hinsicht,* (hg. v. R. Brandt) (Philosophische Bibliothek 490), Hamburg, 2000, p. 42–47, §15–§20. Sometimes it is claimed that the feeling for balance, the locomotive sense also is a sense.

[3] M. JAY, *Downcast Eyes, The Denigration of Vision,* p. 28. "And yet, having thus demonstrated that the Greek celebration of sight was more equivocal than is sometimes claimed, it must still be acknowledged that Hellenic thought did on the whole privilege the visual over any other sense."

he or she is looking at. The fact that one can observe such a wide field, also allows to anticipate things[4].

The dominance of sight does however not imply a total cultural homogeneity. In history different streams and movements acting against this dominance can be indicated. The most frontal attack in philosophy on this hegemony can be situated in the French philosophy during the 20th century. The anti-ocular-centrical discourse started with a critic of Bergson on Zeno, but the protagonists of the resistance are J.-L. Nancy and J. Derrida. In their vision, touch has to be considered as the most important sense.

3.2 Touch as condition for existence

The vision of Aristotle has influenced all thinkers on touch in the western society; therefore let's have a look at his ideas. To Aristotle every sense has to fulfil three conditions: it has to have a sense organ, a medium and an object. To Aristotle, the sense of touch is the most difficult to describe. Even though he tries to elaborate as much as possible an analogy between the different senses, the difference between the sense of touch and the other senses remains to him.

A first difference is that the sense of touch perceives several characteristics, viz. hard and soft, wet and dry etc.[5] Whereas sight is aimed at seeing and ears at hearing, such a simple characteristic cannot be attributed to the sense of touch. What can be felt are the distinguished characteristics of the body such as hot and cold, wet or dry, heavy and light, hard and soft, thick and thin etc.[6] If an object takes a position that does not differ from the body viz. not colder, nor warmer, not dryer nor more wet, then the sense of touch will not register anything. In fact the sense is the neutral point between two opposites. Only when the neutral point is transgressed in any of both directions it becomes a perceivable characteristic.

Another difference is situated around the question of mediation. Sound and sight reach us from a distance and are therefore mediated. Aristotle assumes that the sense of touch is mediated in an analogue manner[7], but still he is deter-

---

[4] H. JONAS, *The Nobility of Sight: A Study in the Phenomenology of the Senses,* in The Phenomenon of Life: *Towards a Philosophical Biology,* Chicago, 1982.
[5] ARISTOTELES, *Peri Psykhès, De anima, De l'âme,* (II,11,424a).
[6] ARISTOTELES, *De generatione et corruptione* II 2, 329B, ed. trad. Mugler, Paris, 1966, p. 47–48.
[7] ARISTOTELES, *Peri Psykhès, De anima, De l'âme* (II,11,423b); Aristotle finds that fish touching each other do not realise that there actually is a substance, viz. water, separating them from one another. The same can be said for the air. Thus according to Aristotle man has the wrong impression that there is no intermediary environment when he or she is touching something. To Aristotle flesh is like the envelope of air around the body.

208 Karlijn Demasure

mining a difference between both. With sound or with something we see, we experience something because the medium produces a certain effect on us. With touch, we are not touched by but through or via the medium, just like a fighting man does not only feel the blow on his shield but simultaneously also feels the blow himself. If one places an object on an eye – the organ responsible for sight – the object is not seen, but conversely, if one places something on the flesh, it is felt. According to Aristotle, the flesh cannot be the organ of touch, but the medium. The question then is where this organ is located. According to Aristotle, this organ can be found inside (wo)man[8]. It however remains unclear with him what exactly the organ corresponding to the sense of touch is? Aristotle suggests a sense in the body, close to the heart. If Plato speaks about hot and cold or hard and soft, he does not name touch, feeling or sense, but he speaks of common aspects of the entire body[9]. Also now philosophers like Nancy will state that the sense of touch is "le sens du corps tout entier"[10].

Although the experience of touching is the contact when the body touches the surface of things, Aristotle seems to indicate that this experience does not imply the nullification of the distance or interval. According to J.-L. Chrétien, Aristotle states that the interval is never deleted but only forgotten[11]. According to Aristotle there is always a body between the one who touches and the thing or person touched. Therefore something untouchable will always remain in contact, even though the experience indicates that this is not the case. In this case, we speak of a phenomenological occultation. Whereas many philosophi-cal reflections stress the proximity of the perception through the sense of touch, contemporary reflections on touch such as Nancy and Derrida – in imitation of Aristotle – stress the persisting distance and the interval. To them, there will al-ways be a distance, how minimal it may be. The untouchable is that what only possesses small tangibility. Besides, it refers to the notion of the limit. We can only touch borders; what is being touched is always the limit, the heart always escapes[12].

According to E. Wyschogrod the efforts that Aristotle has to make in order to place the sense of touch in the enumeration of senses, proves that the sense of touch actually is not a sense[13]. According to her, touch is a metaphor indicating that the world is acting on the subject. To E. Wyschogrod it appears that

---

[8] ARISTOTELES, *Peri Psykhès, De anima, De l'âme* (II,11,423b).
[9] L. CHRETIEN, *L'appel et la réponse,* p. 111. Plato is quoted there, Timée 65B, 4–5 (*koina tou somatos panthos pathèmata.*)
[10] J.-L. NANCY, *Les Muses,* Paris, Galilée, 1994, p. 34.
[11] J.-L. CHRETIEN, *L'appel et la réponse,* p. 106.
[12] J. DERRIDA, *Le toucher, Touch/to touch him,* p. 143, *"To touch is to touch a border, however deeply one may penetrate, [...] and it is thus to touch by approaching indefinitely the inaccessible of whatever remains beyond the border, on the other side."*
[13] J. DERRIDA, *Le toucher,* p. 67. Derrida also is of the opinion that the touch is not a sense, at least, not in the strict meaning of the word. The same goes for J.-L. CHRETIEN, *L'appel et la réponse,* p. 104.

Pastoral care and the meaning of touch in sexual abuse

the sense of touch is the most trustworthy sense. For this, she is basing herself on Berkeley, who states that touching requires no intermediary and so really has access to the other in an immediate way. His discourse states clearly *"[...] that touch provides the warranty for veracity since tactile apprehension re-quires no intermediary; that we aspire to touch because we aspire to a truth that cannot be vouchsafed through representation [...] and thus retains its alterity."*[14]

In the interpretation of Derrida, the sense of touch is the most important to Aristotle[15]. The other senses are aimed at the well-being but constitute no condition for existence as such. Nobody can live without the sense of touch. This goes for animals as for (wo)man. An animal does not die when it has no hearing or sight. It will however die when the sense of touch is missing, when it is unable to feel[16]. Hence, the sense of touch is not present in order to promote the human well-being, but just as the condition for existence. This does not mean that one cannot speak of pleasure and therefore well-being through touch, but it rather has to be considered as a surplus vis-à-vis the condition for life itself. However, the perception of pleasure and its opposite pain cannot be neglected[17]. The body detects those elements that are harmful or beneficial to (wo)man's well-being. What is unpleasant, is very often also harmful and carries the risk of destroying (wo)man. With the sense of touch, the notion of vulnerability also becomes part of the discourse.

An animal does not only die because of the lack of the sense of touch, it will also die when touch is of such an extensive intensity that it destroys the organ of touch[18]. Hence, Derrida's statement that a certain tact, a certain measure is necessary: *"'tu ne toucheras pas trop', 'tu ne te laisseras pas trop toucher' voire 'tu ne te toucheras pas trop'"*.[19] The quoted laws are considered by him to be the primary laws of feeling. Touching has to do with life and death and this in both ways: without touching, (wo)man dies; a violent touch has the same result.

---

[14] E. WYSCHOGROD, *Doing before Hearing, on the Primacy of Touch,* in . F. LA-RUELLE, *Textes pour Emmanuel Levinas,* Paris, Place, 1980, pp. 179–203.

[15] ARISTOTLE, *Per Psykhès, De anima, De l'âme* (II,11,422b–424a) ed. Budé, 1966.

[16] ARISTOTLE, *Per Psykhès, De anima, De l'âme* (II, 435b 4–7) and J. DERRIDA, *Le toucher,* p. 61, 161.

[17] J. DERRIDA, *Le toucher, Touch/to touch him,* p. 127. Aristotle uses the word *aphe* *"which also means tact, grasp, but as well the place of contact, line of joining, blow or wound."*

[18] ARISTOTLE, *Per Psykhès, De anima, De l'âme* (II,11,424a) (II, 435b 10–16).

[19] J. DERRIDA , *Le toucher, Jean-Luc Nancy,* Paris, 2000, pp. 61–62.

3.2 The same and the other

The Greek word *theoria* was translated into Latin by *speculatio*[20]. This word consists of the same stem as *speculum* and *specular,* which means "to mirror". Mirroring refers to the 'sameness', that what is not the difference. It is precisely against this line in history that the French philosophy is resisting by explicitly stressing alterity. Not only are they resisting against the fact that truth is seen as the reflection of reality, they also point out that since seeing happens from a distance, the distinction of the difference gets lost. In addition to that, a person is always looking from a certain perspective, from a certain interpretation repertoire from which some things are lit up and other stay in the dark without being seen.

In the reflection on the same and the difference, the concept of 'se toucher' is essential. This concept is based on the philosophy of Husserl. To Husserl the sense of touch stands for a being in the world and for the completeness of the experience of a presence in the present. Touching is the experience of the prescence in a full, direct, intuitive and immediate manner[21]. His most important example is not the hand as a whole as for many writers. It particularly are the fingers who get to play an important role with him. When touching an object, one experiences two different things, viz. an object located outside oneself and the own body. When fingers touch each other, one notices that the own body can be the object. Thus one only speaks of an own body thanks to the experience of touch. This reciprocity exclusively belongs to touch and not to the other senses. Whereas the person touching someone, is feeling at the same time him or herself, the person seeing or hearing is not necessarily seen or heard by another. Reciprocity is the privilege of touch.

The double given of touching and being touched does not necessarily mean that there is a symmetric relation. Things do not touch a person in the same way that he or she actively touches those things. The same goes for human beings. This is often translated into a male and female polarity as it can be observed with Levinas and Merleau-Ponty. With such an interpretation, the reciprocity of the touch is liable to be pushed aside as the one expressed but the touching of two palms of the hand, symbol for a perfect reciprocity where different dichotomies are neutralised.

Nancy uses the expression "se toucher toi (et non 'soi')", "to self-touch you, and not oneself"[22], or identical "to self touch skin"[23].Through the grammatical intervention Nancy wants simultaneously indicate the reflexivity of the touch as well as the presence of the other. In the heart of the experience of the self,

---

[20] M. JAY, *Downcast Eyes, The Denigration of Vision,* p. 31.

[21] J. DERRIDA, *Le toucher,* p. 186.

[22] J. DERRIDA, *Le toucher, Touch/to touch him,* p. 137.

[23] J.-L. NANCY, *Corpus,* (Suites Sciences Humaines) Paris, Ed. Métailié, 2000, p. 36.

Pastoral care and the meaning of touch in sexual abuse 211

the other intervenes. This other is not introduced in the third but the second person. Not as a mirror of the self, not in the reflexivity of the self but as a vocative, as the unattainable transcendence. In a tactful touch the other makes an appeal to me[24].

L. Irigaray also states that touching allows recognising alterity, to meet the other. It has the potency of recognising the difference without appropriating it. *"It is a gesture which emphasises a passage between, [...] Indeed, it is a form of connection rather than isolation"*[25]. Next to that one can speak of a second passage, viz. from the inside to the outside. *"A phenomenology of the passage between interior and exterior"*[26]. What happens inside man only speaks through gestures, and through these gestures the boundaries are recognised, but nevertheless access is granted to the deepest parts of (wo)man.

Types of touches must also be recognised where the other is objectified and appropriated as an object. It is a type of touching when the other is not recognised as such, the difference is nullified and when he or she is included in *the same*[27].

4. Some starting points for pastoral care

What does this philosophical detour teach us about pastoral care of victims of sexual abuse? We would like to draw three conclusions. First we will see how the condition for the possibility of spirituality is liable to be pushed aside after sexual abuse. Next to that we point out that the sense of guilt is inevitable with sexual abuse, and finally we plead for the elaboration of care on a physical level.

We saw that Aristotle made attempts to indicate that the touch is a sense like all others. But it is rather the condition for existence of (wo)man. (Wo)Man has no chance for survival if he or she is not touched, but (wo)man also dies in case of a violent touch. A 'good' touch would then create the possibility for life or be life-promoting, the 'bad' touch would then be lethal, or diminish the life force. With victims of sexual abuse, we speak of a violent touch. Derrida already

---

[24] J. DERRIDA, *Le toucher, Touch/to touch him,* p. 141. To touch as tact is, thanks to you, because of you, to break with immediacy.
[25] L. IRIGARAY, *An Ethics of Sexual Difference,* p. 61. (134–135, 142*)* The image which Irigaray uses as a symbol for this, is that of two palms of hands touching each other. With such a touch, the dichotomy between active and passive, between subject and object, disappears. A gesture she considers to be more intimate than taking by the hand or walking hand in hand. "The joined hands, not those that take hold one of the other, grasp each other, but the hands that touch without taking hold-like the lips."
[26] L. IRIGARAY, *An Ethics of Sexual Difference,* p. 61, (135).
[27] L. IRIGARAY, *An Ethics of Sexual Difference,* p. 204, (71–80). She refers to male sexuality where women are only considered as an envelope for men.

212 Karlijn Demasure

stressed the fact that there is a law of tact, which is at the basis of all other laws[28]. If the law of touch is not respected, the life-force is brought in danger.

Life force and spirituality have to do with each other. Etymologically the word spirituality is tributary to the Greek *pneuma*, and signifies vital force of life or vitality of the spirit. It is precisely this force of life that is brought in danger by the violent touch in sexual abuse.

Steggink and Waaijman clearly indicate two poles in their definition of spirituality[29]: (wo)man and the transcendent dimension: the other. Our reflection has made clear that touch is precisely that sense that of all senses is allowing to make the distinction between the self and the other, at least when speaking of a 'good' touch. The distinction between both poles is pressurised in the case of sexual abuse. With a 'bad' touch the difference is erased and the other is treated as the same, an object. The negation of the difference, of the acceptance of an alterity places a great strain on the creation of a spirituality where the transcendent dimension is focussed upon.

Next to that the sense of touch is the only sense that supposes reciprocity. Even when they did neither initiate nor want it, they cannot escape feeling. This leads victims to the conviction of being involved in the sexual act and by consequence being responsible for it. That is why they feel guilty and why it is so difficult to convince them that they are innocent: the experience of participation is situated on the existential level.

This leads me to the conclusion that next to a narrative reconstruction a recovery on the physical level is imposing itself. With diverse forms of touching, e.g. in sports, one experiences that the touch can also be beneficent and does not necessarily destroy life, but the opposite: stimulating life. As long as victims have not experienced that the touch cannot only be lethal but also lifegiving, it will remain very difficult to come to a recovery on the spiritual level. Besides they can learn the difference between active and passive feeling and the difference in responsibility and guilt this brings along. Pastoral care should take those givens into account.

The Author

Karlijn Demasure, born 1955, holds the Sisters of Our Lady of the Cross Chair in Christian Family Studies at the Saint Paul University, Ottawa, Canada. Research interests: family studies, epistemology, Paul Ricoeur, narrativity, sexual abuse and trauma, gender topics. Recent publications: Troost het kind in mij. Over incest en

---

[28] J. DERRIDA, *Le toucher,* p. 81–83.

[29] O. STEGGINCK en K. WAAIJMAN, *Spiritualiteit en mystiek*, 1985, 79–108. K. WAAIJMAN, *Spiritualiteit. Vormen, grondslagen, methoden*, Gent, Kampen, 2000, 1–8.

geweld 2007); Baert, B., Bieringer, R., Demasure, K., Van Den Eynde, S., Noli me tangere. Mary Magdalene: One Person, Many Images (2006); Burggraeve, R., Demasure, K., Lagae, E. (ed.), Behoed de geliefden (2006); Familles recomposées. Une perspective de théologie pratique, in Intams (2007) 13, 203–221; Pastoral Care in Marriage and Divorce in Burggraeve, R., Demasure, K., Foket, M., Weber, Ph., Marriage-Divorce-Remarriage. Mariage-divorce-remariage (2007) 191–205.

Brigitte Fuchs

Trend Research – a Tool for Pastoral Planning

The transformation of religious culture is part of an overall process of transformation in societies. To understand the phenomena of religious change, we have to put them into the greater context of long-term global economic, social and cultural change. We must ask how people react to these changes; how does this reaction influence their religious sensibility and their religious search.

The Problem of Relevance

Individuals don't find themes and content important because religious authorities, preachers, or teachers tell them they are. The relevance of Christian beliefs will only be felt when the beliefs demonstrate their importance to real-life concerns.

A 1999 study of religion in Switzerland concluded that for 85% of the Swiss, religion had played an important, if not decisive, role in their lives. However, except for the 12% of respondents which the study qualifies as "exclusive Christians," the Christian offering does not fully answer the needs of what people feel to be relevant to their lives.[1]

The relevance of Christian belief will only be felt if it demonstrates its importance in the life-world. Therefore it is necessary to perceive in which way global change has affected the sensibility, feelings and longings of people in everyday life.

Reactions to developments already accomplished often come too late, disappointed expectations are difficult to correct. It is therefore of great importance not only to state and to analyse the *status quo*, but to find out the directions of developments as early as possible and proceed accordingly.

The Pastoral-Sociological Institute in Switzerland carried out two major empirical studies on the progression of religious attitudes, the first in 1989 and the second in 1999 (cited above), the so-called "Sonderfallstudien."[2] Based on the results of trend research, I interpreted the data of the aforementioned studies and developed suggestions for future pastoral care.

Firstly, let us consider the context of long-term global, economic, social and cultural change (Megatrends).

---

[1] Dubach, A.; Fuchs, B.: Ein neues Modell von Religion. Zweite Schweizer Sonderfallstudie – Herausforderung für die Kirchen, Zürich 2005.

[2] The analysis of the two studies by Dubach, A, in: Dubach, A.; Fuchs, B. 2005.

Megatrends

The term "Megatrends" was developed by John Naisbitt.[3] Megatrends are long-term movements of change:

- They form a change that persists at least half a century.

- Megatrends are global in principle.

- Megatrends concern all parts of human life: technology, culture, human relationships, work environment, consumption.

Of the five megatrends – individualization, globalization, aging, education, and women – I have selected aging, education, and women to show the way they influence religion and religious attitudes and how this change challenges pastoral care.

Aging

The elderly are the most steadfast members of the churches. As the elderly are considered a given, they get little attention in the pastoral care literature dealing with future planning. However, the relative proportion of the elderly to the young is shifting dramatically. The OECD predicts that in 2020, in developed countries, at least a third of the population will be over 60.

This development is generally considered a demographic catastrophe, as it is regarded first and foremost as an economic burden: "Greying means paying" (P. Petersen).[4]

Slowly, aging is being rehabilitated. There are numerous indicators of a change in attitude towards old age. Contrary to the idealization of youth, old age is more and more connected to maturity and spiritual growth. "An older society is a society with changed values. In it, maturity, personal growth and serenity get a different meaning."[5]

This development will have a strong influence on religion and its institutions. The growing presence of the elderly in societies that have viewed aging as negative puts new emphasis on questions concerning the meaning of life. The

---

[3] Naisbitt, John: Megatrends – 10 Perspektiven, die unser Leben verändern, Bayreuth 1984.

[4] Horx, Matthias: Die acht Sphären der Zukunft: Ein Wegweiser in die Kultur des 21. Jahrhunderts, Wien/Hamburg ³2000, 99.

[5] Ders.: Future Fitness. Wie Sie Ihre Zukunftskompetenz erhöhen. Ein Handbuch für Entscheider, Frankfurt a.M. 2003, 83.

216 Brigitte Fuchs

meaning of life has ceased to be a private affair. It has become a topic of public interest.

Horx states, "In a society whose majority is over 50, for many, life is deeply affected by primal human fears and experiences like pain, illness, loneliness, infirmity, dementia and death."[6]

These experiences already influence the younger generation. With regard to longevity, young people now want to age in good health. Today "Health" is a "megatopic" not only with the elderly. The religious dimension of health plays an important role. The booming sector of "wellness" presents itself as part of New Age or esoteric religion.

The elderly form the majority of church-goers. The majority of persons whose central point of orientation is the Christian religion are over 56. Churches and parishes have to reflect their own notion of the elderly. How much of the economically defined discrimination of old age finds its way into language and pastoral offerings for the elderly?

A qualitative survey of people aged between 55 and 88 concerning the development of religious belief concluded that the search for strategies to cope with changes in life prevails over wishes for continuity and stability.[7] Support for a culture of aging cannot begin in old age. As shown above, the evolution towards an aging society already influences the young in their desire for holistic personal growth and their search for meaning.

To solely focus pastoral care on target groups such as the elderly and young people is to lose track of social reality. Cross-generational consideration of the topics of health and meaning, as well as counselling and support in the process of changes in life situations, emerge as important assignments in pastoral care.

Education/Women

The average level of education is rising. The trend towards higher education concerns primarily the rising educational level of women. Persons of a higher educational level turn away from church more consistently than people of a lower educational level.[8] In comparing data from 1989 with data from 1999, the drop-out tendency increased more with groups with higher education.

---

[6] Schirrmacher, Frank: "Das Methusalem-Komplott", München 2004, 132f.
[7] Fürst, Walter; Severin, Burkard; Wittrahm, Andreas: Kooperationsprojekt: Glaubensentwicklung in der zweiten Lebenshälfte und die pastoralen Konsequenzen – eine qualitative Pilotstudie, Abschlußbericht, Bonn/Aachen 1997, 51.
[8] Dubach, Alfred.:Konfessionslose in der Schweiz: Entwicklung von 1960–1990, in: Schweizerisches Pastoralsoziologisches Institut 1998, 11–70, 44.

Amongst women, the self-employed and those in positions of leadership leave church noticeably more frequently than their male counterparts.[9] Women play the decisive role in the religious upbringing of their children. A series of empirical surveys proves that mothers are the most important persons for building a lasting attachment to religion and church.

Churches and theology must address the Megatrend "education," especially in regard to women, to reduce the number of members who leave the church. Persons engaged in pastoral care must receive a well-grounded education and advanced training. They should be prepared to "account for our hope" in postmodern times. Albrecht Grözinger compares the change in local ministries to changes in the general working environment. "The study has turned into the office," and, he adds, "this development has to be reversed. The ministry is a distinguished intellectual institution."[10]

The promotion of self-assured, educated women into leading church positions is crucial to convince middle and higher educated women to remain in or return to the churches.

Summary

The study of Megatrends indicates that developments in religion and the churches are directly affected by radical and long-term developments in societies. The evolution within churches and religion is directly linked to developments in technology, economy, culture, population, social structures and structures of consciousness. The described developments show productive tendencies in regard to religiousness. The sensitivity for religious topics is rising. Religious developments present themselves less as a scenario of downfall than a reflection of temporal disparities between church, social and personal topics.

Socio-cultural trends

Megatrends, as overall and long-term movements, produce counter movements (socio-cultural trends). The significance of certain values increases with their vulnerability. Counter movements emerge at the real-life, socio-cultural level. They are affected by the feelings of people. They are about sentiments and longings, about deficiency-syndromes and unresolved issues of cultural history. They deal with shortcomings of social developments.[11]

---

[9] Ibid., 38.

[10] Grözinger, Albrecht: Die Kirche – ist sie noch zu retten? Anstiftungen für das Christentum in postmoderner Gesellschaft, Gütersloh 1998, 139.

[11] Website Zukunftsinstitut, Hamburg.

Socio-cultural trends include:

- Anchoring,
- Localization,
- Religious anchoring,
- Cocooning,
- Clanning,
- Design,
- Health,
- Downshifting,
- High-Touch,
- Counselling,
- Experience orientation,

I will highlight a few of these.

Anchoring

Localization

Complementary to the megatrend "globalization," the trend "localization" takes place. The more society is globalized by economic conditions and constraints, the more people cling to local traditions.

Local shooting-clubs, music societies, clubs for the preservation of traditional costumes and folklore societies cultivate and revive local customs with new emphasis. More and more town or neighbourhood festivals are organized and become very popular. The trend towards local traditions appears as well in the religious sector. Processions through fields and farmland, praying for favourable weather and rich harvests are "in" again.

In Switzerland and Germany rogation processions are enjoying a renaissance. New local religious traditions arise and meet with enthusiastic response.

The socio-cultural trend of "localization," especially in rural areas, runs contrary to the restructuring of pastoral care into larger parish units to cope with the lack of priests.

Localization as it is described here does not mean going back to the structures of the good old times for the elderly and people with low educational levels. Today, it is mostly the young and middle-aged with medium or higher educational levels who are engaged in localization. It deals with the search for roots and identity (regional and religious) in times of globalization.

Religious anchoring

"The core of the matter is a search for values of the past which endure until today and enable us to confront the uncertainties of the future."[12] Newly reli-

---

[12] Popcorn, Faith; Lys, Marigold: Clicking. Der neue Popcorn Report. Trends für unsere Zukunft, München 1996, 109.

gious and syncretic Christians resort to religious traditions of a multitude of religions and cultures: Germanic, Hindu, Indian and Shamanic rituals and concepts of wisdom are studied and practised. In 1989, 39% of the Swiss population agreed with the proposition: "The future of peoples lies in the natural knowledge of ancient peoples." In 1999 the percentage had grown to 52%.[13]

Even Christian traditions are newly-discovered and revived. Gregorian Chants reach the top of the music charts; angels as helpful spirits are more popular in the New Religion than they are in church. Hildegard of Bingen is revered as a representative of holism; her herbal remedies and healing methods are very popular. The discovery and revival of old Christian and early church traditions mostly takes place outside the churches. We must view the vitality and immediacy of our own religious and churchly traditions through the eyes and needs of people living today.

High-Touch

High-Touch is the reaction to a development that has lost sight of humanity. In the age of High-Tech everything was geared to rationalization and improvement in respect of economics and function. Whether in service, trade, medicine or pastoral care, modern technologies were employed to cut costs and to replace human input by high-tech machines. Face-to-face contact was, wherever possible, replaced by automatons, computers, answering machines, or other impersonal means. Human contact was organized to meet the criteria of efficiency and rationality.

However, human services are not easily replaced or reduced by machines; they always represent elements for which no rationalization or mechanization can substitute: physical presence, closeness, touch, care.

High-Touch constitutes a relativization of economic values. Emotional competence becomes more important in all realms of human contact. High-Touch in pastoral care and deacon services means availability (not of an answering machine), accessibility and personal care.

Developments in many parishes are in opposition to this trend. Many "communities of parishes" can be compared to medium-sized companies with a well organized office and a good management."[14] Face-to-face encounter and personal counselling have become marginalized. The decrease of financial resources brought about a more intense economic orientation.

---

[13] Dubach, in: Dubach, A.; Fuchs, B. 2005.

[14] Kellner, Gerhard: Mein Seelsorgekonzept, in: Seelsorge der Zukunft, PThI 23/2003-1, 59–61, 61.

One of the central findings of the 1989 Sonderfallstudie was affirmed by the 1999 Sonderfallstudie. The communication of religious orientation turns out to be most efficient wherever the churches happen to generate an emotional attachment. The stronger the emotional attachment, the higher the efficiency of preaching. Emotional attachment develops only through personal attachment to an individual pastoral attachment figure. Consequently it requires high-touch in pastoral care.

Summary: Socio-cultural Trends as Counter-Movements and Complements of the Megatrends

Opening the horizon beyond the explicit religious and church debate into areas of life where belief has to prove its life-relevance shows that there is a requirement, grounded in openness, not merely for new, but also for traditional religiousness and spirituality as seen through a new perspective.

Re-Spiritualization

Religion and spirituality is everywhere today. Religion has lost its traditional distinct boundaries. Transcendence is felt in everything. Spirituality in this regard appears as a high sensitivity to transcendent reality and openness in experiencing transcendence. It manifests itself as a preoccupation with the meaning of life in the face of suffering, illness, old age and death. Religion and spirituality manifest themselves in the struggle in the face of maintaining humanity against mechanization and economization. Spirituality appears as well in perceiving human beings as holistic with their physical, intellectual and spiritual dimension. It appears in a new tendency to appreciate wisdom, spiritual growth and maturity. It appears in new forms of asceticism. It appears in the retrieval of the dimension of true and good in aesthetics. Re-spiritualization means a search for meaning, for inwardness, for transcendence, for lasting genuine truth. This new spirituality is not detached from the world; it looks for transcendence here and now. Thus, every aspect of life is a possible locus of spiritual experience, a spa, as well as a pilgrim's journey, a clinic as well as a manager's office, a church as well as a gym. This new way of spirituality is to be understood primarily as an endeavour to live one's life with all its potentialities, as a search for life to the fullest. This search requires counselling and support.

Christianity also strives for life to the full (John 10,10). For many people this life to the full, vigorous life, is no longer or not adequately perceivable in church services, sermons, lectures or activities for seniors. "I only know that life like that is not enough, that I would like to experience more on a metaphysical level," so stated an art historian in the empirical survey of the

EKD 2002.[15] This woman is searching; she feels a "growing need for ritual and meditation."[16] She asks around and hears many suggestions of where to turn. Church is not among them. Though educated in a Christian household and brought up as a church-goer, she herself turned to Buddhism, to Yoga, to Tai-Chi but not to the church.

According to an ecumenical survey of the churches of Basel (Switzerland), what people expect least of churches is religious counselling. In evaluations this service gets the lowest marks.[17] Churches have lost their reputation as competent counsellors regarding the spiritual way of life. In the debate regarding religious meanings the argument of authority or tradition is no longer enough to convince. The search goes on for genuine life and experience. "It is the element of one's own intensely felt inner experience that today is often missed in church."[18]

Re-spiritualization of the culture appears as a search for meaning, for inwardness, for life to the full. That a growing number of people do not find this anymore inside the churches touches the central core of the church.

Concluding remarks

Research into megatrends as well as socio-cultural trends leads to more than an analysis of the religious market. If one perceives the problems, needs and longings of today's men and women as more than indicators of a superficial optimizing of their market-orientation, the results of trend research lead to question life in the churches themselves. It shows that the crisis of western churches is not only a crisis of marketing Christian contents but a problem of the churches' identity, their ability to communicate, their spirituality and their spiritedness. Structural and economic reforms are necessary but they only make sense in a Christian way if they meet people's needs for orientation and religious meaning in their changed everyday world and their search for "life to the full" (John 10:10). Wherever spiritedness and relevance to every-day life is perceptible, whether in celebratory services, in pastoral counselling, in rituals and group experiences, churches are still attractive. Wherever the longing for inwardness and holism, for a spiritual life, is not satisfied, all organizational endeavours will be in vain.

---

[15] Schloz, Rüdiger: Suche nach Lebensgewissheit. Amelies Religion und was Kirche und Theologie damit zu tun haben, in: Pastoraltheologie 93 (2004), 82–98, 92.

[16] Ibid., 88.

[17] Bruhn, Manfred; Lischka, Andreas: Qualitätswahrnehmung und Zufriedenheit der Bevölkerung mit den Kirchen, in: Bruhn, Manfred; Grözinger, Albrecht (Hg.): Kirche und Marktorientierung. Impulse aus der Ökumenischen Basler Kirchenstudie (Praktische Theologie im Dialog, Bd. 20), Freiburg/Schweiz 2000, 43–68, 48f.

[18] de Jong: Glaube, Hoffnung, Heilung, in: Psychologie Heute, 3/2005, 21–25, 25.

According to Hassidic tradition, Rabbi Yitzchak Meir taught:

> 'If somebody becomes a leader, everything has to be there, a school, a room and tables and chairs, and one becomes a caretaker, and one will become a servant and so on. And then comes the evil adversary and tears out the innermost point, everything else stays as before, and the wheel continues to turn, only the innermost point is missing.' The rabbi raised his voice: 'But God may help us: we must not let it happen!'[19]

The Author

Brigitte Fuchs, Dr. theol. habil., born 1958, private lecturer of practical theology at the Faculty of Theology at the University of Würzburg. Research interests: interreligious understanding, religion and health, meditation and health, sociocultural implications of religion. Recent publications: (mit Dubach, A) Ein neues Modell von Religion, Zürich 2005; (mit Kobler, N.) (Hg.):Hilft der Glaube? Heilung auf dem Schnittpunkt zwischen Theologie und Medizin, Münster-Hamburg-London 2002; Eigener Glaube – Fremder Glaube, Münster-Hamburg-London 2001.

---

[19] Buber, Martin: Die Erzählungen der Chassidim, Zürich 1949, 830.

Bonnie Miller-McLemore

Redefining Children's Spirituality[1]

In the last few decades, people have become increasingly invested in children's spirituality. In particular, the emergence of developmental theory led Christian educators to tailor teaching to young children's needs. In other circles, re-surging interest in monastic disciplines and their generalization to everyday life led to new curricula for children and youth experimenting with practices such as centering prayer or *lectio divina*. Yet in the midst of these developments standard assumptions about the nature of spirituality, developed with adults as the standard and model, often go unquestioned.

Do common understandings of spirituality in Christian history and contemporary psychology truncate children's experience and knowledge and, if so, how might fresh perspectives be more inclusive? Closer investigation reveals that Western Christianity has framed spirituality in two general ways – one around *space* and the other around *time* – that have left little *place* for children. Children *de facto* create problems for conventional models of spirituality and faith development. For those who seek the divine in solitude and silence or in organized worship, children – their noise, demands, and distractions – are a major impediment. Children also baffle those who define mature faith around the acquisition of adult reason or knowledge. Where the early Christian tradition perpetuates a spatial dichotomy of inner over outer (mind over body, intellectual over material), developmental theory presumes a chronological divide between young and old (immature and mature, small and big). Models of spirituality shaped by these two views of quiet space and linear growth over time often exclude children and those who care for them.

Space and the Hierarchy of Inner over Outer

When people think of the spiritual life, they often picture silence and solitude. Thinking of children, by contrast, they imagine noise and complication. By and large, these portraits are accurate. The spiritual life requires a kind of extended concentration that children rarely demonstrate. In turn, caring for children is one of the most intrusive, disorienting occupations around. Can children and those who care for them pursue a spiritual life?

---

[1] This chapter is an abridged version of another chapter, "Children's Voices, Spirituality, and Mature Faith," which appears in *Children's Voices: Perspectives in Ethics, Theology, and Religious Education*, Annemie Dillen, ed. (Leuven: Peeters). It draws significantly on two previous publications, *Let the Children Come: Reimagining Childhood from a Christian Perspective* (San Francisco: Jossey-Bass, 2003) and *In the Midst of Chaos: Care of Children as Spiritual Practice* (San Francisco: Jossey-Bass, 2006).

The Western world has a long history of saying *no*. In the Greek context of early Christianity, marriage and children were thought of as a trap for the soul, which ancients understood as yearning for the unchanging immaterial world of beauty and truth. Early church theologians did not have a uniform outlook on families and procreation by any means. But they all agreed on one thing: family life is inferior to the celibate life of religious heroes and saints.

Spirituality as something that happens outside ordinary time and space, within formal religious institutions, or within the private confines of one's soul and mind still pervades Western society. This is true despite recent popular movements and publications affirming everyday spirituality and despite longer standing religious traditions, such as Ignatian and Benedictine spirituality, which have encouraged the integration of faith into daily life.[2] Typical guidance from priests and pastors often affirms the "received" view, as a story recounted by theologian Janet Martin Soskice reveals so well:

> When a young, exhausted Anglican mother found her devotional life in disarray after the birth of her child, Soskice reports, the mother received this advice from three priests: The first told her that if the baby woke at 6.00 A.M., she should rise at 5.00 A.M. for a quiet hour of prayer. The second asked if her husband could not arrange to come home early from work three times a week so that she could get to a Mass. This advice proved threatening to life and marriage. The third told her, "Relax and just look after your baby. The rest of the Church is praying for you."[3]

Children and parents are presumed to be "Christians on idle," taking some years off while others seek God on their behalf.

There is genuine truth about the danger of external attachments. But this spatial bias of inner over outer, which is woven through so much spiritual and psychological advice, also ends up demeaning the external, the bodily, the earthy, and the material and obscuring their actual connection to authentic spirituality. This

---

[2] For efforts in the Christian tradition to bridge contemplation and action, see Ignatius of Loyola, *The Spiritual Exercises of St. Ignatius*, trans. By Louis J. Puhl, S. J. (Chicago: Loyola University Press, 1951); Timothy Fry, ed., *The Rule of Saint Benedict in English* (Collegeville, Minnesota: Liturgical Press, 1982); Marilyn Schauble and Barbara Wojciak, eds., *A Reader's Version of the Rule of Saint Benedict in Inclusive Language* (Erie, PA: Benet Press, 1989); Delores R. Leckey, *The Ordinary Way: A Family Spirituality* (New York: Crossroad, 1982); Esther de Waal, *Seeking God: The Way of St. Benedict* (Collegeville, Minn.: Liturgical Press, 1984) and *Living with Contradiction: An Introduction to Benedictine Spirituality* (Harrisburg, Penn.: Morehouse, 1989); Joan Chittister, OSB, *Wisdom Distilled from the Daily: Living the Rule of St. Benedict Today* (San Francisco: Harper and Row, 1990).

[3] Janet Martine Soskice, "Love and Attention," in: *Philosophy, Religion and the Spiritual Life*, ed. Michael McGhee (Cambridge: Cambridge University Press, 1992), p. 62.

Redefining Children's Spirituality 225

bias against outward forms of spirituality marginalizes many Christians, especially children.

Time and the Hierarchy of Adult over Child

The social sciences have proven only partly helpful here. Even though theorists in psychology and education have made children's emotional and moral development a central subject matter, they reinforce a hierarchy of another sort. Developmental theory perpetuates another problem – a chronological divide between young and old. In some ways, stage theory is a re-instantiated version of the early Greek and Christian division between the unreasonable child and the rational adult.

For over two decades, Christian scholarship on children's faith has been captivated by categories of cognitive development, formulated by psychologist Jean Piaget, elaborated by moral philosopher Lawrence Kohlberg, and systematized by practical theologian James Fowler.[4] In the last quarter of the twentieth century, Fowler's *Stages of Faith* held sway in U.S. in particular.[5] Scholars in religion have voiced general concerns. But few connect criticism of stage theory with an inadequate understanding of children. Three assumptions, however, impede understanding of children.

Foremost, although Fowler makes general claims about children, his primary subject is not quite the child but the individuating adult who is looking back over life to judge where one stands and where one is going. He talks less in *Stages of Faith* about "being children today" or "raising children in faith" and more about "becoming adult," as his second book is titled.[6] Since many adults do not progress beyond the conventional faith of stage three, only the first two stages pertain distinctively to childhood and even these do not refer to children under four. Twenty-eight year old Mary is the capstone case of *Stages of Faith* and many more pages are devoted to her twenties than to her primary years. This subtle shift from childhood to adulthood results in part from the theory itself. It is hard to have a stage theory that does not overvalue the final frame.

---

[4] B. Inhelder and J. Piaget, *The Growth of Logical Thinking from Childhood to Adolescence* (New York: Basic Books, 1958); Lawrence Kohlberg, *The Psychology of Moral Development: The Nature and Validity of Moral Stages* (San Francisco: Harper & Row, 1984); and James W. Fowler, *Stages of Faith* (San Francisco: Harper & Row, 1981). Fowler's theory appears in a myriad of primary articles and secondary publications about faith stage theory.

[5] For more detailed exploration of this problem, see Bonnie J. Miller-McLemore, "Whither the Children? Childhood in Religious Education," *Journal of Religion* 86, no. 4 (October 2006): 635–657.

[6] James W. Fowler, *Becoming Adult, Becoming Christian* (San Francisco: Harper & Row, 1983).

226 Bonnie Miller-McLemore

Fowler's definition of faith as a "verb" or a way of making meaning "prior to our being religious or irreligious" further limits understanding of children.[7] Differentiation between the formal structures of faith (largely cognitive and universal) and the particular content of faith is unwieldy with children. For children, there is no easy distinction between how one makes meaning in a generic sense and the specific practices, rituals, traditions, stories, and convictions that hold meaning. There is no such thing as a faith that is "beyond the specific domains of religion and belief." Children's faith grows precisely in the midst of particular beliefs and practices that Fowler sees as so susceptible of "idolatrous distortion."[8]

One final characteristic impedes satisfactory understanding of childhood. Development theory mostly avoids complicated questions about wrongdoing and sin that still have a place, despite their misuse with children. Sin and transgression are primarily adult categories, Fowler contends. Children are more prone to "befallenness" or the alienation "due to circumstances utterly beyond our control."[9] Although this respects children's vulnerability and difference from adults, it also shortchanges their spiritual complexity and moral ac-countability.

To be clear, I am not arguing that stage theory ignores children or that it does not appreciate their faith or that religious education as a whole has not had an interest in children.[10] Rather I am saying that one particular strand within the academic scholarship of the last two to three decades in the U.S. that has had considerable impact has tended to focus on adults more than children, with a few important exceptions.[11] This strand has overshadowed scholars in prior decades who did explicitly address children.[12] For nearly three decades fas-

---

[7] Fowler, *Stages of Faith*, p. 5. He is following the modern distinction of Paul Tillich, H. Richard Niebuhr, and Wilfred Cantwell Smith between institutional religion and ultimate concern or between doctrinal belief and loyalty to centering values.

[8] Fowler, *Stages of Faith*, pp. 5, 9, 293.

[9] James W. Fowler, "Strength for the Journey: Early Childhood Development in Selfhood and Faith," in: *Faith Development in Early Childhood*, ed. Doris A. Blazer (Kansas City: Sheed and Ward, 1989), p. 34.

[10] Some scholars, such as Catherine Stonehouse, for example, have made up for the deficit by illustrating more concretely how developmental theory can help adults "join children on the spiritual journey." See *Joining Children on the Spiritual Journey: Nurturing a Life of Faith* (Grand Rapids: Baker, 1998).

[11] Similar criticism could be made of the state of childhood in pastoral theology and care, where the focus has been primarily on care for adults in crisis and less so on children with the exception of a few books in the 1980s and more recently.

[12] See, for example, Iris V. Cully, *Christian Child Development* (San Francisco: Harper & Row, 1979) and her earlier book, *Children in Church* (Philadelphia: Westminster, 1960). The situation in the U.S. is different from other contexts, such as Europe and Africa, where there are other scholarly influences and broader political and social commitment to children as a shared responsibility.

cination with stage categories stifled other ways of thinking about children and faith.

New Understandings

We now stand in the midst of a reconstruction of childhood comparable to that which occurred with romantization of children in the eighteenth century, a portrayal that has run its course. We have moved irrevocably beyond the sentimental child toward some other vision, what art historian Anne Higonnet identifies as "Knowing children."[13] Just as the modern construction of innocent childhood caused anxiety and resistance in its day among those who saw children as sinful, so also does the reinvention of childhood today. More than anything, the more realistic, less romanticized child mixes together sexual, moral, and spiritual attributes previously dichotomized and provokes fresh moral and religious questions about the meaning of mature faith, the role of children and adults in faith formation, and the spiritual potential of children. Alternative approaches to children emerging in psychology and philosophy suggest new understandings of children's spirituality and invite further work by those in religion.

Space: Spirituality on the Outside

Children question common assumptions about spirituality as primarily an interior phenomenon, pursued through solitude, silence, and a posture of prayer. This is not to say they rule out the importance of any of these as part of the Christian life. Rather children demand a widening of the circle of faith to include them more fully.

One of the most remarkable aspects of psychiatrist Robert Coles's work with children, captured in his widely recognized trilogy, is not the particular content but rather the method by which he discovers it. He attends to children in a truly remarkable way, partly because of his psychoanalytic training. When he becomes a "field worker" instead of an analyst, he carries into conversation with children a style and demeanor honed through years of patient listening. His method is essentially to offer "acceptance of the immediate, the everyday, the objectively visible and audible."[14] Moreover, he learned from the children themselves, as he admits. One child finally confronted him in "blunt, earthy,

---

[13] Anne Higonnet, *Pictures of Innocence: The History and Crisis of Ideal Childhood* (New York: Thames and Hudson, 1998), p. 207 and chapter 9 as a whole.

[14] Robert Coles, *The Spiritual Life of Children* (Boston: Houghton Mifflin, 1990), p. 21. The other two books in the triology are *The Moral Life of Children* (Boston: Houghton Mifflin,1989) and *The Political Life of Children* (Boston: Houghton Mifflin, 1986).

child's language," saying something like, "You're not interested in my religion, only my 'problems.'" So Coles changed his approach. When he adopts a "truly humble" pose, trying to "learn from this girl," new doors open not only with her but also with other children.[15] Each child "becomes an authority." His job "is to put in enough time to enable a child [...] to have her say."[16] "Prolonged encounter" is the essence of the psychoanalytic method.

In other words, children suggest the need for an understanding of spirituality that embraces the whole of family living in all its beauty and misery. Their spirituality takes shape in the concrete activities of day-to-day and the varied contexts where children and adults live together (e.g., playing, working, eating, talking, learning, fighting, making up, arriving, departing, and otherwise making a home).[17] Children's wisdom entails "an *activity* of knowing" according to Tobin Hart, a psychologist who has spent several years doing empirical research with children. It is not just what they know but how it gets "walked out into" their lives and translated into "character and compassion."[18] The usual focus on the verbal and the conceptual should not prevent notice of the extent to which children's spirituality is tactile, shaped in part by what they sense and know physically, by what they do and how they respond.

Time: Spirituality Beyond Stages

Just as children's spirituality disrupts usual definitions of sacred space (inner over outer), it also defies conventional chronological categories. Religious faith does not develop in the same way as other parts of our bodies and minds from small to large or immature to mature. Growing up, in fact, does not guarantee spiritual development. Spirituality evolves in more curious and less obviously quantifiable ways. In fact, spirituality, like philosophical imagination, rests on a freshness or vitality that is as likely to be lost in adolescence and adulthood as gained. "All too often," philosopher Gareth Matthews observes, "maturity

---

[15] Coles, *The Spiritual Life of Children*, p. 39.

[16] Coles, *The Spiritual Life of Children*, p. 27.

[17] For further comment on faith as a way of life, see Dorothy Bass and Craig Dykstra in Dorothy C. Bass, ed., *Practicing Our Faith: A Way of Life for a Searching People* (San Francisco: Jossey-Bass Publishers, 1997); Craig Dykstra, "Reconceiving Practice," in: *Shifting Boundaries: Contextual Approaches to the Structure of Theological Education*, eds. Barbara Wheeler and Edward Farley (Louisville: Westminster/John Knox, 1991); and Dorothy C. Bass and Don C. Richter, eds., *Way to Live: Christian Practices for Teens* (Nashville: Upper Room Books, 2002). Robert Wuthnow makes a similar argument about the influence of everyday practice in *Growing Up Religious: Christians and Jews and Their Journeys of Faith* (Boston: Beacon, 1991).

[18] Tobin Hart, "The Mystical Child: Glimpsing the Spiritual World of Children," *Encounter: Education for Meaning and Social Justice* 17, no. 2 (Summer 2004): 3, 5.

Redefining Children's Spirituality 229

brings with it staleness and uninventiveness."[19] It also brings, I would add, a desire to conform to convention and a penchant for increasingly inflexible beliefs and opinions. Children by contrast have an eye for incongruity and perplexity. They are receptive, open, and curious. They communicate what they see with candor. Matthews believes that most educational settings actually discourage such attributes and, with them, more imaginative philosophical thinking. The same might be said of spirituality.

As Catholic theologian Karl Rahner argued more than two decades before Matthews, childhood has "unsurpassable" value in itself. That is, it has value that adult faith cannot surpass. He questions our ordinary subordination of childhood. The adventure of faith includes "remaining a child forever."[20] He is not talking about a Peter Pan flight to Never-Never Land but about retaining the "infinite openness" of childhood or the openness to the infinite that adults often squander. If childhood has a "direct relationship with God," then adult faith does not mean moving "away from childhood in any definitive sense," but toward it and its eternal value in God's sight.[21]

Based on five years of research that included interviews, statistical survey, case studies, and examination of historical autobiographies, Hart names five types of spiritual capacities that have escaped sufficient notice by theories focused largely on intellectual growth: wisdom, wonder, wondering, relational empathy or resonance, and "multidimensional perception" or access to the "nonspace, nontime dimensions of existence." Rather than go into each of these capacities here, I simply note Hart's broader assertion that children have spiritual abilities that have eluded previous developmental research. "Adult-centric, rationalistic, and institutionalized understandings of spirituality" have partially misled us. Previous research has often equated spirituality with reason and verbal acuity. It assumes and looks for a certain kind of "abstract thinking and language ability" and a certain kind of "God talk" or way of thinking and talking about God and other religious concepts.[22]

Developments in religious education in the past decade in the U.S. reveal new trends. Scholars, such as Bradley Wigger, Elizabeth F. Caldwell, and Joyce Mercer, draw on their experience as ministers and parents or parenting figures.

---

[19] Gareth B. Matthews, *The Philosophy of Childhood* (Cambridge: Harvard University Press, 1994), pp. 16–18.

[20] Karl Rahner, "Ideas for a Theology of Childhood" from *Theological Investigations*, vol. 8 (London: Draton, Longman & Todd, 1971), pp. 33, 50.

[21] Rahner, "Ideas for a Theology of Childhood," p. 36, 48. See also Mary Ann Hinsdale, "'Infinite Openness to the Infinite': Karl Rahner's Contribution to Modern Catholic Thought on the Child," in Marcia J. Bunge, ed., *The Children in Christian Thought* (Grand Rapids: Wm. B. Eerdmans, 2001), p. 428; and Anderson and Johnson, *Regarding Children*, pp. 7, 9, 20–26.

[22] Hart, "The Mystical Child," pp. 1, 11.

Indeed, they represent a different generation of child rearing.[23] Generally speaking, these scholars stand in greater proximity to children, often assuming a major responsibility for children, and they appeal to a wider audience than conventional scholarship.

Three additional characteristics distinguish recent work in religious education. Contrary to the common assumption that the church educates children, the home occupies a central place, as illustrated most overtly in book titles. Caldwell, for example, has two companion books, *Making a Home for Faith* on children and *Leaving Home with Faith* on youth. Wigger titles his book, *The Power of God at Home*. Parents are encouraged to reclaim their primary role. Wigger's entire book is, in fact, geared toward reclamation of "spiritual territory" within the home.[24] Second, adults should not underestimate the power daily life holds for children. Implicit in this literature is the conviction that sheer participation in any of a rich array of practices can serve to convey important religious values and virtues. Finally, recent scholarship pairs a reinvigorated understanding of parents as "primary faith educators" with an emphasis on the fundamental "partnership between the church and the home."[25] Families and congregations must work together to help congregations become more like families and families more like worshipping communities.

A Concluding Caveat

This leads to a final caveat. As respect for children's religious experience has increased dramatically in the last decade, naïve celebration of their wisdom runs an odd inverse risk of romanticizing them as somehow "other" or "ideal" until tainted by parents, teachers, media, or even institutional religion itself. This idealization particularly tempts those unfamiliar with the study of religion, such as Hart, who now claim expertise about spirituality. Celebrating children's spirituality can create another kind of setting apart or dehumanization.

Most religions, by contrast, have sustained (not always successfully) a difficult tension between children's spiritual gifts and limitations. They identify children as mediators of grace in Catholicism, bearers of the spirit in Native American religions, spiritual provocateurs in Judaism, or little Buddhas in Buddhism. At

---

[23] See, for example, Elizabeth F. Caldwell, *Making a Home for Faith: Nurturing the Spiritual Life of Your Children.* (Cleveland: Pilgrim Press, 2000); Bradley J. Wigger, *The Power of God at Home: Nurturing Our Children in Love and Grace* (San Francisco: Jossey-Bass, 2003); Karen-Marie Yust, *Real Kids, Real Faith* (San Francisco: Jossey-Bass, 2004); Kenda Creasy Dean, *Practicing Passion: Youth and the Quest for a Passionate Church* (Eerdmans, 2004); and Joyce Ann Mercer, *Welcoming Children: A Practical Theology of Childhood* (St. Louis: Chalice, 2005).

[24] Wigger, *The Power of God at Home*, pp. 2, 19.

[25] Caldwell, *Leaving Home with Faith*, p. 10 and *Making a Home for Faith*, p. 40.

Redefining Children's Spirituality

the very same time, they combine such views with a realism about children's frailty and faults, whether through insistence on sinfulness, imperatives about learning respect, convictions about competing inclinations toward good and bad, or beliefs in an inevitably mixed karmic inheritance.[26] While many people react negatively to the idea of children as sinful or depraved, the history of the depraved adultish-child of premodern times and the innocent childish-child of modern times has shown the limits of both views. In other words, we have to contend with the real ambiguity of children's spiritual complexity.

The Author

Bonnie Miller-McLemore is E. Rhodes and Leona B. Carpenter Professor of Pastoral Theology at Vanderbilt University Divinity School. Book publications in progress include: Engaging Practice: The Work of Practical Theology (Eerdmans) and The Blackwell Companion to Practical Theology (Wiley-Blackwell). Recent publications include Children and Childhood in American Religions (Rutgers University Press 2009, co-edited with Don S. Browning); Faith's Wisdom for Daily Living (Fortress 2008, co-authored with Herbert Anderson); In the Midst of Chaos: Care of Children as Spiritual Practice (Jossey-Bass 2006); and Let the Children Come: Reimagining Childhood from a Christian Perspective (Jossey-Bass 2003).

---

[26] See Don S. Browning and Bonnie J. Miller-McLemore, eds., *Children and Childhood in American Religions* (Rutgers University Press, 2008). See also Naomi C. Rose's children's book, *Tibetan Tales for Little Buddhas* (Clear Light Publishing, 2004).

Practical Theology and Liberating Practice

Nancy Pineda-Madrid

Social Suffering, Its Aftermath and Questions of Redemption

On March 6 of this year (2007), not far from Boston, Massachusetts, U.S. immigration officers conducted a raid of a manufacturing company located in New Bedford. These officers aimed to incarcerate and deport some 350 workers who did not have papers proving that they worked legally in the U.S. The overwhelming majority of those apprehended were mothers with young children.

On the day of the raid, the officers shackled many of these women together in three's by their wrists and ankles, and took them to Fort Devens some 100 miles away. These women were denied legal representation and due process. What is ironic is that these female employees were manufacturing safety vests and backpacks for U.S. soldiers in Iraq. The U.S. war effort benefitted from the skills of these Guatemalan and Salvadoran women. Yet, U.S. officials treated these women not as heroines making a contribution, but as traitors. There were countless stories like the one of a young father of an eight month old baby, desperate because his wife was detained. Dehydrated, their breast-fed baby girl cried incessantly for her mother.[1] While the owners of the Michael Bianco, Inc. manufacturing plant were released within hours of their arrest, by and large, the undocumented women employees were not released until days after their arrests.

The children of these women – many of whom were born in the U.S. and thus citizens – endured trauma in the wake of their mothers' forced absence. A full day after the immigration raid, the U.S. federal government permitted state social workers to enter the detention site at Fort Devens. The social workers found 20 female detainees who had not been previously identified – four of whom were nursing mothers or pregnant, nine of whom were single mothers and seven of whom were under the age of 17. These women were dubbed national security threats, reported *Boston Globe* columnist Eileen McNamara. Massachusetts Governor Duval Patrick rightly termed the raid "a humanitarian crisis," when he learned that these women were not only taken to Fort Devens, but many of them were quickly flown to the Texas border, several thousands of miles away. Officials did not bother to consider that deportation hearings just as easily could have taken place in Massachusetts as in Texas. Outraged by the raid, Brookline based child-psychologist Carolyn Newberger asserted that the "abrupt separation of mothers and children precipitated by this raid is child neglect by any definition I know." Further, she argued: "If, as the U.S. Depart-

---

[1] Yvonne Abraham and Brian R. Ballou, "350 Are Held in Immigration Raid, New Bedford Factory Employed Illegals, US Says," *The Boston Globe* (Boston, MA), 7 March 2007.

ment of Homeland Security claims, the Massachusetts Department of Social Services (DSS) 'worked closely' with them prior to the raid on the Bianco clothing factory in New Bedford, then our state agency charged with the protection of children has itself actively collaborated in children's abandonment, starvation, and traumatic psychological injury. The damage to the children left behind is inevitable and incalculable, and the leadership of DSS must be held to account for their roles in this travesty."[2]

El Salvadoran, Ana Alegria was among the detainees at Fort Devens. After three days of detention, federal officials released Ana allowing her to be reunited with her sick 17-month-old son. Having spent three cold nights in the detention center unable to sleep, she shared, "Every day I told myself I had a little son at home and that's what got me through. I came here for a better life, and I worked at that factory for my son to have a better life."[3] Ana Alegria stated that she had entered the U.S. illegally three years ago.

Without a doubt, Ana Alegria's life has been marked by suffering, as is the case for most undocumented women working in the U.S.

Since the inception of the Christian tradition, suffering has remained an enduring theological problem. Fundamental to the problem is the question of understanding. For example, how do we take account of Ana Alegria's experience? Are she and the other undocumented women simply unfortunate individuals who need to figure out for themselves how they will come to terms with their painful lives? Or, does their suffering hold some larger meaning given that it is the by-product of a legal system created by human beings that privileges some at the expense of others? *While Christian theology has often framed suffering in terms that are either exclusively personal or exclusively collective, a "social suffering" hermeneutic foregrounds the interplay of the social and the personal which, in turn, challenges us to consider anew the meaning of redemption.*

In order to develop this claim, we first need to briefly acknowledge how suffering has been typically understood within contemporary theological discourse. This, in turn, sets the context for our consideration of a "social suffering" hermeneutic, a distinctive approach to suffering. This approach will become clear when examined in light of the 2007 New Bedford, Massachusetts immigration raid, which revealed the inhumane and systemic injustices experienced daily by undocumented immigrants. Finally, the theological import of this approach will be considered with regard to questions of redemption.

---

[2] Eileen McNamara, "State Fails Immigrants," *The Boston Globe* (Boston, MA), 11 March 2007.

[3] Maria Sacchetti and Brian Ballou, "DDS Teams Arrive in Texas to Interview Detained Immigrants, Some Say They Were Mistreated," *The Boston Globe* (Boston, MA), 11 March 2007.

Regarding Suffering

In Christian theological discourse today, the problem of suffering has been largely situated within a personal, individual frame of reference, or, within a social, political frame of reference. Without a doubt, suffering presents such unrelenting questions that both of these trajectories remain always pertinent. The range of approaches to suffering within each of these trajectories demonstrates what a complex endeavor it is to delineate suffering.

Even so, in the latter part of the 20th century, definitions of suffering with an explicitly social and political character became more prominent in keeping with the widespread emergence of liberation theologies. These definitions foregrounded the institutionalization of structural violence (e.g., racism, sexism, classism), unmasked the ideologies that served to legitimize these institutions, and identified suffering as an inevitable by-product of these social, political and economic systems. Accordingly, theologians conceived redemption with an implicit understanding of the social, political and economic as integral dimensions of the God-human relation. To varying degrees, the writings of Latino/a, mujerista, womanist and feminist theologians as well as the writing of other liberation theologians, all reflect this worldview.

When theologians situate suffering within a social, political ambit, as liberation theologians do, then theology presumes a public relevance. Here, theology concerns itself not only with the hopes, pains and fears of Christian believers, not only with the intellectual import of age old beliefs, but also with the current state of society and the world, and the impact of theology on these. This impact is understood not merely in terms of personal decisions but just as importantly, in terms of the infrastructures we create – social, political and economic – that give shape to our world. Thus, theology holds itself accountable to furthering the reign of God in this world as well as the next. This theological conviction carries a constant impetus to continuously and critically consider how we delineate suffering. It matters utterly.

A Social Suffering Hermeneutic

Ana Alegria's experience and that of the other undocumented women gives us pause. How best to delineate their experience of suffering. Certainly their U.S. experience carries many different forms of suffering. We can analyze their social, political and economic situation, and develop an understanding of a wide range of factors that put them at high risk for great suffering. Yet, as Rebecca Chopp warns, "Knowledge of suffering cannot be conveyed in pure facts and figures, reportings that objectify the suffering of countless persons. The horror of suffering is not only its immensity but the faces of anonymous victims who have little voice, let alone rights, in history."[4] Analysis alone offers a picture that falls short, which leaves us aware but not engaged.

On the other hand, the personal stories of pain of the Ana Alegrias of the world likely will leave us engaged but not responsible. The interrelated social-political systems that create a middle class lifestyle for some and structural violence for many are not transparent for us. "The dynamics and distribution of suffering are still poorly understood."[5] So, as Robert McAfee Brown tells us, "the world that is satisfying to us is the same world that is utterly devastating to them,"[6] yet we still do not understand this connection well.

Cognizant of this dilemma, some theorists and theologians (e.g., Paul Farmer, M. Shawn Copeland, Rebecca Chopp[7] and others) have sought means of delineating suffering in a fashion that links social, political analysis with personal stories of suffering. The focus here is on "structural violence," on social processes and tragic events that lead to insidious, extreme and, tragically, avoidable suffering. This interpretation of suffering, namely, linking personal accounts of extreme suffering to the social matrix that precipitates them, may be called "social suffering." The lens of social suffering allows us to see in sharp relief how wider social forces coalesce to mar individual human lives. Thus we read individual experience from within the larger social matrix that defines the parameters of that individual experience. To appreciate the significance of this approach, we began with an instance of massive public suffering, namely the experience of undocumented workers whose sufferings were brought into the light of day by the March 2007 raid of the Michael Bianco manufacturing plant in New Bedford, Massachusetts.

Obviously, social suffering refers not only to a particular way of delineating suffering but also to a type of suffering. It is suffering as a social phenomenon brought on by, at the very least, dehumanizing institutional power or by institutionalized power that can only be described as evil. Social suffering may be

---

[4] Rebecca S. Chopp, *The Praxis of Suffering: An Interpretation of Liberation and Political Theologies* (Maryknoll, NY: Orbis, 1986), 2.

[5] Paul Farmer, "On Suffering and Structural Violence: A View from Below," in: *Social Suffering*, ed. Arthur Kleinman, Veena Das and Margaret Lock (Berkeley, CA: University of California Press, 1997), 272.

[6] Robert McAfee Brown, *Liberation Theology: An Introductory Guide* (Louisville, KY: Westminster, 1993), 44.

[7] Paul Farmer, *Pathologies of Power: Health, Human Rights, and the New War on the Poor* (Berkeley: University of California Press, 2005); Farmer, "On Suffering and Structural Violence: A View from Below."; M. Shawn Copeland, "'Wading 'Through Many Sorrows' Toward a Theology of Suffering in Womanist Perspective," in: *A Troubling in My Soul: Womanist Perspectives on Evil and Suffering*, ed. Emilie M. Townes (Maryknoll, NY: Orbis Books, 1993), 109–29; Chopp, *The Praxis of Suffering: An Interpretation of Liberation and Political Theologies.*

an event of public suffering that is widespread (e.g., genocide in Rwanda) or an economic exchange that leads to the ongoing destruction of human lives (e.g., sex tourism). According to Copeland, "torture, genocide, extermination, 'ethnic cleansing,' 'disappearance,' enslavement, cultural decimation, protracted systemic racism," to name a few, are all examples of social suffering.

Specifically, a social suffering hermeneutic calls attention to human suffering that is a by-product of the social systems humans create. In Ana Alegria's case, a legal system created by human beings deems that she has no standing before the law in this country and therefore, can be "legitimately" treated in an inhumane, cruel fashion; and deems that her child though he be a U.S. citizen can be subject "legitimately" to psychological trauma administered by the U.S. government. A social suffering hermeneutic brings the absurdity of this situation into focus. Instead of allowing the social systems which give rise to suffering to remain hidden behind a veil of bureaucratic obscurity, and instead of relegating the experience of suffering to the realm of abstraction by labeling it a "necessary and unavoidable" by-product of society, – a social suffering hermeneutic maintains *in the fore* the integral relation between social systems with destructive fallout, and the resulting personal stories of human tragedy. Such an approach neither reduces all to a collection of personal "anecdotal" experiences of suffering, nor does it allow suffering to remain a concern distant from present life. A social suffering hermeneutic paints a picture of human tragedy that demands a response, social-political as well as personal.

A number of questions begin the process of mapping a social suffering hermeneutic. For example: Which population is most at risk of great suffering? How might we identify those who are most at risk to sustain debilitating suffering? Chronic suffering? Who will likely experience the enduring assault of racism? Sexism? Classism? Rape? Torture? Further, are certain forms of institutionalized violence "demonstrably more noxious than others?" And even more, which population stands the greatest mortal risk? Such questions begin to construct the lens of social suffering.[8] Again, Ana Alegria offers us a telling example. In New Bedford, she is an extremely poor woman in a country with a workforce that is, by and large, skilled and educated. She is a dark-skinned woman in a society where racism and sexism abound. She is an alternately documented woman (a Salvadoran citizen) working in the U.S. where her "papers" afford her no legal status. She is monolingual Spanish in a, by and large, monolingual English world. And moreover, her country's extreme poverty and violence are integrally related to the comparative wealth of the U.S. In short, her risk of suffering is great.

The value of a social suffering hermeneutic most assuredly includes the ability to reveal the close connections between personal problem and societal prob-

---

[8] Farmer, "On Suffering and Structural Violence: A View from Below," 261.

lems. But its value extends further. It draws connections among the experiences of those who live in the favalas of Brazil, in the gang-ridden barrios of south-central Los Angeles, and in the poorest sections of New Bedford. In all these settings the desperately poor and powerless know a life utterly defined by questions of survival at its most basic level. These populations find themselves to be the causalities of a global political economy far beyond their sphere of influence.

What is more, a social suffering hermeneutic requires from all of us far more than pity and charity. When we appreciate the social-political dimensions which foster suffering we are more inclined to feel called to a social trans-formation, a social conversion. Such conversion makes serious demands of us.

Yet, bringing this social-political consciousness into full view remains deeply problematic. Far more often than not the pain of others, particularly that brought on by institutionalized power, remains sequestered from public view. We find numerous ways to keep the social suffering of our time at bay, distant. It slips in and out of our awareness with the passing stories we read in our daily newspapers. Undoubtedly we realize that recognizing social suffering will be personally costly. It is far easier to view the pain of others as a misfortunate occurrence, the poor luck of the draw, rather than a product brought about by our own action and/or inaction. To label the suffering of others "misfortune," of course, trivializes that suffering and leaves us blameless. Indeed, as Law-rence Langer has argued, "We need a new kind of discourse to disturb our collective consciousness and stir it into practical action that moves beyond mere pity."[9]

The plight of undocumented Latinas, like Ana Alegria, remains largely invisible in the public arena. A perduring fear of being discovered marks their lives, and overshadows their experiences of physical violence, economic be-trayals and every manner of abuse. These brutal realities continue unabated be-cause undocumented women are *persona non grata* before the law. Ac-cordingly, their daily lives are marked by unmitigated vulnerability. Their experience of structural violence, in a real sense, defies description. It eludes us because while they live in close physical proximity to us, their culture, their language, their life histories remain distant from that of most of us who are U.S. citizens and professed Christians. Consequently, the experience of undo-cumented Latinas can be, disastrously, less affecting.[10] We cannot relate to it.

---

[9] Lawrence L. Langer, "The Alarmed Vision: Social Suffering and Holocaust Atroc-ity," in: *Social Suffering*, ed. Arthur Kleinman, Veena Das and Margaret Lock (Berke-ley, CA: University of California Press, 1997), 47.
[10] Farmer, "On Suffering and Structural Violence: A View from Below," 272.

On Redemption

Social suffering, like all suffering, can be a portal to questions of redemption. Over time suffering, particularly social suffering, can gnaw at our hope, can gut our driving passion. Recognizing the impact of suffering in our lives, we begin to ask "Why?" We begin to ask, can someone, some reality greater than ourselves, bring relief? Bring healing? Bring meaning? Bring genuine freedom? Bring wholeness?

As we have heard, Ana Alegria and other undocumented Latinas in our world, persist as an invisible presence in our communities, live lives marked by vulnerability in the extreme, and remain silenced by our legal system. They are modern day slaves. Life in the U.S. affords them little to no space in which to shape a meaningful life, in which to create their own history. They are slaves. They embody something other than the U.S. norm for a human being, that is, a person who is a citizen, ideally white, preferably male.

When confronted with the social suffering of undocumented Latinas, theology's response must include the social-political dimension of the human condition. The transition from bondage to liberation, from bondage to greater freedom, no doubt, marks the lives of undocumented Latinas working in the U.S. Ultimately, this universal human drive concerns our desire for communion, with ourselves, with others and with God. Theologians label the true satiation of this drive, "redemption."

Generally speaking, Christian theologians consider redemption to be a basic element in the doctrine of salvation (soteriology). The doctrine of salvation addresses God's saving presence among human beings which was inaugurated at creation, given final expression through the person of Jesus the Christ and continues in the dynamic action of the Holy Spirit in history. Among various approaches to the doctrine of salvation, redemption reflects an approach that emphasizes the transition from bondage to freedom. Such an approach presumes an integral relation between the history of salvation and the history of the world. In the second half of the twentieth century widely influential theologians such as Karl Rahner, Edward Schillebeeckx, Rosemary Radford Ruether and Gustavo Gutiérrez argued that the human quest for salvation entails not a flight from the world but an engagement with the world.

Redemption signifies an ongoing and intrahistorical process of transformation comprised of liberating historical events that tenaciously seek out fulfillment in the present but whose final meaning will become clear only in the fullness of time. For as Gutiérrez rightly argues, "Without liberating historical events, there would be no growth of the Kingdom. But the process of liberation will not have conquered the very roots of human oppression and exploitation without the coming of the Kingdom, which is above all a gift. Moreover, we can say that the historical, political liberating event *is* the growth of the Kingdom and *is* a salvific event; but it is not *the* coming of the kingdom, not *all* of salvation. It is the historical realization of the Kingdom and, therefore, it also proclaims its fullness."[11]

For the Ana Alegrias of the world and for the rest of us, the substance of redemption would have to include an abiding, deepening awareness that the undocumented are not merely props on the stage of human history but rather actors who fashion their historically significant lives. Redemption would likewise involve a critical awareness of history, meaning the larger forces and events – social, political and economic – that have given rise to the present condition of undocumented workers. And it would entail a critical awareness of their enslavement. Most importantly, redemption would also include a place and an opportunity to join with other like-minded people to actively resist the unjust and inhumane conditions of the lives of the undocumented in the U.S., and to actively transform the structures that make slavery inevitable. The coming of the Kingdom demands no less. Redemption demands no less.

The Author

Nancy Pineda-Madrid, Ph.D. in systematic and philosophical theology, is Assistant Professor of Theology at Boston College. Recent publications: "Latinas Writing Theology at the Threshold of the 21st Century." In: Women-Centered Theologies for the 21st Century. Edited by Rosemary Radford Ruether. Minneapolis, MN: Fortress, 2007: 55–65; "Traditioning: The Formation of Community, The Transmission of Faith." In: Futuring Our Past: Explorations in the Theology of Tradition. Edited by Orlando Espín and Gary Macy. Maryknoll, NY: Orbis Press, 2006: 204–226; "Überlegungen im Hinblick auf eine chicana-feministische Epistemologie (und warum sie für feministische Latina-Theologien von Bedeutung ist)." In: Glaube an der Grenze. Die US-amerikanische Latino-Theologie. Raul Fornet-Bentancourt, (Hg.). Freiburg: Verlag Herder, 2002: 180–210.

---

[11] Gustavo Gutiérrez, *A Theology of Liberation: History, Politics, and Salvation*, 1973, translated by Sister Caridad Inda and John Eagleson, 15th Anniversary Edition (Maryknoll, New York: Orbis Books, 1988), 104.

Lothar Carlos Hoch

The Struggle of Practical Theology in its Search for Identity
A Latin American Perspective

If we take a look at the scenario of Latin American churches nowadays, we will notice a wealth and diversity of pastoral practices never seen before on this continent. The most diverse pastoral practices seem to pop up across the whole range of religious denominations around us. No doubt, this is a rich and creative moment for the Latin American pastoral ministry.

Nevertheless, taking a deeper look we will notice that this multi-colored religious scenario is quite confusing. One sometimes gets the impression that there are just as many pastoral practices as there are purposes that guide them and assumptions behind them. It is no easy task to find your way through this labyrinth.

Some questions need to be addressed: What is the difference between Practical Theology and the Ministry of the Church? What is each one's specific competence? Would it be possible for Practical Theology to lend some order to the chaos of pastoral practices, so that the current exuberance of church ministries likewise could be translated into an exuberant period for Practical Theology?

1. The growing awareness of the deficient profile of Practical Theology

Part of the confusing situation among the ministries must be attributed to the rich religious scenario present in Latin America today and to the challenges posed to the churches by the realities of this continent. However, a share of responsibility for this state of affairs must be attributed to the distance between the pastoral practices found within the churches and the theological education offered by seminaries and education centers maintained by the churches. Practical Theology as taught in seminaries today is not attuned to the ministry taking place in local congregations and grassroots social movements.

I suspect that the Practical Theology being taught in seminaries today suffers both from not having a specific theoretical body of its own and from lacking clarity concerning the assumptions under which it operates. I fear that little dialogue is taking place among professors of the different sub-disciplines of Practical Theology, which means that little reflection is taking place about the common ground they share. The difficulty of establishing a common nomenclature (Practical Theology? Pastoral Theology? Applied Theology?) is symptomatic for the lack of clarity that permeates the discipline. Another worrisome symptom is that there is virtually no publication by Latin American authors on the nature of Practical Theology.

Now, if the Practical Theology taught and practiced in seminaries operates without an own theoretical framework, how can we expect the ministry developed within the churches to have any theoretical clarity about what it does? I just want to make sure there are no misunderstandings here, so let me clarify that I do not subscribe to the view that Practical Theology should aim to direct the ministry that is carried out at the grassroots. The ministry at the local church level and the popular ministries do not allow for tutelage from a theology conceived in the seminary classrooms. After all, true to sound Protestant tradition, the people of the church should be co-subjects of the theology they put to practice.

To be more precise, I believe that seminaries, by influence of Practical Theology, should become "resonance boxes," so to speak, for the different pastoral ministries that arise in the midst of the people of God at the local level. That is their vocation. On the other hand, in a sense of reciprocity, the pastoral ministries developed at the local level should be stimulated, inspired and supported theologically by the Practical Theology taught in the churches' centers of theological education. But for this to happen, Practical Theology must bridge the gap that separates it from the pastoral ministry. It must cross the high walls that surround our seminaries and head out to the streets.

Practical Theology is the special interlocutor of pastoral practices developed in the midst of the People of God. These practices need to undergo theological analysis and reflection so they may better withstand the usual criticism leveled at them, such as being overly focused on spontaneity, or of not being methodologically thorough.

In Latin America our own situation as practical theologians is, no doubt, peculiar. We are asked to address issues related to topics that lie at the limit between theology and other areas of human knowledge. To do this, we need to be knowledgeable not only about all the other theological disciplines, but also about the sociological and psychological insights commonly required to approach a given subject. Likewise, we are often asked to address topics related to religious sciences, the media, politics, economics and culture (for instance, issues regarding sexism or racism). As a matter of fact, any area close to theology that does not fit neatly into the traditional disciplines tends to be incorporated into Practical Theology.

This circumstance makes us into all-round persons, jacks-of-all-trade who understand little of everything. And precisely for this reason we run the risk of becoming superficial. To avoid this trap we must clean up our house and find clarity about the statutes that govern Practical Theology as a theological discipline, about its specific object of studies and into what sub-disciplines it is divided. Only when our competence has been clearly defined and when we have carried out thorough studies in our area of expertise we will be able to

The Struggle of Practical Theology in its Search for Identity

contribute in a serious and respectable manner to interdisciplinary dialogue. In other words, in our Latin American context we need to clarify the identity of Practical Theology as a theological discipline.

Indeed, the anecdotes that make the rounds concerning our discipline are not wholly unjustified. The most recent I heard goes like this: A young student asks his professor: "What is Practical Theology?" The professor replies, "It is practically theology". Maybe history can come to our aid and vindicate us!

2. Could the Protestant tradition be of any help?

A short introductory remark. I belong to the Evangelical Church of Lutheran Confession in Brazil, a church which originated from German immigration into the South of Brazil in the beginning of the nineteenth century. Our theology, our liturgy and our theological education have been strongly influenced by German Protestantism. We cannot jump over our theological tradition when we want to enter in dialogue with the dominant Catholic Latin American tradition.

As we know, Practical Theology has been a controversial discipline right from its beginnings. In the nineteenth century in Germany, theology holds a seat at the highest levels of the state universities. Steeped in the spirit of the Enlightenment, theology makes an effort to prove its legitimacy as a science. In this endeavor, it becomes a victim of sterile academicism and distances itself from the life of the church. As a result, there is no longer a healthy relationship between the theological theory taught at the universities and the practice of pastoral ministry and the spiritual life of church members in the congregations.

The need was felt for a theological discipline that would establish an adequate relationship between academic theology and the everyday life of Christians. With this purpose in mind, Practical Theology was instituted as a new discipline beside Biblical Studies, Church History and Systematic Theology.

It is really quite ironic that Friedrich Schleiermacher, the "father of Practical Theology", whom Karl Barth[1] considered one of the greatest, if not the greatest theologian of the nineteenth century, who was in charge of implementing the new discipline at the Faculty of Theology at the University of Berlin, would refer to the discipline in the following terms in 1810: "Let me state my opinion on the matter at once, I feel that creating a specific chair of Practical Theology is not desirable. It would be far better if this task were taken over informally by the professors in charge of the theoretical disciplines."[2]

---

[1] *Die protestantische Theologie im 19. Jahrhundert,* p. 379ff.
[2] Letter to Wilhelm von Humboldt, in Gerhard KRAUSE, *Praktische Theologie,* p. 7 (author's translation)

246 Lothar Carlos Hoch

How is Schleiermacher's hesitation to be explained? It is possibly a result of the Protestant premise that all theology is by its very nature practical. Luther spared no criticism of Aristotle and Thomas Aquinas for their speculative theology. A theology that claims Jesus Christ as its foundation must necessarily be practical, once it follows from taking up his cross. Christian faith cannot be limited to contemplation or to the act of assenting to a system of revealed truths; rather, it implies getting involved with the words and the deeds of Jesus and with following his path of suffering. For Martin Luther all theology is essentially theology of the cross. And as such it can only be Practical Theology.[3]

3. The contribution of Latin American Liberation Theology

The European theologian Johan Baptist Metz recognizes that Liberation Theology brought about a threefold loss of innocence on the part of European theology: a) by breaking its social and historical innocence; b) by taking away the innocence from the Central-European cultural monocentrism and instituting the Third World as a valid hermeneutical reference for theology; and c) by shattering its innocence concerning the poor.[4]

By positioning theology in a social framework, Liberation Theology has opened a unique perspective for an effective relation between theory and practice. Brazilian theologian João Batista Libânio distinguishes three levels of such relations within Liberation Theology:

a. A theoretical relation, where the Christian communal practice is taken as raw material for reflection. In doing so, Liberation Theology becomes a theology of practice.

b. A practical relation, where the theologian places himself/herself in the midst of a practice of communal struggles and is committed to them. This will be a theology within practice, that is, one carried out from within practice.

---

[3] Thomas Aquinas considered speculative knowledge to be divine, and consequently claimed that speculative life was simply better than the active one (*Cognitio speculativa est divina [...] quia est de rebus divinis e vita contemplativa simpliciter melior est quam activa);* cf. Norbert GREINACHER, Theologie im Spannungsfeld von Theorie und Praxis, p. 162. Luther, in an undisguisedly polemic attitude, and with his characteristic bluntness, literally says: "Theology as a speculative science is simply vain" (*Speculativa scientia theologorum est simpliciter vana).* And he adds: "True theology is practical" (*Vera theologia est practica).* "Without practice, no one can be erudite" (*Sine practica kan niemand gelert sein).* Ap. Jürgen HENKYS, Die Praktische Theologie, p.25. *To Luthers Theology of the Cross,* Cf. Walther von LOEWENICH, *A Teologia de Lutero,* passim.
[4] Ap. João Batista LIBÂNIO, op. cit., p. 161ff.

The Struggle of Practical Theology in its Search for Identity 247

c. Finally, the relation between theory and practice in Liberation Theology becomes manifest in the fact that it is a theology for practice: its intention is to provide insights for those involved at the front of the liberating struggles.[5]

With this perspective of relation between theory and practice, Liberation Theology has greatly contributed to theology in general, for it has recovered the truth that had already been emphasized by Martin Luther, namely that all theology is in its very nature practical. In other words, liberation theology did away with the conflict between the wisdom that arises from intellectual knowledge and that which results from the practice of faith. Liberation Theology overcomes the dichotomy between work of the head and work of the hands.[6]

The relation between theory and practice developed by Liberation Theology offers a solid theoretical foundation on which Practical Theology can build its own theory as theological discipline. In spite of this positive summary, in my opinion, Liberation Theology could have drawn a clearer distinction between the specific competences of Practical Theology and Pastoral Theology as distinctive theological disciplines. While the Pastoral Theology reflects on the art of shepherding the people of God, Practical Theology is the academic reflection on the adequate way of witnessing the Gospel in the world. This distinction of competences could contribute to rehabilitate Practical Theology in Latin America as a theological discipline with a unique profile. It could also contribute to provide a common basis for the different pastoral ministries that are currently disconnected in our context.

4. Attempting to define responsibilities

As mentioned above, Practical Theology only finds its rightful place as a theological discipline within a dynamic relation with the other theological disciplines. I understand that the specific task of Practical Theology is to remind the other disciplines about the practical vocation of all theology.

From this assumption I derive the twofold duty of Practical Theology as follows:

1st) Practical Theology as a premise for theological activity

Practical Theology is a basic assumption of all theological activity as it is tuned in to the world and picks up the current subjects and challenges that call for a stand on the part of theology and the church. Practical Theology is to work as a

---

[5] ID., ibid., p. 162ff.
[6] For further study of this issue, see my essay "Reflexões em torno do método da Teologia Prática" in: SCHNEIDER-HARPPRECHT, Christoph (Coord.). *Teologia prática no contexto da América Latina*. São Leopoldo: Sinodal: ASTE, 1998.

listening post for the concerns and anxieties that trouble people and society nowadays. By doing so, it keeps theology from introversion and blindness to the reality that surrounds it. To fulfill this role, Practical Theology seeks to establish direct dialogue with the social sciences and take counsel with them, for only by this an accurate view of things will be obtained. Practical Theology is the principal interlocutor between theology and the social sciences.

Needless to say, the dialogue between Practical Theology and reality must take place within an appropriate theological perspective, which cannot be abandoned lest the dialogue should lose its theological function. Saying that its action is a premise for theology is not the same as saying that its action comes prior to theology. This emphasis is necessary in order to avoid the misunderstanding that has arisen within Liberation Theology, as if "seeing", – the first step in the well-known triad "seeing, judging and acting" – were an objective act, void of any theological premise.

2nd) Practical Theology as critical conscience of theology

Practical Theology inquires to what extent the ultimate purpose of theology can be attained, namely, becoming a responsible and effective practice of Christian faith. Theology that is not destined to transform the world and the church loses its link to the transforming and questioning Gospel of Jesus Christ. It becomes a sterile science. Practical Theology contributes to preserving the relevance of theology and the action of the church in the present.

In other words, Practical Theology determines whether the practice of the church is coherent with the postulates and theological discourse it proclaims. In this sense it acts as the critical conscience both of theology and the church, which must be an ecclesia semper reformanda to remain true to its vocation. Practical Theology asks whether the church as it is today corresponds to the original intention of the Lord of the Church. Or, as R. Bohren[7] puts it, the question asked by Practical Theology for the truth is the question for the true church.

But the church cannot limit itself to hear the criticism that arises from within its midst. Practical Theology must also act as the spokesperson for those who, outside the church, point to consistencies and inconsistencies in its witness. As a listening post for the church, Practical Theology is the advocate of the world before the church.

It is evident that in order to carry out this critical duty efficiently, Practical Theology must be adequately equipped and must develop effective analytical tools. First and foremost, there must be theological criteria and methodological thoroughness to determine whether its critique is warranted. If not, in its zeal to

---

[7] ID., ibid., p. 384.

The Struggle of Practical Theology in its Search for Identity 249

keep the church up-to-date, Practical Theology might end up conforming the church to the world and denying its prophetic mandate.

The great danger of both postulates above is that Practical Theology might become merely an auxiliary instrument to theology, one that gathers questions and then examines whether the answers provided by theology are adequate. It is the risk mentioned above of restricting the task of Practical Theology to something prior or subsequent to theology, properly speaking. To secure a status of theological discipline in the fullest sense, it is paramount to define its task as being simultaneous to theology.

The lack of recognition of a full theological role for Practical Theology derives from the deductive approach usually taken by traditional theology.[8] Theology was something based on lofty philosophical and methodological presuppositions, while at a later stage, Practical Theology was in charge of elaborating ways of putting across those truths in the most comprehensible form possible for the simple folks. That is, Practical Theology became at the end, an appendix to theology. Theology was a one-way science: first came inferences of the revealed truth, of which the church was the entrusted receiver; only then came issues of applicability. At most, Practical Theology was allowed to raise questions which theology then would be expected to answer.

When this scheme of things is scrapped and the social locus and the practice of faith that applies to it is taken into consideration, both pastoral ministry and Practical Theology acquire newfound meaning. The whole people of God, and not only the caste of theologians, becomes the subject of theology. Praxis of the Church now becomes a theological locus and Practical Theology, as its prime interlocutor, regains its theological role along with its practice.

5. Conclusion

We have attempted to determine the specific task of Practical Theology as a critical conscience for the church and for theology itself in the sense of reminding them of their ultimate purpose: the effective practice of faith. Practical Theology is committed to binding both theology and the church to practice.

Practical Theology can only fulfill this role if it is permanently attuned to the needs and aspirations of today's world, which is why it reflects critically on the life and action of the church as it faces the challenges and social-historical conditions of modern times.

Its task is to make sure that the church of Jesus Christ remains a salvific event here and now. Taking up Schleiermacher's tree metaphor, Practical Theology is

---

[8]Cf. João Batista LIBÂNIO, *Teologia da libertação*, p. 159ff.

the foliage canopy that provides its own trunk with oxygen to prevent it from withering. Practical Theology aims to be a vehicle for the Holy Ghost to keep the church in motion.

Practical Theology promotes dialogue between the church hierarchy and the grassroots, between the church and the world, between theology and the social sciences. It is the point of intersection of all these domains.

It is the advanced post of theology, taking theology to the grassroots of the church and beyond its walls, and in doing so keeping theology's agenda up-to-date, while at the same time putting its effectiveness to the test. As it has a theological role, Practical Theology likewise feeds theology with the reflection it carries out regarding the church and society.

Its role of keeping the witness of the church up-to-date must not lead Practical Theology to follow every new fad and constantly undergo a metamorphosis simply in order to appear modern. Its commitment to the world should not lead it to forget its larger commitment to the gospel. For this reason it should avoid activist immediatism but instead, in close partnership with the other theological disciplines, constantly strive to keep a reflective and self-critical attitude. As the practical conscience of theology, Practical Theology must itself be aware of the theological reasons that guide and inspire it.

References

Antoniazzi, Alberto. Planejamento pastoral: reflexões críticas. *Perspectiva Teológica,* Belo Horizonte, v. 21, n. 53, pp. 101–112, 1989.

Barth, Karl. *Die protestantische Theologie im 19. Jahrhundert.* Zürich: EVZ, 1947.

Boff, Clodovis. *Teologia e prática:* teologia do político e suas mediações. Petrópolis: Vozes, 1978.

Bohren, Rudolf. Praktische Theologie. In: Krause, Gerhard (ed.). *Praktische Theologie.* Darmstadt: Wissenschaftliche Buchgesellschaft, 1972. pp. 377–399.

Daiber, Karl-Fritz. *Grundriss der Praktischen Theologie als Handlungswissenschaft.* München: Kaiser, 1977.

Elizondo, V., Greinacher, N. Evolução da Teologia Prática. *Concilium*, Petrópolis, v. 190, n. 10, pp. 33–42, 1983.

Floristan, Casiano. *Teologia Practica: teoria y praxis de la acción pastoral.* Salamanca: Sigueme, 1993.

The Struggle of Practical Theology in its Search for Identity 251

Greinacher, Norbert. Theologie im Spannungsverhältnis von Theorie und Praxis. In: Neuenzeit, Paul (ed.). *Die Funktion der Theologie in Kirche und Gesellschaft.* München: Kösel, s.d.

Henkys, Jürgen. Die Praktische Theologie. In: *Handbuch der Praktischen Theologie.* Berlin: Evang. Verlagsanstalt, 1975. v. 1, pp. 11–56.

Krause, Gerhard (ed.). *Praktische Theologie:* Texte zum Werden und Selbstverständnis der praktischen Disziplin der Evangelischen Theologie. Darmstadt: Wissenschaftliche Buchgesellschaft, 1972.

Libânio, João Batista. *Teologia da libertação*: roteiro didático para um estudo. São Paulo: Loyola, 1987.

Loewenich, Walther von. *A teologia da cruz de Lutero.* São Leopoldo: Sinodal, 1988.

Nipkow, K.E., Rössler, D., Schweitzer, F.(ed.). *Praktische Theologie und Kultur der Gegenwart. Ein internationaler Dialog.* Gütersloh: Gerd Mohn, 1991.

Schleiermacher, Friedrich. *Kurze Darstellung des theologischen Studiums.* Commented edition by H. Scholz, Leipzig 1910.

Schneider-Harpprecht, Christoph (ed.). *Praktische Theologie im Kontext Lateinamerikas.* Münster/Hamburg/London: Lit Verlag, 2003.

Seitz, Manfred. *Prática da fé :* culto – poimênica – espiritualidade. São Leopoldo: Sinodal, 1990.

Tillich, Paul. *Teologia Sistemática.* São Paulo: Paulinas; São Leopoldo: Sinodal, 1984.

VV.AA. *Enciclopédia Teológica: Sacramentum Mundi.* Barcelona: Herder, 1974.

Volp, Rainer. Praktische Theologie bei F. D. Schleiermacher. In: Klostermann, F., Zerfass, R.. *Praktische Theologie heute.* München: Kaiser; Mainz: Grünewald, 1974, pp. 52–64.

Zabatiero, Júlio. *Fundamentos da Teologia Prática.* Editora Mundo Cristão: São Paulo, 2005.

The Author

Lothar Carlos Hoch, Lutheran Theologian, born in Brazil, Doctoral Degree at the University of Marburg (Germany), teaches Practical Theology and Pastoral Counseling at Escola Superior de Teologia in São Leopoldo/Brazil.

Isolde Karle*

Gender Norms and Their Consequences for Body and Soul – a Challenge for the Christian Community

1. Gender as Habitus

When one examines gender identity, it becomes clear how closely body, mind and soul are related to each other. Through his concept of habitus, the French socio-logist Pierre Bourdieu has illustrated how, contrary to popular opinion, it is not the body which presents the objective, causal basis for the derivation of binary conceptions of gender, but it is rather the particular cultural conceptions and typologies which crystallize in the experience of corporeality. The binary differentiation of gender, which would not be possible without our familiar forms of culture and language, is so to speak "embodied". It is "in the embodied state – in the habitus of the agents, functioning as systems of schemes of perception, thought and action."[1] Consequently, with a habitus one is dealing with an unreflected process of internalization, with "embodied" habits, the *incarnation* of the schemes and structures of social praxis.

The asymmetry in bipolar gender relations is thus expressed first and foremost in posture and its corresponding scripts of perception. According to Bourdieu's thesis, this habitus exists primarily in two forms: one male, one female. Each gender-differentiated habitus exists in relation to the other. Accordingly, the habitus is created in the form of two opposing yet complementary *postures* (hexis) together with their respective *principles of vision*. While habitus refers to a deep structure which also encompasses the *schemes of perception*, with the term *hexis* Bourdieu refers to that external and perceivable ensemble of permanently acquired postures and physical movements. This ensemble of permanently acquired postures, which arise through the (unconscious) imitation of particular, gender-differentiated motor movements and behaviors, is a basic dimension of one's sense of social orientation. Consequently, the social aspect is efficiently embodied and naturalized via posture, primarily because posture and feeling correspond with each other. Thus gender norms exist "in the way in which people move, in their gestures, indeed even in the ways in which they eat."[2]

The secret behind the successful production of these two genders lies in the fact that it occurs to the most part "automatically", without conscious direction or reflection. It is anchored in the routines of the division of labour and the routines

---

*Translated from the original German by Stephen Lakkis.
[1] Pierre Bourdieu, Male Domination, Cambridge (Polity) 2001, 8. "The Habitus is the product as well as the producer of practices: repeated experiences condense in bodies as perceptive, cognitive and behavioral schemes and in this way remain actively present".
[2] Judith Lorber, Gender-Paradoxien, Opladen (Leske + Budrich) 1999, 68.

Gender Norms and Their Consequences for Body and Soul

of one's physical body. Each person, man or woman, is required, both implicitly and explicitly, constantly to emphasize those characteristics which correspond to the social definition of his or her gender identity and to carry out corresponding practices, while suppressing inappropriate behaviours.[3] "Early upbringing tends to inculcate ways of bearing the body, or various parts of it ..., ways of walking, holding the head or directing the gaze, directly in the eyes or at one's feet, etc., which are charged with an ethic, a politics and a cosmology."[4] Thus women learn to smile, look down and accept interruptions. In a particular way, women are taught how to sit, occupy space and adopt appropriate postures.

For example, among the emerging bourgeoisie of the 18th and 19th centuries, it was forbidden for a woman to play the cello since it would have required her to spread her legs.[5] When in 1845 a female cellist first performed publicly, it was not her musical skill which took centre stage but rather "the shameful and obliquely-posed question whether this musician would dare to take the instrument between her legs."[6] In bourgeois society a female musician – in contrast to a female member of the aristocracy – was subject to strict regulations. Women in the 18th century in particular were "rigidly subjected" to a newly developed "mimetic ideal"[7] which forbade any overly emotional facial expressions. Yet not only was the choice of instrument regulated, but also the instrumental piece itself. In their performances, women were "not to overstep the boundaries of tender femininity."[8] The piece was to be limited to the higher, "feminine" register; a hearty virtuoso piece performed with the entire body would be regarded as improper.

This example shows the wide-reaching consequences that were drawn from a gender-adequate habitus, particularly in the 19th century – the period when that dichotomous gender metaphysic (with which we still struggle) was developed. Today, a moral importance is still attached to a woman's posture, and this is clearly differentiated from the male perception of the body. The image of a drunken woman in public – who can no longer control her own body – generally strikes us as much more negative than if it were a man. Furthermore, the freedom given a girl or woman to move her body is limited. A woman's own clothing reduces her possibilities for movement. Her clothing "has the effect not only of masking the body but of continuously calling it to order ... without ever needing to prescribe or proscribe anything explicitly ... either because it

---

[3] Cf. Bourdieu, Die männliche Herrschaft, Frankfurt a.M. (Suhrkamp) 2005, 48, translated by Stephen Lakkis.

[4] Bourdieu, Male Domination, 27–28.

[5] Cf. Freia Hoffmann, Instrument und Körper. Die musizierende Frau in der bürgerlichen Kultur, Frankfurt a. M./Leipzig (Insel) 1991, 196ff.

[6] Ibid. 197.

[7] Ibid. 51.

[8] Ibid. 206.

254 Isolde Karle

constrains movement in various ways, like high heels or the bag which constantly encumbers the hands, and above all the skirt which prevents or hinders certain activities (running, various ways of sitting, etc)."[9] The collection of these mostly-implicit 'calls to order' then results in a particular *posture*, which persists even when the clothes no longer demand it: young women in pants and flat shoes still often walk with quick, small steps. These continual, tacit orders lead most women to completely accept arbitrary gender norms and proscriptions as natural and self-evident, "proscriptions which, inscribed in the order of things, insensibly imprint themselves in the order of bodies."[10]

In this way, the social order leads to a significant *transformation of the body and mind* "imposing a *differentiated definition* of the legitimate uses of the body ... which tends to exclude from the universe of the feasible and thinkable everything that marks membership of the other gender ... to produce the social artifact of the manly man or the womanly woman. The arbitrary *nomos* which institutes the two classes in objectivity takes on the appearance of a law of nature ... only at the end of a *somatization of the social relations of domination.*"[11]

2. The opacity and inertia of corporeally-anchored schemes

In western society – unlike traditional societies – male domination works in a very subtle way. It is a *symbolic, gentle and invisible form of violence* which reproduces the asymmetrical order of dual sexuality. It ensures that men and women develop differing habitus and brings women to submit 'voluntarily' to the gender norm and to limit themselves when they become mothers, for example, within the home or within a private female world.[12] "The effect of symbolic domination ... is exerted ... through the schemes of perception, appreciation and action that are constitutive of habitus ... Thus, the paradoxical logic of masculine domination and feminine submissiveness, which can, without contradiction, be described as both *spontaneous and extorted*, cannot be understood until one takes account of the *durable effects* that the social order exerts on women (and men)."[13]

Young girls and boys become familiar with the binary schemes of perception and appreciation through the experience of a gender-differentiated social order, and through socialization and upbringing. Yet this is not accessible to consciousness. "Already at five years old children participate in what they perceive

---

[9] Bourdieu, Male Domination, 29.
[10] Ibid. 56.
[11] Ibid. 23.
[12] Cf. Bourdieu, Die männliche Herrschaft, 64.
[13] Bourdieu, Male Domination, 37–38.

to be normal male or female activities."[14] Generally, this leads them to accept the social order as normal and natural just as it is. Thus most people anticipate their own fate, so to speak, by rejecting those career opportunities which are not allowed for and by pursuing those options which "naturally" suggest themselves. Correspondingly, we find that the appropriate functions or occupations for women are an extension of their domestic function – such as caring, teaching, the raising of children, social networking, assisting and advising. "The constancy of habitus that results from this is thus one of the most important factors in the *relative constancy of the structure of the sexual division of labour*"[15] as Bourdieu points out. Since these processes escape conscious control, we witness the often observed discrepancy between formulated, emancipatory declarations on the one hand, and factual, relatively traditional and gender-typical behavior on the other.

Last, but not least, the *asymmetry in the experience of corporeality* is evident in sexual practices and conceptions. Thus young men in particular describe a sexual relationship completely in the logic of conquest, while young women are socially prepared to experience sexuality as an emotionally highly charged experience.[16]

The creation of gender-differentiated habitus takes place in an essentially unobservable and insidious way. It is carried by a form of power "that is exerted on bodies, directly and as if by magic."[17] This symbolic violence is branded upon the deepest parts of the body in the form of *dispositions*. Dispositions are anchored deep in our bodies. The body is withdrawn from the directives of consciousness when it blushes, shivers or acts reflexively. Thus women often tacitly accept the barriers laid upon them, which leads to the contemporary *self-exclusion* of women in place of those explicit exclusions which are today prohibited by law. The foundation of symbolic violence lies in the dispositions which lend their hypnotic power to social injunctions, suggestions, seduction, threats and reproaches.[18] The question of emancipation is by no means focussed merely upon a 'dawning of consciousness' or enlightenment regarding this situation. Such an approach fails to appreciate the *opacity and inertia* that stem from the embedding of social structures in bodies.[19]

Of course, these observations are also valid for men. Men, too, are prisoners of the dominant gender conceptions and must learn over the long-term what it

---

[14] Helga Kotthof, Geschlechtertypisierung in der kindlichen Kommunikationsentwicklung. Ein Bericht über ausgewählte Forschung, 271, in: Jahrbuch für Pädagogik 1994. Geschlechterverhältnisse und die Pädagogik, Frankfurt a.M. (Peter Lang) 1994.
[15] Bourdieu, Male Domination, 95.
[16] Cf. ibid. 20.
[17] Ibid. 38.
[18] Ibid. 42.
[19] Cf. ibid. 40.

256 Isolde Karle

means to be a man, and thus superior. "Being a man, in the sense of *vir*, implies an ought-to-be, a *virtus*, which imposes itself in the mode of self-evidence, the taken-for-granted".[20] In the male body, too, there is inscribed an ensemble of dispositions, "inscribed in the body in the form of a set of seemingly natural dispositions, often visible in a particular way of sitting and standing, a tilt of the head, a bearing, a gait, bound up with a way of thinking and acting, an ethos, a belief, etc."[21] In this way, a man also learns to accept behaviours as unavoidable and natural – behaviours that for women are hardly possible. Men lay their arms protectively and possessively across the shoulders of a woman – the reverse image is hardly thinkable.

The social became flesh, and works as an *amor fati*, a bodily inclination. Bourdieu compares the construction of manliness with the construction of the noble man. Both forms of identity – to be manly and to be noble – are products of a social practice of transferral which ensures that this social identity becomes "natural", a habitus. As with the nobility, manliness must also be validated by other men and certified by recognized acceptance in the group of 'real men'. Many rites in school, the military, and police force contain such corresponding tests of manliness, which testify to the dependence of one's declaration of masculinity upon the judgement of the group.[22]

Manliness is extraordinarily vulnerable. Why else would so much energy in our society be invested in violent male games, above all in *sports*? Combat sports and the martial arts are particularly good at highlighting the visible signs of masculinity. It is for this reason that women find it particularly difficult to enter these sports. Men must continuously prove themselves in those most serious of competitive games: namely in politics and economics. *Competition* among men, which with the nobility found its classic expression in the duel, therefore plays a central role. To this extent, "*male privilege is also a trap*, and it has its negative side in the permanent tension and contention, sometimes verging on the absurd, imposed on every man by the duty to assert his manliness in all circumstances."[23]

Manliness lives from the fear of the feminine. For this reason, particular forms of courage – as required above all in the military and police force – are finally nothing more than expressions of fear: "*fear* of losing the respect or admiration of the group ... and being relegated to the typically female category of 'wimps' ... What is called 'courage' is thus often rooted in a kind of cowardice."[24] Dicta-

---

[20] Ibid. 49.
[21] Ibid.
[22] Cf. ibid. 52.
[23] Bourdieu, Male Domination, 50.
[24] Ibid. 52.

Gender Norms and Their Consequences for Body and Soul

torships function in a similar way. They live off the fear of men – the fear of being ostracized from the world of "hard men", murderers and tormentors.

To summarize: *it is not the biological body which produces, and is the ground for, gender identity, rather it is the gender order which leads to the feminization and masculinization of bodies, persons, behavioural codes, postures, corporeal experiences, schemes of perception, emotions and sensations.* Our culture directly imprints upon the body its gender via sexually differentiated habitus. In an even more extreme form, this can be observed in cultures which not only imprint upon the body but rather purposefully change or even mutilate it. In Chinese society the feet of young girls were bound into nine-centimetre-long stumps. In some African regions, the clitoris of pre-pubescent girls is excised until today. These are particularly extreme and painful forms of the gender-differentiated imprinting of the body. Yet they display once more the extent to which *the human body is to be understood as thoroughly, socially imprinted.*

3. The transformation of gender

Interestingly, Bourdieu notes that the Jewish culture of the 19th century expressly rejected the violent cult of hegemonic masculinity, even in its ritualized forms, such as in duelling or sport. The devaluing of physical exercises in favour of spiritual exercises promoted the development of gentler dispositions within the Jewish community.[25] Such counter-movements also appeared repeatedly in Christianity. As with Judaism, these movements are not universal, yet Jesus and the early church purposefully distanced themselves from a male dynamic which tended toward hegemony and violence. So, for example, Jesus rebukes Peter when he uses his sword to try and hinder Jesus' arrest. Jesus certainly did not avoid competition with the male elite of his time, yet, due to his deep convictions, he always pursued this on the spiritual level and not by means of physical violence. At the same time, he never allowed himself to be intimidated by the typical signs of male, hegemonic power.

Even more foundational is the baptismal formula from Gal 3:28, which testifies to the fact that in Christ, all former differences – race, class or gender – have lost their validity and relevance. Jürgen Roloff writes: "they are through being the prevailing way in which a person sees him- or herself and being the historical location of one's only definable factors."[26] The removal of barriers between men and women is an expression of the new creation in Christ which brings radical social change with it and which fundamentally relativizes and transforms sexual differences. That Gal 3:28 should be understood in this

---

[25] Cf. ibid. 51 n. 81.

[26] Jürgen Roloff, Die Kirche im Neuen Testament, Göttingen (Vandenhoeck & Ruprecht) 1993, 94.

consequential way can be displayed in the direct and obvious reference to the "old creation" in Gen 1. The Septuagint version of Gen 1:27 is adopted word for word in Gal 3:28c — and is done so as its *antithesis*: "God created them male and female" (Gen 1:27) becomes a direct negation: "no male and female" (Gal 3:28c).[27] As Ruth Heß points out: "Eschatologically, an extremely fundamental transcendence of gender is emphasized here."[28]

In and through Christ, a new creation has been formed. The existing world is consigned to the old creation, to the past aeon (1 Cor 7:31). "The orders of the failing old world are abolished through the 'new creation'."[29] To carry each other's burden (Gal 6:2) and to live in the freedom of the Spirit, which no longer allows any slavery and body-soul justifications of any kind (Gal 5:11ff), is the sign of the new creation. For in Christ the new creation is at hand, the old has passed away, the new is emerging (2 Cor 5:17).

Therefore, the baptismal formula in Gal 3:28 is to be understood as the reflected antithesis to Gen 1:27.[30] By "'putting on Christ' in a type of eschatological travesty (1 Cor 15:53f; 2 Cor 5:2–4), [the believers] are *incorporated* with their entire existence into Christ's salvific sphere."[31] A radical change of identity occurs. Their gender identity is "subversively dissolved"[32]; from a bodily, spiritual and cognitive perspective they have been freed from repressive gender norms.

This leads to the creation of a free space which allows people to live together in a 'de-dualised' and anti-hierarchical way. While the early church community practiced this approach at least partly, they also realistically pointed out that even our most elementary self-perceptions still require transformation in a way that is hardly imaginable to us: "We are now children of God, yet what we will be has not yet been made known" (1 Jn 3:2). This present, fragmentarily experienced corporeality and identity will only be unpacked properly in the eschaton. Yet at the same time, faith in Christ is already breaking apart disastrous and dichotomizing attributions and models of expectation in the present, *setting free new experiences both of body and identity*.

---

[27] Cf. Hartwig Thyen, "... nicht mehr männlich und weiblich ...". Eine Studie zu Galater 3,28, 109, in: Hartwig Thyen/Frank Crüsemann (Hg.), Als Mann und Frau geschaffen. Exegetische Studien zur Rolle der Frau, Gelnhausen u.a. (Burckhardthaus) 1978.
[28] Ruth Heß, "Es ist noch nicht erschienen, was wir sein werden". Biblisch (de)konstruktivistische Anstöße zu einer entdualisierten Eschatologie der Geschlechterdifferenz, 310, in: Ruth Heß/Martin Leiner (Hg.), Alles in allem. Eschatologische Anstöße. FS J. Christine Janowski, Neukirchen-Vluyn (Neukirchener Verlag) 2005. Thus the new figuration of gender in baptism also has a thoroughly bodily dimension. Cf. ibid.
[29] Thyen, "... nicht mehr männlich und weiblich ...", 109.
[30] Cf. ibid. 111.
[31] Heß, "Es ist noch nicht erschienen, was wir sein werden", 311.
[32] Ibid.

Gender Norms and Their Consequences for Body and Soul

This is a great challenge for the liberating practice of the Church regarding women who do not fit gender norms, homosexuals, transgender persons and intersexuals. The church must develop more sensitivity how the church itself has contributed to a gender system that is oppressing and deforming souls and bodies until today. Nobody should be obliged anymore to submit oneself to a certain gender class which is determining and limiting behaviour and the chances of participation in society. Everybody should have the chance to develop her or his own individual gifts and talents independent from gender lines. This would also mean that homosexuals who want to live together in the spirit of Christ, i.e. the spirit of freedom und trust, should have the possibility to get married like heterosexuals. Because: Not the details of anatomy but the spirit of love and freedom are decisive for the credibility of the church community.

The Author

Isolde Karle, Prof. Dr., born 1963; professor in Practical Theology, especially in Homiletics, Liturgy and Pastoral Care, at the Protestant Faculty of Theology at the Ruhr-University of Bochum. Research interests: gendertheory, theory of the pastoral profession, theory of church and the reform of the church, religion and illness/suffering, identity in modern society. Recent publications: „Da ist nicht mehr Mann noch Frau...". Theologie jenseits der Geschlechterdifferenz, Gütersloh 2006; Der Pfarrberuf als Profession. Eine Berufstheorie im Kontext der modernen Gesellschaft, Stuttgart 2008 (3rd ed.); Isolde Karle/Günter Thomas (Hg.), Krankheitsdeutung in der postsäkularen Gesellschaft, Stuttgart/Berlin 2009.

Johan Cilliers

Creating Space within the Dynamics of Interculturality: The Impact of Religious and Cultural Transformations in Post-Apartheid South Africa[1]

1. Introduction: On peeling an onion

The South African society is like an onion. The more skin you peel away, the more layers you discover. But hopefully there is a core somewhere. Our society is indeed a multi-layered phenomenon, with different levels of possible analysis, perspectives and meanings. This reminds one of the latest publication of the prolific German author and Nobel Prize winner, Günter Grass, an intense self-reflexive autobiography called *Beim Häuten der Zwiebel*[2] (On peeling an onion). In this book the onion functions as a metaphor for memory and with each layer of skin peeled away, one is taken back into history. But, says Grass, when you are peeling an onion you easily get tears in your eyes and this can influence the clarity of your vision. And sure enough, when peeling off the layers in search of the kernel, the essence of what constitutes our South African society, tears could often be shed – especially if we peel only with a view to be taken back into our history.

It is indeed a hazardous exercise to try and peel off a few layers of the South African society, endeavouring to reach a deeper level, perhaps a core, from which not only the past, but hopefully also the present and future of the South African society could be viewed. Such an act of peeling can reveal only a fraction of the multi-layered South African society – many other aspects could be presented, offering different angles of interpretation of a country in transformation. This paper represents an exercise in experiential peeling. It does, however, open up possibilities to reflect specifically on how the dynamic relationship between culture[3] and religion[4] contributes towards the trans-

---

[1] Abbreviated version of paper delivered at the international meeting of the International Academy of Practical Theology in Berlin, Germany, 30 March to 4 April 2007.
[2] Published by Steidl, 2006.
[3] Culture could of course be defined in many ways. According to Raiter and Wilson, it is *"those ideas, beliefs, feelings, values, and institutions, which are learned, and by which a group of people order their lives and interpret their experiences, and which give them an identity distinct from other groups"* (2005: 122). We will return to the whole issue of identity in 3. Other definitions of culture: *"Culture is that complex whole which includes knowledge, belief, art, morals, law, custom and any other capabilities and habits acquired by man as a member of society"* (Sarpong 2002: 40). Webb simply compares culture to the air that we breathe or water that surrounds a fish: *"We live and move about in the culture with which we are closely and invisibly enmeshed"* (2001: 21). The word *culture* comes from the Latin *colo*, which means to nurse (take care of), or to transform the earth through a plough (an instrument) in order to live.

Creating Space within the Dynamics of Interculturality   261

formation of a post-apartheid society, and how this relationship is being transformed and challenged itself.

2. Uncovering some (outer) layers of the South African society

The first level, or outer skin so to speak, could perhaps be described as that
which is glaringly evident, painfully visible and graphically depicted in the
public media. At a meeting of South African Christian Leaders (Sacla) held in
Pretoria on 17–20 July 2003, the gravest factors eroding South African
culture(s), and indeed the greatest challenges facing the church, were depicted
as seven Giants – alluding to the biblical narrative of David facing Goliath.
These seven Giants were identified as: HIV/Aids, Crime and Corruption,
Violence, Poverty and Unemployment, Sexism, Racism and the Crisis in the
South African Family.[5]

Obviously these giants are a reality and should be taken seriously. But ultimately they are only symptoms of more fundamental issues, only the outer
skin[6] of the onion. But what then are the *real forces* and *centres of power*

Culture therefore refers to the human achievement and endeavour which try to "cultivate" creation and the cosmos into a human space for living through symbols, metaphors, language, instruments (*techné*). Culture is the human attempt to "re-create" creation through spiritual-religious articulation (transcendency); ethically driven actions
(norms, values, taboos); aesthetic imagination (art), technical intervention (technology); dialogical verbalisation (language and speech) and social/political/juridical restructuring into a humane environment. Religion can therefore also not be understood
apart from its situation within culture (cf. Louw 2006: 9).

[4] Religion, being imbedded in culture, is as difficult to define as culture. Religion is co-
determined by the perspective of the religious person and his or her situation within (a
specific) culture. Religion could be defined holistically as the acts, rituals and ideas of
individuals and societies in which the relationship between the immanent reality and
the transcendent reality (or aspects thereof) becomes visible through word, image and
acts (cf. Hacking 2005: 6). Religion also harbours within itself the dimensions of spirituality and (the search for) meaning. The term "religion" is unfortunately often associated with rigid structures within which religious experiences and rituals are set. Perhaps
the term "spirituality" offers a wider lens to evaluate certain (religious) phenomena
taking place in culture. Spirituality can also be strongly linked to the search for meaning and the creation of "spaces" within which meaning can be nurtured (Cf. further on
in 3 our discussion on the role of space). In the light of our designated theme I will be
using the term "religion", but with a specific view on "spirituality" as an important
component of religion.

[5] Sacla Newsletter 28 May 2003.

[6] The following quotation from J.M. Coetzee's novel *The Master of Petersburg* (published by Secker and Warburg, 1994) puts it well: *"You are appalled by the hideous
face of hunger and sickness and poverty. But hunger and sickness and poverty are not
the enemy. They are only ways in which real forces manifest themselves in the world.
Hunger is not a force — it is a medium, as water is a medium. The poor live in their*

262 Johan Cilliers

behind the emergence of the seven giants in South Africa? There are no quick or sure-fit answers to this. Perhaps it has got to do with a clash and resultant implosion of divergent paradigms,[7] for instance between the phenomenon of so-called "Americanism",[8] and the African spirit of Ubuntu.[9] There seems to be *a vast difference between the Americanist understanding of (extreme) democratisation, which basically rests on individualism and privatisation on the one hand, and, on the other, the "democracy" of Ubuntu, which operates from the basis of community.* It is indeed a valid question whether Americanism, brought to Africa within the context of globalisation, is not slowly but surely eroding that which is typical of the African spirit. *Somehow it has been expected of South Africans to process and digest the workings and implications of globalisation within thirteen years after the dawn of our democracy, and to a*

---

hunger as fish live in water. The real forces have their origin in the centres of power, in the collusion of interests that takes place there."

[7] The whole issue of colonialism could of course be added here. Africa and South Africa in particular, are still bearing the scars of this "clash of paradigms".

[8] *Americanism* could best be described in terms of the keyword: *consumerism.* Globalisation here takes on the form of a materialistic imperialism, a market driven economical manipulation that networks in such a manner that a new "McWorld" is created, a world within which particular cultures are denied their regional and national features. E. Zwingle (1999: 12–13; cf. also Louw 2002: 340) characterises this brand of globalization as the "cultural assault" of McDonalds, Coca-Cola, Disney, Nike, MTV, and the English language. There is of course presently also a rising tide of "anti-Americanism" – in most cases linked to the foreign policies of the Bush Administration, and therefore called "Bushism".

[9] The belief that one is a human being through others ("I am because you are"). The term Ubuntu comes from the Zulu and Sotho versions of a traditional African aphorism, often translated as: "a person is a person through other persons": *Umuntu ngumuntu ngabantu. Motho ke motho ka batho.* It articulates a basic respect and compassion for others. As such, it is both a factual description and a rule of conduct or social ethic, both descriptive and prescriptive. (Ramose, 1999: 49f; Shutte, 1993: 46). Africans, indeed, have a more systemic understanding of life. Life is a dynamic space for holistic relationships, an integral whole of cosmic and social events. Africans adopt a non-analytical approach to our existence on this planet, epitomized in the words of A.A. Berinyuu (1988: 5): *"In Africa, there is no division and/or differentiation between the animate and inanimate, between the spirit and matter, between living and non-living, dead and living, physical and metaphysical, secular and sacred, the body and the spirit, etc. Most Africans generally believe that everything (human beings included) is in constant relationship with one another and with the invisible world, and that people are in a state of complete dependence upon those invisible powers and beings. Hence, Africans are convinced that in the activities of life, harmony, balance or tranquillity must constantly be sought and maintained. Society is not segmented into, for example, medicine, sociology, law, politics and religion. Life is a liturgy of celebration for the victories and/or sacrifices of others."* This differs quite considerably from a Western approach to life. Whilst analyses, solutions and consumerism are typical of the latter, myth and symbol, ritual and rhythm determine everyday life in the African context.

certain extent South Africans themselves have fallen into the trap of trying to achieve this.

But let us peel deeper into the South African society. At another level an intensified clash of paradigms is taking place between the dynamics of a market-driven economy, and a growing spiral of poverty. It is common knowledge that the sound South African economy has been praised as one of the greatest achievements of our country since 1994. Although the original intended growth rate of 6% per annum[10] has not yet been reached, it seems as if though the general condition of the economy is stable and indeed healthy, inter alia because the government has allowed the open market to function and create wealth without too much political interference. One of the paradoxes, however, is that in spite of political freedom gained through democracy, and in spite of increasing economic growth, violence and crime seem to be on the rise, or at least remain unacceptably high – even if statistics suggest a levelling out in terms of certain crime categories.[11] *Why did the dawn of democracy and increasing economic growth not bring with it a decline in crime and a safer and more secure society?*

This is not an easy question to answer. One possible analysis[12] would be that the South African society is in fact at present *not* a unity celebrating her diversity, in spite of constant political rhetoric reminding us of our democratic achievement in 1994 (epitomized in Archbishop Desmond Tutu's colourful phrase: *rainbow nation*), but rather *a nation of mobile, industrialized and individualized consumers.*

For centuries most South Africans were subjected to poverty and discrimination. The dawn of 1994 brought with it enormous expectations of "a better life for all". On the one hand, these expectations have not been met; on the contrary, for the majority the situation has worsened to intolerable levels. On the other hand, the mass media paint a picture of capitalistic bliss in a relentless propagandistic onslaught on all the senses, painfully reminding the masses that they in fact have not reached the goal of a new life, and are still living in abject deprivation. The end result of this scenario is predictable: utter frustration, and in some cases, bloody violence.

---

[10] Currently 4.2%. Projected rate for the next two years: 4.5%.

[11] According to the Crime Information Analysis Centre (CIAC) of the South African Police Service, the (reported) cases of murder were 25,965 per annum during 1994/1995, in comparison to 19,824 in 2003/2004. The (reported) cases of rape, however, increased from 44,751 in 1994/1995 to 52,733 in 2003/2004 – to mention only two categories of crime in South Africa.

[12] Cf., for instance Johann Rossouw in *Die Vrye Afrikaan* 1 Oktober 2004, 4–5; also Bylae by *Die Burger* 30 September 2006, 4.

3. Peeling towards the core – the search for a new identity?

It is clear that South Africa, as a young democracy, is struggling to find its identity.[13] The basic question facing South African society after apartheid is: *can we have both national unity and celebration of our diversity?*[14] Furthermore, what role can religion play in answering this question? According to Villa-Vicencio (1994: 115–126), there are different options for the co-existence of unity and diversity, ranging from unfavourable (in some cases, downright dangerous) to potentially viable.

One option would be that of *cultural assimilation*, in which cultures and cultural differences are assimilated into one another, up to the point where a fully homogenized end product is created, under so-called "social consensus". The problem with this, however, is the role of *power*, with the accompanying question: who determines the process (and even outcome) of the so-called consensus? Cultures that are not in consensus with the rest may be marginalized, or will remain so, being alienated and excluded to the detriment of the richness of our diversity. *This option seems to stress unity to the detriment of diversity.*

A second possibility would be one of *multicultural pluralism*, in which people from different cultures, ethnic and racial origins, as well as genders and religions have the right and freedom to express their identities within the character and the decision-making processes of the public realm (Villa-Vicencio 1994: 117–118). Within this model ethnicity and culture seem to be the driving forces in determining individual and social identity, and it would be a valid question to ask whether these emphases, given our history, will heal our society or rather prompt a regression into apartheid once again. The problem here again is the question of power, the dominant forces and role players, as opposed to the marginalized. *Whilst cultural assimilation stresses unity to the detriment of diversity, multicultural pluralism tends to overemphasize diversity against unity.*

---

[13] Perhaps this is epitomized best in the quest for an *African renaissance*, strongly advocated by President Thabo Mbeki. Although it has become a political slogan and is in danger of being commercialised, this quest still articulates Africa's longing for recognition, acknowledgment and therefore identity. Not only is it aimed at reviving political and economic structures, but also the reconstruction of African culture and self-esteem. It is linked to the notions of *Pax Africana* (African solutions for African problems) as well as *Pan-Africanism* (the social, political ideal of interconnectedness despite divisions on the African continent) (Cf. Landsberg and Kornegay 1998: 16), and intends to rejuvenate the "spirit" of Africa in a quest for dignity and freedom.

[14] Linked to this could be the question of the relationship between the effects of *globalisation* and the call for *glocalisation*. Glocalisation was coined by Robertson (1992) as an indication of the importance of local issues and the impact of culture on local communities. It guards against the tendency of globalisation to homogenize.

Creating Space within the Dynamics of Interculturality 265

A third option could be *cultural engineering*, in which a certain amount of intervention in, or moulding of, cultures could take place. Obviously, although South Africa is presently going through a period of reconfiguration, which entails certain measures to redress the imbalances of the past, for South Africans emerging from apartheid the very thought of cultural manipulation is hard to swallow. The concept of intervention begs the question of power once again: who does the engineering, and with what agenda? *In my opinion, this option could in fact destroy not only the communal discovery of a new unity, but also the richness of our diversity in our quest for a new identity.*

What in fact is needed is an approach that ensures *cultural openness* (Villa-Vicencio 1994: 120). This involves a co-mingling of cultures, which does not mean an assimilation, consummation or fusion of one within the other. Rather it operates with the presumption of equal worth and openness to the possibility of discovering together something that encompasses our particular cultures, but is also bigger than the sum total of that which we bring to the national table.

In my opinion this notion of cultural openness needs to be developed further, specifically with the potential role of religion in mind. Cultural openness could also be described in terms of *interculturality*,[15] as opposed to *inculturality*.[16]

---

[15] Interculturality is a set of processes through which relations between different cultures are constructed on a basis of equality and mutual respect. This concept emerged towards the end of the twentieth century as a correction or expansion of the existing paradigm of *inculturality*. Whilst inculturality emphasizes the fact that interpenetration takes place between cultures, interculturality emphasises exchange. The theological rationale for inculturality can be found in incarnational theology, stressing the fact that in this process the gospel can and should be enfleshed and embodied within the paradigm of a specific local culture (Cf. Louw 2006: 8–9). From a vast body of literature on this concept, the following may serve only as indication: Bennett, Milton (1998). Overcoming the Golden Rule: Sympathy and Empathy. In: Bennett Milton (Ed.), *Basic Concepts of Intercultural Communication. Selected Readings.* Yarmouth & London: Intercultural Press, pp.191–214; Bhabha, Homi K. (1994). *The Location of Culture.* London: Routledge; Brislin, Richard W. & Yoshida, Tomoko (Eds.) (1994). *Improving Intercultural Interactions. Modules for Cross-Cultural Training Programs.* Thousand Oakes, London, New Delhi: Sage; Brocker, Manfred & Nau, Heino H. (Hg.) (1997). *Ethnozentrismus. Möglichkeiten und Grenzen des interkulturellen Dialog.* Darmstadt: Wissenschaftliche Buchgemeinschaft; Cesana, Andreas (Hg.) (1999). *Interkulturalität – Grundprobleme der Kulturbegegnung. Mainzer Universitätsgespräche. Sommersemester 1998.* Mainz, Trier: Gutenberg Universitätsverlag; Demorgon, Jacques (1999). *Interkulturelle Erkundungen. Möglichkeiten und Grenzen einer internationalen Pädagogik.* Europäische Bibliothek interkultureller Studien Bd. 4. Frankfurt a.M.: Campus.

[16] The problem of inculturality could once again be that of power – it can easily happen that inculturation, though meant well, ends up by being "Christianization", in which the dominant culture of those doing the Christianization is imposed on the receiving culture. In the intercultural approach the separation between Christ and culture is no

The concept of interculturality could in turn be refined from the perspective of *interpathy*.[17] The latter denotes more than just sympathy. It is an inclusive compassion that is not only directed towards individuals, but also cultures and values. It operates from an unbiased, unconditional love, taking the ethics of love into systemic paradigms. Interpathy goes far beyond a condescending attitude[18] of a "superior" culture sympathizing with an inferior one, or giving handouts on the grounds of misguided compassion. It does not romanticize either – viewing, for instance, African culture through a rosy tourist lens of tribal drums, wooden artefacts or colourful traditional dresses. Interpathy, as mode of interculturality, operates from the basis of mutual respect, openness to the other, reciprocal understanding, compassion and enrichment. It adheres to a *porous hermeneutics*, in which the supposed boundaries of epistemologies are revisited frequently and crisscrossed in a spirit of genuine teachability.

In this regard religion can make a meaningful contribution – not, as unfortunately happens time and again, functioning as an agent that legitimizes the

---

longer accepted, nor the domination of one (Christian) culture over the other, but rather the interconnectedness between Christ and culture. It focuses on the meaning of Christian spirituality within culture as well as the mutual exchange of paradigms between the two, a sharing with the intention to empower within a relationship of reciprocity. One is reminded of the classical distinctions concerning the relationship between Christian faith and culture (Christ and Culture) proposed by R.H. Niebuhr in 1951. He describes the rejection and anti-model: Christ against culture (58-92); the accommodation model: the Christ of culture (93–122); the synthesis model; Christ above culture, i.e. to maintain both the distinctions between Christ (his Lordship) and culture as well as the relatedness to culture, "both-and" (127–128); the dualistic model: Christ and culture in paradox (154–191); and the operational model: Christ the transformer of culture (192–228). Niebuhr himself believes that, although Christ is above culture (different), He operates through it to transform (convert) it. He still works with the so-called object-subject split in a polar model, i.e. the presupposition that according to the substantial difference between the two, the relationship has to be re-established (cf. Louw 2006: 8).

[17] First used by David W. Augsburger in his *Pastoral Counseling Across Cultures*, Philadelphia: Westminster, 1986. According to him interpathy is *"an intentional cognitive envisioning and affective experiencing of another's thoughts and feelings, even though the thoughts rise from another process of knowing, the values grow from another frame of moral reasoning, and the feelings spring from another basis of assumptions"* (1986: 56).

[18] Often our (body) language reveals our self-absorbing interests. Language, of course, remains a significant element of intercultural communication. *"Language is the medium through which a culture expresses its world view[...] Like culture in general, language is learned and it serves to convey thoughts; in addition it transmits values, beliefs, perceptions, norms, and so on"* (Jandt 2004: 224). *"Vom ersten Moment an hat sich Sprache als wesentliches Element in interkulturellen Begegnung herausgestellt. Begegnung zwischen Menschen unterschiedlicher Kulturen ist Übersetzungsarbeit, die allerdings nur bedingt gelingt"* (Federschmidt et al. 2002: 19).

Creating Space within the Dynamics of Interculturality 267

status quo of cultural boundaries or separateness. Its dimension of spirituality should rather help to safeguard society from changing that which is only temporal into something permanent or eternal, giving that which is transient a rigid, stable value. Religion should serve the movement from stringency to contingency, from status quo to status flux. Religion can help create a *space for graceful neighbouring*.[19]

The notion of *creative and respectful space* [20] might be explored further. The *Institute for Justice and Reconciliation*, which in the past three years has facilitated several interactions in communities across the country, aimed at creating and fostering dialogue between former enemies and ordinary citizens who endeavour to build a common future after generations of violent conflict, has developed an approach that aims at so-called "safe spaces" (cf. Du Toit 2003: 212–217). These spaces originate in relationships where *honesty* is a sine qua non, but held in tension with *respect*. In other words: differences are put on the table and not hidden or masked, but these differences may never lead to disrespect of the other. On the other hand, *acknowledgment* of past and present transgressions is held in tension with *responsibility* – a deep confession coupled with the sincere desire to act and to transform that which was and still is wrong in our society. In this way, through mutual adherence to these four basic values, a framework for dialogue in a "safe space" can be created: honesty, but with respect; acknowledgment, but with responsibility.

---

[19] Diana N. Cheifetz has written a beautiful essay on graceful neighbouring, which she subtitles: *Dancing with our diversity*. She uses the metaphor of dance to illustrate some rules or guidelines for "graceful neighbouring" – one could say, interculturality. The first is simply to be aware of others on the dance floor of society (2006: 16). Not to be so self-focused and engrossed with your "own" movements, but rather gracefully becoming part of the whole. A second rule would be to acknowledge, with respect, the others around you – very much like the curtsy with which medieval dancers opened up the dance. To acknowledge one another is to accept and respect the "otherness" of the other. A third rule could be added to this: to respect the space, and from time to time even to create the space, between dancers. There should be closeness without familiarity, but also space without alienation. Graceful neighbouring can mean honouring the space in between, so we can move together respectfully even with our differences (2006: 22). Of course, dancing must be learnt. Before mastering it, many toes might be stepped on and many egos end up stretched out on the floor!

[20] The notion of space is of course not a new one. The Greeks already referred to the importance of space in our quest for being human. The Greek word *Chora* means space or place and could also be interpreted as the *attitude* through which humans fill space with values, perceptions and associations, resulting in a created relational environment, a systemic and hermeneutical arena for living with meaning and dignity. *Chora* represents a nourishing and maternal receptacle, a womb that defines the quality of the places (*topoi*) where we encounter one another. Indeed, in this space we cannot exist without one another; it is where we meet in our diversity and unity, but also as perpetrators and victims.

The concept "safe space" does not indicate neutrality or inactivity, or a type of securocracy.[21] On the contrary, it intends a spiritual space of intimacy, where reciprocal enrichment can take place. Perhaps we can coin a helpful phrase here, building on the notion of Ubuntu: what is needed in South Africa is an *intercultural and interpathetic space for redefining our identity. Religion, being part of culture, can operate as a definitive and formative space-creator and space-setter within culture.*

Within this space, a new South African identity may be formed. Within this space we have reached a deep level of the South African onion, a core: the search for identity. I am of the opinion that what transpires at this core in the years to come will influence all the layers of our society; that our mutual understanding of our identity will in fact be the most profound factor in shaping our communal future. It is exactly here, in my opinion, that the church and religion face their deepest challenge: either to be a stagnant or even destructive role player, or a heuristic agent that acts as midwife for our country in the fulfilment of her new birth. South African society is like an onion. But peeling it need not only bring tears.

References

Augsburger, D.W. 1986. *Pastoral Counseling Across Cultures.* Philadelphia: Westminster.

Bennett, M. 1998. Overcoming the Golden Rule: Sympathy and Empathy. (Ed.), *Basic Concepts of Intercultural Communication. Selected Readings.* Yarmouth & London: Intercultural Press, pp.191–214.

Berinyuu, A.A. 1988. *Pastoral Care to the Sick in Africa.* Frankfurt a.M.: Peter Lang.

Bhabha, H.K. 1994. *The Location of Culture.* London: Routledge.

Brislin, R.W. & Yoshida, T. (Eds.) 1994. *Improving Intercultural Interactions. Modules for Cross-Cultural Training Programs.* Thousand Oakes, London, New Delhi: Sage.

Brocker, M. & Nau, H.H. (Hg.) 1997. *Ethnozentrismus. Möglichkeiten und Grenzen des interkulturellen Dialog.* Darmstadt: WBG.

Cesana, A. (Hg.) 1999. *Interkulturalität – Grundprobleme der Kulturbegegnung. Mainzer Universitätsgespräche. Sommersemester 1998.* Mainz, Trier: Gutenberg Universitätsverlag.

Cheifetz, D.N. 2006. Graceful Neighboring: Dancing with our Diversity. In *Weavings* xxi: 4 July/August 2006, 15–23.

Coetzee, JM 1994. *The Master of Petersburg.* London: Secker and Warburg.

---

[21] John de Gruchy, referring to the art of reconciliation, speaks of the *creating of space for interfacing* in a post-apartheid South Africa (2002: 148–149).

Creating Space within the Dynamics of Interculturality

De Gruchy, J.W. 2002. *Reconciliation. Restoring Justice*. David Philip: Cape Town.

Demorgon, J. 1999. *Interkulturelle Erkundungen. Möglichkeiten und Grenzen einer internationalen Pädagogik*. Europäische Bibliothek Interkultureller Studien Bd. 4. Frankfurt a.M.: Campus.

Du Toit, F. (Ed.) 2003. *Learning to live together. Practices of social reconciliation*. Cape Town: Institute for Justice and Reconciliation.

Federschmidt, K.; Hauschildt, E.; Schneider-Harpprecht, C.; Temme, K. und Weiss, H. (Hg.) 2002. *Handbuch Interkulturelle Seelsorge*. Neukirchen-Vluyn: Neukirchener.

Grass, G. 2006. *Beim Häuten der Zwiebel*. Steidl.

Hacking, J. 2005. Kunst en religie. In *Wereld en Zending. Tijdschrift voor interculturele theologie*. 1 (2005). 4–17.

Jandt, F.E. (Ed.) 2004. *Intercultural Communication. A Global Reader*. London: Sage.

Landsberg, C. and Kornegay, F. 1998. *The African Renaissance: A Quest for Pax Africana and Pan Africanism in South Africa and Africa*. FGD Occasional Paper No 17 Braamfontein: FGD.

Louw, D.J. 2002. Pastoral Hermeneutics and the Challenge of a Global Economy: Care to the living Human Web. In *The Journal of Pastoral Care and Counseling*. Vol. 56/4, 339–350.

Louw, D.J. 2006. Cura Vitae. *Illness and the healing of life. Guidelines for pastoral care*. Stellenbosch, Faculty of Theology: Unpublished document.

Niebuhr, H.R. 1951. *Christ and Culture*. New York: Harper and Row.

Raiter, M. & Wilson, M. 2005. Culture, Human Identity, and Cross-cultural Ministry: Some Biblical Reflections. In *Reformed Theological Review* Vol. 64, December 2005, No. 3, 121–134.

Ramose, Mogobe B. 1999. *African Philosophy through Ubuntu*. Harare: Mond.

Robertson, R. 1992. *Globalization, Social Theory and Global Culture*. London: Sage.

Rossouw, J. 2004. Kerkwees in 'n veranderde tegniese milieu: Gelowige Afrikaners vanaf die grafosfeer na die videosfeer. In: *Die Vrye Afrikaan* 1 Oktober 2004, 4–5.

Sarpong, K.S. 2002. *Peoples Differ. An Approach to Inculturation in Evangelisation*. Sub-Saharan Publishers.

Shutte, A. 1993. *Philosophy for Africa*. Rondebosch, South Africa: UCT Press.

Villa-Vicencio, C. 1994. Theology and Culture in South Africa: Beyond multiculturalism. In *Theology Today* 51/1 April 1994, 115–126.

Webb, W.J. 2001. *Slaves, Women and Homosexuals. Exploring the Hermeneutics of Cultural Analysis.* Intervarsity Press.

Zwingle, E. 1999. Goods move. People move. Ideas move. And Cultures change. *National Geographic* Vol. 196/2, 12–13.

The Author

Johan Cilliers, Prof. Dr., born 1954; associate professor in Homiletics and Liturgy at the Faculty of Theology at the University of Stellenbosch in South Africa, vice-president of *Societas Homiletica*. Research interests: homiletics and ethics; liturgy and aesthetics; ritual and interculturality. Recent publications: *The living voice of the gospel. Revisiting the basic principles of preaching.* Stellenbosch (2004); *God for us? An analysis and evaluation of Dutch Reformed preaching during the Apartheid years.* (2006); *Binne die kring-dans van die kuns. Die betekenis van estetika vir die gereformeerde liturgie.* (2007).

Claire Wolfteich

Prayer as Liberating Practice:
Theological Complexities in Two Case Studies

Prayer has been integral to many movements for social justice – from the anti-apartheid movement in South Africa to the Civil Rights movement in the United States. Yet, few scholars have reflected critically on the theological complexities of such integration. This paper will explore two case studies in order to open up such reflection.[1] A call for prayer to bring down the South African apartheid government in the mid 1980s argued for an understanding of prayer as prophetic and as integrally, necessarily, related to liberating practice. Cesar Chavez and the farm worker movement in the United States in the 1960s and 1970s embodied a belief that prayer can serve dual, related functions: the inner spiritual renewal of persons and communities as well as the attainment of social, economic, and political ends. These cases contradict an exclusively private and interior understanding of prayer. They also point to the idea that social justice or liberating practice should not be understood apart from prayer. In both cases, however, the linking of prayer and social justice is not unproble-matic; each case involves some controversy and raises practical theological dilemmas.

Case Study: Prayer for an End to Unjust Rule – South Africa

After decades of suffering under the apartheid regime in South Africa, a group of South African church leaders in 1985 called upon Christian congregations to gather on June 16 – the anniversary of the Soweto uprising – to pray for the end of the government. Many of the churches had issued statements condemning apartheid. Some had declared apartheid to be a heresy. Christian leaders in the South African struggle for liberation were clear: apartheid was against God's will.[2] And yet, change had not come. The Botha regime in fact was intensifying the discrimination and violent repression.

Following a rallying cry by Rev. Allan Boesak, a group of South African Council of Church leaders published this theological rationale for the prayer to end unjust rule:

> We have prayed for our rulers, as is demanded of us in the scriptures [alluding
> to, for example, 1Timothy 2:1–3]. We have entered into consultation with

---

[1] This paper draws upon research that I have published in my book *Lord Have Mercy: Praying for Justice with Conviction and Humility* (San Francisco: Jossey Bass, 2006).
[2] World Council of Churches,"Harare Declaration" (1985; repr., World Council of Churches Programme to Combat Racism. PCR Information: Reports and Background Papers: Southern Africa: The Harare and Ai-Gams Declarations: A Call for Freedom and Independence for South Africa and Namibia, no. 23, 1986): 16. Citations are to the World Council of Churches Programme edition.

them, as is required by our faith [...] We now pray that God will replace the present structures of oppression with one that are just, and remove from power those who persist in defying his laws, installing in their place leaders who will govern with justice and mercy.[3]

The call for prayer turned out to be highly controversial. Theologians and church leaders debated it; newspapers printed a running stream of controversy. What was prophetic to some was, to others, going too far, wrong-headed, presumptuous. Not surprisingly, defenders of apartheid resisted the call to prayer. More difficult was the painful, public split among church leaders working for the same anti-apartheid cause. What was at the heart of this controversy?

South African theologian John de Gruchy pointed to an otherworldly, privatized spirituality as the reason for resistance to the prayer. He argued, in fact, that such spirituality led Christians to become passive collaborators with an evil government. Prayer is political, he claimed. It is just a question of which politics prayer supports:

> [...] what is new for many people is that prayer should no longer be harnessed in support of those in power and the maintenance of the status quo, but in the service of the transformation of society. This does not mean that Christians should no longer pray for those in authority, but that they should pray for them on the basis of what the kingdom of God requires of rulers. The priestly, prayerful service which the church renders to the state cannot be separated, as Karl Barth shows, from its prophetic responsibility.[4]

Critics argued, however, that the prayer could unintentionally incite violence, encouraging people to take matters into their own hands to try to remove the government by force.[5] We need to be careful, they said, about the kind of action to which our prayer leads. Was this just another example of the passive, status-quo-supporting church? Or was this a correct word of caution?

The Anglican Archbishop of Cape Town, Rev. Phillip Russell, thought that caution was appropriate. Russell opposed apartheid but did not support the prayer for an end to unjust rule. He argued that one cannot negotiate with a government when one is asking God to remove it from office. If the church entered into this prayer, then, it would need to stop its efforts to meet with and influence the government, an unwise move in his view. Russell also noted that the prayer would require a change in the South African prayer book and liturgy. He did

---

[3] "A Theological Rationale and a Call to Prayer for an End to Unjust Rule," in: *A Call for an End to Unjust Rule*, 26.

[4] John de Gruchy, "Introduction," in: *Cry Justice!: Prayers, Meditations, and Readings from South Africa*, ed. John de Gruchy (Maryknoll, NY: Orbis Books, 1986), 36.

[5] "Statement by Prof. Ben Engelbrecht and some staff members of the Department of Religious Studies, University of Witwatersrand", in: *A Call for an End to Unjust Rule*, 165–167.

Prayer as Liberating Praxis: Theological Complexities in Two Case Studies   273

think that the call had a scriptural justification but, given the profound implications, he refused to commit the Church of the Province of South Africa to
it. The highest courts of the church would need to deliberate about the matter.[6]

Rev. Peter Storey, the head of the Methodist church in South Africa and a key
anti-apartheid leader at the time, agreed that Christian spirituality and a struggle for social justice go hand in hand. And yet, Storey also did not support the
prayer to end unjust rule. As he later wrote: "in terms of the Methodist doctrine
of grace, I did not believe that we were committed 'to pray prayers which limit
the operation of that grace to one option only.' While God might well decide
upon that option, 'it is not our business to limit him to it.'"[7] Some other theologians concurred, saying that the prayer to end unjust rule contradicted scripture and tradition and was "presumptuous both in its approach to God and to
the churches of God."[8] Was it "presumptuous" to pray for the end of the government? Or was it boldly prophetic?

Case Study #2: Cesar Chavez and the Farm Workers

In the spring of 1966, a group of farm workers and supporters set out on a
march from Delano, California to the state capitol of Sacramento. Mexican and
Filipino immigrants, the farm workers were struggling for a decent wage and
humane working conditions. Months before, they had declared a strike against
the grape growers; month after month the strike dragged on and the farmworkers encountered violence and intimidation. The march from Delano to
Sacramento was a dramatic effort to publicize *la causa* and gain support for the
grape strike. It was also, in the word used by Cesar Chavez, a *peregrinación,* a
pilgrimage, an act of penance to recommit the movement to nonviolence.

According to Chavez, the march would be "public penance for the sins of the
strikers, their own personal sins as well as their yielding perhaps to the feelings
of hatred and revenge in the strike itself."[9] For Chavez, the spiritual dimension
of the struggle was critical. He believed that the "success" of the movement

---

[6] Philip Russell, "Pastoral Letter of 7 June 1985", in *A Call for an End to Unjust Rule*,
172–175.
[7] Peter Storey, "Prayer in the Anti-Apartheid Struggle" (unpublished paper, Prayer and
Social Engagement Conference hosted by the Church and Theology in the Contemporary World Project, Berlin, May 27–29, 2004), 5. Storey here quotes directly from his
President's Update which was sent to all Methodist leaders on June 14, 1985.
[8] "Statement by Prof. Ben Engelbrecht and some staff members of the Department of
Religious Studies, University of Witwatersrand", in: *A Call for an End to Unjust Rule*,
165–167.
[9] Spencer Bennett, "Civil Religion in a New Context: The Mexican-American Faith of
César Chávez," in: *Religion and Political Power*, eds. Gustavo Benavides and M.W.
Daly (Albany, New York: State University of New York Press, 1989): 159.

depended on its continual spiritual renewal through prayer, penance, and fasting. The march to Delano was a kind of physical purgation or ascetical practice. Chavez said, "We wanted to be fit not only physically but also spiritually, and we wanted to stress nonviolence even more, build confidence, and have more visible nonviolent tactics."[10]

While Chavez sought a kind of spiritual rededication and purification, he and others in the movement clearly sought economic and political benefits as well – contracts with growers, improved wages, public support, political power. They were indeed somewhat successful in these aims. What began as a small group in Delano swelled to thousands as supporters joined the march to the state capitol. A few days before the procession reached Sacramento, the National Farm Workers Association secured a contract with a major company, the Schenley Corporation. Chavez briefly left the march to negotiate the contract. On Easter Sunday the marchers poured exuberantly onto the steps of the state capitol. Union co-founder Dolores Huerta publicly demanded that the governor call a special session of the legislature to establish a collective bargaining law in California. Was this a pilgrimage? Whereas the destination of a pilgrimage typically is a holy site, here the destination is the center of state government. Is the merging of piety and politics here problematic, or consonant with a liberating understanding of spirituality?

Analysis: Prayer as Liberating Practice

In the particular example from the South African context, proponents of the prayer to end unjust rule saw prayer as itself liberating and as integrally connected to social and political action on behalf of the oppressed. Prayer and political action went together. South African theologian Charles Villa-Vicencio, for example, wrote that the biblical tradition "knows no gap between the sacred and the secular, between prayer and social engagement."[11] He described prayer as a kind of "eschatological symbol": "If politics be the art of the possible, then prayer is the quest for what is not immediately possible but may be possible tomorrow. Such is the nature of Christian hope [...]." Prayer rightfully understood does not lead to passive wishing or waiting but rather calls one forward to work under God's grace for that for which one prays, so that, in the words of the Lord's Prayer, "thy kingdom come." Prayer becomes a "lure drawing one forward to the end for which one is praying."[12]

---

[10] Susan Ferriss and Ricardo Sandoval, *The Fight in the Fields: Cesar Chavez and the Farmworkers Movement* (New York: Harvest/HBJ Books, 1997), 117.

[11] Charles Villa-Vicencio, "Some Refused to Pray: the Moral Impasse of the English-Speaking Churches," in: *A Call for an End to Unjust Rule*, 44.

[12] Charles Villa-Vicencio, "Some Refused to Pray: the Moral Impasse of the English-Speaking Churches," in: *A Call for an End to Unjust Rule*, 45.

Clearly, in the South African case, those who supported the prayer for an end to unjust rule saw prayer as a form of prophetic practice. It named evil (specifically) and called (with specificity) for change that would free a community from concrete political, economic, and cultural oppression. This understanding of prayer as prophetic became more clear several months after the call was issued, when a group of South African theologians published *The Kairos Document.*

The Kairos Document sharply critiqued "state theology" – a "blasphemous" attempt to give a racist, oppressive government theological justification. The document described proponents of state theology as "false prophets." It also denounced "church theology," the inadequate responses of the English-speaking churches that sought reform and reconciliation with the state, compromising with rather than confronting structural injustice. Why have the churches not developed an adequate social analysis and political strategy to combat apartheid?

> The answer must be sought in the type of faith and spirituality that has dominated Church life for centuries [...]. Social and political matters were seen as worldly affairs that have nothing to do with the spiritual concerns of the Church. Moreover, spirituality has also been understood to be purely private and individualistic [...]. And finally the spirituality we inherit tends to rely upon God to intervene in his own good time to put right what is wrong in the world. That leaves very little for human beings to do except to pray for God's intervention. It is precisely this kind of spirituality that, when faced with the present crisis in South Africa, leaves so many Christians and Church leaders in a state of near paralysis.[13]

In contrast, the *Kairos* authors advocated a more radical "prophetic theology"; they argued, Christians need to make a "bold and incisive response that is prophetic, a response that does not give the impression of sitting on the fence but is clearly and unambiguously taking a stand." As opposed to the false spirituality that separates faith and politics, prophetic theology is infused with "a truly biblical spirituality [which] would penetrate into every aspect of human existence and would exclude nothing from God's redemptive will." Prayer is part of a prophetic response, but prayer cannot simply serve the "need of the individual for comfort and security." The prayer of the community, rather, "must be re-shaped to be more fully consistent with a prophetic faith [...]." Prayer must explicitly name the evil forces operating in South Africa and it cannot be separated from active participation in the struggle for liberation, civil disobedience, and mobilization of all Christians to work for a change of government.[14]

---

[13] World Council of Churches, *The Kairos Document: Challenge to the Church: A Theological Comment on the Political Crisis in South Africa* (Geneva: World Council of Churches, 1985), 22.

[14] World Council of Churches, *The Kairos Document: Challenge to the Church: A Theological Comment on the Political Crisis in South Africa* (Geneva: World Council of Churches, 1985), 23, 28, 29.

276 Claire Wolfteich

In the farm worker example, prayer is seen as liberating in a somewhat different sense. Prayer liberates not only from social oppression but also, perhaps primarily, from the chains of our shared human sinfulness. Dolores Huerta described the meaning of Chavez' fast in this way: "I know it's hard for people who are not Mexican to understand, but this is part of the Mexican culture – the penance, the whole idea of suffering for something, of self-inflicted punishment. [...] Cesar has often mentioned in speeches that we will not win through violence, we will win through fasting and prayer." Chavez saw no dichotomy between his spiritual practices and his prophetic work: "I said to myself, if I'm going to save my soul, it's going to be through the struggle for social justice."[15] For Chavez, prayer was a path of repentance and spiritual renewal – seeking freedom specifically from the temptation to respond to violence and oppression with violence. Only with that inner renewal could the liberation from political and economic oppression – the success of the movement – be achieved.

Practical Theological Questions at Stake

The case studies here described call into question understandings of prayer that are largely focused on the personal and interior life. They argue for prayer as a kind of liberating practice – a public lament, a way to give voice to the marginalized as they name evil, a petition for release from oppression. Indeed, they point to a powerful connection between prayer and freedom – not simply in terms of an individual's personal freedom from sin (although Chavez reminds us that this dimension does not drop out in a social struggle for justice) but also as a community's freedom from political and economic oppression. Prayer expresses the needs and hopes of a community that in its suffering nevertheless or even more intensely so trusts in a God of justice and solidarity. Prayer also is a bold call upon God to be not just companion but also the One who must bring about transformation.

It is possible that in prayer communities discover or come to know more fully God as a God of justice, compassion, and power. Here I recall the arguments of Craig Dykstra, Dorothy Bass, and others that practices have epistemological horizons – that they not only reflect belief but that we come to know in and through practices.[16] I think this must hold true particularly for a practice such as prayer. And so, such case studies should lead us to explore what oppressed communities come to know in and through their prayer – and how such knowledge is interpreted and how it becomes liberating (or not) in their particular

---

[15] Jacques Levy, *Cesar Chavez: Autobiography of La Causa* (New York: W.W. Norton & Company, 1975), 277, 276.
[16] See, for example, Craig Dykstra and Dorothy C. Bass, "A Theological Understanding of Christian Practices", in Miroslav Volf and Dorothy C. Bass, eds., *Practicing Theology: Beliefs and Practices in Christian Life* (Grand Rapids, Michigan: Eerdmans, 2002), 13–32.

contexts. It seems clear too that the cases argue for a mutual relationship between prayer and other forms of liberating action: prayer is not "enough" without corresponding action but neither is action sufficient without flowing from and flowing back into the Source of grace and power.

At the same time, these case studies raise practical theological questions for our consideration. I would characterize these questions as related to issues of discernment, the potential danger of instrumentalizing prayer, and the proper place of religious expression in differing public, pluralistic contexts. Reflection upon the case studies prompts one to ask: What exactly does it mean to be "prophetic" in a particular, complex political situation? With what degree of specificity does the prophet know or come to discern the will of God, and when does "prophecy" blur into presumption? How do we distinguish between an authentic integration of piety and a struggle for social justice, on the one hand, and the misuse of prayer as a political tool? Moreover, the place of spiritual practice in a social movement becomes quite complicated in contexts of religious pluralism. In what sense is a movement a spiritual community – or even the church? What is the appropriate place of tradition-specific spiritual practice in a movement that is religiously diverse (in which case the integration of piety could lead to conflicts and even questions of integrity for supporters) and/or in a movement that seeks to effect change in the broader public sphere? As we continue to explore the public and liberating nature of prayer, it will be critical for practical theologians to attend closely to such questions.

The Author

Claire Wolfteich, Prof. Dr., associate professor of practical theology and spiritual formation at Boston University, co-director of the Centre for Practical Theology. Research interests: religion and public life, history of Christian spirituality, American Catholicism, work and faith, spiritual practices, women and religion. Recent publications: Lord, Have Mercy: Praying for Justice with Conviction and Humility (2006); Navigating New Terrain: Work and Women's Spiritual Lives (2002), and American Catholics Through the Twentieth Century: Spirituality, Lay Experience, and Public Life (2001).

Terry A. Veling

Theological Method: A Way of Life

Introduction

For some years now, I've never quite known where to place myself as a theologian. When I am asked (at conferences or conventions, for example), "What is your area?" or "What do you teach?", I always feel a little lost for words. None of the designated areas of theology offer me a ready place to hang my hat.

When I look at the books on my shelves, there seem so few that qualify as "theology books" – unless one considers that books on philosophy, culture, poetry, education, etc, have something to do with theology. I've always had an instinct that theology isn't meant to operate as a discipline unto its own or with a haughtiness that separates it from other human disciplines. If it is a "divine discourse" or a "sacred discipline," then it seems to me that the Christian tradition has always urged the intimate bond between the divine and the human.

When I look at the courses I teach, a lot of them are "theology and ..." type courses (e.g. theology and culture, theology and literature) in which I attempt to connect theology with human concerns and the signs of the times. I like the opening statement from *Gaudium et spes* when it affirms that nothing authentically human is alien to the Gospel.

I was initially attracted to practical theology because of its interests in connecting theories/ideas/texts with practice/life/reality. It seemed to understand the link between theology and life, heaven and earth, question and answer, call and response. I also liked its lack of regard for itself, that it didn't seem too preoccupied with itself. It didn't feel "boxed-in" or "pinned-down." I liked its beautiful ambiguity, its unabashed complexity, its passion, its life, its energy. As Karl Rahner suggests, "*everything* is its subject-matter."[1] Moreover, it seemed to give me a place to hang my hat, so that when someone asked about what I do or what I teach or what my area was, I could reply: "practical theology."

Of course, the next question would be, "what's that?" – but at least a conversation could ensue. Or, people would simply be satisfied, "oh, so you make theology practical and concrete in people's real lives" (the typical stock-standard response).

I have a love-hate relationship with the phrase "practical theology." It's a cold, hard term. It also carries connotations of making theology practical lest it be of

---

[1] Karl Rahner, "Practical Theology within the Totality of Theological Disciplines," *Theological Investigations 9* (New York: Herder and Herder, 1972), p. 104.

Theological Method: A Way of Life

little or no use. I like the Catholic instincts behind the phrase "pastoral theo-logy" – to shepherd each other's lives, to be pastoral people through and through, filled with God's love and mercy. That's much more poetic than being "practical." But of course "pastoral" also has its own connotations of pastoral care, counselling, etc, etc (none of which I am trained in).

In my recent book, *Practical Theology: On Earth as It Is in Heaven,* I was sur-prised to find myself arguing against practical theology as much as I argued for it.[2] There are conceptions of practical theology that are misconceptions. For example, that theology needs to be made practical. Or that theology isn't of much use, unless it can be made useful. Or that we need to take theology – which sits in a rarefied and abstract realm – and turn it into something relevant and applicable. Generally speaking, Western society doesn't like to suffer useless things (or useless people). It likes progress and achievement. It likes concrete facts and ideas that are tested. It likes things that are workable and ef-fective – even though, any trip to the shopping mall will quickly reveal all the plethora of useless things we produce and consume.

Many people are interested in the method of practical theology, as though it offered a secret recipe that could produce successful outcomes. The word *method,* however, comes from the Greek word, *methodos,* which means a *path* or a *way.* Practical theology is a choice to practice a theological way of life – a choice or a decision that doesn't come at the end of a process like an outcome, but rather stands at the beginning, like a true test of faith: "Can I practice *this way of life?*"

What I learnt from writing a book on practical theology is that to venture a theological life is *to live theologically.* It is not so much to ask about the ways that theology can be made practical; rather, it is to ask how the practices of my life can be made *theological.*

Theological Method – A Way of Life

Method and theory are closely related words. According to the early Greeks, one must necessarily have a path or a way (*hodos*) in order to attain knowledge. In other words, anyone who proposes a theory typically brings with them a path or a method of inquiry that helped them arrive at the theory. For this reason, people are often interested in the *path of thought* as much as they are in the resulting *theory.* A person's *method* or *way* of pursuing knowledge is crucial – not simply as a forerunner to great theories or ideas – but as the very "stuff" of theory, the very thing that makes theories interesting, because we are able to

---

[2] Terry Veling, *Practical Theology: On Earth as It Is in Heaven* (Maryknoll, N.Y.: Orbis Books, 2005). A fuller treatment of this paper can be found in chapter eight and the epilogue.

witness the unique and particular paths that have been *traversed* and *travelled* in the pursuit of knowledge and human inquiry. Often, the *path* is so crucial or fascinating that it can even generate bands of disciples who become so intrigued by a particular *method* or *path* that they too want to follow and become disciples (we even have words for such followers, for example, Lonerganians or Thomists, existentialists or Marxists, Franciscans or Buddhists, and so on).

Method, however, can be too closely associated with theory, which is always a great temptation; such that we think that a particular method or way of attaining something is the truth itself. Or we think that our method gives us a certain control that steers everything in accord with our well-worked theory. What is lost in these conceptions of method is the original sounding behind the word that suggests a path – a way, or a search, or a pursuit – but not necessarily a controlled destination or an assured arrival.

To ask the question of method is to ask: What is the way? Methodological questions are questions about the best way to go, the path to follow, the way ahead. To seek a method, therefore, is to ask: What will guide me? What will move me? What will lead me?

According to Pierre Hadot, it is with questions such as these that the ancients approached the task of philosophy. Their goal was never simply knowledge, but the practice of a way of life. Rather than offer abstract principles, philosophical discourse "always intended to produce an effect, to create a *habitus* within the soul, or to provoke a transformation of the self."[3] The philosophical way was always in search of the best way to live. Hadot seeks to remind us that the ancient task of philosophy was always considered as a *way of life*:

> We must discern the philosopher's underlying intention, which was not to develop a discourse which had its end in itself but to act upon souls [...] Whether the goal was to convert, to console, to cure or to exhort the audience, the point was always and above all not to communicate to them some ready-made knowledge but to *form* them. The goal was to change people's way of living and of seeing the world (274).

Hadot notes that the "choice for a way of life" was not located *at the end* of the process of philosophical activity, like a kind of "accessory or appendix"; rather, the choice for a way of life stood at the very beginning: can I practice *this way of life*? The choice meant following "a certain way of life and existential option which demands from the individual a total change of lifestyle, a conversion of one's entire being, and ultimately a certain desire to be and to live in a certain

---

[3] Pierre Hadot, *What is Ancient Philosophy?* Trans. Michael Chase (Cambridge, Mass.: Belknap Press of Harvard University, 2002), p.176. Subsequent references are cited by page number in the text.

Theological Method: A Way of Life   281

way" (3). "The real problem is therefore not the problem of knowing this or that, but of *being* in this or that way" (29).

Philosophy was never conceived by the ancients as a *mastery of life* – borne of speculative theorizing – but always as a *practice,* a *discipline,* a *way to follow,* a *questioning* and a *searching.* While the ancient philosophical schools were guided by ideals and *forms of life* – the true, the good, and the beautiful, for example – these were never considered as remote ideals or detached theories; rather, they were tasks to be enacted in our world. The ancients knew that the great universals such as "the true, the good, and the beautiful" would remain great abstractions unless they were invested with a real weight or "heaviness" that anchors them in actual existence. They considered that humans were the "bearers" of these virtues in such ways that unless we learnt to *practice* them, we would remain mired in falsity and illusion – in lies, in hatred, and in ugliness.

"Go and Study" – "Go and Do Likewise"

In modern thought, practice is often contrasted with theory. Practical theology is an attempt to heal this dichotomy, so that thought and deed can *work together* rather than against each other. David Tracy refers to the dichotomy between theory and practice as a "fatal split."[4] When we divide theory and practice, we injure life, and it is the task of practical theology to heal this fatal wound.

Often, we are impatient with "theories." We can easily dismiss them as heady speculations. We want to get on with life. Unlike theory, or in contrast to theory, we typically associate the word "practical" with things that are *useful, workable, feasible, doable, realistic, sensible, functional, pragmatic, applied, hands-on, effective, relevant.* These "practical" words carry a positive content for our modern ears. We like to feel useful and productive. We like things that are relevant and applicable. Theology would lose its very soul if it were reduced to this understanding of the word "practical."

In a strange twist, however, there is also a sense in which we privilege theory over practice. Theory is the bright light that illumines all we do. Theory represents our "thinking selves," so highly prized in Western philosophy. It comes first and foremost. Practice plays second-fiddle to theory because practice typically comes *after* theory, in second-place. Practice is what remains after theory has accomplished all its winning work – all that now needs to be done is for practice to demonstrate or test how well the theory works. Too often

---

[4] David Tracy, "On Theological Education: A Reflection," in Rodney L. Petersen and Nancy M. Rourke, eds. *Theological Literacy for the Twenty-First Century* (Grand Rapids: William B. Eerdmans, 2002), p.15.

practice functions as the hand-maiden of theory. In terms of theology, we have often considered "systematic" theology as the queen bee, and "pastoral" theology as the worker bee.

Practical theology sees theory and practice as partners that belong together. They are made for each other. They require each other. Action requires reflection. Reflection requires action. They are not one or the other; they go hand-in-hand. The Talmud relates a famous story about the beloved Rabbi Hillel:

> It happened that a certain heathen came before Shammai and said to him, "Convert me on the condition that you teach me the entire Torah while I am standing on one foot." Shammai drove him away with the builder's measuring stick that was in his hand. He then came before Hillel who converted him. Hillel said to him, "That which is hateful to you, do not do to your neighbor. This is the entire Torah; the rest is commentary – now go and study." (Shabbat 31a)[5]

Hillel teaches the entire Torah in a single verse. He makes it sound quite simple: "That which is hateful to you, do not do to your neighbour." There is no great mystery here; this is a very practical command that is within everyone's grasp. However, Hillel reminds us that maybe it isn't as simple as it seems, for there is much commentary on this verse that requires our attention. *To practice the entire Torah requires much study.* We should not be lulled into thinking that the practice of the Torah is easy. Practice also requires reflection. Practice also requires learning. Practice also requires us to "go and study."

There is a story in the gospels that is very similar to the story of Hillel:

> A lawyer stood up to test Jesus. "Teacher," he said, "what must I do to inherit eternal life?" He said to him, "What is written in the law? What do you read there?" He answered, "You shall love the Lord your God with all your heart, and with all your soul, and with all your strength, and with all your mind; and your neighbor as your self." And he said to him, "You have given the right answer; do this, and you will live." (Luke 10:25–28)

Whereas in the story of Hillel it is a "heathen" who comes to test the rabbis, in Luke's story it is a scholar of the law (the Torah) who comes to test the teacher, Jesus. Jesus takes the scholar's question and, in typical rabbinic fashion, bounces it straight back: "What do you read in Torah? What has your study taught you?" The scholar is obviously well versed in Torah and has studied it well, for he creatively brings together two seemingly disparate verses – the first from the book of Deuteronomy (6:5), and the second from the book of Leviticus (19:18). By combining these two verses, he manages to encapsulate the very essence of the Torah, to which Jesus replies, "You have given the right answer; do this, and you will live."

---

[5] Cited in Barry W. Holtz, ed. *Back to the Sources: Reading the Classic Jewish Texts* (New York: Simon and Schuster, 1984), p.11.

Like the story of Hillel, Luke's story ends with a twist. The scholar in Luke's story offers the correct response, but when Jesus says, "do this and you will live," he feels a need to "justify himself" and so he challenges Jesus further: "And who is my neighbour?" (10:29). Jesus responds by offering a *commentary* on the "great commandment." He tells the story of the Good Samaritan. To love our neighbour – to not do what is hateful – is a difficult teaching. If we think it is within easy reach of our comprehension, if we think that we are already fulfilling this commandment, then we are probably kidding ourselves (or trying to justify ourselves). Why else do we say, over and over again, "For I have sinned, in my thoughts and in my words, in what I have done and in what I have failed to do"? Why else do we pray, over and over again, "Lord have mercy"? It is difficult to live the *essence* of the Torah, yet we know it to be a beautiful teaching, as sweet as honey.

To practice the entire Torah will require much study. It will require much reflection on God's word and on the way we are living, and much practice in trying to live according to the ways of God, according to the essence of the Torah.

"Go and study." Go and study the ways of God and learn what God is teaching you, and "go and do likewise" (Lk 10:37). Go and study. Go and do. This *rhythm* is a natural pattern for theology, a natural pattern for the people of God. It is the pattern of discipleship – of listening and responding, hearing and doing, reading and answering, worshipping and going. This rhythm has sustained generations of faithful and prayerful people across the centuries, people who have sought to align their lives according to the ways and purposes of God, "on earth as it is in heaven."

Exemplum Vitae – "A Way of Life"

In one of his Socratic dialogues, Plato notes that the philosophical way of life is often considered a "madness" by those who are comfortably acclimatized to the world's normality. Those who follow the routine ways of the world are often scandalized by the philosopher who follows the inspiration of "divine madness" – "the vulgar deem him mad, and rebuke him; they do not see that he is inspired."[6] Every great "thought-project" that signals a pattern of life has a "madness" to it somewhere – something very attractive and yet maddening at the same time. Jesus was often accused of "raving" and "being out of his mind" (Jn 19:20). Paul also spoke of the gospel as a "madness" or a "foolishness." He seems to say it right up front, rather than try to hide its madness and make it appear more reasonable. He tells the Corinthians he has come to preach "Christ crucified" – a "foolishness" and a "stumbling block" to all those who think themselves wise, or knowledgeable, or successful, or powerful (see 1 Cor 1:18–31).

---

[6] Plato, *Phaedrus,* 64.

Maddening ideas are maddening because they cannot simply be "thought." Rather, they irritate and unsettle by constantly prodding and poking us toward new attitudes and transformed behaviors. Perhaps there is some truth in saying that there is often a "method in madness," as, for example, when Jacques Derrida says that "madness must watch over thinking."[7] We need to keep looking for what is "mad" and "unstable" in systems of thought that have, over time, forgotten the madness and become stabilized and calmly coherent. The gospel message harbours "dangerous memories," as J.B. Metz well reminds us.[8] We need only think, for example, of the mad lives of saints and prophets who were gripped by a wild and foolish passion for God.

It would be a mistake to assume that practical theology is simply arguing for a "practical method" – something that will turn our systematic workings into practical workings. Rather, it is arguing for the somewhat maddening idea that we actually have to live the Gospel message much more than we think. J.B. Metz says: "In itself, the Christian idea of God is a practical idea. God cannot be thought of at all unless this idea irritates and encroaches on the immediate interests of the person who is trying to think it." He then offers this rather maddening statement about the "folly" of Christ: "Christ has always to be thought of in such a way that he is not simply thought of." Rather, "All Christology is nourished, for the sake of its own truth, by praxis and particularly the praxis of the imitation of Christ. It is, in other words, expressed in practical knowledge."[9]

"If God were a theory," writes Abraham Heschel, "the study of theology would be a way to understand him."[10] What if God were not a theory, but a method? What if we were meant to be studying, not the "theory" of God, but rather the "way" of God – God's method, God's ways, God's thoughts, God's hopes, God's desires, God's concerns – or, in traditional theological language – God's will? At its simplest – and yet most difficult – practical theology is a way of life that needs to be practiced. The method of practical theology is this – to become disciples, followers, listeners and doers of the Word, people of faith, people who walk the paths of God, people who seek to know and practice the purposes of God, who desire God and the *ways of God*. "Thy will be done, on earth as it is in heaven" (Matt 6:10).

This is what I understand by a theology that is practical – it requires a "way of life" – living it, testing it, seeking it, treasuring it, daring it.

---

[7] Jacques Derrida, *Points ... Interviews, 1974–94*. Ed. Elisabeth Weber (Stanford: Stanford University Press, 1995), pp.339ff.

[8] J.B. Metz, *Faith in History and Society: Toward a Fundamental Practical Theology*. Trans. David Smith (New York: Seabury Press, 1980), p.184.

[9] J.B. Metz, *Faith in History and Society*, p.51.

[10] Abraham Joshua Heschel, *God in Search of Man: A Philosophy of Judaism* (New York: Farrar, Straus and Giroux, 1955), p.281.

The Author

Terry A. Veling, Dr., teaches in the Faculty of Theology and Philosophy at the Australian Catholic University. He is the author of Practical Theology on Earth as it is on in Heaven, Maryknoll, NY: Orbis Books, 2005.

Valburga Schmiedt Streck

Youth and Spirituality in the Context of Internet:
New challenges for pastoral practices

The purpose of this article is to understand how youth use the Internet as a place where they find meaning in an always more complex world.[1] It seems that the Internet provides for the young generation a vital space where they find meaning and are able to relate to others through virtual communities or *web-blogs*. The new generations are being socialized outside of the traditional patterns, and new personalities, more complex and less self-secure, appear. On the other hand this new generation is able to adapt to new role models that are constantly changing. The new labor market demands more time of men and women, so that time for family life and affective relationships are becoming difficult to negotiate. From early childhood the children have to adapt to strange environments and community life, and neighborhoods atomize into smaller contexts. Instead of belonging to one community, a person belongs to several, and relationships have to be constantly constructed. If traditionally a life cycle was more or less planned and expected to have defined roles, now one is able to choose the roles to be lived. This freedom brings chances and risks because in this world the subject has little to say, and children and youth while becoming "architects of their own future" feel deprived of safe models.[2]

In the midst of major cultural changes and the neoliberal economy in countries like Brazil, social apartheid deepens with an increase in violence, poverty, unemployment and drug trafficking. The Christian communities are constantly being challenged by new religious movements and struggle to survive. In this scenario one can see that neopentecostal churches as well as fundamentalist groups challenge the historical churches and use the latest media technologies and reach out for persons in spiritual need. This brings a new challenge to Practical Theology and Pastoral Counseling, requiring that a new study field should be conceived and developed in this area.

---

[1] This study is part of a larger study project where several youth communities are studied looking mainly at the ways they discuss spiritually and form community by giving support and solidarity to each other.

[2] See BECK, Ulrich, BECK-GERNSHEIM, Elisabeth (ed.) *Riskante Freiheiten.* Individualisierung in Modernen Geselschaften. Frankfurt a.M.: Suhrkamp, 1994; BEEHORST, Joachim, DEMIROVI´C, Joachim, GUGGEMOS, Michael (ed.) *Kritische Theorie im gesellschaftlichen Strukturwandel.* Frakfurt a.M.: Suhrkamp, 2004.

Youth in the Brazilian context

The Brazilian population doubled since 1970, and today we have 182 million inhabitants.[3] 19.6% of them are between the ages 14 and 24; it is the largest youth population in our history. Unfortunately, these youth are more a problem than a solution for our country: the majority are poor, uneducated, and many are drug addicted. It is also the population that has the highest unemployment rate. Crime has been on the rise; the highest homicide rate is among young, black males. From the sociological perspective there is a serious concern that we are exterminating our youth. The films *City of God*, *Favela Rising* and *Falcão Report* point to this reality. Besides, the child and teenager policy implemented in the decade of the 90's was not effective in improving the situation. Poverty, bad schooling, drugs and unemployment are the main reason for this scenario.

On the other side, we have a higher overall life expectancy, and it is estimated that in 2050 we will have a population of 13.7 million old people and 13.7 million children from 0 to 14 years. The rapid urbanization in a country with a rural structure plus a political economy that for decades allowed the concentration of wealth brought the erosion of social networks in civil society. Governmental agencies and non-governmental agencies have difficulties in attending to the growing demand for social services in the country. However, when we talk about youth, one has also to consider the immense differences that exist in the country. Youth in the south will present themselves differently than youth from Rio de Janeiro, for example. Illiteracy is higher among the black male population, and the majority of the illiterate youth live in the Northern part of the country. The so-called *Zapping* generation of the middle and higher classes have access to good schools, to modern communication system, and to travel overseas for student exchange. They wish to live intensely doing many things at the same time. Supported by their parents to realize their dreams, they have better chances than the older generations. Living with their parents often until their thirties, they feel protected by their families. Many do not know how to travel on a bus and to move around in the city where they live.

Christian Communities and Youth

In contemporary society, historical Christian churches live in severe crisis because of religious pluralism. Among their members and pastors one can also find charismatic and fundamentalist orientation as well as the Theology of Liberation. There is a constant challenge for Church leaders to maintain an open dialogue that leads to unity. Most Christian communities struggle to

---

[3] According Revision 2004 the National Projection of Population of the IBGE (Instituto Brasileiro de Geografia e Estatística – www.ibge.org) based on the Census 2000 the number of inhabitants of Brazil was projected to be 182 million people in that year.

288 Valburga Schmiedt Streck

maintain their identities and to hold together, but the younger generation is already socialized in a new cultural model. We still find a strong ethnic profile among members of local communities, which means that it can happen that people from other ethnic background are not welcome to participate. Unfortunately, neither clergy nor laity were prepared for these new conceptions and do not know how deal with them. It is well known that Latin American people are very religious and that "religiosity comes out of each pore of the skin." It is also a fertile soil for emotional religiosity. Local television is crammed with evangelical programs that start early in the morning, offering salvation for the sins, prosperity, and family counseling. The members are constantly being seduced by new religious movements that use free market tactics, such handing out gifts for youth like t-shirts and hats or offering spiritual support like prayers and exorcisms.

A youth survey was published at the end of 2003 with a total of 3501 youth, aged 14 to 24, coming from rural and urban zones.[4] Religion in this study came in 13th place in a ranking of 15 issues of interest. 65% of these youth say they are Roman Catholic and 22% practice an evangelical religion. The fear of God comes in 4th place of important values and religiosity ranks 8th. To speak of God is not the same as to have a religion. The Church still comes after the family, school, street and work as an important place to become mature. It is also the 4th place where one can make friendships. In another survey carried out in the city of São Leopoldo/RS in 2006, with youth aged 15 to 24, religion ranked 7th out of 8 in terms of importance to life. Most of them said that they would not like to have neighbors that are very religious. 17.1% never participated in any religious encounter or activities while 22.1% participate at least once in a week. When they follow a religion the majority say it is the father's religion, in case he is Roman Catholic. If the mother is Pentecostal the children tend to follow the mother. The study concludes that there is a tendency to reject institutionalized religion and that there is a preference for a private faith. This shows also rejection to a traditional Church community life as well.

Virtual Communities and the case of the Orkut

The terminology virtual community is being used for a group of people who relate themselves in the cyberspace. These virtual communities may never meet themselves out of the cyberspace by having face to face contact but they can constitute themselves as a virtual settlement in a social network (Recuero, p. 13).[5] The interaction established in these communities can be of cooperation

---

[4] See www.projetojuventude.org.br under the technical responsibility of "Criterium Assessoria em Pesquisa" in partnership with SEBRAE and the "Instituto de Hospitalidade".

[5] RECUERO, R. ORKUT rede social, see .http://www.facom.ufba.br/ciberpesquisa/ tics/2003/body_suely_2003.htm.

such as a support group, as a competition such as showing popularity by having more friends that appear on the social board of the profile or it can also cause conflicts through persecuting others in case of rival groups. In Brazil social interaction through the Internet is growing and is already being considered a particularity of our society. In the case of weblogs, for example, one can say that our youth never wrote so much as they do in their blogs, which is a specific aspect of the online interaction culture. The social interactions get adapted to the virtual contacts in a rapid way of communication where physical distance is not a barrier. The social networks impose themselves in a horizontal setting against the vertical organization that was based on authority and hierarchy.

Today more and more persons use the Internet to contact different worlds. It can happen that one never will see in real life the person with whom one communicates throughout the time of virtual interaction that can last for years. This is called a "pattern of specific sociability" and does not mean that behind the screen we have someone who never wants to be found, but it is a way one chooses to interact and socialize.[6] One goes online not only to gather information but also to establish relationships, be it on a local or international level. In this perspective, new forms of collective as well as individual communication are created. Many times it has been observed that local relationships improve through virtual communication. People also go online to enjoy themselves through games and other entertainments that are being offered.

It is foreseen that in 2010 two billion of the world's population will be connected. Internet becomes an important instrument of social practices in the sense that it can offer new possibilities for society and the economy to move forward. For example, it can be a way to include in a network persons excluded from society and offer them a possibility of interacting freely without being controlled and watched. It can also help to educate people so that they can process information and generate new data. The Brazilian government has a project to buy laptops for schools in the country at a price of $100US. In many schools this is already a reality. There are experiments of connecting the internet through electricity. This will bring the costs down. Many NGOs are also collaborating and empowering children, youth, and adults to use computers and Internet. In universities there are more online courses.

With more than 14 million members, the Orkut is one of most popular sites of relationship where we can find 72.51% of Brazilians. 56.58% of the members are ages 18 to 24 and only 2.35% are more than 50 years old. Of these 41.9% are single and a total of 83.04% enter the site to search for friends, while 30.22% look for professional contact. The main goal of the site is to offer a

---

[6] CASTELLS, Manuel. *A galáxia da internet*. São Paulo: Zahar, 2003.

290 Valburga Schmiedt Streck

possibility to establish contact among people.[7] The Orkut is considered a "social software" created by Orkut Buyukkoten in 2004. It is free of charge. One can participate by being invited by another member. Persons younger than 18 are not allowed. However, the number of teenagers and children is growing. Many times parents help children to be part of the Orkut. By becoming a member I can have a profile or a community. When I have a profile I can indicate friends and add communities. I can also have discussion forums and receive or send messengers. People can write to me and I write back in a mutual interaction. I can also ask for someone to become part of my community. There are about 140 thousand communities in the Orkut and one always has to see if this information has not changed because it is growing very fast. One says in Brazil that the Orkut is already the *Orkut way of life*. The tendency is that one uses more Orkut as e-mails. In many cases the whole family is on the Orkut. I am surprised many times when I find former class-mates on the Orkut and I can see pictures of their already grown up children.

A relationship site is similar to heavy traffic road and many children, when using this road, can be victims of virtual bullying or other aggressions. Many of them do not know how to defend themselves and the aggressors most of the time are not caught by the law. Children might give their home address and it is easy to get their identities as well as the information when they move around and where they study. However, one has to also see the good side of it. For example at the Orkut people can resume relationships that faded away many years ago, meet new friends, get support and solidarity.

Youth and Spirituality in the Context of Internet

In our research project we searched the Orkut in November 2006 for youth communities of the historical Christian churches and found more than 500 communities with the word "youth." It has probably increased since then as is common with virtual communities. I will make some comments of the major topics of the Lutheran Youth community called *JE-Juventude Evangélica IECLB* (Evangelical Church of Lutheran Confession in Brazil), which had 2.3 million members in March 2007. On the roll of topics for discussion one can find issues such as *Lutheran Identity*; *Why youth has turned away from the IECLB?*; *Luther and ecumenism; I am Lutheran and that is why I am evangelical*. One can also find some curious discussions such as *Can a Presbyterian love a Lutheran?* Another curiosity seen in looking at this community is that the leaders as well as many of the people who interacted most in the forums had a personal profile showing that they interacted also with other communities that

---

[7] According to the survey realized by Nielsen/Netratings, Brazil is the country that got most residential users in the month of February, a growth of 10%, totaling 13.2 million users (March 27, 2006 – www.terra.com.br).

had IECLB identities as well as communities that were linked to other religious movements. For example most participated in the *Aldeia Gospel* with no identification with the IECLB except that some members of the Church did participate in this band. Some members also participated in a community called *Gospel Band*. This shows a tendency of today's youth to belong to different groups and youth cultures, depending on the occasion and situation. Apparently this is also done with religion.

In the discussion forum *Why has youth turned away from the IECLB?* youth blamed not only the Church's leadership but also their parents and themselves for not participating in the community life. Are adults – including their parents – busy doing other things? By reading the other postings we find that the discussions have pretty much the same tone. The tendency seems to be geared to a more fundamentalist orientation where the world is not so nice and one has to hold together against evil. One posting condemns the ecumenical movement in the Lutheran Church with strong comments against the Roman Catholic Church.

None of the communities are official ones of the Church, and the Church does not interfere in these discussions. Also the youth assessment group does not interfere in the discussion, trying to keep out as much as possible. There are serious concerns for a Church that is open to an ecumenical dialogue. The question has to be asked regarding a possible intervention in such discussion forums.

Concluding Remarks

Cyberspace is not merely a place to go anymore, but it is becoming a place where people live. Virtual communities more and more resemble real life communities. One wonders about how churches can be in the virtual world to support and clarify the discussions of their members and interact in communities. It is much more than having an official site and offering counseling on-line. Maybe one day there will be a possibility of choosing where one goes to church on Sunday morning by choosing the preacher, the Church and the friends one wants to meet. For example, it could be that I decided to attend a service at the Lukas Church in Munich, where I will meet my friends who live there but also invite other friends from other parts of my country to join us. The preacher could be one of the pastors of my church in Brazil or not. This all will happen in front of my computer and we interact online by seeing each other online, or one could get an avatar as in one of the virtual games. For many people virtual communities are becoming a way of life. I don't think one can deny it.

Back to the issue of youth and spirituality – in virtual settlements in the Brazilian context one has to look further to understand how other young people from other churches organize themselves and deal with their spirituality. We need to ask the question of how they can be helped to find ways to live the commitments of faith in this new world. How can the Gospel of Christ be understood without turning persons against each other as we see in so many instances, be it in the virtual world or in real world? For Practical Theology, mainly for pastoral counseling, one has to see ways of helping to empower the new generation to become protagonists as members of a Christian community – be it online or off-line – so that they can deal with the radicalism of Christ's Gospel.

References

BECK, Ulrich, BECK-GERNSHEIM, Elisabeth (ed.) *Riskante Freiheiten*. Individualisierung in Modernen Geselschaften. Frankfurt a.M.: Suhrkamp, 1994.

BEEHORST, Joachim, DEMIROVIC, Joachim, GUGGEMOS, Michael (ed.) *Kritische Theorie im gesellschaftlichen Strukturwandel*. Frakfurt a.M.: Suhrkamp, 2004.

CASTELLS, Manuel. *A galáxia da internet*. São Paulo: Zahar, 2003.

Newsweek, February 12, 2007.

RECUERO, Raquel. ORKUT e rede social. http://www.facom.ufba.br/ciberpesquisa/ tics/2003/body_suely_2003.htm.

Revision 2004 the National Projection of Population of the IBGE (Instituto Brasileiro de Geografia e Estatística – www.ibge.org)

www.projetojuventude.org.br.

www.terra.com.br, Marck, 27, 2006.

www.uol.com.br, March 04.2007.

The Author

Valburga Schmiedt Streck, Prof. Dr., Professor of Practical Theology at the Lutheran School of Theology in São Leopoldo, Brazil. Research interest: Urban pastoral practices and new methods of counseling with families in the context of poverty; New identities, social changes and pastoral counseling; On-line and Of-line communities and social networks in the Brazilian context. Recent publications: Seelsorge angesichts von Zerbrechlichkeit und Zerstörung In: Helmut Weiß, Klaus Temme (ed.) Schatz in irdenen Gefäßen Reihe: Ökumenische Studien/Ecumenical Studies. Bd. 34, 2008; Jugend im Brasilianischen Kontext: Überlegungen zu einem neuen Forschungsfeld. In: Jahrbuch Jugendforschung, 2005; Internetseelsorge mit Jugendlichen – Wege zum Menschen, 2006; Families in Transition: Challenges for Society and Church. Estudos Teologicos, 2007.

Daniël J. Louw

Reframing masculinities and femininities in the gender debate. From the body as social text (narcissistic model tyranny) to the body as religious text (compassionate intimacy) in a practical theology of human embodiment and sensuality

The *gender debate: masculinity/femininity?*

Scholars accept the fact that *gender* is to a certain extent mostly a social construction (Harris 1995:1). Gender is distinguished from sex, which refers to the physiological differences between men and women. "In contrast to sex, gender refers to culturally constructed systems of meaning that identify various things – persons, ideas, gods, institutions, and so on – according to the binary categories of 'women/men' or 'feminine/masculine' (Jones 2000:8). Bird (1997:172) defines gender as a demorfic classification based on observed genital differentiation[1].

Sexual features are imbued with symbolic content and social meaning that, among other things, attempts to differentiate between men and women. Every *culture* has a *gender* system that contains shared expectations for appropriate female and male behaviour, social norms or roles[2], different messages[3] that vary from culture to culture.

It is accepted by scholars that currently there is what they call a "gender crisis". "There is also a *gender* crisis – the beginning of the ending of *patriarchy* as a way of organizing male-female relations and distributing social power" (Thatcher 1999:27). Beck et al. (1995:22–24) points out that prescribed gender

---

[1] To complicate the gender debate further, scientists are more and more working with the concept of intersexuality (Looy 2002:12). The term "*intersexuality*" has been introduced to replace the older terms "*hermaphrodite*" or "*pseudohermaphrodite*". It refers to a diverse set of conditions that have in common an ambiguity in biological sex. The sex chromosomes, gonads, reproductive organs, genitals, or hormones are not consistently female or male. The process of sexual differentiation is therefore enormously complex and has a profound influence and implication for a person's experience of gender and sexuality.

[2] It can be expected that fathers and mothers are playing in this regard a fundamental role. The more harsh, judgmental, controlling and punitive a father is the angrier and rebellious the son will be. (Harris 1995:50).

[3] For the different male messages, see Harris 1995:12–13: i.e. adventurer; dad as role model; the best (achievement); protector (breadwinner); being in control; accomplishments; money maker; sportsman and nature lover; the playboy being sexually aggressive, attractive and muscular; the rebel; ignore *pain* (stoic); be perfect without admitting mistakes (superman); Mr. Fixit; tough guy; prove yourself and take risk (warrior); workaholic.

294 Daniël Louw

roles which are being subverted in the 19th century were the basis of industrial society and should not be seen as some traditional relic which can easily be dispensed with. People are shaking off rigid gender roles, bourgeois maxims in the process of establishing a new kind of gender freedom.

To a great extent the famous declaration of Simone de Beauvoir, "One is not born, but rather becomes a woman" (See Mirsky 1996:27), fueled the *gender debate*. It is the contention of Mirsky (1996:27) that both the academic field of men's studies and the various politically and spiritually oriented men's groups active today owe their existence, directly or indirectly, to *feminism*.[4]

It is indeed the conviction of many feminist scholars and researchers that the dominant traditions have always favoured men (Krondorfer 1996:3). Men are normative in theological discourses and enjoyed unrestrained access to *positions* of political, socio-economic, and sacred power. Even still in contemporary interpretations, the male body itself is treated preferentially and projected onto a male God[5].

Within the context of *feminism* Elisabeth Schüssler Fiorenza (1998:3) argues that even to use or to refer to the concept 'feminism' exposes women researchers to *stigmatisation* because in the minds of many a feminist characterizes a person as a fanatic-biased, man-hating, and crazy. The point is that 'feminism' should be understood against the theoretical framework of "sexism" and "*patriarchy*", which is connected to the domination of all men over all "*wo/men*" in the same way (Fiorenza 1998: 7–8)[6].

---

[4] While entering the gender debate, one should therefore always bear in mind the cultural phenomenon of *patriarchy* and hierarchy. For example, many assess femininity as a man-made construct and that it has nothing to do with femaleness. "Femininity, as the gender ideal assigned to women under the terms of patriarchy, has come to be seen as a mark of women's oppression in a system organized around the interests of (putatively masculine) males" (Mirsky 1996:28–29).

[5] It is the contention of Krondorfer (1996:8) that the notion of God with a male body is the reason why, in all male institutions, Christ was time and again represented in highly sensuous and androgynous images.

[6] Fiorenza (1998:13–14) refers to the Athena complex as a heuristic feminist concept that not only refers to the myth of the Goddess Athena who emerged from the head of Zeus as a war goddess, but also to articulate "what is not spoken of" in feminist discourses, i.e women as the "motherless" offspring engendered from the brains of powerful fathers due to the subconscious fear that women's *wisdom* can surpass the knowledge and power of "intellectual fathers". To a certain extent *feminism* is not so much about *gender* as such but about the oppression of "*wo/men*". It is therefore indeed a question whether gender is in itself a "thing" (independent phenomenon), and whether it is more about relations, functions and behaviour. Gauntlett (2002:139) sees gender as performance and nothing more. Gender, then, is what you do at particular times, rather than a universal who you are. Gender is then more performatively consti-

Reframing masculinities and femininities in the gender debate

Mass media[7] and images of maleness/femaleness

The core of the *gender debate*[8] is about the meaning of our being human as either male or female. Due to cultural images, maleness[9] is determined by *masculinity* and femaleness by *femininity*. These images correlate with specific gender role functions in society. They are culturally determined and lead to specific perceptions and typology of maleness[10] and femaleness. In this regard mass media plays an important role in projecting the stereotypical masculine and feminine differences. These images are then internalised by both males and females.

A good example of the impact of communication technology and the mass media on being male/female, is the concept of *hegemonic masculinity*: the athletic male body as a mark of power and moral superiority. It becomes a dominant, global idol in Western thought: white, middle-class heterosexuals (Dworkin et al. [6]2004:508)[11].

---

tuted by socio-cultural expressions. However, over a period of time the images gain the meaning and status of identities.

[7] Wermke (2006:199–213) points out the role of the media in projecting a very specific image of maleness: the mythical role of the hero and the impact of power and violence in this regard. The mythical role of the hero is closely related to the motive of adventure and journey. The hero is forced to act as a savior and conqueror.

[8] From a sociological point of view the *sex/gender debate* and system is a patterning of social relations. Carrigan et al. 2004:152.

[9] It is the contention of Capps (2002:xvi) that males should be understood in terms of their separation *trauma* in early childhood. Emotional separation from the mother in early childhood can lead to melancholy. In women it tends to be more *depression*. The religiousness of men tends to be invisible and is directly related to their melancholy self, a sort of disconnection within the self due to the fear of abandonment – separation trauma (10–19). The latter is connected to the son's failure to bond with his father (56–57).

[10] Smith 1996:10 points out that the cultures having a pronounced manhood ideology seem to be the ones that have chosen fight as a survival strategy. Without a genetic imprinting, men in those cultures have to be conditioned to be brave in order to fight.

[11] Other variations include the *Adonis Complex* which describes male-image and *masculinities* in terms of a preoccupation with building muscles, a lean body, appearance and *good* looks in terms of clothing and grooming, and often in terms of the size of the *penis*. Another concept is metrosexuality where the male is in contact with the female component of his being, but freed from the strict categories and classifications of masculinities in the past. The metrosexual person lives in the metropolis within the different options of a Man's World". The David Beckham icon opens up the world for the metrosexual from the gym to the hairdresser. *Metrosexuality* within a postmodern paradigm beyond any past "isms" and stereotypes becomes even nowadays the *Übersexual* where men are portrayed in terms of categories such as quality and the positive aspects of being male; maleness as excellence and something to be proud of.

296 Daniël Louw

Gender issues (as indicated in terms of the previous mentioned developments in male-images) are closely linked to stereotypes and in this regard the media plays a decisive role[12]. For example, Gauntlett (200:38) refers to the phenomenon of *"scopophilia"*. Scopophilia is the voyeuristic gaze directed at other people as part of the pleasures of cinema. The pleasure in looking leads to the male gaze projecting its fantasy onto the female figure which is styled accordingly, and vice versa. In their traditional exhibitionist role women are simultaneously looked at and displayed, with their appearance coded for strong visual and erotic impact so that they can be said to connote to-be-looked-at (Gauntlett 2002:38)[13].

The most determining factor in *masculinity*[14] and *femininity* is the current, dominating philosophical paradigms, which determine perceptions pertaining male behaviour and female behaviour. These perceptions are embodied in *gender* role functions and become prescriptive for the expression of masculinity and femininity.

Patriarchy and Patriarchalism

A *good* example of the impact of a philosophical paradigm within the gender debate is the paradigm of *patriarchy*[15] as related to a hierarchical understanding of human value and identity[16].

In order to partake in the *gender debate*, one must realize that *femininity* is in many cases a deliberate reaction over against patriarchy and the power status of men. In this regard Reid-Bowen (2004:197) argues that when men fight patriarchy, they are to a significant degree, also fighting themselves (and this necessarily includes their male desires and interests).

---

[12] The media even creates a new sense of religion, i.e. a human's search for meaning. For the role of the internet in this regard, see Meier 2006:276–284.

[13] For the role of magazines in stereotyping, see Gauntlett 2002:187–191: pretty self-evident women who are very lean and skinny. Men should be well built with muscles, *good* in bed, happy in relationships, witty, considerate, skilled in all things, sex with a lot of attractive women (159–163).

[14] According to Carrigan et al. (2004:153) the differentiation of *masculinities* is psychological, but also institutional and an aspect of collective practice. Hegemonic *masculinity* is to impose a particular definition on other kinds of masculinity (154).

[15] It is the contention of many researchers on gender issues and counseling males that that caregivers should be able to understand the dynamics of patriarchy and its contradictory messages for men's lives and be able to help men sort out what is true and faithful for their lives in community. Neuger & Poling 1997:44.

[16] For a discussion on the male-headship tradition and the so-called Biblical mandate for wives to submit to husbands and the influence of Aristotle's Nichomachean Ethics and politics, see Browning 2004:4.

Reframing masculinities and femininities in the gender debate 297

Currently gender issues are raised within the context of processes of democratization. The debate therefore emphasizes the importance of the notion of equality[17].

In this regard the gender debate must take cognizance of the role of what can be called patriarchalism. Culbertson (1994:22) refers to Augsburger who points out that patriarchalism is the product of four interlocking premises:

- First, that male physical strength is part of intended natural law.
- Second, that families and societies are naturally based on aggression, domination, procreation, and spouse and child protection.
- Third, that property, production, and the distribution of goods are the natural domain of men.
- Fourth, that male superiority, dominance, and privilege are a part of received religious revelation.

These four interlocking justifications – biological, cultural, economic and religious – form the cornerstone of patriarchalism. The further problem with these premises is that they often feed oppressive behaviour and social structures and lead to the domination of one gender over the other.

Patriarchalism emphasises the presence of male power and control in intimate relationships as well as discrete acts of behaviour. It leads to the abuse of power and what Poling (1997:140) calls *male violence*[18]. According to Poling, male violence to women encompasses physical, visual, verbal, or sexual acts[19] that are experienced by a woman or girl as a threat, invasion or assault, and that have the effect of hurting her or degrading her and/or taking away her ability to control contact (intimate and otherwise) with another individual.

Male fears and violent behaviour

Patriarchalism is connected to the interplay between fear and resistance. The following fears play a decisive role in patriarchal masculinity:

---

[17] See in this regard the argument of Bird (1997:165) that the creation narrative in Genesis 1 and Genesis 2 contains no statement of dominance or subordination in the relationship of the sexes, but its narratively constructed emphasis is on the equality of the sexes. The Yahwist sees the disobedience of the man and woman to the divine command as the root sin that disturbs the original harmony of creation. The consequence of sin is alienation. The estrangement introduced into the divine-human relationship works itself out in every other relationship, especially between the sexes.
[18] Male violence therefore emphasizes themes of power, control, and dominance of men over women, children, nature, and the competition of men for dominance over one another, which lead to racism, sexism, war and economic oppression. Male violence feeds on gender inequality and is socially constructed as a hierarchy, that most men base their personal identities on being members of the dominant class.
[19] On sexual violence, see Fortune 1983.

- The fear to disclose emotions and to be exposed to the affective. *Patriarchal masculinity* denigrates and trivalises the world of inner experience, feeling and intuition. This inner world is deemed weak, making men too vulnerable. "Men have been taught to value independence over interrelatedness, measurable objectivity over inner reality, linearity over the circular character of emotionality" (Culbertson 1994:13)[20].
- The fear to loose face. This fear is related to shame and the cultural notion of man's role in society. Men fear to loose face when he falls short of role expectations assigned by society or he violates the rules of conduct or breaks communal customs. This fear can lead to aggressive behaviour in order to gain control. When males believe they need to act as procreators, protectors, and providers, the fear of being stripped naked before the judgement of the public eye explains the concept of male shame.
- The fear of powerlessness. Being a male means to work and be strong. The only option for males is full-time employment. They ought to prove their masculinity over and again with no other accepted arena in which to work out their masculinity. When this fear of powerlessness is related to poverty and unemployment, one can understand why so many males end up by crime[21].

Whether preconditioned or socially and culturally constructed, two issues are in the gender debate paramount: the notion of power and the notion of sensitivity.

In order to capture the essence of the *gender debate*, *masculinity* will be discussed with reference to the *P-factor* (the dominant projections and portrayals of being male), and *femininity* with reference to the *S-factor* (the dominant projections and portrayals of being female).

Cultural Masculinity: the P-factor

As a product of *culture* one can say that *masculinity* in the past went hand in glove with social role functions as well as personal and public self-esteem. Due to cultural differences sociologists prefer the plural *masculinities*.

Personal self-esteem, for a male, required public performance. In this regard boys grew up[22] with the notion of the pre-eminence of men.[23] It is then un-

---

[20] The fear of being weak or called a woman, can quickly spill over into *misogyny*, the hatred of things associated with women. Men bypass emotions even in their conversation patterns. Men generally limit their conversation to five topics: sports, politics, women, their professional successes and toys (such as guns, boats, politics, computers, and electronic equipment) (Culbertson 1994:16).

[21] This fear of powerlessness explains to a large extent the violent crime in the townships of South Africa as well as the phenomenon of gangsterism.

[22] See in this regard Driver (1996:43–64) on growing up Christian and male.

Reframing masculinities and femininities in the gender debate

manly to be ill, unmanly to complain, and unmanly to ask for help and show emotion. It is manly to be powerful[24] and erect (the *phallic syndrome*). This image was enforced in the church, because to worship an all-powerful, omnipotent and self-contained male God, extends to male *narcissism* supremacy and the quality of even something religious. The homophobia in the church is then an inevitable outcome of such a stance. Thus the categorical condemnation of *homosexuality*[25] as sinful with the exclusion of any so called female mannerisms to be associated with *masculinity*.

In the *gender* discourse about *masculinities*[26] and the notion of maleness, the *P-factor* is still very dominant in the general public discourse. We even confuse maleness[27] (biological sex) with *masculinity* (gender) at our peril[28]. The P-factor refers to dominant, cultural gender symbols and role functions in our society. They are inter alia:

---

[23] Males should therefore be the head of everything. Notions like "male supremacy", "male chauvinism", and the cultural archetype of the "super *macho*" refer to the dominant *positions* of males in society. Super macho sports of violent body contact sport such as wrestling, football, rugby and boxing enforced this rigid macho-image because in the eyes of viewers the crowds will respond after coming back on the field after an injury: "What a man!"(See Goldberg 1976:112–113). To be a "man" is the epitome of an upbringing which taught boys that it is "sissy behaviour" to complain of body pains and the encouragement to resist the fact of *illness* and injuries as long as possible, because "cowboys don't cry".

[24] Driver (1196:55) thinks of chauvinism as attitude men have toward each other, leading to competition for renown and influence, so that their associations almost always result in a pecking order. Where one stands in the pecking order indicates one's degree of *masculinity*. In such a condition, masculinity is always a performance, something put on like a theatrical role or a priest's vestments. Masculinity became narcissistic and self-referential. In the church this image was enforced by a God-image that is predominantly male and all-powerful.

[25] Stemmelet (1996:95) calls the term *homosexuality* a "gemixtepickle" including such prejudices terms as faggots, dykes, and fairies.

[26] It is indeed difficult to pinpoint what is meant by *masculinity*. Scholars therefore rather refer to "*masculinities*" due different social patterns of masculinity (Harris 1995:104). There are for example the image of the hard worker and the breadwinner (standard bearer); the faithful husband, lover or playboy; the influential boss and leader; the rugged individual as the rebel, tough guy or superman. Each of these patterns of masculinity connotes a specific way of looking at the world. Indeed some patterns of masculinity support *patriarchy* but also encourage men to rebel against the destructive aspects of patriarchy (Harris 1995:105).

[27] The search for the "deep masculine", a sort of primal vitality and distinctly *masculine spirituality* is the endeavour of mythopoetic men's movements. Mirsky 1996:34–35.

[28] Some researchers differentiate between anatomical sex (men), *gender* identity (maleness) and gender performance (*masculinity*). Men's studies explore how anatomical men are gendered male within the society and perform or do not perform masculinity according to society's norms, Mirsky 1996:1.

- P-enis = *masculinity* is connected to the impulse to control[29]. This urge is symbolised by the connectedness between the male organ (*penis*)[30] and its function: penetration.
- P-ower = the male is seen as the stronger component[31]. Thus the quest for physical strength and fitness. The male is then the dominant factor (authority) and the female the subordinate factor that leads to the notion of submission. The notion of women's subordinate position is strengthened by Biblical interpretations portraying the male as representing "headship", mind and reason, requiring that males dominate women (Mowrey 1996: 119).
- P-hallus[32] = maleness is expressed in courage and dominionship while femaleness is valued in terms of vulnerability and subjugation. The *phallus* symbol[33] is closely connected to procreation, (fertility) and erection. The display of the phallus leads in our *culture* to the consumerism of male sexuality (Kibby et al., 2004:214).
- P-erformance = maleness is connected to the courage to act and to produce (pleasure production and *sperm* production). Sexuality becomes the technique of "seizure." In the quest for performance, the body-image plays a fundamental role.

The danger in these male *gender*-symbols is violence. The effect of the symbols on male sexual behaviour is that it feeds aggressive behaviour, often expressed in violent actions[34]. For example, in the case of rape and sexual

---

[29] In our *culture* the *penis* has come out of closet (Bordo 1999:32). Underwear advertisements explore the impact of the phallic mythology of Superman *masculinity* as a vital image in our culture: the cultural equation of penis=male (37); the "proud member" and "throbbing manhood". Nonerect, the penis suggests vulnerability, and fragility. (44)

[30] It is the contention that of Haldeman (1996:115) that the touch of the *penis* and masturbation can, at least, serve to put men back in touch with themselves. The renewal of a man's relationship with his body is related to, and a part of, a man's image of his sexuality. Men think of their penis as the definitive sign of their identity as men.

[31] It seems as if all *masculinities* share two central components: the negatively defining characteristic of being not feminine, or like women; and the positively defining characteristic of having more power (social, physical, cosmic) than that is feminine, or women. Mirsky 1996:31.

[32] Bordo (1999:43) refers to the link between the phallic god Fascinus, worshipped by Romans and the fascinum attached to the worship of the *phallus* as a magical being. Phallus is the *penis* that takes one's breath away because of its majesty (87); projecting generic male superiority the phallus is an idea and not merely a body part.

[33] In religion the *phallus* symbol played an important part in the cult. Eilberg-Schwartz (1996:41) refers to the Greek gods Poseidon, Apollo, and Zeus who were frequently sculptured in Greek art with their penises fully displayed. The divine phallus is also of concern in ancient Near Eastern mythology.

[34] Masculinity becomes roughness and toughness. It is therefore quite understandable that Du Toit (2003:64) concludes that men must refuse to be men in as far as the popular conception of *masculinity* views it as the enforcing of one's will against opposition.

Reframing masculinities and femininities in the gender debate 301

abuse, male dominance plays a decisive role. The alarming statement has been made that the "male sex" requires injustice in order to exist[35].

Cultural Femininity: the S-factor

In the *gender*-debate about femaleness, the *S-factor* is still very dominant. (The S-factor in this case refers to symbols and role functions in our *culture* and media projecting and promoting a specific image of desirable women).

- S-ubtle = women are projected as geared to the art of sensual flirt[36] (being sexy). Women's magazines support this image. "entice men" (Smith 1985: 217).
- S-ubmission = females and women are the weaker link. To a certain extend they are therefore inferior to male superiority and always on the passive, receiving end of sexuality.
- S-eduction = it is the challenge to femaleness to catch the attention of males by means of tempting. In this regard females are forced into the "art of seduction." Females become sex objects.
- S-ensual = females/women represent the emotional and sensitive side of our being human. Femininity equals tenderness. Women are therefore due to motherhood, forced into the position of server and caregiver.

The above-mentioned stereotypes[37] feed the existing discourse on *gender*. On the other hand, they shape the dominant gender images that determine gendered identities[38].

---

[35] See in this regard, Du Toit 2003:36. It is clear that rape refers to irresponsible male behaviour. It includes torture. "I came to the conclusion that rape is first and foremost an assertion of power through an act of supreme humiliation." Du Toit 2003:25–46. Rape is sexual terrorism (49).

[36] That women's bodies are exploited in the media to project the image of flirtation, see Bordo 1999:28–29.

[37] The stereotypes are fed and strengthened by the following presupposed dualism (Mowrey 1996:121): Masculine/Feminine; active/passive; mind/body; rational/emotional; independent/dependent; dominate/subordinate; objective/subjective; judging/nurturing; strong/weak; logical/intuitive; competitive/cooperative; risk-taking/safety-seeking; self-interested/self-sacrificing; controlling/supporting; assertive/deferential; achievement oriented/relationship oriented; culture/nature.

[38] Mowrey (1996:121) points out that according to this familiar dualism, the human characteristics we most value we attribute to *masculinity*, and we define *femininity* as it's opposite. The male is the paradigmatic human, the generic human, and masculinity is the norm. The female is the deviant human, so that femininity is whatever masculinity is not.

302 Daniël Louw

A crisis? Towards a reframed masculine spirituality?

When they refer to *gender* issues, some researchers are convinced that we are heading for a crisis, very specifically, a crisis in *masculinity*. Albeit, it is the contention of Gauntlett (2002:7) that it is not really a crisis but a question whether men do not fit into their traditional roles and that they will have to find a new, modern, useful place for themselves in the world. Men need to change. "Emotional communication, and the expression of love and vulnerability, is important. Men don't need to become 'like women' but can develop a new form of masculinity which places 'a greater value on love, family and personal relationships' and less on power, possessions and achievements' (Gauntlett 2002: 7).

In order to facilitate change, Culbertson (1992:110) uses the phrase *masculine spirituality*, i.e. that which is appropriate to those males who have taken seriously the opportunity for their own liberation from gender stereotypes and have in the process begun to seek a new and more sensitive self-understanding in light of the feminist critique[39].

Even our God-image in a spiritual approach to *gender* should be addressed. According to Ramshaw (1995:5) the task for feminist Christians is to detect which language speaks more of male power than of divine mercy[40]. Nobody

---

[39] In this regard the following stumbling blocks can be identified:
- The image of God as controlling Father (hierarchical dominionship).
- The fear of the affective and the feminine.
- The male dominated tradition even in spiritual direction (office); the suppression of human emotions (the affective=weakness).
- Self-sufficiency and the fear of powerlessness; independency with the devaluation of interdependency in reciprocal relationships.
- The insistence that to do something is categorically manlier than to be something, or simply to be.
- The inability to integrate the body with ensoulment.
- The obsession with order and control, and the fear of both chaos and spontaneity.
- The fear of failure.
- The pre-occupation with male anatomy and *phallocentrism*.

[40] From a more conservative and reactionary position it is proposed that feminist Christianity is impossibility. Feminist thought and behaviour will inevitably divorce itself from Christian trinitarianism and turn to neopaganreligion or secular ideology (Ramshaw 1995:4). According to Ramshaw there was a tendency to develop Christianity in the El/Jupiter tradition, imaging God as the powerful Survivor (11–12). The noun God must be overhauled; Christians must re-deify their conception of God, and Christian language must reflect a renewed appreciation of divinity. Such deifications require degendering the word God. (19). God should not be depicted as a male creature. The second task is unhumanising the connotations of God. The divine should not be replaced by the superhuman. In this regard Ramshaw finds the notion "God as

Reframing masculinities and femininities in the gender debate 303

can deny that images of a strong, patriarchal God did not play a role in the Christian tradition to project force and male superiority[41].

The challenge for "gender healing" is not to censor all hierarchical religious language because then it will be impossible to refer to divine transcendence. The theological challenge is to reframe and redefine God's power in terms of a *theologia crucis* (vulnerability) and a *theologia resurrectionis* (empowerment and transformative affirmation) In terms of an eschatological reframing of gender issues, the implication is that our new being in Christ (ontology of re-creation) is more fundamental than cultural images and role functions.

Towards a theology of sensual and erotic *embodiment* and *compassionate intimacy*

It is always a question how to merge faith with the body. In the history of Western Christianity the body and its desires were not assessed favourably. *Moral theology* put heavy restrictions on the sexual pleasures of clergy and even the laity. Believers were subjected to the enigma of spiritual perfection (the absent *penis*/phallic presence in Roman Catholic theology) by degrading the erotic sensuality to the domain of the obscure[42].

In the twentieth century pornographic language dominates the sex scene and the discourse on the male and female body. The dominant ideal for example for *masculinity* in Christian cultures has shifted from denying the *penis* to over-sexing it, albeit never challenging the power and the presence of the *phallus* (Krondorfer 1996:12). In extreme feminist circles this emphasis on the male

---

Friend" helpful as a partial corrective to other inadequate categories, such as "God the judge" (21).

[41] For example, Augustine argues the man alone is the image of God and that will be completed if the woman too is joined to him, but separately she is not the image of God (see Mowrey 1996:120). "Regarding God's necessarily male characteristics and their hierarchical applications, here I believe the issue is the need to salvage the authoritarian image of God. Authority in the ancient world was almost universally associated with the male – so much so that queens who wielded absolute authority were regarded as honorary males as evidenced by the false beards ceremoniously worn by Egyptian queens of some periods." (Ross 2005:28).

[42] Moral theology viewed intercourse mainly for procreative purposes. Some regulations for example in Roman Catholic moral reflections, permitted intercourse on special days only and contraceptive devices and intercourse during menstruation were prohibited. Some regulations singled out laymen, such as the notion of copula sicca (dry intercourse) or coitus reservatus, the withdrawing of the penis after pleasuring the woman (Krondorfer 1996:9).

304 Daniël Louw

phallic leads to *misandry*[43] (misandry as a new disease in the health discourse: the hatred of men).

The challenge[44] for theology and pastoral care is the following: rather than rejecting eroticism, is it possible to embrace the sensuality of an embodied spirituality and to introduce the body as a space for human encounter? Instead of the instrumentalisation and commercialized exploitation of genitals and penises can even the genitals be part of a spiritual enrichment, and become "bodily tools" to be used for the empowerment of human beings (identity) within faithful relationships? Are genitals "bodily ingredients" of unconditional love, trust and fidelity?

Over against the exploitation and commercialisation of *eros*, I want to opt for an embodied and *compassionate intimacy*. The critical question will be whether Christian spirituality can be connected to such a category or not.

Conclusion

In order to move beyond the unilateralism of a cultural assessment of being male (masculinities) or female (femininities) I would rather opt for a theology of embodied intimacy and sensual spirituality. This option in a practical theological approach implies the following paradigm shifts:

- From the *soul*-body dualism to an integrative and *compassionate intimacy*.
- From *gender* performance to human empowerment. The body is not anymore viewed and handled as a machine but holistically enjoyed as a living organism.
- From merely autoerotism to personal sensitivity and sensuality. Embodiment as erotic attachment and humane affirmation.
- From narcissistic phallicism to an inclusive *inter-corporality*. The body and its genitals are then assessed as valuable and primary tools/vehicles for the establishment of a human encounter and the *disclosure* of meaning and peaceful and faithful satisfaction.

---

[43] See in this regard the reference of Krondorfer (1996:13) to Patrick Arnold's book, Wildmen, Warriors, and Kings: Masculine Spirituality and the Bible 1991:52. For a more constructive theological evaluation of human sexuality, see Nelson 1990, and Nelson 1996.

[44] Against this cultural background one can now understand the challenge that contemporary bodyism and *healthism* put before theology. The fundamental question is whether we can proceed from a dualistic paradigm that locate the body, its desires and functions, in the negative area of sin (sin-fragmentation) and obscurity (the *despiritualisation of bodily desires*), to the constructive area of spiritual-integration (the *respiritualisation of bodily desires and sensuality*).

Reframing masculinities and femininities in the gender debate

- From the body as the beast (body heat) to the body as the beauty (the *aesthetics* of body enjoyment as well as genital morphology)[45].
- From the assessment of the body as a manufactured subjectivity (media manipulation), to the body as ethical subjectivity; i.e. the awareness of bodily responsibility
- From some-thing to some-body. This paradigm shift is about the personification and ensoulment of the body beyond the cultural limitations of the social classification/role functions of masculinities and femininities. The body is a being quality (ontology) and part of our total *human dignity* as affirmed by the Spirit of God (pneumatology) through the inhabitational presence of God in human corporality.

References

Beck, U. et al. 1995. The Normal Chaos of Love. Cambridge: Polity Press.

Bird, P. 1997. Missing Persons and Mistaken Identities. Women and Gender in Ancient Israel. Minneapolis: Fortress Press.

Bordo, S. 1999. The Male Body. A New Look at Men in Public and in Private. New York: Farrar, Strauss & Giroux.

Browning, D. 2004. The problem of man. In: D. Blankenhorn et.al. (eds.) Does Christianity teach Male Headship? Grand Rapids: W.B. Eerdmans, 2–12.

Culbertson, P. The Future of Male Spirituality. New Adam. Minneapolis: Fortress Press.

Capps, D. 2002. Men and their Religion. Harrisburg: Trinity Press International.

Carrigan, T. et al. 2004. Toward a new Sociology of Masculinity. In: P.F. Murphy (ed.) Feminism and Masculinities. Oxford: University Press, 151–165.

Ceyson B. et al. 2006. The Great Tradition of Sculpture. In: G. Duby, J.-L. Daval, Sculpture. From the Renaissance to the Present Day. Köln: Taschen, 698–703.

Du Toit, L. 2003. Rape Understood as Torture: What is the Responsibility of Men? In: E. Conradie, L. Clowes (eds.) Rape. Rethinking male Responsibility. Stellenbosch: EFSA, 36–67.

Dworkin, S.L. et al. [6]2004. The Morality/Manhood Paradox: Masculinity, Sport, and the Media. In: M.S. Kimmel et al., (eds.), Men's Lives. Boston: Pearson: 507–521.

---

[45] "For the human body, an image of the divine, contained a small part of divinity and hence of beauty." (Ceyson et. al. 2006:702)[45]. Embodiment is then more than merely a *good* or bad issue, but about the aesthetics of being human through *embodiment*. The body should be valued and admired as part of being the image of God. The body attains religious meaning as the concrete space to embody and enflesh the presence and grace of God. Grace is beautiful because it heals the beast in oneself and in the other.

306 Daniël Louw

Driver, T.F. 1996. Growing up Christian and Male. In: B. Krondorfer (ed.), Men's Bodies, Men's Gods. Male Identities in a (Post-) Christian Culture. New York/London: New York University Press, 43–65.

Eilberg-Scwartz, H. 1996. God's Phallus and the Dilemmas of Masculinity. In: B. Boyd et al. (eds.), Redeeming Men. Religion and *Masculinities*. Louisville: Westminister John Knox Press, 34–47.

Fortune, M.M. 1983. Sexual Violence. The Unmentionable Sin. Cleveland: Ohio.

Fiorenza, E.S. 1998. Sharing her Word. Feminist Biblical Interpretation in Context. Boston: Beacon Press.

Gauntlett, D. 2002. Media, Gender and Identity. London: Routledge.

Goldberg, H. 1976. The Hazards of Being Male: Surviving the Myth of Masculine Privilege. New York: Nash Publishing.

Haldeman, S. 1996. Bringing Good News to the body. *Masturbation* and Male Identity. In: B. Krondorfer (ed.), Men's Bodies, Men's Gods, 111–115.

Harris, I.M. 1995. Messages Men Hear: Constructing Masculinities. London: Taylor & Francis.

Jones, S. 2000. Feminist Theory and Christian Theology. Minneapolis: Fortress Press.

Knox-Seith, E. 2005. Sexuality and death. In: OneBody. North-South Reflections in the face of *HIV* and AIDS. Vol 1. Copenhagen: The Nordic-Foccisa Church Coperation, 22–27.

Krondorfer, B. 1996. Introduction. In: B. Krondorfer (ed.), Men's Bodies, Men's Gods, 3–27.

Looy, H. 2002. Male and Female God created Them: the Challenge of Intersexuality. In: Journal of Psychology and Christianity, Vol.21, no.1, 10–20.

Meier, G. 2006. Religion meets Internet. Plädoyer für einen differenzierten Umgang mit einem neuen Forschungsfeld. In: Berliner Theologische Zeitschrift, 23, Heft 2, 177–284.

Mirsky, S. 1996. The Arguments for the Elimination of Masculinity. In: B: Krondorfer (ed:), Men's Bodies, Men's Gods, 27–43.

Mowrey, M. E. 1996. The Accomodating Other: Masculinity and the Construction of Feminine Identity. In: B. Boyd et al. (eds.), Redeeming men. Religion and *Masculinities*. Louisville: Westminster John Knox Press, 118–129.

Nelson, J.B. 1990. Sexuality, Christian Theology and Ethics of Sexuality. In: R.J. Hunter (ed.), Dictionary of Pastoral Care and Counseling. Nashville: Abingdon, 1154–1158.

Nelson, J.B. 1996. Epilogue. In: B. Krondorfer (ed.), Men's Bodies, Men's Gods, 311–319.

Neuger, C.C. & Poling, J.N. Gender and Theology. In: C.C. Neuger & J.N. Poling (eds.), The Care of Men. Nashville: Abingdon, 32–45.

Poling, J.N. 1997. Male Violence against Women and Children. In: C.C. Neuger & J.N. Poling (eds.), The Care of Men, 138–162.

Ramshaw, G. 1995. God beyond Gender. Feminist Christain God-Language. Minneapolis: Fortress Press.

Reid-Bowen, P. 2004. Reflexisive Transformations: Research Comments on Me(n), Feminist Philosophy and the Theological Imagination. In: U. King, T. Beattie (eds.), Gender, Religion and Diversity. London: Continuum, 190–200.

Ross, T. 2005. Can we still speak to God the Father? In: R.L. Platzner (ed.), Gender, Tradition and Renewal. Oxford: Peter Lang, 13–33.

Smith, S. 1996. Fear and Power in the Lives of Men. In: B. Boyd et al. (eds.), Redeeming Men, 7–19.

Stemmelet, M.L. 1996. Empowerment: The Construction of Gay religious Identities. In: B. Krondorfer (ed.), Men's Bodies, Men's Gods, 94–107.

Thatcher, A. 1999. Marriage after Modernity. Christian Marriage in Postmodern Times. New York: New York University Press.

Wermke, M. 2006. Mythos, Gewalt und Religion. Ein Beitrag zur mythentheoretischen Analyse des populären Kinofilms. In: Berliner Theologische Zeitschrift, 23, Heft 2, 199–213.

The Author

Daniël J. Louw, Prof. Dr., Professor for Practical Theology at the Department of Practical Theology and Missiology at the University of Stellenbosch/South Africa. Recent publications include: Meaning In Suffering: Mature Faith: Spiritual Direction & Antropology in a Theology of Pastoral Care & Counseling (1999); A Theological Reflection On The Cross And The Resurrection For Pastoral Care And Counselling (2000); Dreaming the Land in Hope: Towards a Practical Theological Ecclesiology of *Cura Terrae*, in: H.-G. Ziebertz, F. Schweitzer, Dreaming the Land. Theologies of Resistance and Hope (2007).

Ottmar Fuchs

How can Christian communities claim their "better truth" without violence against others, even more for the sake of solidarity with them? Some considerations reflected on Biblical traditions

1. Introduction[1]

Quite unsurprisingly, since September 11, 2001, Christian believers have been facing a deluge of knowledgeable reproaches regarding specific Biblical texts, namely those that do not only legitimize violent destruction and murder of people who think differently but actually call for it. The frightful ambivalence of all revealed book religion has become a talking point.

We shall need to both counteract this particular sentiment and take it seriously, by giving account of how *we* intend to handle those texts from the Bible. For the existence of such passages cannot be denied. But people allege that we apply a hermeneutics of imitation to them: Whatever the Bible says Christians are allowed to, and indeed have to imitate – in doing so they will please the God of their Bible. The fact that – unlike in the past – they do not do so (and in fact shamefully avoid such texts in their liturgy and everywhere else) is due to modernity, the Enlightenment and the universalisation of human rights, but not to the Bible.

This problem cuts right to the heart of practical Biblical hermeneutics, and its resolution, though delicate, must not be delayed. Because such a fundamental criticism of Biblical hermeneutics retrieves exactly those problematical texts from our own unconscious denial and places them squarely in the public domain. We are left wondering at our own helplessness and inability to properly account for them, and indeed at our failure to even start to identify conceptional hermeneutic solutions to these issues.

Yet there aren't any easy answers; at the most there are pointers to a constructive hermeneutics of violent Biblical texts. For we can neither eliminate the passages concerned from the revelatory canon by branding them un-Biblical, nor reconstruct their reception in the horizon of a positivist, nonlinear understanding of revelation. Inner-ecclesial attempts to defuse the issue by downplaying it will no longer do either. All these cop-outs lack an appreciation of the profound ambivalence of God and humans themselves. Those texts are

---

[1] Cf. concerning the following considerations more detailed (especially concerning the problem of God's violence as an ambivalent token of his inapprehensible mystery) Ottmar Fuchs, Praktische Hermeneutik der Heiligen Schrift, Stuttgart 2004, 438–461 (444–448).

How can Christian communities claim their "better truth" 309

not archaic, inhumane stories that we might smugly bring ourselves in distance to, deeming ourselves more "advanced". Down to the present day, the lesson of history is a different one. The Bible confronts us remorselessly with the hidden depths of humans as well as with those of God. What will remain true is St. Paul's statement from Romans 15:4: "What ever was written, was written for our instruction." But how is it meant? Definitely not as a training in wickedness![2]

2. Hermeneutical explorations

2.1. The signature of God's eschatological power over history

The Biblical texts about God's violent intervention hold a lesson for us: Tendencies to reduce belief in God's power over history to stories about a God that helps individuals must be reversed, thrown open and universalized into collective (concerning the people and all peoples, just like collective lamentation) and cosmic (concerning the whole world, as did the Flood at Noah's time) dimensions. At the core of such lamentation lies, no doubt about God's ability to intervene because he does not exist or is too weak, but distress at his failure to intervene even though he could. Why does he not step in mightily? Why does Jesus not call on the heavenly hosts (cf. John 18:36)? The belief that he will never intercede because he cannot intercede is tempting for the victims to resign to and the perpetrators to be reassured by. But that is a delusion. Here the Biblical texts about his violent interventions remind us never to forget that he can intercede and surely will do so ultimately, with unimaginable might (described in Revelation), wiping out violently and uncompromisingly all destructive violence, destroying the freedom of evil and the "violence of injustice".

This eschatologisation of God's power to intervene at the end of history is, at the very least, what must not be suppressed. Otherwise there would be no hope of justice, and the victims would be lost forever. This would be so if there was no resurrection of the dead. Yet as death is the last and ultimate violence

---

[2] Which are the texts concerned here? Some brief examples will give a flavour of their forcefulness. A survey of the material reveals the following scenario among others: The Lord himself wages a war against the enemies and destines them to total destruction (Isaiah 34:1–17; 63:1–6). God calls for revenge upon other peoples and for their annihilation (Numbers 31:1–20; 1 Samuel 15; Deuteronomy 20:10–20; 25:17–19); God chastises his own people and shows his wrath by delivering them to their enemies (Lamentations 2; Deuteronomy 28: 15–68); God uses violence against individuals (Job 16:6–17; Psalm 88); a curse calling on God to destroy the enemies (Psalm 109; Psalm 137:7–9; Psalm 139 19–22); God restores his servant who accepts violent humiliation to atone for the sins of others (Isaiah 52:13–53:12); God judges and scolds "before the eyes of the lamb" those who "worship the beast" (a reference that arguably includes the imperial cult) (Revelation 14:9–11, also 19:11–21).

310 Ottmar Fuchs

against life, only a more powerful force can lead to the resurrection of the dead and put an end to death.

2.2. Not imitation but delegation

There is a number of texts, among them the cursing Psalms, that delegate the violence to God because those concerned are themselves victims lacking any capability for it: "O God, break the teeth in their mouths!" (Psalm 57:7; cf. Psalm 3:8). But do such delegation strategies apply also in cases where those concerned do have such power? Is God's power called on only to compensate for one's own weakness? Is this a matter of principle applying to all situations? Clarification will come only from a hermeneutics that generalizes the semantics of those texts on a meta-contextual level. As a matter of principle, even in situations of acute hatred, the cursing Psalms' demand to renounce becoming a source of violence and to delegate violence to God applies to those capable of violence as well. This is certainly not the highest form of spirituality, but still a necessary one that can prevent the worst in a potentially violent situation and, above all, block knee-jerk reaction. Those not yet ready to turn the other cheek will at least hold back their own violence in appealing to God for it. But does this not mean to instrumentalise the relationship to God to satisfy instinctual drives? But perhaps He wishes to help with this particular historical problem? The questions remain open.

Again, relevant texts are not only from the Old Testament but from the New Testament, too. St. Paul radicalises the issue in Romans 12:17–21: The prospect of divine revenge does not only prevent violence, but on its back makes possible love of the enemy, or more precisely, loving action towards the enemy, which, eschatologically speaking, actually amounts to hatred of the enemy. Again, this is hardly the pinnacle of anti-violent motivation. But it does offer a Biblical strategy for dealing with the violence of texts and of human desires in a constructive way, preventing at least violence of *human* origin from affecting others. And ultimately, delivering someone to God's wrath means delivering them to his mercy, which leaves the question unsettled for the moment. In the end, everything is left to His autonomy and thus to the justificatory activity St. Paul described so intensely.

Those reflections on a delegatory hermeneutics of violent Biblical texts leaves us with the renewed realization that those who rely on a revelation must in no case take violence into their own hands. There can never be a nonlinear hermeneutics in relation to the violent texts, neither one of discipleship, nor of comprehension, nor of approval.

2.3. Being alarmed at ourselves

There is thus no uniform hermeneutics that could be applied to all Biblical texts. Woe to the people if we get our categories mixed up and, for example, read violent texts in the category of a hermeneutics of imitation. Rather, given the variety of texts in the Bible, we should expect hermeneutic approaches to vary correspondingly, ranging from imitatory hermeneutics to hermeneutics of confrontation and challenge where the Biblical texts disclose to us our real or potential nature, leaving us *alarmed at* it and *revolting against* it. Being mutually dependent, the hermeneutics of self-explication and the hermeneutics of confrontation constitute the sinner's repentance! Both may be termed forms of confrontative hermeneutics provided that two aspects are kept in mind: explicative confrontation with self and self-activating confrontation with violence.

Then, our reading of the violent texts will have an all the more forceful impact as, in the light of repentance, through self-critical "identification" they will reveal our own part in being actual or potential perpetrators. Thus, our horror at the texts merges with horror at ourselves and at our temptation, on reading the texts, to wish for such a violent God and such violent solutions to our problems!

Thus, the texts facilitate self-knowledge and also disclose to us our own susceptibility to violence in order to warn us in time and protect us against outbreaks of violence. There is no use – especially not to others – suppressing them if we do not want to face them, and this includes violence that others inflict upon others. Is it fair to say that our refusal to face violent texts reveals our refusal to face our own hidden depths or actual (especially structural and global) realities of violence? The resulting marginalization and scorning of the Old Testament (because of the allegedly low level of ethicality of its violent texts) has always been tied up with an actual proclivity towards violence against the Jewish people! Hence these texts have indeed been written for our education, in order that from the catastrophic rifts of revelation we may come to see our own flaws and may open ourselves up to those violent texts which present the severest of all criticisms of violence at the same time.

Therefore, eliminating specific violent texts from the Bible on account of their incompatibility with a particular image of God revealed in other passages is no solution. This would be to repeat Marcion's mistake of making the Bible "holier" than it is. If, then, we stay true to the Church's tradition of seeing all those texts as integral to the Biblical canon of revelation, we need different hermeneutical approaches in order to take the various texts seriously in exactly the way they are to be taken seriously. In this way, we reaffirm that all Biblical texts have revelatory status while their content is plural and sometimes contradictory and must be accessed through a corresponding plurality of approaches.

312 Ottmar Fuchs

Hence the notion of Biblical revelation as something entirely good, holy and salvific is discredited. Holy Scripture makes no pretenses about the unholy. Its character as revelation derives from the fact that it presents encounters with God in a variety of situations and against the backdrop of the ambivalence of human longing and thinking. The Bible is God's revelation as reflected in humans, their evil and their bad traits, their hatred and their love, their oppression and their justice. As soon as God enters this ambivalence through his actions they become part of it and their divine "purity" is tainted.

The Bible has not been purged of the profound ambivalence of creation and human existence; rather, they are integral elements of the multi-faceted encounter of God and man. It abounds with instances where humans misunderstand God (and vice versa) and in this is no different qualitatively from the later history of the churches, the history of the ambivalence of the religions and of the encounter of man with God and vice versa. The Bible reveals the misunderstandings, the dark sides, the often explosive ambivalence of encountering the divine, to later generations so that they may become aware of the ambivalence of their own faith: alarmed at themselves and fearful of God. The dark mysteries of humanity, creation and God are not banned from the Bible. Rather, in the stories of the Bible, we encounter the mystery of our violence and of the power which God has over history and which in the present eon cannot be explained without ambivalence.

2.4. A martyrial criteriology

Finally, I want to highlight a certain attitude which can be found within the Bible itself, even though it calls for an active decision on our part. Wherever someone accepts to suffer violence in someone else's stead and does not respond with violence, we see a different kind of "violent texts": for example, the suffering servant in Second Isaiah, the suffering Son of God praying for his violent tormentors even from the cross (cf. Luke 23:34), returning the violence he suffered as love. Both scenes presuppose a context of violence in reality and could, especially for Christians, suggest a specific hermeneutics of violent Biblical texts which Horst Eberhard Richter put in these words: Those who don't want to suffer must hate![3] So do the violent texts seek to educate us about self-discrimation for the sake of others, even the perpetrators, in other words, to endorse martyrdom? Not the martyrdom of suicide bombers who, rather than breaking free from the vicious circle of violence, augment it *ad infinitum*. One of the "signs of the time" may be found in the increased necessity for Christianity to take a stance in a wider argument about the correct understanding of Christian martyrdom vis-à-vis an emerging societal interest in the concept, and to bring out the specific nature of Christian martyrdom: It is

---

[3] Cf. Horst Eberhard Richter, Wer nicht lieben will, muss hassen, Hamburg 1993.

How can Christian communities claim their "better truth" 313

better to suffer defeat than to prevail by violence. Those in view here are those who, for the sake of justice, share when there is time to share, to avoid having to kill later (cf. Matthew 2:13–18), those who, for the sake of keeping violence in check, suffer and withstand more (direct and structural) violence than they inflict, starting right from the first small discriminations. Those who ultimately, and consistently, prefer being killed to being a killer.

Are those the violent texts that provide an authentic inner-Biblical key to Christians and for all other violent texts indicate the "centre" of meaning and interpretation? This perspective establishes an interrelation between the different texts, maintaining their multiple perspectives, and at the same time it drives on a particular dynamic which cares about their equal validity while challenging hermeneutic carelessness. Here we have a hermeneutics acknowledging all forms of human and religious violence. It is also critical because it undermines violence by surrender, euphemizing neither active nor passive violence, or rather: neither the violence inflicted nor that actively suffered.

They are counter-texts of intransitive against transitive violence: Servant and Son of God inflicting violence upon themselves, allowing it to be inflicted upon them, juxtaposing the non-violent force of their own bodies. The body is their resistance. The "heroes" and protagonists here are not the subjects of violence, but those subjects who non-violently rise against the violence wrought by others and who expose themselves to it (vicariously) for the sake of others. They are not objects in this process because they are and will be in charge of their decision. They could decide otherwise: run away rather than hold out; call for or apply violence rather than resist with their own life and body (which the opponents need to clear away before carrying on or, indeed, deciding to refrain from doing so); destroy the perpetrators rather than protect them. After all, Cain has a mark put on him so no-one would kill him without attracting the sevenfold revenge of God (cf. Gen 4:15).

Still the question remains: The approach outlined remains an externally applied set of options, because as they stand the texts are presented with no valorization or prioritization. What is the basis for prioritizing our critique of violent texts away from transitive and onto intransitive violence? From inflicting onto accepting suffering? For the texts of martyrdom too portray violence, albeit substantively and perspectively different: with a view to the victim rather than the perpetrator. The texts that criticize violence are part of the Bible, but what prevents readers from prioritizing those legitimizing violence over the martyrial ones? The Bible itself, for one, does not. The ambivalence it contains is that of life itself, that of our lives.

Nevertheless, it is important to establish an intra-Biblical authenticity for this perspective and identify relevant texts. Once this perspective is adopted, we discover significant texts taking it up and grounding it within the Bible. I will try to sketch the line from the Flood to the Gospels – the crucial rainbow, as it were, considering that in Genesis 9:17 YHWH promises never again to intervene with such violence, and that in the Gospels Jesus gives the command to love one's enemy rather than calling on the heavenly hosts. The relevant intra-Biblical dynamic appears to be notably robust, all the more so since there are no positive texts capable of establishing a reverse counter-dynamic of equal validity.

3. Outlook

3.1. The path of the Church

Though we might find evidence for this dynamic, there is one question that remains as yet unanswered: What is the basis on which believers take the decision for such prioritizing in dealing with Biblical revelation? How can we talk of the will of God in a criteriologically sound way, given the variety and diversity of texts? There is only one answer to this, and it is an ecclesiological and pneumatological one: as and when believers read the Bible in the spirit of the God whom they believe to be love and freedom, in the spirit of the risen one and his judgment on human violence. For this transformation to be firmly and plausibly established (against many of the plausibilities of Church and society), a social context is needed that *sustains* this perspective, this "hierarchization" of the Biblical texts, through internal and external interaction.

The more God's people tell each other the relevant stories (or hear them told about "Saints" and exemplary figures past and present), the more there will develop that *willingness to delegate all violence, current and eschatological, to God and to God only – conscious of the permanent danger and temptation of taking violence into their own hands*. The Biblical message exposes our profound sinfulness, that is, our violence, and at the same time proclaims a God who accepts sinners back into his love and justice and, at least according to St. Paul's theology of justification, refrains from violent punishment. Those who in their proclamation and belief are able to join God in this unconditional love will from the very heart of their being no longer be driven to violence. Grace alone can conquer violence.

Once more, the social forms of the Church emerge as the external condition for the possibility (or impossibility) of this perspective on the Bible's internal variety. There is no hermeneutics of the text without such prior hermeneutics of the context. Social hermeneutics leads to Biblical hermeneutics and vice versa. If Christian and ecclesial existence accepts discrimination for the benefit of the less fortunate in the name of God, rather than chasing their personal advantage, certain Biblical texts (and their context) will disclose their meaning quite differently. People treat the Bible the same way they treat each other and out-siders.

Can we find a "plausibility" for this in our faith and proclamation? It would be high time, so that a millennium of mainly violent Christianity may be suc-ceeded by a millennium where Christian existence embraces surrender and "vicarious" existence rather than the subjugation of others, empowerment rather than the exerting of power.

3.2. ... towards the Bible's fourfold conception of violence

Thus in the Bible we find a fourfold conception of violence: Firstly, one that makes perfectly plain to us our profoundly violent nature; secondly, one that embraces the compromise of forcibly expressing human hatred and desire for violence but delegating its implementation to God; thirdly, one where the Ser-vant of God on the cross endures our violence in all its fierceness, returning it as reconciliation; and finally, one that makes unambiguously clear that the omnipotent God has both the power and the intention to eventually use violence to put a stop to the violent and destructive forces of the world and establish an eternity of surrender and non-violence.

Corresponding to these conceptions of violence, there is a hermeneutics of *confrontation* (in exposing our violent nature and triggering resistance against it), a kind of hermeneutics of *delegation* (as the compromise between expressed aggression and abdication of violence), a properly theological hermeneutics of *martyrdom* (a willingness to pay with one's life for one's renunciation of violence), and an *eschatological* hermeneutics (in hope for and awe of God's powerful intervention to destroy violence at the end of time). These her-meneutic perspectives contain partially interlocking and overlapping triggers that are paramount if anyone is to open themselves up for the Biblical message and form their lifestyle correspondingly.

The Author

Ottmar Fuchs, Prof. Dr., born 1945, Chair for Practical Theology at Cath.-Theol. Faculty in the University of Tübingen. Main researches: Fundamental questions between Practical Theology and Human science; Religion solidarity; Theology of diaconical institutions; Theology and Church in front of the challenges of Modernism, Postmodernism and Pluralisation of life; Theology of the Second Vatican Council; Pastoral responsibility in the horizon of eschatology; Constitutive interdisciplinary relations between practical theology and Biblical resp. systematic Theology. Recent publications: Das Jüngste Gericht. Hoffnung auf Gerechtigkeit, Pustet, Regensburg 2007; Praktische Hermeneutik der Heiligen Schrift, Kohlhammer, Stuttgart 2004; mit Franz Weber: Gemeindtheologie interkulturell. Lateinamerika-Afrika-Asien, Grüne-wald, Ostfildern 2007.

Susan Adams

Southern Perspectives:
Theological Education, Community Development and Leadership Empowerment[1]

Introduction

This paper is part of a larger research project exploring the philosophical and pedagogical underpinnings for a model of theological education enabling the development of transformative community leaders. The primary case study for this research is the Ministry Training Unit (MTU) of Trinity Methodist Theological College in Auckland, Aotearoa-New Zealand.[2] In this paper I introduce some of the ideas that give shape and coherence to the work of the MTU programme.

The Background

Aotearoa-New Zealand is nation of migrants. From our earliest history the peoples who settled here came from 'overseas'; from somewhere in the islands of the Pacific. In 1840 the Treaty of Waitangi[3] established a formal set of expectations and relationships for the colonial settlers from Britain and the 'indigenous' Maori settlers. This treaty still shapes life in Aotearoa-NZ. Migration is still a major feature of life in Aotearoa-NZ.

One of the motivations for the early British settlers who colonised Aotearoa-NZ was the move to 'escape' the religious strictures and practices of 19th century Britain. Early legislation was passed to ensure that matters of religion and faith were left aside from the public sphere so as not to specifically influence the values and decisions of those shaping the moral and ethical values of the emerging nation.[4] The 1877 Education Act enshrined these sentiments and provided for education that was 'free and secular'. In this way, Aotearoa-NZ developed as a 'secular' nation. Pacific migration to Aotearoa-NZ con-tinues to

---

[1] The contents of this paper have been discussed with Tongan and Samoan people from the Methodist Church in Aotearoa-New Zealand as part of my commitment to transparency and accountability. There was no request to delete or modify any aspect.

[2] I will use the term Aotearoa-New Zealand to indicate recognition of the name used for this land by the original inhabitants linked to that used by European 'discoverers'. Aotearoa-NZ is a commonly accepted abbreviation.

[3] The Treaty of Waitangi is the covenant entered into between many of the indigenous tribes and the British Crown. Its significance is still debated.

[4] Davidson (2005:311–313) describes the 1854 & 1855 debates in the new House of Representatives which eventually agreed that a prayer should be read but that this 'not be a declaration in favour of a State church'.

Southern Perspectives

be significant today. This wave of migration brings with it the moral and ethical values of 19th century English missionaries who were active in the Pacific Islands. Methodism for example, is the state religion in Tonga and this influences the expectations of Tongan migrants to Aotearoa-NZ. A similar pattern of 20th century missionary influence affects migrant Korean Christians. Both Pacific and Korean migrants arriving in Aotearoa-NZ cluster together in church communities aimed at maintaining the ways of 'home' and helping new migrants from 'home' to settle.

The 2001 census revealed that 92% of Tongan people reported an affiliation with a Christian denomination, of which 45% identified as Methodist.[5] The Samoan profile is similar, though the numbers of Methodists is considerably smaller. In post-Christian, post-colonial Aotearoa-NZ we are seeing the breakdown of many of the positive influences the 'neo-village' structures exercised. This is exacerbated by the children's engagement in a western styled education, so the once strict adherence to cultural and church traditions is now being questioned. One result is a stronger insistence by the elders on the ways of 'back home', and a consequent censuring or silencing of those who question. This censuring is often undertaken by religious leaders: ministers and stewards imported from the islands, leaving the NZ born generation without relevant church-based leadership.

'Practical Theology' has a concern for community health and wellbeing and theological engagement relevant to the issues of specific contexts. It is therefore a significant move by the Methodist Church of Aotearoa NZ to have developed a primary ministry education programme using the critical concepts and philosophy of Practical Theology. This model for theological education has the potential to develop leaders who are competent in engaging their com-munities, in dialogue around social development and identity, spirituality and hope. These are core issues in Aotearoa NZ today. Ministry leaders equipped with the skills of reflective practice (praxis) characteristic of practical theology will be able to respond creatively to the current issues of our increasingly mobile and ethno-culturally diverse society.

Anecdotal evidence suggests that graduates from the MTU are demonstrating an ability to encourage an openness of mind and facilitate the participation of church communities in the critical issues of their neighbourhoods. Their experience confirms that a shift in perception is frequently required by people in these communities to enable engagement in the 'secular society' that is now 'home'. The critical work of a theological/ministry education programme in the current climate of migration, identity search, and rapid change is to assist mi-

---

[5] Statistics New Zealand: www.stats.govt.nz/analytical-reports/pacific-profiles/tongan/ religion. 7/08/2006. At the time of writing there are no updated figures available from the 2006 census.

nistry leaders to develop the skills of 'attending' to the communities in which they work and to the 'signs of the times'. Connecting the present with the stories of faith in ways that proclaim hope in our time relevant to specific cultural contexts becomes critical if the communities that are struggling with difference and change in a 'new' host culture are to develop trust and engagement. Their work to create the space for dialogue can enable participation rather than perpetuating fearful withdrawal into isolated communities seeking to limit the impact of secular influences on traditional ways.

Leaders who encourage awareness and engagement through open dialogue and critical debate on the deep questions that face us socially and spiritually and where appropriate to lead change, are 'transformative' leaders. They will be leaders who

1. are open to substantive change
2. facilitate interpretation of current events and ideas
3. shape a theological perspective
4. take lived experiences as their starting point
5. have a vision of a sustainable healthy society
6. engage in dialogue in terms of both content and process
7. point toward hopeful futures.

We need leaders who take seriously the spiritual and religious experience of migrant communities if we wish these communities to engage in shaping this nation.

As a nation seeking a new way forward that will include rather than isolate migrant communities, we are increasingly aware that *assimilation* or even *tolerance of difference* is not adequate. But as yet models for effective *integration* and ongoing participation have not emerged.[6] It is into this place of engagement, theological education from within the particular frame of 'Practical Theology' can play a positive part in equipping transformative leaders and leading a move to sustainable integration.

A Response

As 'not for profit' players, the churches can claim a place in the public contest for popular support between market forces, ecological sustainability and community wellbeing currently being played out. The MTU Practical Theology programme is itself caught in this contest. The particular expression here is between an established university and an independently accredited private

---

[6] Freire (1974:4) indicates his understanding of integration noting the 'integrated person is subject while the adapted person remains object'. Integration indicates the critical capacity to 'make choices and to transform reality'.

teaching establishment (PTE).[7] It has been suggested that Practical Theology can never be undertaken within a university setting, as in that context it must necessarily be pulled toward a theoretical emphasis and in support of institutionalized knowledge shaped by the dominant hegemony. Mudge and Poling contend that this bias is inevitable, as theory is the priority of the academy. So, while it may be possible to teach the theory of Practical Theology it will not be possible, from situations of community engagement, to embody the processes of reflective action leading to transformation. A basic structural analysis of Aotearoa-NZ society will reveal the 'compromised' role of a state-funded university weighted with a research commitment to the business and corporate sector in the promotion of a 'knowledge economy'. The niche that a 'public-private' education establishment, such as the church is able to develop is therefore significant in keeping in focus human and community wellbeing.

In a relatively 'new' society such as Aotearoa-NZ, the time is right to promote educational processes for Christian community leaders that offer alternatives to traditional western training models. It is critical in Aotearoa-NZ that we avoid any suggestion of engagement in processes of re-colonisation. In multicultural educational environments such as ours the co-creation of knowledge that leads to change is essential. Trust must be demonstrated if partnership is to grow. This is particularly relevant for the denominations whose early missionaries were engaged in the Treaty negotiations, and in the interests of orthodoxy and tradition have since that time largely contained critical thinking within the professional body of the academy.

The way educational programmes are planned, both in curriculum design and pedagogy, need to be consistent with the fundamental philosophy on which the programme sits. Therefore the 'outcomes' we are seeking for our students, for the church, and for the wider community need to be reflected in the way we interact with each other as teachers and learners. This need pushes us in two directions simultaneously: to embody what we wish to be, that is to be the subjects of our own concern, while at the same time being agents of that concern amongst those with whom we live and minister. It is important that the processes we use to achieve our learning outcomes reflect this tension.

The MTU was inaugurated seven years ago. Its design and subsequent practice has attempted to remain faithful to the principle of coherence. The development of the site, the curriculum and the pedagogy was undertaken holistically, with the adult learner and the current context of Aotearoa-NZ at its heart. The opportunity to design a programme from the ground up, with the clear purpose of targeting contextual engagement was an exciting challenge. Physical space and space in the curriculum was provided in which people could find empowerment to engage

---

[7] PTE is the term used to identify teaching establishments accredited by the Aotearoa NZ Qualifications Authority to teach and award diplomas and degrees.

320 Susan Adams

with the processes of reflective practice which we believe leads to transformation. This development reconnects the educational priorities of the Methodist Church of Aotearoa-NZ, Te Hāhi Weteriana, with the social responsibility and transformational priorities of Methodism's foundational years. It also enables Te Hāhi Weteriana to fulfil its moral obligations, following the Church's participation in missionary activities in the Pacific and in Aotearoa-NZ.[8]

The Plan

The design of the MTU demanded a holistic approach that would take account of the person, the place, the programme, and the purpose. The educational philosophy of Paulo Freire and the initiatives of liberation movements toward conscientization influenced the shaping of a place in which students could feel at home and with the right to speak. 'Home' in this instance is a metaphor for the place of security and love where we know that our 'best interests' are of concern and our shortcomings will be handled with sensitivity; where we recognise our environment, and where we can get our bearings and our voice will be heard. 'Home' provides for a sense of belonging as of right, and with the right to engage in shaping its environment, identity and concerns. Emerging from this 'community of mutual concern' comes a desire to participate in the care and nurture of the home place and the 'others' with whom it is shared. Evidence of the 'home' culture is provided in décor and music and dance. Being 'at home' also enables from time to time the use of the first language in collegial learning situations. The invitation by Samoan and Tongan leaders to 'unfold the mat' in the seminar room is indicative of the importance of cultural symbols and of 'being at home'. The development of differently styled spaces and the use of stimulating colours for the general décor and comfortable chairs is consistent with contemporary adult educational theory and practice regarding positive learning environments for adult students. We sought a 'home' feeling in which students would be free to participate. We sought to overcome any sense that it was 'back to school': back to a place of possible failure. This was to be 'our place', and the learning endeavour we were to be engaged in would be something we would do together. Participants are not being sent back to school to be re-educated or trained in the ways of Aotearoa-NZ society. We planned for a cooperative learning environment where we are simultaneously teachers and learners.

'Home' provides a theological motif and a primary model of hospitality. 'Home' resonates with the experience of an environment conducive to trans-

---

[8] John Wesley sought to locate the concerns of the Methodist movement in the migration to the urban centres of industrialising Britain. He took into account the current scientific and theological developments of his day. The provision of access to information and knowledge through a wide range of 'popular' educational opportunities was part of the movement's genius.

formative learning.[9] I am proposing that transformative learning occurs most effectively in the safe environment of 'home' and that this is particularly so in a cross cultural situation. The work of ministry is an offering of hospitality; enabling 'guests' to be 'at home' and providing the circumstances and information where they can contribute to the 'home-making'. It focuses our attention 'here', 'now', in Aotearoa-NZ, *this* unique place we are learning to call 'home'. We seek to facilitate a shift in longing from the places of 'before' off shore, or the 'after-life'; heaven, to this life here, now in Aotearoa-NZ.

Discovering *who we are* in our difference and diversity, and figuring out how to engage with 'the other' is an implicit as well as explicit part of the programme. Theory and practice emerge from the group's experience of the diversity represented in the group itself, and in the prior experiences of members. The security of a safe and trusting environment makes it possible to speak about the embedded ideas brought with us, to re-evaluate and rethink, to re-theologise. From places of security and belonging we can engage positively in processes of change and identity shaping rather than withdrawing, resisting and self-isolating.

Students from the Pacific have expressed dismay at what they experience as the reluctance of many Tongan and Samoan church leaders and their communities to engage with the surrounding neighbourhood and its issues. The eyes of many of the current older generation of leaders look back to Tonga and to Samoa. Key concerns have been the provision money for church building projects, remittances back 'home' to the Islands and meeting the needs of the ministers and newly arrived migrants. Graduate and current theological students are beginning to engage in the debates on these issues that are beginning to take place. They are finding mutual support amongst a wider group of Aotearoa-NZ-born Pacific young people for the work of change. A challenge has emerged to the practice of importing ministers from the islands.

Encouraging many theological students, particularly from the Pacific and Asia, to engage theologically with global concerns for environmental and economic sustainability can be challenging. Yet as awareness of human mobility and the global-local tension develops there comes an urgency to know more about what is going on in the world, the 'global village' and how we can participate in promoting its health. The threat to the islands as a result of climate change is a powerful motivator. For many students our earth-home takes a new place in their perception of where the activities of God can be seen and of what is

---

[9] Jack Mezirow (1990) & (1991) provides for an extensive discussion on the nature and conditions of transformative learning in his two foundational and influential texts on the subject in relation to the adult learner.

322 Susan Adams

sacred and where the sacred is located.[10] The previous paradigm based in maintaining, with as little contamination as possible, the attitudes and mores of their places of origin, seems to shift in their priorities and perception.

A Process

The development of skills in critical theological reflection is fundamentally important for ongoing leadership effectiveness. Developing skills and competence in becoming reflective practitioners forms the centrepiece of the MTU programme design. Student engagement and experience of selected current contextual issues provide the primary data for reflection. A simple model has been developed for collecting and analysing relevant data. Significant time is spent in developing the 'OARRs'[11] model with which the students navigate the unfamiliar waters of critical theological reflection. Observation, Analysis, Reflection and Response provide the basis of the process. This way of imaging the process seems to connect readily with students from the South Pacific, where nations comprise islands connected by the sea and where boats are a fact of life. The use of image and metaphor, symbol, sign, drama, dance and liturgy and open debate are essential tools in a local theological education programme.

Awareness is growing that to live and work responsibly in this 'new land', the Pacific voice, along with the voices of others who are making this place home, needs to be heard within the dialogue. Enabling participation requires from the Pacific leadership both a level of consistent engagement in current issues and a re-evaluation of effective leadership. Pacific communities will inevitably be influenced by their church ministers. The opinion of ministers is weighty and influential. The attitudes and skills of reflective practice, core to Practical Theology, can equip ministers educated in this model, to make a unique contribution to the public dialogue. To exclude the theological perspectives that are emerging from the experiences of this significant group of Pacific people is to alienate Pacific church communities from participation and to force them into a

---

[10] The concept of 'kaitiakitanga' embedded within Maori culture and translated roughly into 'stewardship' seems easily absorbed and readily engages students in environmental concerns. It seems to have the potential of generating a critique of capitalist consumerism and the embedded missionary ideas of dominion over the earth and all creatures by man [sic].

[11] I have developed a simple mind-map for use with the OARRs model for the collection and organising of data. It includes the identification of the theological issue, the contextual factors, the traditions and the implications. Models of reflection provided by the work of Killen and de Beer (1999), Lartey (2000), Thompson and Pattison (2005) Green (1990), Graham (1996) are other sources to be drawn on. A rolling hermeneutical spiral developed from Segundo's hermeneutical circle and also Kolb's learning cycle are also useful models to give shape to the task and a way for students to engage immediately with some confidence.

reactionary and defensive mode. While to question and critique faith and its supporting theology and practice represents nothing less than a paradigm shift for many grass roots Pacific Christian church-goers, to back away from the task will only exacerbate the isolation of the church communities. Not to engage in this serious transformational work is to further alienate the second generation Aotearoa-NZ born from the 'village culture' found in these church communities. It sets them 'adrift' in the sea without oars.

Conclusion

Practical Theology as it is being expressed in the MTU programme is about discovering and naming the emerging dynamic power that is being experienced in culturally diverse as well as multicultural communities. Empowerment for engagement is being found in equipping people with information and reflective processes that enable an honouring of the past and participation in current issues. A contextually based paradigm for theological education, such as the MTU, shaped by the priorities and perspectives of Practical Theology assists these processes.

References

Davidson, Allan (2005). "Chaplain to the Nation or Prophet at the Gate? The Role of the Church in New Zealand Society" in John Stenhouse (ed) *Christianity Modernity and Culture*. Adelaide: ATF Press.

Freire, Paulo (1972). *Pedagogy of the Oppressed*. Great Britain: Sheed & Ward.

(1974). *Education for Critical Consciouness*. 2005 edition. London: Continuum.

Graham, Elaine (1996). *Transforming Practice*. London: Mowbray.

Green, Laurie (1990). *Let's do Theology*. London: Continuum.

Heyward, Carter (1995). *Staying Power*. Cleveland: The Pilgrim Press.

Killen, Patricia, and De Beer (1999). *The Art of Theological Reflection*. New York: Crossroad Pub.

Kolb, David (1984). *The Art of Experiential Learning*. Englewood Cliffs, NJ: Prentice Hall.

Lartey, Emmanuel (2000). "Practical Theology as a Theological Form" in *The Blackwell Reader in Pastoral and Practical Theology,* edited by James Woodward and Stephen Pattison. Oxford: Blackwell Publishers.

Mezirow, Jack and Associates (1990). *Fostering Critical Reflection in Adulthood: A Guide to Transformative and Emancipatory Learning*. San Francisco: Jossey-Bass Publishers.

Mezirow, Jack (1991). *Transformative Dimensions of Adult Learning.* San Francisco: John Wiley & Sons.

Mary Elizabeth Moore (2004). International Journal of Practical Theology Vol. 8, Issue 2.

Mudge, Lewis & James Poling, eds. (1987). *Formation and Reflection.* Philadelphia: Fortress.

Ritzer, George (2004). *The MacDonaldization of Society.* California: Sage Publications.

Segundo, Juan Luis, S.J. (1979). *The Liberation of Theology.* Maryknoll New York: Orbis.

Statistics New Zealand (2006). www.stats.govt.nz/analytical-reports/pacificprofiles/tongan/religion. 7/08/2006

Swinton, John and Harriet Mowat (2006). *Practical Theology and Qualitative Research.* London: SCM Press.

Thompson, Judith and Stephen Pattison (2005). "Reflecting on Reflection: Problems and Prospects for Theological Reflection" in *Contact,* 146:8–15

Walker, Alice (1983). *The Colour Purple.* London: The Women's Press.

The Author

Susan Adams, Rev. Dr., is an Anglican priest in the Diocese of Auckland, New Zealand, who has developed and led a number of innovative programmes for the training of persons for formal and informal ministry. At the time this paper was presented, she was the Director of the Methodist Church of NZ's Ministry Training Unit. She is now engaged in an Anglican Parish-based community-focused programme in Auckland, and is working on further development of the theoretical issues raised in each of the innovative training programmes in which she has been involved. Publications include Social Capital and the Education of the Practical Theologian as a Community Leader, to be published in Contact, 2008; Towards a Reshaped Church, Auckland, New Zealand: Women's Resource Centre, 1991; Being Just Where you Are (with John Salmon), Melbourne: JBCE, 1987; Struggle and Hope: is it Enough? In: Keeping our Heads above Water, Auckland women's Resource Centre, 1998.

Mary Elizabeth Mullino Moore

Non-Theological Discourse in Theological Practices of Peacebuilding

Secularization is commonly understood as a movement away from religious affiliation and participation, diverging from religion, which binds people (*religio*) to particular communities and life patterns.[1] Secularization is portrayed as freeing, religion as narrowing. The work of peacemaking problematizes this distorted bifurcation because the phenomena labeled as secular and religious are enmeshed in one another. Deep conversation is needed if we are to understand the complex relationships and to draw upon religion *and* secularity for the sake of peace. The central question of this essay is how the contributions of non-theological language can thicken human discourse and relationships, serving as a theological resource in peacebuilding. To that end, we turn first to religious resources, then, to the power of process philosophical discourse to inform theological conceptions and practices of peacebuilding.

Religious Resources in Peacebuilding

Many scholars engaged in peacebuilding acknowledge the value of religious resources in resisting violence and building positive relations. Marc Gopin, a Jewish peace leader, recognizes diverse ways in which religion contributes to conflict and peace, sometimes a contributing factor in both, sometimes a veneer over otherwise non-religious motivations. John Paul Lederach, a Mennonite, argues similarly that religion plays diverse roles, but cannot be dismissed; it is vital in realizing the potential for peace. He argues that appraising global violence awakens the need for moral imagination and constructive change.[2] The sources for imagination and change are often religious.

The value of religion was highlighted for me in an interreligious panel on peacemaking. The Buddhist panelist challenged others to consider that religious traditions are not always text-based and discursive. Further, peacemaking is not purely discursive: protesting, proclaiming, and negotiating with words. Describing Buddhist practice, she asked, "What is the role of *meditation* in peacebuilding?" I remembered these words later when I stood on a street corner with signs to protest the United States' threat to enter war with Iraq. A pro-war contingency gathered on the opposite corner and a group of Buddhist monks on

---

[1] Three definitions of secularization are offered by Jose Casanova, *Public Religions in the Modern World* (Chicago: University of Chicago, 1994). The popular definition offered here fits one of Casanova's three, and bears resemblance to a second definition of secularization in terms of the marginalization and privatization of religion.
[2] John Paul Lederach, *The Moral Imagination: The Art and Soul of Building Peace* (Oxford: Oxford University, 2005), 54–60.

a third corner. Two of the monks played small drums while others stood in meditation postures. They used no words, but their presence was powerful.

The Buddhist meditative witness awakened me to the value of religious diversity in peacemaking. Diversity includes the richness of people in *diverse* religions working together and the richness of *each* religious tradition. The richness transcends words and worldviews to include rituals, symbols, affections, ethical values, patterns of daily life, and art. Marc Gopin echoes this, saying that religion's contribution to peacebuilding has less to do with discourse than with ritual, symbol, and art – aspects of human life in which religions are particularly rich.[3] Gopin supports his position with physiological and psychological research on the human brain. People experience the world through many brain functions – a phenomenon that Howard Gardner has named as "multiple intelligences" – and we need to address *all* of these functions if we are to build peace.

Non-Theological Resources for Peacebuilding

If religion has a major role in peacemaking, how do people of diverse religions and diverse perspectives on religion's role in peacemaking work together? Here I consider the potential of non-religious resources in this work, which some identify as "secular." Such resources can create space to relate across difference without requiring agreement on the roles of religion. My purpose is to create that space, and not to resolve definitional questions about religion and secularity, or to draw sharp distinctions between them. The "non-theological" source that I explore is the process-relational philosophy of Alfred North Whitehead. Though the philosophy has shaped process-relational theologies, I focus here on Whitehead's metaphysics rather than the theological constructs developed later by others.

In a Whiteheadian worldview, everything in the world is dynamically related to everything else. This view resonates with Gopin's insistence that peacemaking requires a worldview in which "everything is fundamentally dynamic." Peacemakers recognize that, "when one thing changes, it affects everything else."[4] Such a view engenders hope: positive change is always possible and small

---

[3] Marc Gopin, *Holy War, Holy Peace: How Religion Can Bring Peace to the Middle East* (Oxford: Oxford University Press, 2005). Karl Ernst Nipkow also taps the riches of religious traditions, with particular attention to Jewish and Christian traditions, in his educational approach to peace. See: Karl Ernst Nipkow, *God, Human Nature, and Education for Peace: New Approaches to Moral and Religious Maturity*, in Explorations in Practical, Pastoral, and Empirical Theology (Aldershot, UK: Ashgate, 2003).

[4] Marc Gopin, Lecture, Emory University, 21 March 2007. See also: Gopin, *Healing the Heart of Conflict: 8 Crucial Steps to Making Peace with Yourself and Others* (Emmaus, Pa.: Rodale Press, 2004); Nipkow.

changes can lead to larger ones. These tenets are also a sober reminder that change can move against peace. Gopin's own efforts are to detect "early warnings of peace" in order to build upon them in the long, sometimes invisible journey toward peace.[5]

This view bears remarkable resemblance to process-relational philosophy. Even the most stubborn situations of violence and war are held in place through trajectories of memory, habitual practices, beliefs about the world, and assumptions about what is and is not possible. In a process view, however, all reality is in a process of emerging. Even the most stubborn war heritage holds seeds of novelty and change within itself, Gopin's "early warnings of peace." Other aspects of heritage also exist, such as moments of peaceful coexistence, cooperation, and strong personal and cultural relationships. These seeds of hope can be uncovered and magnified as sources for peacemaking. Five accents of Whiteheadian cosmology are particularly helpful.[6] Each can illumine practical theologians' work of peacemaking.

1. Vision of Peace

A vision of peace is central to process philosophy. A-political in its origins, this vision was not initially focused on political peace processes. It referred to a potential harmony in which all beings live in synergistic, life-enhancing ways. For Whitehead, peace is an ideal that pulls individuals *and* the world toward their finest:

> [Peace] is a broadening of feeling … Its first effect is the removal of the stress of acquisitive feeling arising from the soul's preoccupation with itself. Thus Peace carries with it a surpassing of personality … It results in a wider sweep of conscious interest.[7]

Peace is a vision invoking a sense of wideness, a cosmic vision. It enables people to transcend themselves, to transcend acquisitiveness and value the wellbeing of the entire world. It enables people to let go of fears and other emotions that inhibit, and expand their concerns for others. This vision is larger than the absence of war; it is an active way of knowing and being in the world. Peace is not "anesthesia"; it is "a positive feeling that crowns the 'life and motion' of the soul."[8] It includes reason and feeling. It can be cultivated through actively engaging the world. Thus, peace is the presence of hearty relationships with the wider world.

---

[5] Gopin, Lecture, Emory University, 22 March 2007.
[6] I developed some of these in an earlier essay, found in: "Imagine Peace: Knowing the Real, Imagining the Impossible," in: *Handbook of Process Theology*, Jay McDaniel and Donna Bowman, eds. (St. Louis: Chalice, 2006), 201–216.
[7] Alfred North Whitehead, *Adventures of Ideas* (New York: Free Press, 1967, 1933), 285–286.
[8] Ibid., 285.

328 Mary Elizabeth Moore

Whitehead's view of Peace alerts people to tragedy and the unrealized ideals to which it points – "what might have been, and was not."[9] In this way, tragedy can itself be transformative, awakening people to new vision. Peace does not arise from human effort and reason, however; it "comes as a gift" – a gift to be expected and received. [10] Practical theologians are thus challenged to cultivate expectation and wonder, even in tragic moments. They are challenged to mine their religious traditions for the spirit of awe and for rituals, symbols, and art that open people to hope and its Source.

2. Creativity and Creative Advance

For Whitehead, the principle of creativity permeates the universe; thus, everything is imbued with creativity, whether micro-realities or meta-movements. The creative process is exemplified by the process of concrescence, in which the "many become one and are increased by one."[11] Elements of past experience enter into a new unity in each new occasion; this occasion then enters into later occasions. Through this subatomic process, repeated billions of times every millisecond, everything comes into being. The process takes place in rocks and trees, animals and seas, tiny plants and human beings; thus the entire universe is continually becoming, opening possibilities for the creative advance of the world. Alternatively, the possibilities for destruction are also magnified by this creative process, as when something is created that snatches life from others.

Whitehead accented creativity throughout his writing, especially the creative interplay of past and present with novelty in the ever-becoming processes of the world.[12] For him, the nature of the world *is* creativity; hence, he urged people to participate in, and equip others to participate in, the creative process. He hoped to counteract "minds in a groove" and to instill "habits of aesthetic apprehension" or "the habit of enjoying vivid values."[13] These emphases in process-relational philosophy challenge practical theologians to throw open the doors of creativity and imagination as they engage in present action, theological reflection, and visioning. They accent the role of *phronesis* in practical theology, focusing on future vision and action, as Bernard Lee urges.[14] For peacemaking, these emphases call practical theologians to address realities of

---

[9] Ibid.

[10] Ibid.

[11] Alfred North Whitehead, *Process and Reality: An Essay in Cosmology* (New York: Macmillan, The Free Press, 1978, 1929), 21; cf: 21–22, 40, 56–57.

[12] Whitehead, *Adventures*, 192–193.

[13] Whitehead, *Science and the Modern World* (New York: McMillan, The Free Press, 1967, 1925), 197, 199–200.

[14] Bernard J. Lee, S.M., "Practical Theology as *Phronesis*: A Working Paper from/for Those in Ministry Education," *APT Occasional Papers*, no. 1 (Winter 1998).

violence in ways not envisioned heretofore: to engage with creativity and hope that their efforts, alongside others, will contribute to creative advance.

3. Propositions as Lures for Feeling

A third metaphysical accent is the function of propositions. Whitehead understood propositions as lures for feeling – ideas or constructs that invite fresh perspectives and draw people into hope, curiosity, or the world of possibility.[15] Whitehead was more concerned that a proposition be interesting than it be true. He saw the primary value of truth claims as adding to interest, which fosters intense feeling and value.[16]

In this view, the practice of reason is an aesthetic, life-giving practice: "The function of reason is to promote the art of life."[17] It takes many forms, even traditional logic, which Whitehead encouraged for precise investigation and philosophical rumination.[18] He said, "Logic, properly used, does not shackle thought. It gives freedom, and above all, boldness."[19] Reason is a way for people to explore the heights, depths, and breadth of life, thus awaking to complexities, connections, and new possibilities. The practice of reason can break open abstractions that prevent people from "straying across country" with new ideas and combinations of ideas.[20] It can counteract "inert ideas"; encourage fresh encounters with the world in its immediacy and wholeness; and support painstaking analysis and fresh interpretation.[21] Reason is a way to engage the world through multiple senses and intuitions, and to practice many forms of analysis, yielding new conclusions and contributing value to the world.

Practical theologians need to offer propositions that evoke fresh reasoning, disrupting habitual ideas and attitudes and replacing familiar practices of war and fruitless approaches to peacemaking with more promising approaches. The new approaches may "work" or "not work" in the most pragmatic sense, but even those that do not work as intended may open space for new patterns of relationship. This view parallels Marc Gopin, who says that peacemaking involves "insertion of doubt about what people think definitively about their enemies," which can eventually contribute to a paradigm shift.[22] Propositions can shift paradigms, encouraging the religious value of "holy foolishness" and ethical risk-taking.

---

[15] Whitehead, *Process and Reality*, 25, 184–185.
[16] Ibid., 259.
[17] Whitehead, *The Function of Reason* (Boston, Beacon Press, 1958, 1929), 4.
[18] Whitehead, *The Aims of Education and Other Essays* (New York, The Free Press, 1929), 89.
[19] Ibid., 118.
[20] Whitehead, *Science*, 197.
[21] Whitehead, *The Aims*, 13; *Science*, 199; *The Aims*, 30.
[22] Gopin, Lecture, 22 March 2007.

4. Overcoming Dualisms – Converting Opposition into Contrast

Process-relational thought resists dualisms ingrained in Western culture. Whitehead's integrative impulses led him to a philosophy of organism, exploring complex wholes. He sought to "accommodate scientific theory and practice, and our social, aesthetic, and religious experience."[23] In all things, he resisted reductionism and dualistic contradictions as explanations of reality.[24] Thus, Whitehead could make sense of contradictory realities, inspiring others to seek knowledge through multiple approaches and continual integration. The metaphysical process for embracing complexity is "converting opposition into contrast" – transforming realities assumed to be opposites into wholes that preserve the uniqueness of each, while binding them in relationship.[25] Contrasts include order and chaos, freedom and necessity, permanence and flux, sadness and joy, God and the world. This view of opposition diverges from human practices of compromise – blending into unity with something from each part. The idea of contrast is better depicted in the process of negotiation, or constructing a unity that retains diversity. Contrast is a convergence that contains each part *and* the distinctions among them.

With such a view, either/or thinking is unthinkable; one can never fully separate and choose between oppressor and oppressed, comedy and tragedy, right and wrong. This view suggests that the act of imagining peace requires consideration of all parties in a conflict, each with distinctive histories, hurts, and values, and all in relationship with one another. On a global political scale, this view is embodied more by South Africa's Truth and Reconciliation Commission than by the Nuremberg Trials following World War II. The former dealt more fully with the complexities, evils, and tragedies of diverse peoples and political communities; the latter targeted one particular group as war criminals.

This discussion has considerable relevance for practical theology. Whitehead did not address theologians, but he did address cultural sweeps of history, noting that order can function either "as the condition for excellence" or "as stifling the freshness of living."[26] Dangers arise when distinctions are not preserved – degeneration, triviality, and loss of intensity. This challenges practical theologians to maintain a rich matrix of theological passions and perspectives, embrace conflict, and engage in diverse approaches in dialogue with one another. It challenges political leaders to uphold the values and power of diverse peoples, lest one becomes so powerful that it dominates others. According to Whitehead, "The moment of dominance, prayed for, worked for, sacrificed for, by

---

[23] Victor Lowe, *Alfred North Whitehead: The Man and His Work, Vol. I - 1861–1910* (Baltimore: John Hopkins University, 1985), 5; cf: Whitehead, *Process and Reality*, 3–17, 266–281, 342–351.

[24] Whitehead, *Process and Reality*, 16–17, 274–275.

[25] Ibid., 109, 111, 338–341, 348, 350.

[26] Ibid., 338.

generations of the noblest spirits, marks the turning point where the blessing passes into the curse."[27] In short, no society's order is adequate to preserve and enhance life permanently over time, just as no particular religious order or theological system is adequate. Whitehead concludes, "The art of progress is to preserve order amid change, and to preserve change amid order."[28]

To convert opposition into contrast is to move away from judging one side of a conflict as fully right or wrong, or more oppressed or oppressive. It moves away from sharp divisions between religion and secularity. It encourages practical theologians to draw upon *all* available resources, including those that emerge from theology, "secularity," religious communities, aesthetics, grass root practices, and academic discourse. The practice of converting opposition into contrast encourages peacemakers to move beyond scapegoating and simple answers. It is a way of imagination and negotiation, hard work and bountiful possibility.

5. An Open Future

The process of converting opposition into contrast also suggests a relation between inheritance and novelty, both contributing to an open future. Peaceable breakthroughs of the past (inheritance) are evidence that change is possible in the most conflict-ridden situations of the present (novelty). Every effort at peace in the history of humankind can potentially contribute to a decision for peace in the present moment. Any regret for violence, or tragic awareness of the devastations of war, can contribute to a decision for peace. Novelty enters as well, through the unique integration of past inheritance or through God's initial aim. The combination of inheritance and novelty opens endless possibilities for building peace. The past – with its tragedy, ambiguous successes, and complex moments of peace – is a valuable resource; yet the future is radically open.

Because of the "fully and radically open" future, progress is always possible.[29] This view is easily misunderstood, either by asserting a deterministic past or inevitable progress. Neither is adequate to capture the cosmology of Whitehead. After many years as an agnostic, Whitehead posited the participation of God in the universe because his metaphysical analyses required a transcending explanation of the world's movements. He came to view God as the source for ideals and possibilities, inviting people to sense a goodness that is "attained or missed, with more or less completeness of attainment or omission."[30] For White-

---

[27] Ibid., 339.

[28] Ibid.

[29] John B. Cobb, Jr., and David Ray Griffin, *Process Theology: An Introductory Exposition* (Philadelphia: Westminster, 1976), 112.

[30] Alfred North Whitehead, *Religion in the Making* (New York: Fordham University, 1996, 1926), 60–61.

332 Mary Elizabeth Moore

head, this Source makes it possible to hope for progress, but not to be naïvely optimistic. The future is open, but global progress is not insured.

People can never make peace if they cannot imagine it as a real possibility. The possibility of peace indwells most religious traditions, though religion is sometimes used to reject that possibility, even to postulate a future of religious war. Mark Juergensmeyer describes how religious imagination sometimes projects "images of cosmic war," as in some descriptions of conflicts between Arabs and Jews.[31] Indeed, imagination about the future needs to be subjected to critical analysis, as does *any* form of thinking. Its power can be used for good or ill. Practical theologians cannot be content with occasional dreams and contributions to peacemaking. We need to make a lifelong commitment that we continually analyze, critique, reshape, renew, and restore.

Conclusion

This chapter has been a first step in reflecting on one non-theological system, process-relational philosophy, as a resource to enrich the intellectual constructs, practical theological analysis, and peacemaking practices of practical theologians. I propose that process-relational philosophy, together with the richness of religious traditions, has potential to broaden our understandings of the world; deepen religious experience and convictions; and enhance intellectual, aesthetic, and practical wisdom. With such resources, we might contribute to peacemaking in ways we have not yet envisioned.

The Author

Mary Elizabeth M. Moore, born 1945, is Professor of Religion and Education, Candler School of Theology, Emory University. Beginning 1 January 2009, she will be Professor and Dean, School of Theology, Boston University. Recent publications include: Teaching as a Sacramental Act, Pilgrim, Cleveland 2004; Chris Hermans/Mary Elizabeth Moore (eds.), Hermeneutics and Empirical Research in Practical Theology: The Contribution of Empirical Theology by Johannes A. Van der Ven, Brill, Leuven 2005; Mary Elizabeth Moore/Almeda Wright (eds.), Children, Youth, and Spirituality in a Troubling World, Chalice, St. Louis 2008; "The Ethics of Institutions: Compassion, Critique, Creativity, and Form-Giving," in: Theodore Walker, Jr./Toth Mihaly (eds.), Whiteheadian Ethics, Cambridge Scholars, Cambridge 2008, 83–100; "Education as Creative Power," in: Michel Weber/Will Desmond (eds.), Handbook of Whiteheadian Process Thought, Ontos Verlag, Frankfurt 2008, 199–214.

---

[31] Mark Juergensmeyer, *Terror in the Mind of God: The Global Rise of Religious Violence* (Berkeley: University of California, 2000), 242, 153.

Stephanie B. Klein

The Charismata of Women. An Empirical Case Study

I. The Project and the Empirical Case Study on the Charismata of Women

I would like to report here on an empirical project about the Charismata of women which I carry out on behalf of the kfd (Katholische Frauengemeinschaft Deutschland), an official women organisation of Roman Catholic Church in Germany. The kfd organises the work of more than 620.000 women; its structure contains approx. 6.000 parish groups in whole Germany. It is (according to its own publications) the largest women association in Germany and it is the largest association of the Roman Catholic Church in Germany.

The process "Charismata of women"

In a campaign within the local committees over several years, women developed strategies to become aware of Charismata of women and did their best to create a sensibility for them. On the one hand, women should become conscious of their Charismata, and on the other hand, equally important, the Charismata of women should primarily become visible for the office bearers and the leading men in the church. They shall be perceived and appreciated in theology and church. This process in the parishes is accompanied by two empirical studies: A qualitative case study (by Stephanie B. Klein, Lucerne) and another one on a quantitative base (by Anton A. Bucher, Salzburg). These studies will be introduced to the public in autumn 2007. Both studies are aimed at initiating and promoting discussions in church and in theology.

The qualitative case study

I would like to report on my qualitative case study here. The process is not completed yet and not all results are available now. However, it is possible to formulate some findings already.

The structure and method of the case study

Twelve Narrative Interviews were carried out with Roman Catholic women between 27 and 71 years of age, coming from various and indeed very different social and private situations.

The interviews lasted between one and a half and three and a half hours. After transcription, the data material contains 372 pages. The interviews are being

334 Stephanie Klein

evaluated with methods of the Objective Hermeneutics (Ulrich Oevermann) and the Conversation Analysis (Fritz Schütze).

II. The Concept of Charisma - Some Theological Considerations

The general meaning of Charisma given in the Bible is "present", gift, favour. Charisma is derived from *charizomai*: to give, and *charis*: present, gift. The suffix formation of a noun and -ma emphasizes the result of a plot and points to a concretum – a usual language formation in Koine.[1]

Charisma is frequently brought synonymously to or also in change with *charis*. It puts more emphasise on the result of giving, of what is given by God.

The concept *Charisma* is preferentially used by Paul who picks up a rare and not often used concept from his environment.

- The Old Testament provides only two (unsecured) pieces of evidence (Sir 7.33; 38.20).
- In the New Testament the concept occurs, except for the letters of Paul, only three times in the pastoral letters (1 Petr 4.20, 1 Tim 4.14, 2 Tim 1.6). Paul uses the concept more frequently, but only in Rom, 1 Cor und 2 Cor.
- In the contemporary surrounding of the New Testament the concept does not appear frequently, it is very rare.
- It is rare as well in the writings of the early church.

Paul's concept of Charisma

Paul uses the concept Charisma only in three Epistles (the 1st and 2nd Epistle to the Corinthians, the Epistle to the Romans).

- 1 Cor 1.7: You don't have any lack of any present, (one's gift) to this take (understand) the revelation
- 1 Cor 7.7: Charismata of the different life-forms (unmarried life and marriage)
- 1 Cor 12.1–11: a list of various Charismata (cf. V.4)
- 1 Cor 12.27–31: different presents and the striving for the "bigger" presents (V.28. 18f)
- 2 Cor 1.11: the present of the rescue

---

[1] Vgl. Norbert Baumert: Charisma – Taufe – Geisttaufe. Bd.1: Entflechtung einer semantischen Verwirrung. Würzburg 2001; Karl Rahner: Das Charisma in der Kirche. In: LThK (2.Aufl.) Bd.2, Freiburg 1958, 379–381; Karl Rahner: Das Dynamische in der Kirche. QD5, 1958.

The Charismata of Women

- Rom 1.11–13: the (spiritual) present which he wants to bring to the Romans and share with them to promote the mutual building of the Christian community
- Rom 5.15–17: the present of justice
- Rom 6.23: life in Christ is (undeserved) present of God; unlike: (rightful) pay of the sin is death
- Rom 11.29: God doesn't regret his presents and his vocation (to Israel)
- Rom 12.3–8: list of various Charismata and their fruits.

Charisma can be the present of life in the succession of Christ (Rom 6.23); a life which may contain different lifestyles (e.g. unmarried or married, 1 Cor 7.7).

Charisma in its original Pauline meaning is a single present from God – in almost all cases very concrete. In 1 Cor 12 Paul lists presents, all given by the same Spirit:

- a word of wisdom (*logos sophias*)
- a word of knowledge (*logos gnoseos*)
- faith/confidence (*pistis*)
- presents of healing powers (*charismata hiamaton, pl.*)
- the effects of strength (*energemata dynameon*)
- a prophetic word (*propheteia*)
- distinctions between messages of the spirit (*diakriseis pneumaton, pl.*)
- different kinds of language prayers/glossolallie (*genes glosson*)
- an interpretation of language prayers (*hegmeneia glosson, singl.*).

A main question in the community of Corinth was, whether the striking *glosso-lallie* was the clearest sign for the presence of the Holy Spirit. Corinth had a special reputation for this Charisma. Apparently there was a rank quarrel bet-ween the different gifts. Paul intervenes by stating that there are many various gifts and that all gifts are given by the same Spirit of God and thus are equal. He underlines this opinion with the picture for the unity of the body with its many members (1 Cor 12.12–31a). Here he emphasizes that the members con-sidered as weaker are also indispensable and that even those members regarded as dishonourable have to be treated with decency. With respect to the rank quarrel he refers to love (1 Cor 12.31b – 13.13). The Charisma of everybody has a place in the community (1 Cor 14.26.) The principle according to which the Charismata are brought into the community is one of a certain order: one after the other, and in mutual consideration. The aim is the comprehensibility for others and the mutual on-building and encouragement (1 Cor 14.26–33).

Paul picks up his considerations about different Charismata once again in the later letter to the Romans (Rom 12.1–8). Here he deals rather with the life in and by the Spirit than with questions of the structure of a Christian community. Paul starts with an encouragement to the turning to God. He talks of changing a life completely: in all spiritual and physical aspects. He lists the following Charismata:

- prophecy
- service
- instruction/teaching
- comfort
- giving
- standing up for one another
- compassion.

Again, the picture of the body illustrates equivalence and indispensability of the Charismata.

The concept of Charisma in the further theological development

In the history of the church the concept played a subordinate role. The concept experienced a renaissance only by the sociologist *Max Weber* who newly stamped it by his theory of the charismatic power and the charismatic personality of a leader. This typically modern shift of meaning influences the contemporary use and understanding of Charisma. Charisma is not merely a gift of God here, but becomes connected with the modern concept of subject and its abilities.

Charismata of women

Related to the question of Charismata of women the biblical information can be summarised as follows:

- Charismata of women are non-disposable presents of God.
- Holy Spirit herself manifests herself in these gifts (cf. 1 Cor 12.7).
- Every woman in the community of the *Ekklesia* has got Charismata given by the Holy Spirit, she distributed them "as she wants to" (1 Cor 12.11).
- These Charismata don't have to be equated with social roles of women. They don't correspond to the planning stipulations of the church but may very well mess them up.
- The Charismata of the women are various ones, they can be inconspicuous or obvious. They are all important according to the picture of the many members of the unite body.
- All Charismata shall be allowed to come to the unfolding in the community.
- As presents of God all Charismata of women must be respected and appreciated, church develops from and lives in them.

The Charismata of Women

III. First Allusions to the Charismata of Women: Results from the Interviews

Which Charismata do women live today? What do women tell about their Charismata? The material isn't completely evaluated yet. I would like to give first notes here (under reservation of the definite evaluation). In general, it has to be noticed that these women have a consciousness of their gifts given by God, and they articulate this awareness in a plain and simple everyday language.

The Charisma of the communication and translation of faith

A lot of women mention their ability to translate traditional beliefs (biblical, dogmatic, pious experiences etc.) into nowadays language and the world of experience we live in. They also see the necessity for this arrangement which is not perceived frequently in inner church circles at all.

> "I think the love for the Bible is something I am particularly good at, and then I find the right words to tell it to people, let them feel it, what this Bible and pious traditions are all about." (Mrs Münther, 51 years)

Mrs Dornbach, 71 years, sees her gift in the passing on of beliefs, too:

> "[...] translating these faith statements which are sometimes a little difficult, or what is in the Bible into the language of our ordinary world."

The Charisma of the life-form

Already Paul speaks about different Charismata regarding the life-form: "I wish that all men were as I am. But each man has his own gift from God; one has this gift, another has that" (1 Cor 7.7).

The questioned women live in various life-forms and represent a variety of living Christian female Charismata today.

- The education of own children seems so natural and "normal" that it isn't mentioned especially as a Charisma. But often the formation of a family is connected with privations for the women. The renunciation of professional unfolding is often described with melancholy, and there is a renunciation of time for own interests and in some cases the renunciation of the possibility to continue theological studies.
- One woman emphasizes that her lifestyle in the community of an order provides her with a great acceptance and reliability when she deals with people in today's society. She realises that this is partly due to the traditional image of Christian orders. At the same time the order community gives her safety and a cushion for negative experiences.

338 Stephanie Klein

- One woman, Mrs Kaufmann, 71 years, refers the question of Charismata directly to her lesbian lifestyle and her task of dismantling prejudices by the passing on of her example, a homosexual way of life. She regards it as her Charisma to live freely and without hiding:

> "I think that my abilities lie in this to be able just to live liberal and openly. I live out of the faith now so as I am, as I feel, as I am convinced that God also wants to have me. He then wouldn't have allowed this form of lives certainly, if it wasn't so. I think it is a challenge to accept that for one self... I will not live a lie anymore. That can not be his will […] I think that comes out of my faith".

She considers the removal of taboos from the lesbian life-form as her task: "Public relations. Dare to do things. I think that this is my ability and that I have to use it".

The Charisma of service: commitment for others

Commitment for others is described in multiple ways. Caring for parents and parents-in-law when they are old and sick is mentioned according to the Pauline term "service" repeatedly. A woman calls her work for multiple handi-capped persons in special facilities explicitly her Charisma.

Care, comfort and acceptance of the others

Many women talk about her Charisma to be able to listen, to signal to the people that they are accepted and understood, and to provide comfort and a feeling of well-being. Again Mrs Dornbach:

> "This sensitivity has been given to me during my illness. And I think, this is a gift and if I still carry this one actually which has befitted me from someplace and which is now with me for twenty years. Therefore this sensitive develop-ment for the so called everyday histories, which we see no more and ignore in the hectic rush, grew in me. It's actually simple: to take the time to realize these are the miracles anyway, these are small, tiny miracles, therefore miracles happen not only in the Bible but today, too [...] I have experienced this also in many conversations with people suffering from an illness".

Organization and working with chaos and inadequacy

Many women mention their organizing ability but also their ability to work with inadequacy, provisional situations and even chaos as their Charisma. Mrs Ebert (70 years) connects her organizing ability explicitly with her faith:

> "I am one which can organize well, can design structures and keep up any necessary work, and this is related to my activities in the parish which I carry out in faith […]."

The Charismata of Women

Two women explicitly mention their ability to handle chaos.

> "[...] I can bear chaos therefore well, I can bear mess in the youth work... well, untidy tents and a chaotic office and also dirt, this is quite important, if it must be, that one can leave things as they are sometimes. Things can be in a chaotic state before clarity is achieved, it cannot always already be ready [...]." (Mrs Münther, 51).

Mrs Fuhrmann (45 years) told the interviewer about her efforts to make everything as good as possible, but also about her experiences with her own limits. She had to admit weaknesses and defeats. She connects the acceptance of weakness with her faith:

> "How does my faith come to an expression here? (*thinks over*) [...] As I said, I try to make everything as good as it is possible [...] However, one also must admit I sometimes don't know things perhaps so well, and mistakes happen, or if things went wrong, you learn in the church to accept that, to accept defeats or weaknesses, that one doesn't have to be perfect in everything".

Charismata in the liturgical area: processes of changing

Many interviews show quite well the exclusion of women from the liturgical area: The chancel, the sacristy and the gallery were locked for them during their childhood and they felt a great shyness when working in "sacred" places and with some pieces of equipment. Cleaning the church and the liturgical equipment was the only entrance for Catholic girls and women.

Nevertheless, the material does reflect a rapid change in this field. Many women overcame their shyness and feel her Charismas to take on liturgical tasks today as well.

Summary

Central structures of the Christian life and of being Christ's church come to expression in the Charismata of women: They have got Charismata in the spiritual welfare (*diakonia*), in the passing on of the faith and its transformation into the present time (*martyria*), in the organization and the creation of community (*koinonia*). In the area of liturgy (*liturgia*) we witness a change, at least in the daily practice of many parishes: Catholic women do involve themselves more and more.

340 Stephanie Klein

Prospects on the finished case study

These are only some first allusions to the results from the case study. A central focus is the question, which factors supported the women with respect to the unfolding of their Charismata and what impeded them.

Another crucial question will be, how the various Charismata of women as God's gifts can be brought to full theological and churchly appreciation, how they can be integrated structurally in the church so that the church can develop through them.

As a matter of fact, it seems so as if the women form and build up the church with their activities and Charismata at the base. However, this is not inserted conceptually, neither by theology nor by the official churchly organisation. I do not think church can afford this ignorance any longer, can no longer ignore the various presents of the Holy Spirit for half of its members. To speak in Paul's picture again: The body needs both halves of its members.

The Charismata of women must be respected and appreciated as given by God. They build up the church because the church lives by these gifts which God gives to the women. Wherever the Charismata of the women are promoted and developed, church will develop and flourish.

The Author

Stephanie B. Klein, Prof. Dr. theol. habil., born 1957, is Professor for Pastoraltheologie at the Katholische Fakultät of the Universität Luzern, Switzerland. Recent publication: ‚Jede hat ihre Gnadengabe von Gott, die eine so, die andere so' (1 Kor. 7,7). Die Charismen von Frauen. Eine qualitativ-empirische Studie. In: Katholische Frauengemeinschaft Deutschlands (Hg.): Jede hat ihre Gaben. Studien, Positionen und Perspektiven zur Situation von Frauen in der Kirche. Ostfildern 2008, 64–123.

Practical Theology and Ministry Formation

Neil Pembroke

Spiritual Care by Physicians: Maintaining the Integrity of Religion and Finding an Appropriate Form

The process of secularization means the rejection of a major role for religion in central social domains such as healthcare, education, politics, and the arts. Though it is widely recognized that religion has a role to play in all of these areas, the secular society views it as a minor one. The principles that shape the theories and practices in these central social domains are drawn almost exclusively from secular sources. However in the healthcare field, especially in the United States, there is a move to once again establish a central place for religion and spirituality. The argument is that the mind-body paradigm, while constituting an advance beyond a strictly biomedical approach, does not go far enough. The new era of medicine, some are claiming, will be founded on a mind-body-spirit or "theosomatic" (Levin, 2001) paradigm. There is now quite a large body of empirical evidence supporting this claim. Physicians who subscribe to this new model of healthcare take the view that spiritual care is an essential part of their work.

Some, perhaps many, in the Christian community will want to champion this new approach. It looks like one important area of societal life in which religion is making a comeback, so to speak. Theologians interested in the healthcare field tend to welcome the valuing of the spiritual dimension, but at the same time express a concern, rightly I will argue, that the new thrust carries with it an unintended degradation of religion. The reason for this unfortunate "side effect" has to do with the link that is made with the empirical research on the health benefits associated with religious belief and practices. The rationale supporting the move to spiritual care by physicians tends to run like this: There is strong scientific evidence that religion has a salutary effect on health; we should therefore do what we can to encourage and support the spirituality of our patients. This instrumentalist approach to spiritual care, I will argue, is inappropriate. It is my contention that it is much more desirable to see support for the patient's spirituality as part of holistic care.

The Religion and Health Connection

There is now a substantial body of research literature that claims to show the generally positive effects of religious involvement on a wide range of health outcomes. One of the leading figures in religion and health research, Harold Koenig of Duke University, notes that of the more than 850 articles on religious involvement and mental health over two thirds show an advantage for the religiously active, and that of the more than 350 articles on religious involvement and physical health over one half show an advantage for the religious (Koenig, 2000). Another key figure, the epidemiologist Jeff Levin, puts the number of empirical studies showing a positive relationship between religion and health even higher at 75–90% (Levin, Chatters & Taylor, 2005). Among the physical diseases and issues that have been examined are heart disease, hypertension and other circulatory disorders, cerebrovascular disease, cancer, gastrointestinal disease, immune system, physical disability, pain and somatic symptoms, overall self-rated health, and self-reported symptomatology (Ellison & Levin, 1998; Koenig, 1999; Koenig, McCullough & Larson, 2001; Levin, 2001). Research on religion and mental health includes religious coping, hope and optimism, self-esteem, bereavement, social support, depression, suicide, anxiety, psychosis, alcohol and drug use/abuse, marital instability, personality, and general mental health (Koenig, 1999; Koenig et al., 2001; Levin, 2001). Thoresen and Harris (2002) and Kliewer (2004) provide useful summaries of the research findings on the advantages for the religiously involved. They include the following:

- Lower rates of coronary disease, emphysema, cirrhosis, and suicide.
- Lower blood pressure.
- Lower rates of myocardial infarction.
- Better immune system function and lipid profiles.
- Improved physical functioning and medical regime compliance.
- Higher levels of self-esteem and lower levels of depression.
- Reduced levels of pain in cancer patients.
- Less medical service utilization.

Though there are some who are very skeptical (see Sloan, Bagiella, & Powell, 1999; Sloan et al., 2000; Sloan & Bagiella, 2002), it does seem that there is growing epidemiological evidence that religion has a salutary effect on health.

The Religion and Health Connection and Spiritual Care

A large number of papers have appeared over the past ten years exploring the clinical implications of the religion and health link. The rationale that they tend to follow is this. If there is scientific evidence indicating that religious persons have a health advantage then it behooves us as clinicians to support and encourage patient spirituality. The following statements are typical of the approach: "We believe that there are sufficient, research-based reasons for clinicians to provide basic spiritual interventions…" (Larimore, Parker & Crowther, 2002, p. 70) and "Spirituality is an important, multidimensional aspect of human experience…[and] convincing evidence in the medical literature supports its beneficial role in the practice of medicine" (Anandarajah & Hight, 2001, p. 87). Spirituality is viewed by these proponents of spiritual care as an "adjunct to therapy" (Lawrence & Smith, 2004, p. 626) and as part of "the arsenal of treatment" (Larson in Mita, 1998, p. 1896) of the clinician.

Spiritual Care by Physicians

Already you may be sensing that from a theological point of view there is a problem with this approach. Religion and spirituality are approached in utilitarian terms. Spirituality is seen as simply one more weapon to add to the therapeutic arsenal. Doctors have long advised patients to eat a balanced, nutritious diet and to exercise regularly in order to promote health. The scientific evidence indicates these medical interventions. Now that the scientific research is mounting for a religion and health link, doctors should, so the argument goes, support and encourage "good spiritual hygiene." One medical writer actually equates nutrition and spirituality: "Compare spirituality with nutrition... Inadequate nutrition is costly. If people are not fed properly, resistance weakens and wounds do not heal. Evidence is growing in volume and quality that this holds of spiritual sustenance too" (Culliford, 2002, p. 1435).

A number of writers with a theological perspective have quite rightly objected to this tendency to treat religion as a commodity (VandeCreek, 1999; Cohen, Wheeler & Scott & the Anglican Working Group in Bioethics, 2000; Cohen, Wheeler & Scott, & the Anglican Working Group in Bioethics, 2001; Shuman and K.G. Meador, 2003). It is never legitimate to use religion as a means to an end; it is an end in itself. In the Christian understanding, the end of religion is a joyful, faithful, and courageous participation in the Kingdom or Realm of God. Scripture scholars are virtually unanimous in their view that Jesus' primary understanding of the mission bestowed on him by the Father was the establishing of God's Reign in the world. In the new era of divine grace, love, righteousness and reconciliation would win out over the evil, hatred and division that so distorts the true purpose of human existence. Jesus came into the world as an expression of the hospitality of God, inviting all persons to share in God's love and healing (Byrne, 2000). The Christian faith is not something that can be used for this or that purpose – no matter how noble or worthy the purpose may be. It is a way of being in the world that is shaped by one's encounter with Jesus Christ and his invitation to participate in God's Reign.

The central problem we are encountering is that the issue of spiritual care by physicians is wrongly framed. When the fact that the empirical research indicating a religion and health connection is used as the starting point, it is inevitable that the movement will be in the direction of instrumentalism. The first step in the process is the observation that there is this emerging body of scientific evidence. The second is the question: How can we use this in clinical practice? Then comes the answer: We should support and encourage religion and spirituality. This way of approaching the religion and health research leads to some unfortunate and misguided suggestions. Consider, for example, this proposal for the spiritual care that a family physician might offer:

> ...[F]amily physicians can encourage patients to make use of potentially health-promoting religious resources from patients' own religious traditions. Where appropriate, religious patients might be encouraged to pray more –

346 Neil Pembroke

> whether individually or with others. If already attending a church, synagogue, or mosque, they might be encouraged to continue. They might be encouraged to meditate. They might be encouraged to attend worship, engage in religiously based mourning rituals, seek and ask forgiveness from significant others, or read holy writ (Matthews et al., 1998, p. 123).

This suggestion that doctors should express their spiritual care by encouraging patients to be more spiritually active is by no means an isolated case. Harold Koenig includes it in many of his publications (see Koenig, 1999, pp. 277–280; Koenig, 2002, pp. 25–26). When offering his proposal, he indicates that the physician "may even point out that there is indeed evidence from scientific research suggesting that religious beliefs do help people cope and may affect their health outcomes" (Koenig, 2002, p. 25). Larimore et al. (2002), to give one final example, advise clinicians to "encourage positive spirituality with their patients" (p. 72).

There seems to be clear evidence indicating that linking the empirical research on religion and health to the question of spiritual care inevitably leads to a degradation of religion. This does not, mean, however, that there is no warrant for physicians engaging with the religious and spiritual concerns of their patients. The philosophy of holism is well established in medical theory and practice. A holistic approach is one in which the patient is approached as a unity of physical, psychological, social, and spiritual aspects. One medical practitioner illustrates this approach very well: "Until M's account of his inner world of meaning was heard, acknowledged and affirmed, until he had felt this spiritual dimension of himself to be understood, the totality of his person had not been addressed and cared for" (Bacon in Todres, Catlin & Thiel, 2005, p. 2735). It is here that we find a legitimate rationale for spiritual care by physicians (Cf. Cohen et al., 2001; Shuman & Meador, 2003). The religion and health research has no place in the conversation. Including it can only lead to a distortion of the meaning of religion.

Appropriate Spiritual Care

Medical practitioners are not pastors; they have neither the expertise nor the time to engage in spiritual counseling with their patients. That is not to say, though, that they cannot empathically engage with their patients' spiritual values and concerns. They can, for example, take a short spiritual history that (quite apart from its practical use in relation to medical care) communicates to the religious patient that this dimension of her life is honored. There are a number of useful models of spiritual assessment available (Pulchalski & Romer, 2000; Anandarajah & Hight, 2001; Koenig, 2002).

The question of physicians and prayer is more controversial. There are two categories involved here, namely patient-initiated and doctor-initiated prayer.

Provided a healthcare provider is comfortable with it, there seems to be no ethical reason for her not to accept a patient's request for prayer. If she is ill at ease, she can demonstrate her respect for the patient's spirituality by re-commending colleagues or chaplains who would be happy to share in prayer (Cf. Cohen et al., 2000).

The issue of doctor-initiated prayer needs to be framed around questions of the power differential between patient and doctor and the consequent possibility of coercion (See Cohen et al., 2000; Post, Puchalski & Larson, 2000; Astrow, Puchalski & Sulmasy, 2001; Koenig, 2002). There is a clear asymmetry in the relationship between the doctor and the patient. The doctor possesses a high level of medical expertise and the patient's healing is in her hands. The patient, on the other hand, is beset by pain, uncertainty, anxiety, and feelings of loss of control. Moreover, physicians are accorded a privileged position within the health care institution and therefore possess considerable social power over the patient. When a doctor asks a patient if she or he would like to share in prayer, then, the possibility that the patient will feel coerced is strong. I am of the opinion that the threat of unintended coercion is so real that physicians should only pray publicly with a patient when she has made an explicit request.

Conclusion

The fact that more and more physicians are viewing spiritual care as an essen-tial part of their work is in and of itself a good thing. However, it often carries with it an unfortunate "side effect," namely the degradation of religion. The re-ligious life is not a means to the end of good health. Rather, it is an end in itself. I have argued that it is imperative to keep the religion and health research out of the issue of spiritual care by physicians. Practices such as the taking of spiritual histories, responding to requests for prayer, and making links with chaplains and other religious representatives should be affirmed. If someone needs a rationale for spiritual care by physicians, they need look no further than the principle of holistic care.

References

Anandarajah, G. & Hight, E. (2001). 'Spirituality and medical practice: Using the HOPE questions as a practical tool for spiritual assessment,' *American Family Physician* 63, 81–88.

Astrow, A.B., Puchalski, C.M. & Sulmasy, D.P. (2001), 'Religion, spirituality, and health care: Social, ethical, and practical considerations,' *The American Journal of Medicine* 110, 283–287.

Byrne, B. (2000). *The hospitality of God: A reading of Luke's Gospel.* Sydney: St. Pauls.

Cohen, C.B., Wheeler, S.E., Scott, D.A. & the Anglican Working Group in Bioethics (2000). 'Prayer as therapy: A challenge to both religious belief and professional ethics,' *The Hastings Center Report* 30, 40–47.

Cohen, C.B., Wheeler, S.E., Scott, D.A. & the Anglican Working Group in Bioethics (2001). 'Walking a fine line: Physician inquiries into patients' religious and spiritual beliefs,' *The Hastings Center Report* 31, 29–39.

Culliford, L. (2002). 'Spirituality and clinical care,' *British Medical Journal* 325, 1434–1435.

Ellison, C.G. & Levin, J.S. (1998). 'The religion–health connection: Evidence, theory and future directions,' *Health Education and Behavior* 256, 700–720.

Kliewer, S. (2004). 'Allowing spirituality into the healing process, *The Journal of Family Practice* 53, 616–624.

Koenig, H.G., (1999). *The healing power of faith*. New York: Simon & Schuster.

Koenig, H.G. (2000).'Religion, spirituality, and medicine: Application to clinical practice,' *Journal of the American Medical Association* 284, 1708.

Koenig, H.G., McCullough, M.E., & Larson, D.B. (2001). *Handbook of religion and health*. Oxford: Oxford University Press.

Koenig, H.G. (2002). *Spirituality in patient care*. Philadelphia: Templeton Foundation.

Larimore, W.L., Parker, M. & Crowther, M. (2002). 'Should clinicians incorporate positive spirituality into their practices? What does the evidence say? *Annals of Behavioral Medicine* 24, 69–73.

Lawrence, R.T. & Smith, D.W. (2004). 'Principles to make a spiritual assessment work in your practice,' *The Journal of Family Practice* 53, 625–631.

Levin, J.S. (2001). *God, faith, and health: Exploring the spirituality-healing connection*. New York: John Wiley & Sons.

Matthews, D.A., McCullough, M.E., Larson, D.B., Koenig, H.G., Swyers, J.P. & Greenwold Milano, M. (1998). 'Religious commitment and health status: A review of the research and implications for family medicine,' *Archives of Family Medicine* 7, 118–124.

Mita, M. (1998). 'Getting religion seen as help in being well,' *The Journal of the American Medical Association* 280, 1896–1897.

Post, S.G., Puchalski, S.G. & Larson, S.G. (2000). 'Physicians and patient spirituality: Professional boundaries, competency, and ethics,' *Annals of Internal Medicine* 132, 578–583.

Pulchalski, C. & Romer, A.L. (2000). 'Taking a spiritual history allows clinicians to understand patients more fully,' *Journal of Palliative Medicine* 3, 129–137.

Spiritual Care by Physicians

Lawrence, R.J. (2002). 'The witches' brew of spirituality and medicine,' *Annals of Behavioral Medicine* 24, 74–76.

Shuman, J.J. & Meador, K.G. (2003). *Heal thyself: Spirituality, medicine, and the distortion of Christianity.* Oxford: Oxford University Press.

Sloan, R.P., Bagiella, E. & Powell, T. (1999). 'Religion, spirituality, and medicine, *The Lancet* 353, 664–667.

Sloan, R.P., Bagiella, E., VandeCreek, L., Hover, M., Casalone, C., Jinpu Hirsch, T., Hasan, Y., Kreger, R. & Poulos, P. (2000). 'Should physicians prescribe religious activities?' *The New England Journal of Medicine* 342, 1913–1916.

Sloan, R.P. & Bagiella, E. (2002). 'Claims about religious involvement and health outcomes,' *Annals of Behavioral Medicine* 24, 14–21.

Todres, I.D., Catlin, E.A. & Thiel, M.M. (2005). 'The intensivist in a spiritual care training program adapted for physicians,' *Critical Care Medicine* 33, 2733–2736.

VandeCreek, L. (1999). 'Should physicians discuss spiritual concerns with patients?' *Journal of Religion and Health* 38, 193–201.

The Author

Neil Pembroke is Senior Lecturer in Pastoral Studies and Coordinator of the Doctoral Program in Pastoral Studies at the University of Queensland, Brisbane, Australia. His recent publications include: *Moving Toward Spiritual Maturity: Psychological, Contemplative, and Moral Challenges in Christian Living* (New York: Haworth Pastoral Press, 2007); 'Conjugal Loss and Ambivalent Feelings: A Theological Reflection and a Pastoral Sermon.' *Practical Theology.* Forthcoming; 'Covenant, Trust, and Management-Labour Relations', *International Journal of Practical Theology.* Forthcoming; 'The Spirituality of Presence in Midwifery Care.' *Midwifery* 24 (Sept. 2008), pp. 321–327. (with J.J. Pembroke); 'Empathy, Emotion, and *Ekstasis* in the Patient-Physician Relationship.' *Journal of Religion and Health* 46, no. 2 (June 2007), pp. 287–298.

Edward Foley

Ministerial integration

Introduction

Organized religion has not been immune to the fragmenting, secularizing, and redefining trends of post-modernity. The new millennium has witnessed the unraveling of many religious organizations and the decline of religious authority and influence. Two of the most publicized examples of such disintegration in the US have been the highly charged sex abuse scandal within the Roman Catholic Church which led to the resignation of Cardinal Bernard Law in December of 2002; and the threat of schism within the Anglican communion, whose symbolic trigger was the ordination of Gene Robinson as the first openly gay bishop in 2003.

Besides the impact on ecclesial structures and institutions, individual Christian ministers serving in such ecclesial and societal contexts during times of such rapid change and upheaval often experience their own fragmentation, disorientation and confusion. Numerous studies have examined the growing rates of depression, isolation and burnout of contemporary clergy. Such studies indicate that the sources of this stress are broad and deep. Common factors include the diverse and sometimes staggering multitasking required of a contemporary minister, the general decline in respect for and the authority of clergy in secularized societies, the lack of professional and spiritual support systems for clergy, the inadequate preparation for the real life demands of ministry, as well as the personal and psychological unpreparedness and even unsuitability of some candidates for ministry.

This situation is challenging both for the individual minister, as well as for those individuals, institutions and adjudicatories responsible for preparing and sustaining present and future ministers for work in the Church. In response to the significant ecclesial and societal changes of the past 40 years, there have been seismic changes in places like the US in most initial and continuing formation programs for clergy, as well as the reshaping of seminaries and clergy support systems, and multiple new initiatives for shepherding the ministry candidate in the critical transition from seminary to parish or congregation. Some schools, for example, have shaped their entire curriculum around a central theological theme or ministerial practice; many groups of ministers have banded together in personal and spiritual support groups; some leaders have created high profile programs for helping folk to make the transition from the classroom to the congregation; there are even mainline churches which have mandated such programs for those transitioning from seminary into full time ministries.

Ministerial integration   351

One critical issue that often arises in the nurturing and sustenance of Christian and other ministers who offer their service in the midst of significant contextual change, social ferment is that of integration. Many authors, specialists and authorities charged with ministerial formation are deeply committed to and concerned about this idea. The United States Catholic Conference of Bishops, for example, employs the term 31 times in their relatively brief 2000 document "The Basic Plan for the Ongoing Formation of Priests," and in the introduction of that plan, notes that

> "The unifying thread for both parts of the plan is the grace and the task of integration, which fosters the living synthesis of priestly identity and priestly service. Integration is at the heart of ongoing formation, as priests grow in bringing together who they are and what they do. Their growth is really a growing integrity or connectedness of their ministry and their life."[1]

One of the fundamental challenges surrounding the integration agenda, however, is an apparent lack of consensus on what exactly constitutes integration. In a highly competitive workplace, for example, integration is sometimes understood as an ability to balance critical personal and professional skills in a multitask environment deemed necessary for both hiring and retention. For those concerned with the education of first degree students at colleges or universities in the US, integration or "integrative learning" is an ability to make connections. Researchers from the Carnegie Foundation for the Advancement of Teaching argue that this ability for connectivity is central to scholarship broadly conceived, "whether focused on discovery and creativity, integrating and interpreting knowledge from different disciplines, applying knowledge through real-world engagements, or teaching students and communicating with the public."[2] In a previous study of my own on the concept of integration,[3] conducted at ten Roman Catholic Seminaries in the United States, while the vast majority of the faculty and students interviewed held integration to be "very important" or "important for effectiveness in ministry," most (approximately 65%) defined integration as what one interviewee described as

> "cognitive integration, i.e., a student sitting in a Bible class and thinking about preaching, or a student in a eucharist class and making connections with what the student learned in a dogmatics class." This same interviewee hoped for a

---

[1] At http://www.usccb.org/plm/ongoing.htm [accessed 9 December 2006].
[2] Mary Taylor Huber and Pat Hutchings, *Integrative Learning: Mapping the Terrain* (Washington DC: American Academy of Colleges and Universities, 2004), 1–2.
[3] For this study, focused on Roman Catholic ordination candidates preaching and presiding at Eucharist, integration was defined as "an obvious level of development in the priest-presider that combines 1) solid knowledge of the liturgy with 2) competence and ease in performance skills (e.g., gestures, proclamation, etc.) for enacting the rite, and 3) a clear pastoral sensitivity for the assembly and other ministers."

352 Edward Foley

"more holistic type of integration that we performance skills, faith, and ethics to the cognitive."[4]

The Research Project

Because of the significance of the issue for both initial and ongoing ministerial formation as well as the disparate ways of thinking about integration, and in light of the rich and varied programmatic efforts towards fostering and sustaining integration, I and my colleague Herbert Anderson, have undertaken a study of this topic. The issue of integration, especially the integration of theory and practice in ministerial students, has been an active topic of conversation at Catholic Theological Union for over a decade. Out of various projects, consultations and discussions, a series of theses about integration have been formulated. These are the theses that we wish to test in our research:

1) Integration is a dynamic reality: There could be an implicit problem with the English word "integration" which, as a noun, could give the impression that integration is some kind of static reality or capacity that can be achieved. In response, we are exploring the language of "integrating habitus" or "integrating trajectory" as alternative ways of conceptualizing the dynamic [= verb] rather than static [= noun] foundations of this reality.

2) Integration has multiple forms: Given the dynamics of integration, and the flux of the social and ecclesial environment where the integrating habitus needs to be exercised, there is no "pure" or "right" form of integration. Rather, every authentic integrating habitus is a hybrid, a unique form of hyphenation or even bi-culturality, especially for the religious working offering service in the context of a secularized world.

3) Integration could be considered a form of contextual adaptation: Some research has shown that people who live in a hybrid or bicultural situation do not embrace elements from both cultures that constitute their identities to the same degree at the same time. Instead, as their self-identities vary depending on the social situation, so is the balance between their cultural resources realigned to address the new social situation. Similarly the minister on an integrating trajectory is one who has cultivated the habitus of contextualization and adaptation.

4) Integration is an imaginative act: In order to act holistically in the midst of fragmentation, we need to imagine the whole as we connect the parts. Because integration is an imaginative act, it is also a dangerous activity, breaking boundaries and making something new. It requires the willingness of individuals and institutions to conceive of themselves in new ways. When the

---

[4] "The Teaching of Worship in Roman Catholic Seminaries: A Case Study in Integration." *Liturgical Ministry* 10 (Summer 2001) 163.

Ministerial integration 353

integrating trajectory is experienced in this imaginative manner, it more often invites wonder rather than satisfaction.

5) Integration requires a balance between head, heart, and hand skills. The ability to think in an integrated way is not sufficient for an integrating habitus. Rather, nurturing this habitus requires a combination of cognitive, affective and performative skills open to the working of God's Spirit.

6) Integration is best discovered, fostered and sustained in the practices of ministry. Since ministry is ultimately an activity rather than simply an idea, ministerial performance is of prime importance in discovering the dynamics of an authentic integrating habitus, testing the correlation of those dynamics, and nurturing a deepening of this integrating habitus. This is especially true of public performance because it respects and witnesses to the public context in which ministry is enacted.

7) Integration is an institutional issue: In theological education there is a prejudice that this is a student issue. Integration, however, is a pervasive issue and the forming or sustaining of ministers with an integrating habitus is not a task that can be confined to a classroom, program or curriculum. Institutions cannot expect integration in ministerial students and the growth of an integrating habitus if such integration is not modeled by schools of ministry, sponsoring adjudicatories, and faith communities which provide internships and become the source of a minister's call. Every aspect of an institution has the potential to contribute to or inhibit the integrating process.

8) Integration cannot occur *ex nihilo*: Since the development of an integrating habitus requires a new vision of oneself, those who are launching into an integrating trajectory are in need of broad modeling and support across institutions, denominations, and communities of faith for the development of this pastoral imagination.[5]

9) Integration serves mission: The development and exercise of an integrating habitus is integration is not a goal in itself, but is for the transformation of ministers, of institutions, and ultimately for the transformation of the world. An integrating habitus is thus fundamentally missiological.

10) Integration is a life's work: While ministerial students can be initiated into an integrating habitus during seminary training, most of their integrating work

---

[5]Craig Dykstra explains the pastoral imagination as "an internal gyroscope and a distinctive kind of intelligence .... a way of seeing into and interpreting the world which shapes everything a pastor thinks and does .... [which] requires a particular intelligence that involves specific capacities of mind, spirit and action, that are specific to pastoral ministry itself." Craig Dykstra, "The Pastoral Imagination," *Initiatives in Religion* 9:1 (2001) 1.

occurs after they leave. Thus institutions need to expend significant energy not only assessing current trajectories of integration in a ministerial candidate, but also parallel resources in preparing candidates for an integrating habitus that unfolds throughout their ministerial lives.

11) Integration belongs as much to a community as to an individual: Western concepts of integration, that focus on the individual in an egocentric way and see integration as a personal goal, need to be critiqued by the dynamics of integration modeled in more sociocentric societies where integration is a community task and need.

The Research Process

Initially the plan for testing these theses was to engage in an extensive longitudinal study tracking individuals and their respective schools, congregations, adjudicatories or other institutions, to discover something of the dynamics of the integrating habitus revealed over time. After broad consultation, however, it was agreed that it would be a better use of our resources to draw upon the vast amount of work already done on the topic of integration, rather than engage in fresh field work on the topic. Since wide consultation is vital to the success of the project, it was decided that, as part of that consultation process, we would gather a small group of gifted colleagues at the outset of this venture, so that the topic is considered in all of its richness.

After the initial consultation, the primary researchers will take responsibility for a review of the literature, and the shaping of a book addressing the subject. We will also conduct twenty-six extensive interviews with individuals whom our consultants have helped us to select. These interviewees will be selected to exemplify the integrating habitus in its dynamic diversity. These flesh-and-blood stories will be employed to punctuate the book, as both illustrations and interpretations of what the integrating habitus can be.

After drafting the book, envisioned as a 12–14 month process, the primary researchers will forward the draft to the consultants two to three months in advance of a second gathering of them. The second consultation is designed to offer feedback, critique, commendation and recommendation on the proposed written work. Since it is presumed that several trajectories pursued in the volume will have been generated by the consultants, it seems both ethical and properly collaborative to return to them towards the end of the project for their review and final input. After the close of the second consultation, the primary researchers will finish the volume for publication.

A Preliminary Conclusion

While a published volume is the most tangible foreseen outcome of this project, in some ways it is of least importance. Of much more significance is a sustained and ever broadening conversation on this potent and sometimes illusive topic. There is wisdom to be harvested here, as many individuals and some institutions have broached this topic with varying degrees of intensity and depth. Engaging leaders in theological education as well as the ministerial leadership we hope to target as our interviewees, has the potential for creating an every widening and influential circle of ministerial theologians and practitioners who can provide increasingly effective frameworks and strategies for understanding and nourishing the integrating habitus.

The Author

Edward Foley, Capuchin, Prof. Dr., born 1948. Professor of Liturgy and Music, Founding Director of the Ecumenical Doctor of Ministry Program at Catholic Theological Union, Chicago. Research interests: liturgical history, homiletics, worship and the arts, ritual and spirituality. Recent publications: Journey to Holiness (2007), Commentary on the General Instruction of the Roman Missal (2007, ed. with Nathan Mitchell and Joanne Pierce), From Age to Age (2008).

André Beauregard

Impossible Challenge between Church Institution and Society in Fribourg: Experience of the Ecclesial Power, Neglecting the Issues of Secularization

Introduction

My experience in Fribourg, Switzerland, will be useful to apply the subject of our conference: Secularization Theories, Religious Identity and Practical Theology. Insisting on the process of decision, I will describe a way to challenge the relation between two institutions: Church and Society. It is a way to analyze the link between the autonomy of Society and the privilege of ecclesiastic Institution. Knowing that Switzerland is a Confederation, founded on the respect of people's wills, I was expecting a same relation between believers and their institution. My intuition was that the experience of ecclesial power collapses the issues of secularisation, helping by close connection between all institutions and money in this country! Fribourg, as a Canton, represents something very special to deal with this kind of challenge. Each citizen has to pay a special tax for the Church (Reform or Catholic), used for ecclesiastic staff and activities. And the Affairs Committee, a special committee checking directly the expenses of Church and money coming from other governments, can only approve the budget, without blaming the management of the ecclesiastical institution. In 1999, a specific agreement authorizes the Bishop to control everything by himself in Fribourg, ignoring the fact that it should be important to clarify policies, contracts, projects, and staff's requirements with the civil administration, opening to a lot of inequality between authorities and all kinds of workers (priests, lay people, nuns, etc.). It seems that many factors (other than only work) interfere to create a weird link between most of them. Working for God seems to be a specific appeal to accept some conditions, different of the secular life. The priesthood's habits set the pace keeping a distance with the modern life!

According to this situation, I was impressed by the emphasis on the Bishop's authority, imposing his direction for understanding, analysing, and acting in different roles and functions. His power seems to be, for many believers, unswerving. A large disparity appears between a kind of ecclesiastical spirit with narrow-minded visions and wills of people. Unfortunately, this situation is emphasized by the fact that many parishioners contribute to this situation without criticism, at least publicly. The clergy is sometimes listened to, often absentmindedly, not necessarily followed! One point seems very interesting: religion became for most of the Catholic people a social agreement and not a real challenge of their own Faith. Why do they accept this kind of arrangement?

Rules of "Hierocraty"

Authorities like to inspire respect in their "flock", forcing workers to follow one way direction, usually very narrow. When they want to impose something, they conceal the real reasons, arguing that it is in the name of God, of the Pope, or of Vatican II. When they want to conciliate people, they play a transparency game, claiming that they respect the Lay People. The problems mostly refer to a kind of believers, not ready to accept new deals! And they hate making discussion public: everything needs to stay secret, at the limit of impropriety most of time. Members of the clergy, leaving aside Lay people, usually without prior consultation, only make the real decisions!

Likewise one characteristic of this diocese is the origin of many members of the clergy: Africa, Asia, France, Poland, etc. This situation creates a huge impact on the mentality. As Quebecer, I felt a stranger, having to follow the official rules, irrelevant with some situations. And as a huge and old institution, they always follow the beat of the slower! So I can demonstrate that the practice shows clearly the iniquity between a strong organization, still close by a conservative tradition, and the realistic situation of the parishes. One example illustrates well my puzzlement of this detail.

Sacramental and Liturgy are both and sole ways to express their major act to communicate their wills. By the way, with help by some parents, each year they start again Sacramental preparations of many kids and teenagers to be baptised, confirmed, etc. The families push on them. They have to, as their brothers or sisters did before! And the authorities never take care about the pursuance of these approaches, creating a ditch between preparation and intentions of their users. Catechists know that is, for more of them, a social tradition, without Faith aspect.[1] How can we explain this obedient acceptance of this kind of power? Is it possible to conciliate this type of government and a secular society? At least, can we try to identify this whole picture of it?

This management of Church's authority can be named "Hierocraty"! This type of government forces people (indeed the clergy and religious staff!) to act in the narrow way of their competence, more sacramental and liturgical. The problem of justice, poverty, workers situation, and other "secular" fields are neglected by the practice of the official Church, even though some discourses make sometimes connection with these situations. Of course, some incursions of very few subordinates try to bring up to date people about justice (Lent for example). But daily practices seem to ignore them!

---

[1] For example, one of the mothers, mandated to prepare children for the first communion, never goes to Sunday Mass because she does not believe in this kind of public display! "It is too boring", she said!

358 André Beauregard

They sometimes use their authority to persuade their herd about some issues, like it was done many years ago. In June 2006, the Bishop of Fribourg tried to convict people, on television, to vote against the project to stop immigration, political issue for the citizens. In fact, 67.8 % of the country voted in favour on September 24th, 2006! Big defeat for the Church! In fact, many individuals gave up Church! They don't feel concerned by it, feeling that all this "ecclesiastic stuff" is irrelevant! They don't pay attention about what the ecclesiastical institution put forward.

The exercise of power between politic, economic, and ecclesiastic background is very thin. Here and there, we assist to a discontinuity between what it said and what is done! Could we imagine that one of the challenges is to create good conditions to mix some issues of capitalism and religious practices? Agreements with both sides toned down the iniquity between two kinds of authorities. Tradition is something very deep and respected by most of parishioners. But the goals of the authorities on some rules of liturgies or sacramental preparations do not fit with the habits of the people. In other words, official authorities listen, agree with; but then they do what they want to, ignoring most of time new challenges. They enrol some believers, encouraging to practice and act repeatedly aiming to transmit a deep tradition outdated from generation to generation, leaving aside some modern issues. This example of promiscuity between Clergy and Society has something vicious. It became the rule of supply and demand like a kind of "religious business and marketing"!

Ecclesiastical Power

It is easier for Bishop's staff to frame the pastoral activities more turning toward the past than the future. According to a pattern of "hierocraty", all new ideas, personal initiatives, critical discourses, appear a real threat to the authorities. Continuity is more secure than innovation. On one side, the discourse reminds the fact that Church is People of God! On the other side, the controlling frame of action contributes to keep people under domination of authority, blowing away all interesting personal initiatives. Thereof some pastoral practices stay secluded from the reality of their modern life. Consequently the new priests, young and well obeying, are not prepared to deal with this complex modern situation. Most of them hide themselves behind outfit, conservative discourses, and physical distance with people without showing any soul! They feel frightened of adult believers and mostly of modern challenges, refusing that it comes public by petition, newspapers, debate, etc. And they repeat what the older did and do without wisdom! About the old ones, they fear of ending up alone. Stress, solitude, physical, and intellectual incapacities become the worst situation for them, ignored by the authorities when they are not very productive and enough manageable! This type of vocation is not highly marketable outside of few exclusive clubs of conservative believer fans! My understanding of it shows the profound will-power to maintain authority and control on the conscience of their sheep. It is mostly required to keep distance with the "dangerous" modern world.

When someone feels diminutive, the reflex is trying to affirm with emphasis power on the people around. In this case, they impose some power out of the world, power coming from God or Pope. In fact, their influence becomes "powerless" in front of the people. Weber had insisted on the tinny link between "power and domination"[2]. That explanation clarifies some knowledge of administration in this diocese. Power, domination, and discipline become a kind of survival! These aspects confront radically the options of Secularization and Modern Society. In Disillusion of the World, Michel Gauchet[3] explains the fact that each believer can survive without Church or religious frame. "A complete exit of religion is possible", he said in his conclusion. Do the authorities prefer to ignore it?

"Ex-cultivation"[4]: A Way to Explain a Chasm

The expression "ex-cultivation" seems to fit very well to my topic. We know the meaning of "in-cultivation", describing the agreement from the Church to let coming in the aspects of the civil society inside of this own understanding of the "Word of God". If Public Theology implies to concrete a discourse in link with the societies, it means that the subjects concerned are supposed to be in link with the people, with their preoccupations, and their quest of truth. This expression suggests also a discourse that can be heard, understood, and written in link with the experience of the people. They do not share two opposite worlds. They live in one.

The conservative reality is something very deep in our occidental society. We try to evacuate obligations for living well. In the fact, we feel more insecure and we need to find some life buoy to survive. One of them is Religion. My impression is Catholic Church's Authority (Benedictus XVI for instance) uses this situation to withdraw from our modern culture all aspects going against orthodoxy and modernity! That is why I use the word "ex-cultivation" to explain a kind of dumping of our modern habits outside of the official discourse and practice of the Authority. The moral characteristics of the dialogue between ecclesial authorities and believers try to negate the reality, as it is, and to

---

[2] Max Weber, *Economy and Society*, edited by Guenther Roth and Claus Wittich, University of California Press: 1977, p. 53.

[3] I suggest to read the wonderful book by Michel Gauchet, *Le désenchantement du monde. Une histoire politique de la religion*, (Bibliothèque des Sciences humaines-nrf), Paris: Ballimard.

[4] You find the expression and the clarification in: *Catholicisme, la fin d'un monde*, Paris, Bayard, 2003, p. 90ff.

360 André Beauregard

promise a false paradise where everyone loves everyone without impure situation! And the circumstances push to sweep away the contradictions of the modern world and come back to an irrelevant tradition for the actual believers.

According to this point, the orientations of the diocese seem to support this kind of return to the past. Their action, their discourses, their leadership, and their training look as if they do not take into account the implication in the modern world, closing the eyes to the real world, in the name of the real Truth![5] Believers want a frank discourse, real information, and arguments. They want and they need to know more and well! They react, in making their own individual religion, their own spirituality far away from official doctrine! We have more and more believers without Church! Talking about "ex-cultivation" includes cultivation. How can we neglect Secularization, refusing Modern Society and Secular Authority as a main part of the People of God?

The personal appropriation of Faith by each believer generates a distance between public and private approaches of Faith, Religion, and Institution. A new generation emerges from the Swiss society, afar off the preoccupations of the ecclesiastic authorities, looking for an individual mysticism, more conventional with their own believes and their own life. Church became a kind of dropout of the Swiss society. If one day, the civil society of Fribourg decided to cut money, I think that Church will be pushed to confront each other to real challenges of credibility.[6] The cover using spirituality keeps believers in a kind of stasis, isolated from the real problems of the Society: youth, social injustice, young couples, conflicts with official marital situations, religious education, oldness, etc.

Did we support a quest of Truth into a question of marketing more than a question of contents? It is easy to settle it, referring to something external (for indeed, Bible, discourse of the pope, etc.). But this behaviour does not convict people to follow the shepherd!

A Public Theological Discourse for a Required Dialogue

The last *Motu Proprio* from Benedictus XVI embodies this dysfunction between Modern World and Church. The problem is where is the point of tolerance? Where do we have to stop and how? We can make a long description of Secularization, Modernism, and Post-Modernism. It is easy to describe the opposite visions of both sides. But the understanding of the

---

[5] In May 2007, the bishop decided to spend 40.000 CHF (25.015 € or 34.545 US$) to hire someone for Latin sacramental services concerning few conservative people, without consultation of the pastoral staff.

[6] For indeed, in Geneva, deprived of money's resources, Church has to deal with less people following the voice of the Authority, and renouncing to all kind of practices.

situation is more complicated than a simply virtual reality. We maintain a kind of ambiguity. The question is not only about Faith, Religion, and Church but about Power, Control of Conscience, and Singularity of Catholic Church. The authorities make a grand sweeping gesture about the reflection of theologians, of pastoral workers, and of People of God. They keep a strong position against modernity to be fair with their own thinking. In a "hierocraty", the communication is on one way. This is a typical contradiction with the goals of all modern societies. And keeping this option kills all effort of *aggiornamento* in our Church. Vatican II seems to be a bad dream!

New Challenge for Theologians, Plugging in the Modern World

My topic had explained some contradictions of the understanding of the link between Modern Society and Authorities in the diocese of Fribourg. I can resume my argumentation by these points:

The deep power of the Bishop short-circuits something new, modern, and critic, something exclusive, by staying out of the modern World. Secularization implies a dialogue, equal to equal, to put on the table all arguments to understand, to analyze, and to prevent some practices in link with our world.

The rules have been written but the "under-rules" conduct the real action. Pastoral practices show a lot of contradictions. A real frank dialogue, opportunity of a Secular Society, should be effective. It is not!

In the diocese of Fribourg, the mix of the Authority's competences (political, economic, and religious) appears vicious. It deconstructs the possible appropriation of the modern World by the believers themselves and consecrates the ditch between religious factors and modern life. For many of them, traditional practice is done more by repetitive behavior patterns than by conviction.

Everything coming against the official doctrine seems to be menacing. In a modern society, doctrines should be to serve people and not to be imposed, letting each of the citizens the choice of their action. Ignorance is not acceptable. Interrogation is a part of modern habits.

The time of fear is over. It negates the contribution of cultivation. We cannot accept the fact to level by the top all opinions, criticisms, judgments, freedom, and trusts of their flock of sheep. That is why I used the expression "Excultivation".[7] And all public debate cannot appear as irrelevant and dangerous.

---

[7] If you walk on the street in Fribourg, you will see frequently some religious people, men and women, dressed in their religious vestment and teaching with it. Some students are dressed the same.

362 André Beauregard

This reaction has also an impact on the civil society. Keeping distance with modern world, it promotes a vision of other epoch, representing a way to maintain a kind of power very "powerless"! Involvement is a specific aspect of our societies. When decision is made only by one side, (in this case few members of the clergy), they keep a severe eye on behaviors and doctrine of their flock.

Actual situation insists on the fact that the behaviors of the ecclesiastic authorities will not change soon! Secret, incompetence, power, ignorance, ditch between the Sacred and the Secular life, will confirm the difficult mission to link Church and Modern Society. The question is: How long can we tolerate a divorce between these two realities? Is a dialogue possible?

Conclusion

According to my own experience in the diocese of Fribourg, I discover a "hierocratic" Church in a secular society. As I have shown, this typical "rural" culture is restrained to some traditional behaviors, including ones around Church. Most of these people work, watch television, discuss, read, and go to school and university. And then, they can make their own opinion and distinguish what is good or bad for them. The main problem is the ignorance or the fear of the authorities to construct their discourses and practices in link with the real preoccupations of the people. One condition seems to be strongly important to realize this project: a staff very well educated (not only repeating some old discourses but able to assume a real criticism and dialogue). Training, education, and teamwork become the minimum conditions to make real and pertinent an intense evangelical project. My opinion is to turn into this way; Authority needs to be attentive to the contents of a dialogue, the criticism of the civil society, and to a return to the fundamental mission. But the challenge is huge! That is why my conviction is the fact that "this" Church has to pass away to let emerge a new one, in link with the roots of our Christianity, evangelical project, in dialogue with modern world. The genuine originality of Christian tradition is the capacity, throughout the ages, to adapt to many societies. It seems that the main goal of Vatican II, asking to be in link with the issues of our societies, became irrelevant. That is why, on my point of view, the ditch will be more and more impassable between conservative authorities of Church and believers. These authorities will be marginal and dropout from their own tradition and the wills of the people. According to this will of Jesus, the fundamental acts (often political) of the Church's Government seem out-of-the-way! It is not only a question of values and attitudes: it is a choice of type of World, adapted to the modern challenges in link with freedom of Faith!

As it said above, we need to find some theological resources not only to frame our reflection but also to affirm our convictions publicly by some ways. We need a real debate to stop the conservative invasion. The interest of this challenge is to find not only arguments but also a political way to be understood, considered weight, and listened by these authorities, often blaming, as theologians, about our points of view.[8] By the way, Social Sciences represent interesting fields, contributing to understand the reality. Theology is only one of them, trying to propose a "Special Transcendent Knowledge [...] General transcendent knowledge is the knowledge of God that answers the basic questions raised by proportionate being, namely, what being is and whether being is the real".[9] The contribution of our debate is to submit the official discourses to the same rules of the modern World: dialogue, discussion, criticism, analyze, and democratic debate. All theses terms not be involved with the act of official Church. And the reality shows that Church is far away from modern Society. Can we do something else together?

The Author

André Beauregard, Ph.D. (Theologie-Etudes Pastorales), born in 1950, was Associate Professor to St.Paul University, Ottawa, Canada until 2000. Co-founder of IAPT and Société internationale de Theologie pratique. Member of the American Academy of Religion, Société canadienne de Théologie. Recent publications: "Writing a Public Theology Challenging with a Pluralistic Society: The Experience of the English Speaking Catholic Mission in Zurich" pp. 152–163, in Dreaming the Land: Theologies of Resistance and Hope International Academy of Practical Theology – Brisbane 2005, (edited by Hans-Georg Ziebertz, Friedrich Schweitzer) (Collection International Practical Theology v.5), Berlin: Lit Verlag, 2007. "Ritual Expressed through Sacraments: Main Expression of the Person or of the Tradition?" pp. 235–248, in Creativity, Imagination and Critics. The Expressive Dimension in Practical Theology (edited by Paul Ballard and Pamela Couture), England: Cardiff Academic Press, 2001.

---

[8] The Congregation of Faith has condemned Jon Sobrino, theologian of liberation, a few months ago. How is it still possible?

[9] Lonergan, Collected Works of Bernard Lonergan: *Insight: A Study of Human Understanding*, edited by Frederick E. Crowe and Robert M. Doran, Toronto, Buffalo, London: University of Toronto Press, 1992, p. 709.

Cornelis N. de Groot

Theological issues in fluid ways of being church

1. Liquid religion?

Can there be such thing as religion in liquid modernity? Zygmunt Bauman (2000), taking up insights of Ulrich Beck, Manuell Castells, Michel Foucault, and Anthony Giddens, sketches a world where fixed class and status boundaries are vanishing, people have more choice than ever, and identity is no longer pre-scribed, but to be constructed. In solid modernity, people were determined by their role in the production process; in liquid modernity, they are determined by their role in consumer society. The market has become more powerful than the state, the church, or the family once were. We are tempted to buy the products that provide elements of an "authentic" identity. We have to choose: what to wear, what to do, what to eat, what to believe. Even leading a traditional life, and clinging to a religious tradition must be by choice. Religion, however, does not receive much attention in his work.

According to Bauman (1997, 197), liquid modernity, or post-modernity as he used to put it, does not generate a demand for religion but for identity experts. Following Kolakowski, Bauman identifies religion with the awareness of human insufficiency. People living in risk society (Beck), do no appreciate the reli-gious message of vulnerability, but are longing for the reassurance that they are able to deal with the uncertainties and need a short introduction in the way they can do this. They need experts.

Elsewhere, Bauman is equally negative about the possibilities for community (2001). On the one hand, people are forced to be, and to act as, individuals. On the other hand, large proportions are only individuals *de jure*. They suffer under their dependency of structures beyond their influence, but their suffering does not create solidarity – at least not by itself.

Taken together, these two analyses imply that in liquid modernity only two options are left for religious communities, such as churches.

Firstly, the church may serve as an institution where a *community of equals* is invented and imagined in religious rituals, beliefs, and ethical behaviour. Like an ethnic community, this religious community does not address the actual social networks. In the real world, people of different backgrounds and of different religions are interdependent. The unification of one segment of the population means segregation, a flight from reality, as long as the existing inequality is not addressed. This church provides the experience of belonging. It is a surrogate community, however, since the people in the church are not the people one works with, lives with, exists with.

This 'ghettoization' corresponds with the only 'specifically post-modern form of religion' Bauman discerns: *fundamentalism*. In accordance with the dominant point of view in sociology of religion, Bauman considers this phenomenon as a fully contemporary, both embracing and resisting against modern developments. Bauman focuses on a particular inconsistency: the choice for fundamentalism liberates individuals from the agony of choice. The submission to God and the group promises to unload the individual from the uncertainty of choice-making.

The second option for the church would probably be the *aesthetic*, "instant" community. Gathering to participate in a spectacular event may provide a sense of being part of something that transcends the individual. For a moment, the togetherness of individuals may provide a sense of community without ethical commitments and long-term commitments (Bauman 2001, 69–70). Community, however, cannot be found in these cases. According to Bauman's judgment, a person does not join a community temporarily. Therefore, "cloakroom" communities and "carnival" communities are not "genuine" (comprehensive and lasting) communities, but symptoms and, sometimes, causal factors of the social disorder of liquid modernity (Bauman 2000, 199–201).

In one sentence: Bauman does not leave room for religion in liquid modernity, *except* for fundamentalism. There is, however, a third option. This option is implicit in Bauman's own vision of how people can live together in less misery or no misery at all: 'If there is to be a community in the world of the individuals, it can only be (and needs to be) a community woven together from sharing and mutual care; a community of concern and responsibility for the equal right to be human and the equal ability to act on that right.' (Bauman 2001, 149–150) Clearly, there are parallels between his concerns and those of Christian theology. The community of individuals that is needed according to Bauman reminds the church of its mission. A theological reading of the concept of liquid modernity challenges the church to adopt a hermeneutic reconstruction of its mission. Elsewhere, I have suggested that this reconstruction should connect the desire for ontological security with the struggle for social justice (De Groot 2006a, 100).

The characterization of the current phase in the modernization process as "fluid" or "liquid" has recently received a place in the theological plea for a late modern church reformation. An example is Pete Ward's (2002) popular call for a *liquid church*. Although Ward does not really respond to Bauman's critical analysis, he does challenge us to stop identifying 'being church' with a particular historical phenomenon. Instead, he draws attention to the ecclesial qualities of what is happening in contemporary Christian culture, such as small Christian communities and large-scale events. I regard contemporary Christian culture as one context in which a fluid way of being church happens, beside others. Ward's examples are derived from outside the institutional church, or

366 Cornelis N. de Groot

what is usually associated with it, but they still refer to the (Christian) religious field. A second category consists of ecclesial initiatives in a secular setting, such as a religious service in a hospital or in a prison. A third category consists of secular-religious phenomena, such as particular (gospel)rock-concerts or the multicultural interfaith-project I will be discussing here. Thus, fluidity has to do with the blurring of boundaries between Church and the religious field, and between the religious and the secular domain.

2. Liquid church in contemporary Christian culture

A well-known example of the first type is constituted by the World Youth Days. Interviews and a survey among German participants indicate that the World Youth Days produce the experience of being part of a worldwide Christian community, an experience that stands in contrast with the every day experience of being an exception within a secular world (Scharnberg & Ziebertz 2002). Besides providing the opportunity to have religious experiences with peers, this international youth meeting has effects in life after the World Youth Days. Dutch research among participants in Cologne (2005), confirms that youngsters make friends and keep in contact with people they have met, often using email (Kregting 2005; Kregting & Harperink 2005). German participants at the WYD in Toronto (2002) indicated that not only did they feel motivated to cooperate with the WYD in Cologne, but they also felt encouraged to testify their faith. To a certain extent, the event may be characterized as a post-traditional type of community: a short-term meeting of strangers among whom one may have the experience to 'be oneself'.

Bauman would perhaps call this a cloakroom community. Yet, this is only half the story. What is left out is the tension between the organizing 'solid' Roman Catholic Church and the fluidity of the event. This tension between 'prescribed order and actual practice' became apparent in the concluding celebration of the Eucharist in Cologne. Before an audience of wearied youngsters, Benedict XVI (2005) rendered a well-wrought sermon in which he criticized religious seekers for turning religion into a commodity: 'People choose what they like, and some are even able to make a profit from it.' It is interesting that the leader of the Roman Catholic Church while performing at the centre of a religious youth event criticizes this very culture of fluidity. Solid church and liquid church seem to be entangled in a complex relationship at the World Youth Days. The institutional church and the various new religious movements it cooperates with, facilitate an event that generates its own dynamics of merchandizing, providing spectacle, and satisfying needs.

The World Youth Days represent both the event-culture and religion, with its emphasis on respectively hierarchy and life transient. It is hard to put this in Bauman's two categories: the World Youth Days are at the same time an example of an aesthetic community and of a community of equals. One may say: this event illustrates the dominance of consumerism. It is proclaimed that it is a personal choice to give expression to a Catholic identity. Religious experts teach young people how to live as Christians. At the same time, they are taught to submit to the will of God, which is expressed by the clerical hierarchy, because of the individual insufficiency. Thus, this event has con-sequences for everyday life. As such, this event would rather fit Bauman's category of fundamentalism.

3. Ecclesial initiatives in a secular milieu

The second fluid way of being church can be detected in meetings which have been initiated by the church in a secular setting, are attended by believers and non-believers alike, and generate a particular experience of religious community. One example is the continuously changing community of patients, volunteers, staff and other participants of a church service in a hospital (Steinkamp 1997, 242–243). Another example is the same experience of the more permanent group of detainees who participate in church services in prison. Although these participants are usually hardly familiar with the Christian faith, they tend to be actively involved, especially in prayer (Oskamp 2004).

From the perspective of solid church, this type of soul care would be categorized under the label of special chaplaincies, such as the hospital, military, student, or industrial chaplaincy. The perspective of liquid modernity draws attention to these religious services as celebrations of a particular (permanent or momentary) community, and to pastoral counselling as a practice that serves the individuals in this community. The distinctions between believers and non-believers, various religions and various denominations loose their all-determining status. In those pluralistic and/or secularized cases where ministers can hardly maintain a strictly denominational orientation, a post-denominational, or even post-Christian, orientation may turn out to unite diverse (religious and non-religious) definitions of the situation. (Examples of this liturgical creativity may be found in Post et al (2003).)

This phenomenon raises the theological issue how the momentary experience of community is valued in comparison with the enduring community of the institutional church. From the latter, *solid* perspective, contacts with outsiders are of value in the context of evangelization or charity. Thus, these are activities *of* the church, rather than constitutive elements of being-church. Proponents of the former, *liquid* position, often refer to the verse 'Wherever there are one or two gathered in My name, I am in their midst'. (Matthew 18, 20) Thus, more formal ecclesiological arguments are put between brackets (cf. De Groot 2006b, 2006c).

368 Cornelis N. de Groot

This issue is related to another ecclesiological question: is the church for initiates only or open to all those willing to participate? In these settings, different choices are being made. Dutch hospitals often have ecumenical services, including Holy Communion/the Lord's Supper. In prison-services, these sacraments are seldom celebrated, probably because they would exclude large proportions of those present.

In these cases, a community of people living together is present as opposed to an ascribed community, or congregation, consisting of people of the same denomination. From Bauman's perspective, these settings may provide the better opportunities for a 'community of individuals'.

4. Secular-religious phenomena

The third fluid type of being of church would be those communities and meetings in a secular setting without ecclesial involvement that resemble religious communities. Examples can be found in rock-concerts, theatre plays and management courses (cf. Post 2005, 85-87). Another example is a multi-religious project in a Dutch suburb near The Hague (De Groot & Van der Ploeg 2006). Chore of the project was an exposition about more than 50 residents from various religious and atheist backgrounds. Other activities were lectures, inter-religious meetings, and touring the sacred sites of the town. This project was initiated by the staff of the Zoetermeer City Museum and a journalist of the local newspaper (*Haagsche Courant*). They were strongly motivated not only to pay attention to religion in Zoetermeer as an interesting theme, but also to encourage people from various cultures and religions to meet and to get to know each other. Soon, a third party joined them, a minister from the local Dutch Reformed Church. He perceived the opportunity to make use of the secular space of the museum to organize the inter-religious meetings that he had wished for a long time. Together they planned a half year program. At the closing event a new project was kicked off that continued the inter-religious dialogue in the City Museum and organized a 'peace mission' to Morocco in fall 2006, in order 'to learn from the Moroccan tradition of religious tolerance'.

A plurality of believers brought together within the neutral setting of a museum stimulated the definition of religion as a personal matter. By defining religion as a personal matter in a neutral public space, filled with various religions, people of different faiths are encouraged to getting to known each other, including their religious orientations. This definition of the situation is threatened on one hand by a tendency to transform this neutrality into an ideology of syncretism, and on the other by defining particular believers as representatives of a (religious) community. In other words: the experience of community is threatened by re-embedding in a new structure and by existing structures that tend to close off or incorporate this liquid phenomena.

Rather than labelling this as an instant-community, I would be inclined to regard such experiments as grass roots impulses to a community of individuals. Further research should provide indications of its effects.

In conclusion

Apparently, religion is capable of transforming into a liquid modern phenomenon, just like it transformed into a modern phenomenon. The concept of liquid modernity has great value as a sensitizing concept for highlighting important aspects of contemporary culture, although Bauman himself underestimates the position of religion. The interplay of solid and liquid religion, or institutional and non-institutional forms of religion, deserves our continuous attention.

The concept of 'fluid ways of being church' stimulates theological questions (Brouwer et al. 2007; cf. Ammerman et al, 1997, 36–62). Firstly, how do these phenomena relate to their *context*? Does their fluidity entail a cognitive surrender to modern consumerism? Or is a liquid church possible that seeks an understanding with contemporary culture (cf. Berger 1992, 41–46)?

Secondly, liquid church challenges to rethink the relation between church and *culture*. Ward's conception of liquid church corresponds with the blurring of the boundaries between church and culture in the evangelical milieu. Elsewhere, church seems to 'happen' in various cultural settings. What is the theological evaluation of assemblies where people experience a momentary sense of belonging? Does the concept of church require a foundation in a solid community? The theological concept of *koinonia* seems to correspond to the experience of taking part in a collective ritual that binds people together in their commitment to transcendence. A 'liquid' conceptualization of koinonia would open up the possibility to value momentary types of community, in which people take part in various degrees (De Groot 2006b).

Thirdly, what is the relation between theology and *structure*? An exclusivist soteriology may appreciate fluid structures from the perspective of evangelism, whereas inclusivist soteriologies may appreciate them without further motives.

Fourthly, the emergence of these fluid types of being church is influenced by certain actors and factors. Which are the driving forces behind the liquid church? How is *leadership* practiced? How do fluid styles of leadership relate to theological thinking about ministry?

The concept of liquid church with all its ambivalences opens up wide horizons for future practical-theological research. I suggest that fluid ways of being church may correspond with God's hidden presence in the world, with the conviction that the Word can be heard – not only in the (solid) church, and that

370 Cornelis N. de Groot

the Spirit may be experienced in the relationships between people. This suggestion, of course, calls for more systematic theological research and reflection.

References

Ammerman et al., N.T (1997). *Congregation and Community.* New Brunswick. NJ: Rutgers University Press.

Bauman, Z. (1997). *Postmodernity and its Discontents.* Cambridge: Polity.

____. (2001). *Community: Seeking safety in an insecure world.* Cambridge: Polity Press.

____. (2000). *Liquid Modernity.* Cambridge: Polity.

Benedict XVI (2005). Homily of His Holiness Pope Benedict XVI (Cologne, 8/21/2005) www.Vatican.va [accessed: 9/12/2007].

Berger, P.L. (1992). *A Far Glory. The quest for faith in an age of credulity*, New York: The Free Press/Macmillan.

Brouwer, R., C.N. de Groot, H.P. de Roest, E. Sengers & S. Stoppels (2007). *Levend lichaam. Dynamiek van christelijke geloofsgemeenschappen in Nederland.* Kampen: Kok.

Groot, C.N. de (2006a). 'The Church in Liquid Modernity: A Sociological and Theological Exploration of a Liquid Church'. *International Journal for the Study of the Christian Church* 6(1), 91–103.

____. (2006b). '"Wij zijn de kerk!" Maar wie zijn wij? In discussie met het congregationalisme', *Collationes* 36, 303–320.

____. (2006c). 'At your service: a Congregational Study in Dutch Catholicism', *International Journal of Practical Theology* 10(2), 217–237.

Kolm, G. J. van der (2001). *De verbeelding van de kerk: Op zoek naar een nieuw-missionaire ecclesiologie.* Zoetermeer: Boekencentrum.

Kregting, J. (2005). *Achtergrond en motieven WJD-gangers 2005* [rapport 539]. Nijmegen: KASKI.

Kregting, J. & S. Harperink (2005). *Doorwerking WJD en bezoek Katholieke Jongeren Dag* [rapport 543]. Nijmegen: KASKI.

Oskamp, Paul (2004). *Overleven achter steen en staal: vieringen en geloofsbeleving in de bajes onderzocht.* Meinema: Zoetermeer.

Ploeg, Jouetta van der & Kees de Groot (2006). 'Towards a city museum as a centre of civic dialogue' In R. Kistemaker (ed.), *City museums as centres of civic dialogue?*

Proceedings of the Fourth Conference of the International Association of City Museums, Amsterdam, 3–5 November 2005. Amsterdam: Edita/Amsterdam Historical Museum, 90–96. www.knaw.nl/publicaties/pdf/20051108.pdf [accessed: 12/09/2007].

Post, Paul, et al. (2003). *Disaster ritual: explorations of an emerging ritual repertoire* [Liturgia Condenda 15]. Leuven: Peeters.

Post, P. (2005). 'Ritual-liturgical movements. A panoramic view on ritual repertoires in Dutch Catholicism after 1950/1960'. In E. Sengers (ed.), *The Dutch and their gods. Secularization and transformation of religion in the Netherlands since 1950.* Hilversum: Verloren, 75–100.

Scharnberg, Christian & Hans-Georg Zieberz (2002). *Weltjugendtag 2002 Forschungsbericht zur Fragebogenuntersuchung.* Universität Würzburg. www.afj.de/download/wjt2002forschungsbericht.pdf [accessed: 9/12/2007]

Schulze, Gerhard (1992). *Die Erlebnisgesellschaft. Kultursoziologie der Gegenwart.* Frankfurt/New York: Campus.

Steinkamp, H. (1997). 'Gemeinde jenseits der Pfarrei'. In H.-G. Ziebertz (ed.), *Christliche Gemeinde vor einem neuen Jahrtausend.* Weinheim: Deutscher Studienverlag, 233–346.

Ward, P. (2002). *Liquid Church.* Peabody/Carlisle: Hendrickson/Pater Noster.

The Author

Cornelis N. de Groot, dr., born 1966, studied sociology and theology and is a lecturer in Practical Theology at the Faculty of Catholic Theology of Tilburg University. Research interests: Pentecostalism; psychotherapy and religion; Roman-Catholic parishes; religion and media; religion in popular culture; social theory of religion. Recent publications include a textbook in congregational studies: (with R. Brouwer/H. de Roest/E. Sengers/S. Stoppels) Levend lichaam. Dynamiek van christelijke geloofsgemeenschappen in Nederland, Kok, Kampen, 2007; a study in church and media (with H. Blommestijn/T. Elshof/E. Hijmans/J. Maas) God in je huiskamer, Kok, Kampen, 2006; and (with J. Kregting/E. Borgman) 'The Positioning of the Parish in a Context of Individualization' in Social Compass (2005).

Rodney J. Hunter

Ministry in Depth: Three Critical Questions in the Teaching and Practice of Pastoral Care

Basic Idea

As a teacher of pastoral care and counseling for many years, it became increasingly clear to me that one of the basic aims of such a course was to restrain and redirect the student's first impulse, in all pastoral situations, to decide what to do and how to do it – that is, to take action. No doubt student anxieties have much to do with their reflexive compulsion to focus on action, usually accompanied by a wish for cookbook recipes for "how to handle" or "how to deal with" one kind of situation or another.

This reflexive preoccupation with action is almost always wrong, in my view, because it fails to allow pastoral action to engage situations of human need and difficulty critically, creatively, and in depth, as appropriate to a ministry of religious or spiritual care. Thus one of the basic aims of my course was to enable students to bracket the "action question" temporarily in order to reflect first, with their parishioners, in depth, on "what is going on" in the situation and what good or even profound spiritual ends might be envisioned for it through continued pastoral involvement. Thus I would teach my students to ask, in every situation of pastoral care, three fundamental questions, each of which can potentially open into a rich, profound inquiry appropriate to a spiritual ministry of care:

1. What is going on here?
2. What do we discern to be God's will for this situation?
3. How might we then best proceed?

These three questions were not necessarily to be asked in the literal form as stated here. They could take many forms. What was important is the essential ideas behind them, discussed more fully below, which together guide the pastoral conversation in a naturally flowing sequence.

In general, I sought to teach students to pursue these questions in as much depth as possible, appropriate to the circumstances, and normally to do so in the order given. This allowed the third or "action" ("how to") question to emerge creatively out of reflection on the situation and its possible *telos*. Thus, in actual practice, these questions were asked, and provisionally answered, not once but repeatedly in a continuous process that circled back from action to situational analysis and ends-analysis to action again in what one hoped to be an ever deepening and clarifying pattern.[1]

Moreover, it is not the pastor alone who is taught to engage in this triadic questioning. Good ministry, in my view, is ideally a shared search for the divine will in the midst of human circumstances. Thus the art of pastoral care, or any act of ministry, involves, at a fundamental level, inviting everyone who is involved in the situation into this triadic structure of reflection and action, with all parties taking as much appropriate responsibility for finding their way through the perplexity of the moment – discerning God's will – in a movement toward "answers" and "actions" that both express faith and fit the practical circumstances.

In classroom settings I taught this approach first by presenting it conceptually in a simple lecture with brief illustrations, then used the method repeatedly through the semester in the analysis of role plays, verbatim case reports, and more generalized or abstracted discussions of pastoral topics. I also required students to make explicit use of the method in their papers, and I determined a paper's grade by separately grading their discussion of the three questions (or further differentiated versions of them) and combining the part-scores according to an announced formula.

My purpose in this short, simple paper is to demonstrate the necessity and potential value of asking and seeking to answer these elemental questions in depth in every situation of ministry. I am aware that this pedagogical proposal, which is also a small theory of pastoral practice, though seemingly simple if not naive, floats on a deep ocean of philosophical, theological, ethical reflection

---

[1] This simple statement belies a set of complex underlying questions concerning how description, normative judgment, and action are related to one another, how each is defined, and how they are to be distinguished and interrelated in theory as well as practice. My intent in framing these questions so simply and with such apparent naïveté is not to espouse a particular theory or theology of practical knowledge and action. I have left these categories deliberately broad and ambiguous in order to accommodate a variety of possibilities. However, I do not regard the three questions as categorically distinct, but rather as approximately and partially distinguishable "phases" or "moments" within an organic understanding of human action. How we regard the situation (Question 1) is influenced by our moral and religious values and beliefs (Question 2), as well as by our past and prospective actions (Question 3). In this respect I am in agreement with Critical Theory (and its liberation counterparts in theology) that argues a fundamental unity between description, normativity, and action, rejects the concept of value-neutral theory and science, and equally rejects concepts of practical or instrumental reason devoid of moral and philosophical meaning.

374 Rodney Hunter

with a long, complex history, in addition to the specific tradition and literature of pastoral and practical theology.[2]

Elaboration

I taught my students to seek answers to all three questions "in depth," meaning answers that were not, perhaps, immediately apparent but that provided illuminating and unifying insight into the welter of a situation's particularities and possibilities in relation to the general purposes and resources of ministry. This entailed, at least in part, using either a paradigmatic story or a conceptual scheme or theory that helps one understand and make sense of the situation in terms that open up possible modes of response to it. Thus students needed to know the narratives of faith (primarily scriptures and traditions) and various psychological and social theories and be able to relate them to circumstances at hand. With respect to theories in particular, I found it helpful to note that the English word "theory," and its French and German cognates, derives from a Greek root meaning "to see" (from which also comes the "theatre" – a place of seeing). A theory is therefore a set of ideas that enables one to see something that otherwise would not be seen or the significance of which one might miss.

Though this method may appear complicated and "heady," in actual practice it is fundamentally simple, flexible, and unobtrusive. As a method to guide pastoral action, each of the questions can usually only be touched upon briefly, and one moves from one question to another as gracefully as possible, without rigid or heavy-handed articulation. As questions are repeatedly explored in the continuous loop of reflection, they can and often do grow deeper in insight and significance, and yield an ever richer, more significant ministry. Moreover, students can gradually become more adept and artful at employing these questions as guiding principles in their caregiving, moving from the ability to use them only retrospectively, as they look back on caregiving events in class discussions of cases and role plays and in papers, to employing them more proactively and

---

[2] I refer to the history of philosophical, theological, and ethical reflection on the nature of human action, specifically moral and spiritual action. Philosophical topics include *phronesis, practical knowledge and reasoning, wisdom, praxis,* and the *theory or philosophy of action*, all of which entail numerous other issues such as the nature of volition and freedom, judgment and decision, responsibility, conscience, virtue, and the theory/practice relation, as well as general theories of epistemology and the good. Other relevant non theological disciplines include cognitive science and the psychology of human action, the philosophy of the social sciences, and theories of professional practice (e.g., Donald Schön's seminal work, *The Reflective Practitioner* [New York: Basic Books, 1983]). Theologically, this proposal is obviously situated primarily within practical theology, and thus indirectly within theologies of church and ministry, and theologies of the nature of divine action and its relation to human action, and the nature of sin and grace.

Ministry in Depth   375

intentionally in the work of caregiving itself. The old adage holds true, that with practice, we can gradually move from

> Unconscious incompetence, to
> Conscious incompetence, to
> Conscious competence, to
> Unconscious competence!

Question 1. "What is going on here?"

The first question to ask in any situation of ministry is at once descriptive, explanatory and/or interpretive in nature: "What is going on here?"[3] This is actually a broad and profound question that is not to be taken lightly. It includes attending to one's immediate impressions and the "presenting problem," as well as looking under the surface of things to perceive the psychological, social, cultural, and historical dynamics, the communal narratives and interpretive frameworks that appear to be operative, and ultimately the question "Where is God in this situation?" Question 1 does not need to be pursued exhaustively before moving to the second question, however. On the contrary, it is best to keep an initial inquiry simple and focused on the most important questions ("When did your mother die? Were you close to her?"); the situation can be explored in greater depth as the ministry progresses over time.

Those involved in the situation should be encouraged to participate in articulating what they are experiencing and how they themselves understand it. The pastor's depth perception, guided by story and theory, is not necessarily the same as that of the parishioners or necessarily superior to theirs. Nor is it generally useful for pastors to articulate their detailed theoretical understanding to those with whom they minister. Depth understanding informs and guides good pastoral work but should seldom be made explicit. The desire to do so is a common student temptation, however, and one that is often driven by the anxiety of inexperience and a desire to affirm one's sense of competence and authority – motivations that can be usefully identified and discussed in class. It should also be noted, however, that all attempts to articulate situations change them in the process, however subtly, and often with significant consequences.

---

[3] For purposes of classroom instruction I do not distinguish interpretation (hermeneutics) as a separate fundamental question, but roll phenomenological description, explanatory insights, and interpretations together into a single "phase" or "moment" of situation-analysis. I do note the differences between these ways of saying "what is going on here," however, and focus individually on them as seems appropriate, especially after the general scheme has become familiar to students. Pedagogically, it seems best not to complicate instruction early on with too many fundamental categories (or underlying philosophical and theological issues), though these can all be noted in due course.

It is also important for pastors to include themselves in their "situation analysis." "What is my particular role here? How am I part of this congregational system? What are my needs, fears, concerns, and institutional interests? How does my own emotional and social history, my "story," and my personality, both *enable* and *limit* how I can minister here? How is this situation an opportunity or challenge for my own faith and spiritual growth as well as for my growing competence as a pastor?"

Finally, depending on one's theology, it is also pertinent to ask "Where is God in this situation?" This is critical if one understands ministry as a participation in the comprehensive and fundamental, ongoing work of God in human life. Such a question, of course, points to larger questions about the nature and role of God in history, the "marks of the Spirit," the relation to individual ministry to church, sacrament, tradition, and so on – all of which can and should be noted in discussion or lecture. In any event, Question 1 is not to be identified exclusively with a social scientific perspective. None of the three questions is in fact exclusively correlated with particular disciplines. Both theological and non theological disciplines can and ought to be employed in articulating and answering each question.

Question 2. What do we discern to be God's will for this situation?

As stated, this question is implicitly deontological, though it can be asked in other forms, such as teleologically ("What might we hope and pray for in this situation?") or in terms of an ethic of responsibility ("What is the responsible or morally fitting thing to do here in terms (say) of an ethic of love and justice or virtue ethics?"). The intent of this question is to open up a consideration of the *evaluative* or *normative* dimension in contrast to the expository, explanatory and interpretive intent of the first question.

The *way* this question is asked, and the answers given to it, obviously presuppose an ethical and theological perspective. Thus discussions of Question 2 inevitably lead students not only to consult their personal faith but to recall biblical, historical, systematic and moral theology in specific ways, however fragmentary. This is also true of Question 1 ("What is going on here?") which, as I have noted, can and ought to be considered a theological as well as a non theological question. And as with Question 1, I have encouraged students to share the asking and answering of this question with those to whom they are ministering, and to include themselves as participants in the situation for which the divine will is sought.

Ministry in Depth

Question 3. How might we best proceed here?

The question of what to do and how to do it, Question 3, emerges in part from a creative convergence of the considerations stemming from the first two questions, but it also draws upon practical knowledge of ways and means which can never be derived entirely from situation analysis or normative reflection. Practical knowledge as I use the term includes both simple and complex skills as well as methods and traditions of doing things practiced and learned by communities of practitioners over time. In ministry it also includes traditional "means of grace" – scripture, sacrament, and prayer – as well as the particular skills, attitudes, values, beliefs, and qualities of mind, heart and soul that suffuse, enliven and concretize any practical art in its traditional as well as idiosyncratic, expressive forms.[4]

There is, I maintain, at bottom, no single right way to proceed in most situations; each pastor, each student, each community must forge its own distinctive convergence of reflective insights, practical traditions and methods, and idiosyncratic qualities, abilities, and limitations. At the same time, in most situations of ministry there is, arguably, a range of approaches consistent with communal norms and judgments, and pragmatically conducive to facilitating certain appropriate and desirable outcomes. Some methods of ministry are in this rough sense "better" than others, and it is this range of communally shared methods and perspectives that students study and attempt to master through practice. However, it is not sufficient to learn pastoral methods appropriate to answering Question 3 without engaging reflectively in the first two questions, if one's ministry is to be responsive to the particularities of human situations, deeply accountable to one's religious norms and traditions, artfully creative, and spiritually significant.

Moreover, "how to proceed" rests ultimately not on practical abilities and methods alone, but more fundamentally on the exercise of *judgment* by all participants. Bringing together the insights from Questions 1 and 2 with an eye toward future directions, strategies, and steps to be taken requires judgments about how various interpretive and normative considerations are to be interrelated and prioritized. Religious tradition, community norms, and the "rules of thumb" that guide communities of practitioners may provide rough guidance in choosing priorities and exercising judgment, but in the end, each community and pastor must make such decisions without complete information or clarity, choosing directions that others may dispute or decide differently. Ambiguity, risk, and uncertainty are inescapable in life and leadership, and certainly in ministry. Experience may lessen risk and render decisions more likely to succeed in the end. But even seasoned practitioners recognize the element of

---

[4] See Hunter, Rodney J., "The Future of Pastoral Theology," *Pastoral Psychology*, 29:1 (Fall, 1980): 58–69.

risk and uncertainty and the unavoidable need to move ahead in one direction or another, even if one elects to do nothing, which is itself a direction. Thus, learning pastoral care or any practical art of ministry requires the cultivation of good judgment on the basis of a knowledge of relevant disciplines, accumulated experience (especially experience that has been critically and repeatedly reflected upon), and the formation of values and character that provide the deepest level of orientation in ambiguous circumstances.

I would further suggest that pondering the three basic questions in all situations of ministry, if one includes oneself in the situation, also provides a significant framework for the requisite spiritual formation of pastors themselves: "What is going on with me? What is God's will for my life? How can I best move forward in light of these reflections?" Spiritual and character formation, including an ever deepening and critically conscious self-knowledge, can therefore be a naturally and continuously integrated dimension of the teaching of pastoral ministry through this pedagogical method.

Larger Issues

"Why these three questions, and why in this order? What grounds this proposal theoretically?"

My starting point with this proposal is the intuition that all of us ask these three questions all the time in everything we do, as fundamental to the practical working of the human mind. We cannot survive without cognitive maps of our environments, however incomplete, inchoate, or distorted. Nor can we function without making evaluative judgments, formal or informal, reflective or reflexive, on our circumstances. We are constantly scanning, interpreting, and evaluating our worlds, shaping our actions on the basis of what we believe to be the case, whether or in what respects the situation is positive or negative in relation to our needs, concerns, goals, and obligations, and the repertory of relevant practical methods we have accumulated.

Therefore, what I propose here as a method of ministry is in fact a differentiation and elaboration of natural psychological and social processes. Sophisticated pastoral care and other expressions of ministry differ from their folk versions only in the degree to which these fundamental questions are brought into focus and pursued "in depth," singly and together, through the use of specific theoretical and traditional resources (theological and non theological), and to the degree that judgment is shaped creatively and wholistically through these assessments.

It is precisely because we identify and individually pursue these questions that we can have a ministry that helps the mundane and superficial level of everyday experience become transparent to the profounder issues of human life and the presence of God, which, I would maintain, is a fundamental aim of ministry. This framework, I have found, deliberately ambiguous and diffuse though it is, offers a practically effective way for students to grasp the possibility of pastoral care or any act of ministry as a truly spiritual practice, informed theoretically, and responsive to both the practical needs and particularities of situations and the wider and deeper, and ultimately ineffable reality in which we live and move and have our being.

The Author

Rodney J. Hunter, Ph.D., born 1940, Professor emeritus of Pastoral Theology, Candler School of Theology, Emory University, Atlanta, Georgia, USA, and Presbyterian minister. Research interests: theology of pastoral care and counseling; pastoral theological methodology; practical theology; theology and personality; theological anthropology; psychology and religion; theory of personality; psychoanalysis; analytical (Jungian) psychology; personal commitment. Major publications: Dictionary of Pastoral Care and Counseling, gen. ed. (1990, 2005); Pastoral Care and Social Conflict, co-ed. (with P. Couture) (1995). Selected recent publications: "The Power of God For Salvation: Transformative Ecclesia and the Theological Renewal of Pastoral Care and Counseling," J. of the Interdenominational Theological Center 25:3; "Religious Caregiving and Pedagogy in a Postmodern Context: Recovering Ecclesia," J. of Pastoral Theology 8; "Transformational Commitment as Practical Theological Problem," in Pamela D. Couture and Paul Ballard, eds., Globalization and Difference – Practical Theology in a World Context (1999); "Pastoral Theology: Historical Perspectives and Future Agendas," J. of Pastoral Theology 16:1.

Elisabeth Christiansson & Tomas Fransson

Dialogue as a Reply to the Modern.
The ideas behind the Church of Sweden closely related Sigtuna Foundation at the time of its establishment

The role of Christianity in Western Europe during the 19th and 20th centuries has in the last few years been much discussed. It has been pointed out that the process of modernization not only led to secularism. It also led to Christian innovations, which aimed to renew the church and rechristianize the society.[1]

The Sigtuna Foundation is an example of Christian innovation which appeared as an answer to the modernizing. It started in 1917 and has its roots in the so called Young Church Movement – a renewal movement within the Church of Sweden, which started at the turn of the 20th century. The foundation became a centre for a cultural and societal dialogue where representatives of different political, social and religious movements were brought together for discussions that were of great importance, not only within church. A great number of actual questions were brought up for discussion: society, science, culture, education, church, theology and religions. S.F. has been of significant importance as a an actor close to the Church of Sweden in the 20th century but it is also a representative example of a Christian attitude toward the challenges of modern society that had many followers, namely the attitude of dialogue.

After the Second World War a great number of so called Evangelic Academies appeared all over Europe, especially in Germany. They were inspired by the S.F. and they had similar aims. With the dialogue as a means they worked for the Church to take an active part in post-war debates of ideas and society.[2] In other words, the S.F. is not to be looked upon as an isolated phenomenon, but as an example of a Christian innovation, related to other Christian innovations, which appeared as a result of the modernization.

In this presentation we focus on the years when the foundation was established. Two items are central. How was the societal and churchly situation that formed the basis of the dialogue activities at the S.F and what overall motives did the

---

[1] I.e. Olaf Blaschke, "Das 19. Jahrhundert: Ein Zweites Konfessionelles Zeitalter?" in *Geschichte und Gesellschaft* 2000:1, Olof Blaschke, "Der ‚Dämon des Konfessionalismus'. Einführende Überlegungen" in *Konfessionen im Konflikt. Deutschland zwischen 1800 und 1970: ein zweites konfessionelles Zeitalter*, Olaf Blaschke (ed.), Göttingen, Callum Brown, *The Death of Christian Britain. Understanding secularisation 1800-2000*, London & New York, 2001, Hugh McLeod, *Secularisation in Western Europe, 1848–1914*, London, 2000.
[2] Rulf Jürgen Triedel, *Evangelische Akademien im Nachkriegsdeutschland. Gesellschaftspolitisches Engagement in kirchlicher Öffentlichkeitsverantwortung*, Stuttgart/Köln/Berlin, 2001.

Dialogue as a Reply to the Modern 381

spokesmen of S.F. have, when they wanted to bring different groups of people in society together for a dialogue?

The ideological differentiation and the dream of the new human being

Related to the international discussion about the impact of Christianity in Europe during the 19th and 20th centuries the church historian Anders Jarlert has introduced the concept "pluralistic confessionalism" regarding the Swedish situation. According to Jarlert the secularization of society enforced reactions from the Christian side that led to an increased confessionalism, which in its turn had "pluralistic effects". These pluralistic effects were manifested in the fact that church from the middle of the 19th century and onwards was split into many different communions and that in the different communions – especially in the Church of Sweden – the religious activities increased. A contributory cause was that different church directions with varying confessional profiles, such High Church, Low Church and different kinds of "People's Church" appeared.[3]

The thesis about the pluralistic confessionalisation could be widened so that it also includes other social domains. The diversion into different Christian communities and church directions took place in an environment where many different ideas and concepts of reality – which can be related to Modernity – were in full plat both as competitors and as complements. Examples are confidence in science, striving for sobriety and public health and opposing political ideologies. Especially the expanding socialism with its atheistic basic outlook and its belief in a future classless society created by the people themselves was a distinct alternative to Christianity. Like the church the socialistic movement was split into a great number of groups on "confessional" basis.

The first decades of the 20th century were marked by great tensions between different ideologies and groups. When S.F. initiated its activities – in 1917 and in 1918 – the antagonism came out strongly. All over the country there were demonstrations and food riots. The working-class movement demanded reforms and the Swedish right-wing government feared that there would be a revolution in Sweden, comparable with those in Russia, Finland and Germany.[4] The social tension continued with varied intensity till well into the 1930s.

At the same time as the Swedish society was marked by social opposition and competition between different religious or political confessions there was an all over discourse, comprising most of them – dreams and visions which were cur-

---

[3] Anders Jarlert, "Det ‚långa' 1800-talet som en andra konfessionell tidsålder" in *Nåd och sanning. Församlingsfakulteten 10 år*, Rune Imberg och Torbjörn Johansson (eds.), Gothenburg 2003, p. 89f.

[4] Carl Göran André, *Revolt eller reform. Sverige inför revolutionerna i Europa 1917–1918*, Stockholm 1988, p. 267f.

382 Elisabeth Christiansson & Tomas Fransson

rent in society but were given varied interpretations by different groups. One of them was nationalism, another was the belief in popular adult education. There was also the idea of a new human being and a new society, which would be achieved by struggle, in the first place led by promising, young people.[5]

Sigtuna Foundation as an answer to and a Mirror of Time

S.F. can be looked upon both as an answer to and a mirror of the societal and churchly situation during the first decades of the 20th century. For Manfred Björkquist, the young church movement and the review called *Vår Lösen* [Our Parole] the Motive of struggle played a prominent part at the time of the establishment of S.F. This was in a way characteristic of the period. The struggle aimed at creating a new kind of human being and a new society, summed up in the parole "The people of Sweden – a people of God".

According to contemporary ideas young people were of major impact in the building up of a new world. "New, young people" with "new life prospects" were needed to prevent "the night and hopelessness from falling over us".[6] According to Björkquist education was of great importance in the struggle for a new human being and a new society. In connection with a democracy reform some years before the start of S.F. Manfred Björkquist claimed that the breakthrough of democracy was both "deeply sad " and "binding" since it needed a complement of "education and a unifying power from the inside" which he meant was missing. Therefore it was a central duty for "the Christians" and "others" to ask for "profound, educational powers" "with increasing zeal". [7]

When the S.F. was being planned it was actually with the ambition to work as such an educational power. The intention was that S.F. was to be "a centre for voluntarily church educational work." Courses should work for "advanced religious education" especially among the so called "higher classes", carry on written information campaigns and organize series of lectures in the bigger towns of Sweden. Very important was also to run a folk high-school that concentrates on the building up of character to achieve a true Christian mind.[8]

The nature of the S.F as a centre of the dialogue mainly manifested itself in the folk high-school work and conference activities which would expand a lot in

---

[5] Henrik Berggren, *Seklets ungdom. Retorik, politik och modernitet 1900–1939*, Stockholm 1995. The fact that the Movement from which the Sigtuna foundation aroused was called the Young Church Movement must be seen as more than just an occasion.
[6] Manfred Björkquist, "Ny ungdom", Koncept VI, anföranden och föredrag (tilläggsvolym), Manfred Björkquists samling, Sigtunastiftelsens arkiv. The speech was probably held in the Church of Karlskoga in 1918.
[7] Manfred Björkquist, "Demokratiens genombrott" in *Vår Lösen* 1912, p. 18.
[8] "Sigtunastiftelsen" in *Vår Lösen* 1915, p. 362–363.

Dialogue as a Reply to the Modern 383

course of time. The basis was the ideological differentiation connected with the modernizing. The dialogue activities at the foundation were a direct and conscious answer to this differentiation.

Manfred Björkquist saw the differentiation and schism between different groups as a very serious social problem. He argued that the western society was in a critical state because "somewhere in the inner of culture something has burst where it isn't allowed to burst". Culture was devoid of unity.[9] Politics, science, working-life, art, moral and religion followed their ways in a "bursting process" that had been going on since the Renaissance. By that the connection between the different fields had been lost.[10] As for religion the churches had "resigned themselves to secularization".[11] Secularization and cultural dissolution were consequently closely connected, according to M.B. The dissolution expressed itself in people's "decadence" and "moral fall", their practical materialism and "unfaith" and not least their "class conflicts".[12]

The folk high-school was to counterbalance the schism and the dissolution. Together with the church it was meant to work as a "unifying power in people's lives".[13] It shouldn't be a "party school" but a centre where people from different classes and with different ideologies – Christian and non-Christian – learn to live together and to see the heart in each other so that they later on will be prepared to work together fighting for the ideal values that our culture absolutely not can do without.[14]

Alluding to the Marxist parole "Workers of the World, unite!" Björkquist suggested an alternative parole implying the right-minded to find each other beyond "party- and class limits": "Idealists from everywhere unite!"[15] The atmosphere at S.F would make it possible for this ideal to be realised.

As a matter of fact various kinds of people have met at the school from the very start – left-wing Socialists and Conservatives, followers of High Church and Low Church, atheists and orthodox, and they have in many ways, also in their own press, expressed their respect and pointed out, that S.F. was a centre of spiritual freedom may have been our most valuable experience to see how the spirit of Christ in a truly human way affects the souls and often creates a unity of spirit over and through all separating walls.[16]

---

[9] Björkquist, *I den andliga krisen*, p. 79.
[10] Björkquist, *I den andliga krisen*, p. 79–85.
[11] Björkquist, *I den andliga krisen*, p. 84.
[12] Björkquist, *Kristendom och pacifism*, Uppsala 1924, p. 9.
[13] Björkquist, *I den andliga krisen*, p. 73.
[14] Manfred Björkquist, *Sigtunastiftelsen. En konturteckning*, Stockholm 1928, p. 26.
[15] Björkquist, *Sigtunastiftelsen*, p. 12.
[16] Björkquist, *Sigtunastiftelsen*, p. 27–28.

The ambition to unify representatives of different ideas and groups was also significant for the conference activities. It was hardly a coincidence that this work started with a conference with representatives from the church and from the working-class movement (labourers and university graduates). The conference was a continuation of the meetings which had been arranged in Johannisdal, outside Köping, by representatives of the Young Church Movement in 1912, 1913 and 1915.[17]

The driving force of the meeting, Axel Lutteman, summarized clearly what it all was about in a description of the socialistic labourer: "For him socialism is not only a view of society but a religion". At the same time as there was something righteous in what the socialistic worker was burning for and believed in, his commitment was to be led into the right ways. He had to be shown the insufficiency of his belief, the mistakes of his sentences at the same time as his "zeal", "ability to react against injustice", "his courage to believe and his power to let himself go" had to be won for "the sake of the good thing, that we all are fighting for" namely the church struggle.[18]

Socialism was looked upon as a religious alternative to Christianity that threatened to keep the workers out of church.[19] Therefore it was important within a dialogue for the sake of church. Manfred Björkquist described it retrospectively as follows: "How would it be possible to build up a church of the people if the workers were being left outside?"[20]

But the dialogue was also important for the sake of society. As it has already been pointed out the class struggle was regarded as an element of cultural and social dissolution. Therefore you had to find forms for mutual understanding over ideological- and class limits. At the conference in 1922 a very far-reaching dialogue activity concerning the labour market was initiated. The meetings between labourers and theologians, which took place almost every year in the 1920s and in the 1930s were complemented with conferences between employers and theologians and between employers, labourers and theologians. The latter are said to have contributed to the long industrial peace between the parties on the labour market, which found expression in the agreement in Saltsjöbaden in 1938.[21]

---

[17] Concerning these meetings and their background, see Tergel, *Från konfrontation till institution*, p. 108–152.

[18] Axel Lutteman, "Han måste vinnas" in *Vår Lösen* 1910, p. 6–8.

[19] Manfred Björkquist, "Möten, konferenser och kurser" in *Sigtunastiftelsen. Tjugofem år*, Harry Johansson (ed.), Stockholm 1942, p. 200.

[20] Manfred Björkquist, "Möten, konferenser och kurser" in *Sigtunastiftelsen. Tjugofem år*, Harry Johansson (ed.), Stockholm 1942, p. 200.

[21] Hans de Geer, "Arbetsfreden i Sigtuna" in *Scania* 1976, p. 2.

Dialogue as a Reply to the Modern

In the 1920s the conference activities mainly dealt with the labour market in a wide sense but in the 1930s it expanded and eventually comprehended other fields. "Conferences about co-operation and agreement" were arranged between priests and physicians, between poets and theologians, between representatives of the sports movement, between representatives of the political youth leagues.[22]

At the same time as the S.F. worked as a mirror of time concerning agitatorial rethoric, educational ideals and the belief in a new human being and a new society, it was an answer of time. In a culture, which in M.B.s world of ideas, was threatened by dissolution, it worked like a unifying bond because of its folk high-school and its conference activities. It answered to the conceptual differentiation of society by bringing representatives of different ideas and groups together for a dialogue.

The Vision of the new unity culture

What was actually the aim of the dialogue activities? Was there a comprehensive vision? When Olov Hartman in the 1960s writes about it he argues that "you can see that the purpose from the very start is double; a conversation in which church and theology is one of the parts and a dialogue that "throws bridges" between other parts in cultural and social life".[23] Both aspects are quite evident when you look at the early conference activities and at the work of the folk high-school.

Besides, there was however a more far-reaching vision than just organizing comprehensive meetings and make Christianity a part of the dialogue. Parts of this vision become clear when you look at the invitations to the conferences in the 1920s and the 1930s. The most frequent topic – irrespective of those taking part – is unity round a general goal. When the workers were invited it could be said that "It won't do to act at random. We must know and be in agreement with our goals and principles".[24] In an invitation to a course for employers and academics it was emphasized that it was very important to find methods for the tensions between "the materialistic and the spiritual powers to be solved in a synthesis."[25]

In an invitation to a poetry conference in 1935 you can read that "time demands a modelling of life problems in different cultural fields. Maybe will also the

---

[22] Björkquist, "Möten, konferenser och kurser", p. 199–216.

[23] Olov Hartman, "Konferensinstitutet" in *Öppen horisont. Uppsatser till Sigtunastiftelsens 50-årsjubileum*, Eric Lilliehöök (ed.), Stockholm 1967, p. 46. Olov Hartman was the director of the S.F. between 1948 and 1970.

[24] Program för Samvaron i Sigtuna å Sigtunastiftelsen [konferensen mellan arbetare och akademiker] 26–28 maj 1922. Bilagor till styrelsens protokoll 1916–1928, Sigtunastiftelsens arkiv.

[25] Inbjudan till möte mellan akademiker och arbetsgivare 24–26 oktober 1923. Bilagor till styrelsens protokoll 1916–1928, Sigtunastiftelsens arkiv.

need grow to make oneself familiar with a more integrated view of culture and a more competent vision of the future guiding principles."[26]

Behind the ambition to unite round a special goal there was a rather extensive vision of future namely the vision of a "Christian united culture".[27] To stop the present process of dissolution culture needed "guidance" – or as M.B. himself expressed it: "Modern culture must seek its centre in the image of Christ if it wants to escape catastrophy".[28] How did this vision of a Christian united culture correspond to the talk about "the atmosphere of spiritual freedom" and the concentration on a dialogue over the party limits? The answer is quite likely to be found in the apprehension of Church – or of Christ – being so wide that everything can be included. What Bishop J.A. Eklund as the chairman of the S.F. said at inauguration of the foundation is here significant:

> Culture without Christ becomes a deserted land, where people spiritually are lost like in Babel. In his name we want to gather so deeply round the thought that we find the source of life, which is rich enough to water the entire world of life: belief and knowledge, activity and writing, State and Communion.[29]

In his book *Kyrkotanken* [the Idea of Church], which was published for the first time in 1909, he briefly describes the fundamental view of church under the parole "the People of Sweden – a people of God". The mere thought of Church is big enough to be able to incorporate every truth that exists outside the church. This truth was to be inserted into "her own life context".[30]

Björkquist didn't mean that a united culture under guidance of the church was to be the leader of all parts of culture. Instead the church was to act in the world of heart, where she is commissioned and in there she is going to administer this mission, so that the different cultural circles may freely deepen, each one according to their binding, history and law.

The guiding mission of the Church was to offer "a new profound cultural inspiration" and by this" Christianity" will be able to maintain its place deep in the heart of the cultural world. And in the presence of "an inspiring guidance everything surrenders willingly and happily in obedience".[31]

These ideas make up the background for the understanding of the growth of the dialogue activity at S.F. The church was big enough to embrace all kinds of truths. Therefore there had to be place for all sorts of "right-minded idealism

---

[26] Program för diktarkonferensen i Sigtuna den 1–3 oktober 1935. Bilagor till styrelsens protokoll 1931–1936, Sigtunastiftelsens arkiv.
[27] I.e. Björkquist, *Kristendom och pacifism*, p. 4.
[28] Björkquist, *I den andliga krisen*, p. 90.
[29] "Sigtunastiftelsens grundinvigning den 16 juni 1916" in *Vår Lösen* 1916, p. 214.
[30] Manfred Björkquist, *Kyrkotanken*, Uppsala 1916 (second edition), p. 7.
[31] Björkquist, *I den andliga krisen*, p. 91–92.

Dialogue as a Reply to the Modern 387

and consequently its atmosphere had to be that of the dialogue" and "the spiritual freedom".[32] The mission of the Church and Christianity was to be the unifying bond and the inspiring leader in "the cultural life of heart". All cultural and social fields in society were therefore relevant for Christianity – labour market, sports, politics, poetry – all subjects that were discussed at S.F.

S.F. was party-politically independent, but the ideas of unity over all class conflicts more answered to the vision of the young right-wing movement than that of socialism. S.F. was not a confessionally profiled institution. Confession was not demanded, neither regular participation in the services, that were arranged in the chapel. But behind the dialogue direction as an answer to the differentiation of modern society there was a vision: a vision that the whole culture should become rechristianised. Or, as Manfred B. himself formulated it, "the vision of a world, where the church once again stands in the middle of life" and "on the inner ways of life" for "its leading will into all kinds of cultural life".[33]

The Authors

Elisabeth Christiansson, Dr. theol., born 1965, is Head of the Department of The Institution of Diaconal Studies, Church Music and Theology at Ersta Sköndal University College in Stockholm. Recent publications: "Diakoni och samhällsförändring" in Blennberger & Hansson, *Diakoni – tolkning, historik, praktik* 2008, Verbum, p. 119. "Samförstånd som politik och religion" in *Svensk kyrkotidning* 2008 p. 459. Together with T. Fransson. "Gud bortom genus. Två perspektiv på Gud" in *Svensk kyrkotidning*, 2007 p. 268. "Ideologi i frivilligorganisationer" in *Loop. Tidningen om organisation ledarskap och personal*, 2007, nr.6, p. 53. *Reform in Church and Society. The Justi-fication of Diaconia in Sweden 1845-1965.* 2006.

Tomas Fransson, Dr. theol., born 1968, is vice principal at the folk high school of Vadstena, Sweden. Recent publications: "Samförstånd som politik och religion" [Mutual understanding as religion and politics]in *Svensk kyrkotidning* 2008, p. 459–463 (together with E. Christiansson), "Kristen enhetskultur på modernitetens villkor. Visionen bakom Sigtunastiftelsen vid tiden för dess grundande" [A Christian culture of unity adjusted to modernity. The vision of the Sigtuna foundation at the time of it's establishment] in *På spaning...från Svenska kyrkans forskardagar 2007*, Anne-Louise Eriksson (ed.), Stockholm 2008, p. 397–407 (together with E. Christansson), "Rosendal, individualismen och det katolska" [Rosendal, individualism and catholicity] in *Svensk Pastoratstidskrift* 2008:5, p. 121–126.

---

[32] Cf. Lars Åstrand who, concerning the ambitions of Björkquist to, on the basis of Christian faith, give culture a "form and direction of unity," says that this aim was to be realised "in respect for the different goals and meanings of the others". Lars Åstrand, "Nuets brusande liv. Om det humanistiska anslaget i Vår Lösen 1910–19" in *Tradition i rörelse*, p. 28–29.

[33] Manfred Björkquist, "Kulturskymning" in *Vår Lösen* 1916. The cited words could, according to Björkquist, "be seen as programmatic words concerning the Sigtuna foundation." Björkquist, "Tanken och uppgiften" in *Sigtunastiftelsen. Tjugofem år*, p. 17.

Leo Karrer

Social forms of the Church in relation to medial publicity
Do the media constitute or communicate "religion"?

1. Medial transmission of civil society is the place of the church(es) in the first place and not primarily that of the state.

The approach to people and to their existential and social living area has become pluralized. This changes and speeds up the comprehension of the pastoral activity and the question concerning the places of the churches. The closed milieu and church institutions no longer primarily dictate conditions of membership and religious practice. Every individual decides for himself his closeness or his distance from the Church. Medial offers can also affect his choice of religion. Naturally, the adaptability of the Church to this ideological market and the media is ambivalent. There is the positive possibility and the danger that an uncritical and forced adjustment can also attract the damage and the disadvantages of the so-called post modern era. The Catholicism of the 19th century was already an adaptation. Except that, through organisation and media it placed itself, so to speak, in opposition to the state and its fundamental forces. Today the state remains only a partial opposite of the church. The plurality and multicultural ways of life form a society in which the church is only one of the many groups of interest. These ways of life are transmitted mainly by the media who shape the image of the church(es) and marginalise the bygone Christian press.

2. Which strategies?

The church will have to find a way of linking the two poles of the social market situation and traditional loyalty to the gospels.

The Church as an organisation in the sense of a bureaucratic service (cold form of organisation)

Should the church behave, within the framework of social differentiation and subsystems, as a big customer-oriented organisation, providing the religious market with efficient customer service, looking after ritual stages of life and civil religious needs and assuring social welfare work? This model would to a certain extent comply with the "churchifying" of Christianity. Medially, this form of organisation would quite quickly react on the market/online communication, dialogue with the public media.

Precisely such a cold form of organisation would lead to the distancing between people and institution and church and lose the critical approach to the

Social forms of the Church in relation to medial publicity 389

contradictions of the modern world to the advantage of a market dependent balance of offer and demand.

Confessional church (hot form of organisation)

The opposing model would be a church aware of its responsibilities, attracting convinced believers, offering them a religious home and thus protect them from the crises of the so-called modern society. This would rather be a *hot organisation*, guaranteeing unity in fundamental as well as evangelical circles and institutions, but with the tendency to keep the modern world and its challenges at a distance and precisely losing the capacity of communication. At a time of confused church-going and insecurity such radical proposals would find a positive response with a tendency to fundamentalism. Medially they would no doubt dispose of their own transmission methods.

Popular church (tepid form of organisation)

The popular church in the conventional sense, that the church and its duties are shared by state and society, can no longer be seen as a future possibility. However, the popular church is not to be entirely excluded, even if it is considered a tepid solution. It consists of a basic plurality capacity to integrate an alternative church model, and is thus quite open to differentiation. Medially it can lead to a model of partnership cooperation.

The "popular church" as a basic variety of flexible networking

Public communication culture is decisive. Inside the church it allows plurality on the basis of understanding and for the society with it's cultural, political and social questions and challenges, it remains capable of communicating. Medially and structurally a network of multiple forms of communication and places must be organised with corresponding equipment (staff, coordination…). Such a flexibly networked basis or popular church could permit plurality and would be open for "hot" forms of organisation and for coalition with civil groups, for communicative social milieus and informal meetings, etc. Above all a flexible network is important in order to be present critically and prophetically, locally and regionally and to find the ways and means for doing this.

Rather than having central authorities and organs, it would be more a question of partly church forms of open communication and the search into the future by way of synods, events or regular church meetings, etc. For such instruments of dialogue it would be important to keep closely to relevant themes (forum) and to have the courage to discuss also burning internal church questions. The medial publicity would lead to a forum, which would oblige facing the question of inter-church communication and participation.

3. Medially or only personally?

There is no "either-or", only "as well as". When the Christian distinction becomes the decisive human one, then the dimension of communicative media is the condition and path for religious orientation. Religion should reach out to the individual person and be present in a public critical-prophetical way.

If the Church wants to develop future strength, then it must also take into consideration the partially opposing positions and polarising streams within itself of the plurality and diversity which have become obvious in the secular field. From this can be concluded that the problem of transmitting the Christian message is not primarily the contents of faith. Rather the question is whether the church can be taken into consideration by people in their lives and how the burning questions of people, the contents of faith and the ethical implications can be perceived.

In a society which is institutionally highly differentiated and largely ruled by the media the church cannot follow its obligations only in small groups. Rather it must become responsible for its social presence in an organisational public way.

4. Evangelical or catholic identity?

Is it really identity? Or should we rather speak of profile?

The comparison of religion respectively Christianity and "publicity" has always accompanied church history openly or latently. Right from the beginning the Christian church has always been a complex or global way of communication, either by its mission or its obvious presence. "As a local and global, private and public entity, the church was and is a process of communication, using the necessary media and in so doing becoming media productive itself" (R.Schmidt-Rost). In former times, the internal church communications were marked by instructions and control, for the transmission of the faith went in a linear way from the active sender (clergy) to the passive receiver (layman). Today however publicity is transmitted medially in a plural, multicultural and democratic way as well as marked by sub-social groups of interest.

Today the Catholic Church for example can no longer maintain pure internal communications. As a result the public discourse has penetrated even into the inner rooms of the church, and internally also demands a participatory social form and a new communicative culture. On the other hand, the centrally guided church, with its ritual and sacramental wealth in a visual media world, enjoys a unique place, especially as the search for religious models and symbols is uni-

Social forms of the Church in relation to medial publicity 391

fying. There are colleagues from evangelical faiths who ask if the papal journeys will define "Christianity" in the public conscience in a far-reaching manner.

5. What do the media show and hide on the subject of religion ?

Here religiosity and Christian contents hover between church obligations, personal decisions and media vision and considerations.

Audiovisual media mark also our religious experience. Even religion can become noticeable via media and often not more than our immediate experience. Presumably there are different tendencies:

- Dulling of the mind: people take the virtual world as the real one, with a resulting collapse of the power of judgment. "We are enjoying ourselves to death" (N. Postman).

- Education: everyday and media experiences supplement each other, which sets corresponding demands on the person.

- Boundary confusion: the media transmission becomes the model for interpreting life and for everyday reality. Models simulate ideal fictions causing the individual person to see only problems within himself.

On the other hand, media allows access to themes and experiences which could not be made individually. They give information which can be critical of the church or are found to be anti-church, but they also pick out as a central theme religious contents and questions, discussions in which the church may enter without reservations. The aesthetics of the media can of course lead away from the aesthetics of a church service or church symbols, so that the form can simplify or estrange the religious contents or market orientation, but it can also give an impulse.

6. Media competence = theological professionalism

It is clear, that theological professionalism requires a minimum knowledge of media publicity and its background social conditions, but also competence in dealing with printing media and with audiovisual media.

The Author

Leo Karrer, Prof. Dr., emeritus professor of Pastoral Theology at the University of Fribourg (CH). Recent publications: Die Stunde der Laien. Von der Würde eines namenlosen Standes, Freiburg 1999; ed. with Charles Martig: Eros und Religion. Erkenntnisse aus dem Reich der Sinne, Marburg 2006; ed. with Charles Martig: Traumwelten. Der filmische Blick nach innen, Marburg 2008.

Kathleen A. Cahalan

Beyond Pastoral Theology: Why Catholics Should Embrace Practical Theology

It is time for Catholic theologians to take a fresh look at practical theology as a legitimate and important area of theology. For too long Catholics have persisted with the curricular designation of "pastoral theology" as the courses that pertain to ministry, disregarding the problems that have persisted in this area. Does adopting practical theology in place of pastoral theology solve the problem? Practical theology needs to be considered anew in Catholic theological education, not for academic legitimacy, but because practical theology is a creative theological enterprise that is exploring issues related to the lived Christian faith and the practice of ministry.

In the 1980s, Sandra Schneiders argued that the discipline of spirituality could be distinguished from a discourse or field about spirituality. A discourse is "an ongoing conversation about a common interest" that includes professionals, specialists, teachers, and practitioners. A field pertains to "an open space in which activities which have something in common take place." But a discipline is distinct from either discourse or field as it pertains to: "teaching and learning, including research and writing…in the context of the academy."[1]

Schneiders' categories can be used to describe how pastoral theology has been understood since the Second Vatican Council. First, the Council was pivotal in claming "pastoral" as an ecclesial discourse pertaining to the church's relationship to the world, most notably in *Gaudium et spes*, the only constitution given the title "pastoral." "Pastoral" means the church's mission in the world, making the theological task more open and directed to society rather than traditional scholastic categories.

Pastoral theology is also a *field* pertaining to the teaching and practice of "pastoral" ministry, which includes pastoral ministers as well as theologians and bishops. Since Vatican II information related to ministry has expanded through the development of professional organizations, conferences, journals, and continuing education for ministers. But "pastoral theology" in regards to ministry is not without its vagueness. The category pertains to four areas: the "theoretical and practical training of the clergy" especially in regards to their "shepherding" or "pasturing" role in relationship to the local community; pastoral

---

[1] Sandra M. Schneiders, "The Study of Christian Spirituality: Contours and Dynamics of a Discipline" in *Minding the Spirit: The Study of Christian Spirituality*, ed. Elizabeth A. Dreyer & Mark S. Burrows (Baltimore, Md.: John Hopkins, 2005) 6–7.

care and clinical pastoral education; ascetical and spiritual theology; and theological reflection.[2]

Pastoral theology is a very large field. Training for ministry has expanded beyond seminaries to include colleges, universities, and dioceses.[3] Expanding ministry training, as well as specialization and professionalization of areas in ministry, was unforeseen at the Council, and yet marks a significant post-conciliar development. A brief glance at the past 40 years reveals that the field of pastoral theology is everywhere.

Pastoral theology as a discipline is more difficult to identify. The sub-disciplines commonly associated with pastoral theology each operate independently from pastoral theology. Pastoral theology is a quite recent addition to seminary curriculums and functions primarily as a catalogue heading.[4] Despite the Council's vision and the expansion of education for ministry, pastoral theology as a discipline can be found nowhere: academic journals, professional organizations, and doctorate-level training do not exist. Schuth points out pastoral studies is "subdivided into distinct areas of study and in many cases employs part-time faculty engaged in the ministry associated with their particular discipline. Perhaps for that reason, pastoral studies are emphasized less than Scripture, systematic, moral or sacramental theology." Ministry has the "most varied requirements, ranging from no credits to as many as fourteen, and including courses as disparate as the practice of collaborative ministry, social analysis, ministry to families, leadership in parish settings, and ministry to the multicultural community...In almost all theologates, pastoral field education...carries the burden of providing the knowledge and skills necessary for ministerial service."[5]

The training of pastoral theologians is a serious issue when considering the facts. A 2001 Auburn Center study reported that the practical areas will experience the largest number of retirements in the next 10–15 years.[6] In examining practical theologians hired from 1992 through 2000, the study revealed that Catholics are in an alarming situation: only 22 Catholic schools hired new pastoral faculty over the eight years; Catholics hire the largest

---

[2] Peter Phan, "Karl Rahner as Pastoral Theologian," *Living Light* 30 (Summer, 1994) 3–12.

[3] Mary L. Gautier, *Catholic Ministry Formation Enrollments: Statistical Overview for 2005-2006* (Washington D.C.: Center for Applied Research in the Apostolate, April 2006) 3–24.

[4] T. Howland Sanks, "Education for Ministry Since Vatican II," *Theological Studies* 45 (1984) 481–500.

[5] Katarina Schuth, *Seminaries, Theologates, and the Future of Church Ministry* (Collegeville, Minn.: Liturgical, 1999) 187.

[6] Katarina Schuth, *The Recruitment and Retention of Faculty in Roman Catholic Theological Seminaries* (National Catholic Educational Association, 1992) 60.

number of part-time pastoral theologians (38%) as compared to Protestants (10%), and are less likely to hire in tenure-track positions (85% were contract hires) or candidates with doctorates (18% of Catholic hires had doctorates).[7] The data would suggest that Catholic seminaries are in a crisis but the opposite is the case: this is the way pastoral theologians have always been hired.

There are two sources for pastoral faculty: candidates hired in the sub-disciplines with expertise in a particular pastoral area, but often unable to teach outside their specialty, and graduates of Protestant practical theology programs. Catholic candidates trained in Protestant programs may not be formed in the pastoral thinking that shape Catholic ministry and find the adjustment to Catholic theological education quite difficult. However, they are most likely to identify as practical theologians and perhaps find ways of introducing a newly conceived "practical theology" into Catholic theological education. Regardless, doctoral education of Catholic pastoral theologians is an enormous challenge.

Furthermore, pastoral theology suffers from a reputation problem. As Schuth points out, pastoral theology is a new discipline and among seminary faculties is the most controversial, the area about which there is strongest disagreement and greatest concern about what and how to teach.[8] Two attitudes seem to plague Catholic pastoral theology: its low status can be partly attributed to its encroachment into the traditional curriculum, often times reducing the number of courses taught in other areas.[9] Since the Council, pastoral courses have increased: on average 24 credit hours are given to pastoral courses, and 12 hours for field education.[10] Because of this, 20% of Catholic faculty referred to the regrettable "erosion of the academic" due to the increase in pastoral studies courses.[11] Pastoral theology is not viewed as academic, rigorous, scientific, or theoretical; it is perceived to contain little theological substance and instead is an application of ideas established in other areas. Catholic theological educators have been slow to give up the notion that theology is essentially a theory-to-practice enterprise, but a diminished notion of the practical persists even today.

Are attempts to make pastoral theology into a viable discipline remote? Does "pastoral theology" convey the current hope to improve and strengthen "teaching and learning, research and writing" about ministry? One disadvantage to "pastoral" is its root "pastor," not because a pastor's work is unworthy of study, but because it portrays the field too narrowly. In the past pastoral theology

---

[7] *Recruitment,* 62–63.

[8] Katarina Schuth, *Reason for the Hope: The Future of Roman Catholic Theologates* (Wilmington, Del.: Michael Glazier, 1989) 171–84.

[9] Barbara G. Wheeler, "Signs of the Times: Present and Future Theological Faculty," *Auburn Studies,* No. 10 (February 2005) 5.

[10] Schuth, *Theological Education,* 171; *Seminaries,* 156.

[11] Schuth, *Reason for the Hope,* 171.

attended to the tasks of pastors but today many ministers are not pastors and function in diverse ministries. Furthermore "pastor" has strong connotations with male ministers, and in the U.S. majority of ministers are probably women. Another disadvantage is that "pastoral" is limiting insofar as it pertains to the shepherding function of the pastor, which is one aspect of ministry.

It is obvious that pastoral theology is at the same time everywhere and nowhere. Because of its widespread usage as discourse and field, is there any merit in attempting to reinvent "pastoral theology" as a discipline? Are the wide-spread perceptions about pastoral theology in fact true? Perhaps pastoral theology suffers from its low status in theological education precisely because it never became a discipline and did not develop standards of research and performance commonly adjudicated through academic journals and professional societies. What would it take to strengthen the "teaching and learning, research and writing" about the practice of ministry into a disciplined search for knowledge that is informed by practice for the sake of practice?

In a recent essay, "Mapping the Field of Practical Theology," James Nieman and I define six features of practical theology that provide a way to understand practical theology as a field as well as a discipline:[12]

1. Practical theology engages Christian ways of life and therefore takes as its basic task the promotion of faithful *discipleship*.
2. Practical theology offers leadership for such discipleship by giving sustained attention to various forms of *ministry*.
3. Practical theology brings wisdom to the formation of ministers and the study of ministry in its approach to *teaching*.
4. Practical theology as a discipline involves the relationship between several distinctive domains of *research*.
5. Practical theology focuses in every instance especially upon the *current events* and the *concrete settings* that must be faithfully encountered.
6. Practical theology employs that focus in order to *discern* existing situations of life and *propose* eventual directions for action.

This way of conceiving practical theology goes far beyond how pastoral theology has been understood. As a particular form of theology (not just a particular method) that Catholics can contribute to and learn from, it is not a proposal for "Catholic practical theology," but rather the challenge that all theologians bring their distinctive perspectives to the task.

---

[12] Kathleen A. Cahalan and James R. Nieman, "Mapping the Field of Practical Theology," in *For Life Abundant: Practical Theology and the Education and Formation of Ministers*, ed. Craig Dykstra and Dorothy C. Bass (Grand Rapids, Mich.: Eerdmans, forthcoming 2008).

Nieman and I claim that practical theology begins by attending to the immediate realities of discipleship as it is being lived out in social/historical contexts and proposing normative claims for how it should be lived out in the near and distant future. Practical theologians study what is and what is coming to be in order to articulate a theological understanding of how the Christian community, individually and as an ecclesial body, can live more faithfully. Because of a particular interest and focus, practical theologians pay close attention to the particular, local, contextual, existential, actual, and specific dimensions of lived Christian faith. Practical theologians address a specific community in a particular situation, and through the lens of Scripture and tradition, seeks to guide the community by placing its situation into dialogue with these sources.

Practical theologians who take up issues of discipleship have a range of interests and represent a diverse group of interests, methods, and theological positions. Attention to the lived faith includes addressing questions that range from everyday life, to cultural, social, political, and economic realities; and to religious practice. Catholics can bring to practical theology rich interpretations of discipleship through its sacramental and incarnational perspectives as well as the social teaching and spirituality traditions. Catholics do not lack for sociological descriptions of our situation, but Catholic practical theologians could offer interpretations of the demands Christians face and constructive resources that point to more faithful ways of life in families and parishes.

Nieman and I also claim that practical theology must retain its focus on the practice of ministry precisely because of its relation to discipleship. Because ministry's purpose is the stewardship of discipleship, the study and teaching of ministry must be placed in the broader framework in which aspects of ministry are directly related to the lived reality of Christian disciples in local communities. The practice of ministry is not an end in itself, but rather how such ministry addresses the way of life for particular Christian communities. Further, practical theology must attend to all aspects of ministry, providing theological ways of understanding what constitutes the whole of ministry.

Catholic pastoral theology never provided a theological framework for a theology of practice. What would practical theology be in relationship to the study and teaching of Catholic ministry? Three issues are crucial today: (1) What accounts for the practice of ministry and how do we understand it theologically? (2) What accounts for theological education for ministry today? (3) What studies of ministry are most needed to advance the practice of ministry?

Only recently have Catholic theologians attempted to define ministry.[13] Historically, Catholics equated ministry with priesthood and ordination, but today eccle-

---

[13] Kathleen A. Cahalan, "Toward a Fundamental Theology of Ministry," *Worship* 80/2 (March 2006): 102-20.

siologists are defining ministry through a theology of ordered communion that takes account of the diversity of ministers serving in the Catholic community.[14] However, this effort remains focused on a theology of the *minister*, and not on the embodied practice of ministry. Catholic practical theologians can bring to this conversation not just concern for *who* is doing ministry, but *what* they are doing. What constitutes the practice of ministry today amid its varied contexts? What is continuous in the tradition and what has changed? What is essential to the practice ministry and what is distinctive about its various parts?

Defining what is essential to the practice of ministry leads to questions of education. Can Catholic practical theologians overcome highly specialized sub-disciplines by offering an integrated understanding of ministry? Because ministry takes place in several contexts, we have little substantive research about under-graduate and certificate-level training, both of which account for the majority of ministers. What constitutes ministry education today and how can it be improved? Who are the pastoral theologians teaching and with what qualifications? What can be done to address the weaknesses in doctoral education and research as it pertains to ministry education?

Catholic practical theologians can take up a collaborative research with ministers about the practice of ministry. Ministers serve as sources and resources about ministry, but they also need conversation with researchers on how best to interpret findings for their work.

Can practical theology become a disciplined form of theology? No one would have imagined 15 years ago that spirituality would be viewed an important academic area that no curriculum would be without and that now features several doctoral programs at prominent institutions. Can Catholics embrace practical theology as "teaching and learning, research and writing in the academy" that pertains to lived discipleship and the practice of ministry for the sake of the church's mission in our world?

The Author

Kathleen A. Cahalan is associate professor of theology at Saint John's University School of Theology·Seminary in Collegeville, Minnesota. Recent publications: "Mapping the Field of Practical Theology" (co-authored with James Nieman) and "Introducing Ministry and Fostering Integration: Teaching the Book-ends of the Masters of Divinity Program" in Craig Dykstra and Dorothy C. Bass, editors, For Life Abundant: Practical Theology, Theological Education, and Christian Ministry (Eerdmans, 2008). She has authored two books: Projects That Matter: Successful Planning and Evaluation for Religious Organizations (Alban Institute, 2003), and Formed in the Image of Christ: The Sacramental-Moral Theology of Bernard Häring (Liturgical Press, 2004).

---

[14] Susan K. Wood, ed., *Ordering the Baptismal Priesthood* (Collegeville, Mn.: Liturgical Press, 2003).

Bonnie Miller-McLemore

The Academic Paradigm and the Denigration of Practical Theological Know-How[1]

Negative comments about "tips and hints" are common among those in practical theology in the United States and beyond. Practical theologians often frown on "applied theology" and "rules of thumb" as leftovers from the days of the "clerical paradigm" when theological education focused solely on equipping clergy. Claims about the problem of the clerical paradigm, first suggested by systematic theologian Edward Farley, established a major precedent for how practical theologians tell the history of the field. As an introduction to one major edited volume in theological education observes, the idea is "so widely held that it is often taken to be self-evident."[2]

Why did the phrase *clerical paradigm* gain such staying power? This chapter looks at the source of this term and asks what was helpful about the portrait and what dilemmas it left unresolved. The concept has so dominated the discourse, I will argue, that it has distorted our perception, misdirected blame, and left other problems unattended, particularly the rise of what I will call the "academic paradigm." Theologians eager to revitalize practical theology inadvertently denigrated congregational and pastoral "know-how." This was not their intent, but it was a consequence of the increasingly careless usage of an initially useful term.

The Clerical Paradigm as *the* Problem

Several scholars contributed significantly to the repositioning of practical theology as a respectable academic enterprise in the 1980s.[3] They agreed almost

---

[1] This chapter is an abridged version of "The "Clerical Paradigm": A Fallacy of Misplaced Concreteness?" in: International Journal of Practical Theology 11 (2007): 19–38.

[2] Barbara G. Wheeler, Introduction, in: Shifting Boundaries. Contextual Approaches to the Structure of Theological Education, ed. Barbara G. Wheeler/Edward Farley, Louisville (Westminster John Knox) 1991, 9. Some scholars take issue with Farley, but the debate has rarely questioned this basic category. "Nothing published so far has challenged either Farley's explanation of the almost universal experience of fragmentation or the terms he uses to analyze theological education's malaise," David H. Kelsey / Barbara G. Wheeler, New Ground. The Foundations and Future of the Theological Education Debate, in: Theology and the Interhuman. Essays in Honor of Edward Farley, ed. Robert R. Williams, Valley Forge, Pa. (Trinity Press International) 1995, 183. An exception to this claim might be found in: Joseph C. Hough/John B. Cobb, Christian Identity and Theological Education, Chico, Calif. (Scholars Press) 1985, 3–5. They briefly deny that confinement by the clerical paradigm is the crux of the problem and assert that the key dilemma is confusion in the church about ministerial leadership.

[3] For an excellent bibliography, see: Theological Education 30/2, 1994, 89–98.

The Academic Paradigm   399

universally that previous eras, dating back to Friedrich Schleiermacher in the
nineteenth century, had defined the field too narrowly. "Clerical paradigm" became the code term for this problem. Farley first proposed the phrase as a way
to characterize the troubling preoccupation of theological education and
practical theology with ministerial skills of individual pastors.[4] He was not
alone in raising this concern. Others before him, such as Alastair Campbell,
had already done so.[5] With this phrase, however, and a powerful historical
portrait to match, Farley codified it. The clerical paradigm soon became a
widely used shorthand for everything that was wrong with previous understandings of theological education and practical theology.

Farley's *Theologia* is indeed a pivotal text.[6] It offers a detailed history of theology's displacement as the "unity, subject matter, and end of clergy education"
and its replacement by the clerical paradigm.[7] Culminating with Schleiermacher's *Brief Outline of the Study of Theology* but continuing well into
twentieth century curricular structures, the attempt to establish the study of
Christianity within the modern university led to the elaboration of a
"theological encyclopedia" dividing theology into subdisciplines of Bible, dog-
matics, history, and practical theology. Theology was portrayed as a science,
comparable to its companion sciences of medicine and law, with religion as its
object, clerical education as its aim, and several specialized areas as its components. Practical theology became a culminating cluster of courses directed
toward the task of ordained ministry. In a footnote, Farley clarifies:

> Hereafter, this expression, *clerical paradigm*, will be used to refer to the pre-
> vailing (post-Schleiermacher) Protestant way of understanding the unity of
> theological education [...]. Although this paradigm will be questioned as an
> adequate approach to theological education's unity, the author wishes to avoid

---

[4] Edward Farley, Theology and Practice Outside the Clerical Paradigm, in: Practical
Theology. The Emerging Field in Theology, Church, and World, ed. Don S. Browning,
San Francisco (Harper & Row) 1983, 21–41; and Edward Farley, Theologia. The Frag-
mentation and Unity of Theological Education, Philadelphia (Fortress Press) 1983, 87.
Although he continues this argument in later work, this paper focuses primarily on its
initial appearance in these earlier publications. See: Edward Farley, The Fragility of
Knowledge. Theological Education in the Church and the University, Philadelphia
(Fortress Press) 1988.
[5] See Alastair V. Campbell, Is Practical Theology Possible? in: Scottish Journal of
Theology 25/2, May 1972, 217–227.
[6] Although I begin with an analysis of Farley's proposal, I do not take issue so much
with its original formulation as with its subsequent use. Nor do I focus on the institutional or empirical question of whether or not seminaries are teaching ministerial skills
and practices. Instead, I am interested in the shared rhetoric about the problem and solution in theological education that has subtle and not so subtle consequences for institutional life.
[7] Farley, Theologia, ix.

the impression that this is a questioning of either the validity of clergy education itself or of the validity of education for specific activities and skills.[8]

Is the Clerical Paradigm the Main Culprit?

Did Farley succeed in avoiding these pitfalls observed in passing in this foot-note? Even if he did, have those who followed him maintained the importance of educating clergy for "specific activities and skills?" In a later chapter in *Theologia*, he makes mono-causal statements about the problem of the clerical paradigm that seem to betray his good intentions. The reason Protestant churches do not see theology as meaningful, he insists, "is *simply* the triumph and narrowing of the clerical paradigm."[9] The clerical paradigm is also "responsible for" a truncated view of practice and even for the alienation of ministry students from "praxis, that is, from issues of personal existence and social justice." Indeed, the clerical paradigm "appears to be one of the historical forces at work in the American exclusion of 'theology' from the university."[10]

One upshot of such claims is that the clerical paradigm, and in time practical theology and the church in general, begin to take heat that rightfully belongs elsewhere. What has been overlooked in Farley's aftermath is his incisive critique of the whole of theology. With the rise of rationalism, historical critical method, and separation of different theological sciences, the focus in theological education on "sapiential and personal knowledge" of divine being and the promotion of "a Christian *paideia*" or cultivation of this divine wisdom was lost. Theological understanding was dispersed "into a multiplicity of sciences."[11] Two types of theology continue but now in deranged form:

> Theology as a personal quality continues ... not as a salvation-disposed wisdom, but as the practical know-how necessary to ministerial work. Theology as discipline continues, not as the unitary enterprise of theological study, but as one technical and specialized scholarly undertaking among others; in other words, as systematic theology.[12]

In short, practical theology was not the only area blighted. All areas lost touch with their rightful theological meaning.

Farley himself loses sight of this. Later in *Theologia*, he states the problem as simply the "'clericalization' of theology." He says, "in the clerical paradigm, theology...is something for the clergy alone."[13] Yet one could easily argue, or

---

[8] Ibid., 98, original emphasis.
[9] Ibid., 131, emphasis supplied.
[10] Ibid., 133.
[11] Ibid., 14, 15, 49.
[12] Ibid., 39.
[13] Ibid., 130, 169.

The Academic Paradigm   401

perhaps should more accurately argue, that in the *academic paradigm* theology became something for the academy alone. Congregations avoid theology not because they see it as clerical, as he argues, but because they see it as intimidating and reserved for learned academic experts who have influenced clergy. The problem is not just "clericalization," in other words, but an equally troubling "academization."

Theology is not just "*perceived* as technical," as Farley says. It has *become* technical, and not just because of the clerical paradigm. In the last several decades, theologians have tried to retain a place in the university by becoming ever more sophisticated. They began to write for a public removed from Christian life and ministry. Few parishioners saw such activity as something in which they engaged. When they wanted to understand their religious lives, they turned instead to scholars better able to provide meaningful language: psychologists, economists, political scientists, and even authors of spiritual memoirs. Thus, in the "academic paradigm," theology faced a no-win situation. Too pious for the academy, it became too academic for the church.

In other words, Farley actually exposes an academic paradigm as virulent and problematic as the clerical paradigm. Perhaps if he had so labeled theology's plight, preoccupation with the clerical paradigm might have been tempered and some of the unhelpful consequences avoided, including a phraseology that bestowed a subtle negative connotation on *clergy* and largely ignored the *academic* dilemma. Ironically, in some cases the practical areas became even less relevant to ministry and more removed from practice, lest faculty be accused of merely promoting clerical skills.[14] Theologians in both systematic and practical theology underestimated the intelligence involved in practice and overlooked the limitations of merely academic knowledge.

What Happens to Application in the Academic Paradigm?

Fixation on the clerical paradigm as the key problem has had the odd consequence of further devaluing the already questionable status of congregational life, ministerial practice, and clergy competence. This is unfortunate and probably not the end Farley or others had in mind.

---

[14] This can be illustrated by curricular conclusions like the following: "Seminaries need to resist the pressure to do a quick curricular fix to 'prepare' pastors to be better leaders of Christian education programming in local churches. Such a response ignores the validity of the critique of the 'clerical paradigm.' Rather, seminaries need to become…communities of reflective activity seeking wisdom about 'the believer's existence and action in the world' (Farley)." Barbara Brown Zikmund, Theological Seminaries and Effective Christian Education, in: Rethinking Christian Education. Explorations in Theory and Practice, ed. David S. Schuller, St. Louis (Chalice Press) 1993, 121–22.

What then was the end Farley desired, if not an enhancement of clerical practice? He recommends the recovery of *theologia* or an "education which centers on a *paideia* of theological understanding."[15] "*Paideia*" implies the holistic involvement of the learner and includes all Christian believers. However, the context and cultivation of *paideia* go largely unexamined. Instead, the emphasis falls heavily on the cognitive. The general goal of theological education is facilitating theological "thinking." There is nothing wrong with emphasizing intellect in ministry, a highly desirable good. A problem arises, however, as Craig Dykstra points out, when intelligence receives a narrow definition as primarily linguistic, logical competence. This ignores a range of intelligences related to somatic, spatial, kinesthetic, aesthetic, and personal knowing.[16]

The problem is not just a limited definition of intelligence, however. Ultimately, few people attempt to challenge the one-directional relationship between theory and practice evident in Schleiermacher and the gradual devaluation of practice that resulted.[17] Theory drives practice, acting is ultimately subordinate to thinking, and critical reflection occupies a more important place than practical competence, a conviction that continues to shape theological curriculum.

In descriptions of practical theology, interpretation has been key. Action and implementation are often afterthoughts, even though both are important elements in the science of hermeneutics. Practical theologian Don Browning, paraphrasing Richard Bernstein and Hans-Georg Gadamer, says that in the practical wisdom necessary for ministry, "understanding, interpretation, *and application* are not distinct but intimately related."[18] But major spokespersons have had more interest in the first two elements than the latter. The use of knowledge in practice is basically left to the various subdisciplines of practical theology. Since "clerical tasks" have been defined as part of the problem, little attempt is made to fit them back into the picture at all.

---

[15] Ibid., 181.

[16] Craig Dykstra, Reconceiving Practice in Theological Inquiry and Education, in: Virtues and Practices in the Christian Tradition. Christian Ethics after MacIntyre, ed. Nancey C. Murphy/Brad J. Kallenberg/Mark Thiessen Nation, Notre Dame (University of Notre Dame Press) 1997, 177, n. 29. This article first appeared in: Wheeler/Farley, Shifting Boundaries, 35–66. Most recently, Dykstra has talked about this intelligence in terms of "pastoral imagination" and "pastoral excellence."

[17] John E. Burkhart, Schleiermacher's Vision for Theology, in: Practical Theology. The Emerging Field in Theology, Church, and World, ed. Don S. Browning, San Francisco (Harper & Row) 1983, 52–53.

[18] Don S. Browning, A Fundamental Practical Theology. Descriptive and Strategic Proposals, Minneapolis (Fortress Press) 1991, 39, emphasis supplied.

The Academic Paradigm 403

Is There Anything Commendable about Practical Know-How?

In the last few years, several people have begun to question cognitive definitions of theology. This is most apparent in the far-reaching discussions about practice. Farley's work itself alongside more recent developments in anthropology and moral philosophy helped propel others, such as Dykstra, Don Browning, Elaine Graham, and Dorothy Bass, to "reconceive practice."[19] Theology is fundamentally a practical and "performative discipline" where the focus is right practice or "authentic transformatory action" rather than right belief.[20] Properly understood, practice requires not only cognitive insight but also "judgment, skill, commitment, and character."[21] Practice requires and gives rise to knowledge, requires community, exists over time, and involves people of all sorts.[22] Since religious practices shape wisdom, education must take place in closer proximity to them. An impoverished understanding of practice is a serious part of the problem in theological education, including the failure to include practice in the areas of Bible, history, systematic theology, and ethics and to see that such disciplines are themselves a form of practice.

Such scholarship, however, still leaves largely unaddressed the standing of practices that are particular to clergy. Are such skills too narrow or has their value been fundamentally misunderstood? I do not want to re-inscribe practical theology as only concerned with ministerial technique, but are there any particular tasks for which pastors ought to be prepared and with which theological education ought to grapple? Is there any know-how that is not, as Dykstra and others so readily repeat, "*mere* know-how?"[23]

In the late 1970s Rodney Hunter identified a problem that remains unresolved despite attention others have given it in the intervening years. The "distinctive character of practical knowledge in relation to other kinds of knowledge has not been clearly enough understood."[24] He attempts a brief but helpful phe-

---

[19] Dykstra, Reconceiving Practice. Although he identifies several influential scholars such as Robert Bellah, Hans-Georg Gadamer, Stanley Hauweras, and Jeffrey Stout, Dykstra says that the "most important single text" is: Alasdair C. MacIntyre, After Virtue. A Study in Moral Theory, Notre Dame (University of Notre Dame Press) 1981.

[20] Browning, Fundamental Practical Theology, ix, 6, 7 and Elaine L. Graham, Transforming Practice. Pastoral Theology in an Age of Uncertainty, London (Mowbray) 1996, 7.

[21] Dykstra, Reconceiving Practice, 176, n. 28.

[22] Dorothy C. Bass, ed., Practicing Our Faith. A Way of Life for a Searching People, San Francisco (Jossey-Bass) 1997 and Miroslav Volf/Dorothy C. Bass, eds., Practicing Theology. Beliefs and Practices in Christian Life, Grand Rapids (W. B. Eerdmans) 2002.

[23] Dykstra, Reconceiving Practice, 180.

[24] Rodney J. Hunter, The Future of Pastoral Theology, in: Pastoral Psychology 29/1, Fall 1980, 65, 69.

nomenology. "Whereas descriptive knowledge tells about what is," he observes, "and normative knowledge tells what ought to be, practical knowledge gives information about how to do things." This knowledge is not just about skill but it "must be gained pragmatically" through repeated exercise of skill and testing of rules of thumb.[25] Although it involves more than memorizing a set of simple sequential instructions, it does require initial step-by-step "trial and error" activity by the learner and "show and tell" between virtuoso and amateur. Through such apprenticeship, one acquires a kind of "wisdom of experience." Here Hunter is not talking about "experience" conventionally understood as personal growth in self-awareness but as a "form of knowledge that has accrued and matured through a history of practical, contingent events."[26]

This exegesis suggests that learning practical theology has as much affinity with learning an art or sport as learning law or medicine. Art and music offer intriguing alternative ways to think about the Christian life as an "ongoing, communal improvisatory performance," as liturgical scholar John Witvliet argues.[27] Music is an embodied art that one learns at least initially through repeated practice of particular gestures and body movements, including how to stand, where to position one's hands, mouth, arms, and so forth. In particular, "music and art education give more sustained, habitual attention to the basic 'skills' than does theological education." He continues, "in piano and violin, you never graduate from playing scales. These exercises are fundamental in shaping and maintaining muscle memory."

What then, Witvliet asks, "are the scales we need to practice in theological education?"[28] This is an excellent question and is precisely the question that has been dismissed in the concern about the clerical paradigm. What are the scales needed for faithful practice of ministry and how do those in theological education teach them? Just as technique and musicianship in art education are interdependent "right from the start," so also are skills and *theologia* interdependent from the beginning in theological education. Indeed, the best mentor embraces "scales" *and* "artistry," "hard work *and* soaring vision."[29]

---

[25] Ibid., 65.

[26] Ibid., 67.

[27] John Witvliet, Music/Practical Theology Comparison, unpublished manuscript, Seminar on Practical Theology and Christian Ministry, 8–9 October 2004, 1.

[28] Ibid., 16.

[29] Ibid., 7–8; Witvliet quotes V. A. Howard: "All that I describe here stands in marked contrast to two extremes: drudgery, on the one hand, or means without dreams; and fantasy, on the other, or dreams without means. My overall purpose is to show how means and dreams get connected." V. A. Howard, Learning by All Means. Lessons from the Arts, New York (Peter Lang Publishing) 1992, xiv. Witvliet also quotes Bennett Reimer: "…technique now, musicianship later [is a misconception that] has plagued performance teaching in music education throughout its history. [This] ac-

The Academic Paradigm 405

My youngest son has been trying to learn guitar. For good and then for ill, he hears his oldest brother playing fluently and he quits practicing. He seems to assume that guitar playing entails instant good music and that consequently he is, as he concludes, "no good at it." He displays an all too human desire: he wants to skip the tedious intervening steps – chord repetition, chord progression, finger strengthening exercises, missed notes, poor performance – and just play guitar. The discussion in theology seems stuck right here also. Scholars and students want to skip over practice, scales, and skills, and just play *theologia* in church and society.

Reclaiming Theological Know-How

In *Theologia* and work that built on it, Farley and others do a service for the academy. They call attention to the reduction of theological education to the training of clergy and question its institutional compartmentalization. They reclaim theology as a responsibility of the entire curriculum and the church.

Subjugation by the clerical paradigm is not, however, *the* problem that we once thought. My argument is not so much with Farley himself as with the continued unquestioned use of clerical paradigm as code language for what is wrong with theological education and practical theology. Many people latch on to the critique of clericalism but miss the important depiction of theology's demise. Had Farley named the reduction of theology to the rational, orderly study of doctrine the "academic paradigm" or the "cognitive captivity" of theology perhaps some of the problem might have been alleviated. Instead, the clerical paradigm and its message – that theological education is *not* about teaching pastoral skills – became our narrative. Despite good intentions, the monolithic concern about the clerical orientation has tended to cast a negative shadow over practice, particularly clergy practice, and has hidden intricate interconnections between wisdom and practical know-how.

Recognizing this leads to new questions awaiting further investigation.[30] What is theological know-how? What forms does it take for clergy? How do different areas of study contribute to its enhancement? How does one teach know-how? There are also relational questions. What is the relationship between "scales"

---

counts for much of the convergent, rule-learning-and-following, technique-dominated, rote nature of the enterprise… The solution is to recognize and cultivate their interdependence right from the start." Bennett Reimer, A Philosophy of Music Education. Advancing the Vision, Upper Saddle River, N.J. (Prentice Hall) 1989, 130.

[30] I thank James Nieman for his helpful response to my essay in fall 2005 and, in particular, his articulation of the general and specific moves of my analysis of the clerical paradigm and the proposals and questions it raises. I also thank other members of the Seminar on Practical Theology and Christian Ministry, sponsored by the Lilly Endowment, Inc., for their general comments and help in response to reading an earlier draft.

and "artistry" in ministry? What is the connection between know-how and other kinds of knowledge, knowledge and action, and practical knowing and the kind of knowing necessary for knowing God? We also need to learn more about how people embody knowledge and effect change. What are the connections between knowledge, practice, action, application, and transformation? We need to explore the shape and practice of a pedagogy of know-how not only within seminary programs, but also in doctoral institutions that shape teachers of ministry students, as well as in congregations from which many of us come and go. Such work will help pave the way for a day when we are entrapped by neither the clerical nor the academic paradigm, and no longer view *thinking about faith critically* and *embodying it richly and effectively* as mutually exclusive enterprises.

The Author

Bonnie Miller-McLemore is E. Rhodes and Leona B. Carpenter Professor of Pastoral Theology at Vanderbilt University Divinity School. Book publications in progress include: Engaging Practice: The Work of Practical Theology (Eerdmans) and The Blackwell Companion to Practical Theology (Wiley-Blackwell). Recent publications include Children and Childhood in American Religions (Rutgers University Press 2009, co-edited with Don S. Browning); Faith's Wisdom for Daily Living (Fortress 2008, co-authored with Herbert Anderson); In the Midst of Chaos: Care of Children as Spiritual Practice (Jossey-Bass 2006); and Let the Children Come: Reimagining Childhood from a Christian Perspective (Jossey-Bass 2003).

Daniel S. Schipani

Interfaith Pastoral Care in the Hospital
A Project in Practical and Pastoral Theology

What follows is the description of a research and publication project undertaken as a collaborative endeavor between the Associated Mennonite Biblical Seminary–Pastoral Care & Counseling Program and Lutheran Hospital of Indiana–Pastoral Care Division.[1] The Hospital served as the main *hosting clinical setting* for the study, which started on September 1, 2006, and was completed in December, 2007. The following sections include brief presentations of the rationale for the project, the four-fold purpose of the study, the methodology employed, and implementation steps.

The challenge: Pastoral caregivers encounter diverse faith traditions and expressions

The unfolding process of globalization[2] together with the manifestations of post-modernity[3] are key factors that inform the social context of pastoral care practices in our time. The growing presence of a plurality of faith expressions

---

[1] Chaplain Leah Dawn Bueckert, Spiritual Care Coordinator with the North Eastman Health Association in Manitoba, Canada, was my research partner in this project.

[2] The globalization process under way includes political, economic, technological, and cultural dimensions. Interconnected systems of communication, transportation, and political organization tend to weave our world together into a single global locality. Indeed, globalization is restructuring the ways we live in diverse areas such as sexuality, family life, and the socialization of youth. See, Anthony Giddens, *Runaway World: How Globalization is Reshaping Our Lives* (New York: Routledge, 2000). For a comprehensive introduction to the subject of globalization, see David Held, Anthony McGrew, David Goldblatt, Jonathan Perraton, *Global Transformations: Politics, Economics, and Culture* (Cambridge, U.K.: Polity Press, 1999). We agree with authors such as Robert J. Schreiter that "globalization" is the broad category to use in describing the signs of the times, "postmodernity" needing to be viewed within such a larger conceptual framework. See, for instance, Schreiter's *The New Catholicity: Theology Between the Global and the Local* (Maryknoll: Orbis Books, 1997), especially chapter 1.

[3] We are working with a straightforward account of postmodernity: a pluralist society in which not only are many theories and worldviews tolerated and accepted but there is also a profound suspicion of grand theories and theologies, of systems which make claims to truth (which are viewed as inadequate to reality and coercive). As an ideology, *postmodernism* celebrates the pluralism and fragmentation of so-called postmodern societies as a condition in which "true freedom" is possible. Further, postmodernists typically highlight alternative ways of knowing and restate the human value of emotions and feelings, wonder and mystery. For an overview of the different sources and expressions of postmodernism, and an evaluation from a Christian perspective, see Stanley J. Grenz, *A Primer on Postmodernism* (Grand Rapids: Eerdmans, 1996).

(religious as well as non-religious)[4] in our culture is indeed a major dimension of the social reality. Christian pastoral care specialists, both as practitioners and as pastoral theologians, need to work within, and reflect upon such reality in the light of normative claims of the Christian faith tradition (e.g. convictions about Jesus Christ, the church, the Bible, the Holy Spirit, and the Reign of God). Actually, pastoral caregivers have always had to engage in interfaith communication even if they have not always reflected critically and constructively on such phenomenon in a systematic way.[5] Some of them, however, have taken advantage of the contributions of *intercultural* study to pastoral care and counseling, which offers an opportunity for further exploration of *interfaith* pastoral caregiving as a structurally analogous experience.[6]

The main question that the study addresses concerns the effective practice of *therapeutic*[7] *communication* that becomes "good news" (i.e. gospel) of hope

---

[4] We adopt the understanding of *faith* as a human universal that may or may not find expression in terms of a specific religious tradition and content (beliefs and rituals). It is the understanding articulated by James W. Fowler in his classic work: *Stages of Faith: The Psychology of Human Development and the Quest for Meaning* (San Francisco: Harper & Row, 1981). See also, *Weaving the New Creation: Stages of Faith and the Public Church* (San Francisco: Harper, 1991); *Faithful Change: The Personal and Public Challenges of Postmodern Life* (Nashville: Abingdon Press, 1996); and *Becoming Adult, Becoming Christian*, rev.ed. (San Francisco: Jossey-Bass, 2000).

[5] An exception is the collection of essays in Robert G. Anderson and Mary A. Fukuyama, eds. *Ministry in the Spiritual and Cultural Diversity of Health Care: Increasing the Competency of Chaplains* (New York: The Haworth Pastoral Press, 2004). See also, Sue Wintz and Earl P. Cooper, *Learning Module for Cultural and Spiritual Sensitivity and Quick Guide to Cultures and Spiritual Traditions* (2000) *www.professionalchaplains.org*. These valuable resources, however, do not include a systematic consideration of theological foundations and perspectives for interfaith spiritual care; further, they do not address the epistemological and methodological issues involved in the interplay between the human sciences and theology, which is essential for an adequate understanding and an effective practice of interfaith caregiving from a Christian perspective.

[6] During the last two decades a number of books addressing the challenges of intercultural caregiving have been published, especially in the areas of counseling and psychotherapy. Recent research connects issues of cross-cultural communication and spirituality, as documented, for example, in Mary A. Fukuyama and Todd D. Sevig, *Integrating Spirituality into Multicultural Counseling* (Thousand Oaks, Ca.: Sage, 1999). On the one hand, *interfaith* spiritual caregiving can be viewed and practiced as a special form of *intercultural* caregiving, as caregivers and care receivers share meaning and values. On the other hand, the former presents unique features pertaining not only to the specific content of the verbal and non-verbal interactions between caregiver and care receiver but, especially, to the norms that guide and help to evaluate the very quality and effectiveness of those interactions.

[7] "Therapeutic" is here used with the twofold denotation of *ministerial* as well as *clinical*. Simply put, then, *therapeutic communication* denotes the kind of verbal and non-verbal interaction experienced by the care-receiver as deeply caring in the senses of nurturing, supporting, guiding, reconciling and healing.

Interfaith Pastoral Care in the Hospital | 409

and healing in the pastoral care setting of health care institutions in the midst of such cultural and social reality. It is our thesis that Christian pastoral caregivers can engage effectively and consistently in the practice of therapeutic communication in interfaith situations as a special way of *caring Christianly*.[8] Such a practice may necessitate the transformation of Christian religious and theological language while remaining focused on the communication of good news for care-receivers regardless of their religious affiliation (or lack of religious affiliation), the nature of their faith, broadly speaking (including, for instance, religious humanism) and the overall quality of their spirituality.[9]

Purpose of the Study

The project was designed to address the question of what is desirable and appropriate (that is, pastorally effective as well as theologically sound) therapeutic communication in interfaith pastoral care encounters. Such overall purpose determines the fourfold focus of the study, as indicated below in terms of key sets of issues to be addressed.

First, there was the need to characterize pastoral caregiving situations with care receivers who represent a variety of faith traditions (including non-religious faith traditions). Second, we considered philosophical and human science foundations of interfaith communication. Third, we articulated biblical, theological, and ethical norms that support and guide interfaith communication in pastoral caregiving. Finally, we identified factors such as personal dispositions (values and virtues, attitudes), competencies, and approaches conducive to effective therapeutic communication in interfaith caregiving situations.

Methodology

Consistent with the statement of purpose and the fourfold focus just described, we undertook the study with a practical-theological strategy. Such strategy consisted of the four phases and tasks described in the next paragraphs.[10]

---

[8] By "caring Christianly" we mean the kind of spiritual caregiving that stems from a vision of reality and the good life, a disposition to care as a form of love of neighbor, and a sense of vocation, that caregivers identify as dimensions of their Christian faith that define their identity and ministry. This project included a systematic reflection on the notion of caring Christianly.

[9] The term "spirituality" is meant here as the overarching construct, connoting a fundamental human need for meaning and value and the disposition for relationship with a transcendent power. "Faith" is used by us as denoting patterned ways of being "spiritual" in terms of Fowler's contribution.

[10] For the descriptions of the fourfold pattern of practical theology, we are indebted to Richard R. Osmer and Friedrich L. Schweitzer, eds., *Developing a Public Faith: New*

Empirical and descriptive observation of the dynamics of interfaith communication in pastoral caregiving. Simply put, we addressed questions such as these: What actually goes on in interfaith caregiving?; what are the key issues we can identify in a given interfaith encounter, especially focusing on the caregiver as a ministering person? We did so by gathering information systematically and in standardized ways. The main source of information was visits with patients and their families. Other research activities included semi-open interviews with hospital spiritual caregivers focusing on their experience of, and reflection on, interfaith care; interviews with other caregivers (e.g. nurses, or medical doctors) who are interested in, or regularly include a dimension of spiritual care in their practice; and interviews with other-than-Christian hospital care-givers.

Interpretive analysis of the interfaith care dynamics being observed. Pertinent questions at this point included, why do interfaith care dynamics happen in certain ways?, or, why don't they take place as expected?; what is the psychological and theological significance of the practices involved?; what is the caregiver seeking to accomplish?, and so on. Those and related questions were considered in the form of a hermeneutical analysis involving the interplay between human science (especially psychology) and theological perspectives and conceptual tools. Epistemological as well as methodological questions pertinent to the practice of interfaith spiritual care were a major focus of attention. In addition, the particular character of the care-receivers´ spirituality, together with their own practical wisdom was, of course, a major concern as well. See the APPENDIX for an illustration of the practice of a competent chaplain offering pastoral care in an interfaith situation.

Articulation of ethical and theological norms regarding interfaith pastoral caregiving. This was the normative dimension and task in our practical theological strategy, and it dealt with the key question, what criteria do we identify for "excellence" and "faithfulness" in interfaith spiritual care from a Christian perspective?; are there alternative ethical and theological norms that should be applied? In other words, on this level we considered the professional and moral imperative of finding the best possible forms that the practice of interfaith care should take under specific circumstances. The main challenge that we faced had to do with the integration of norms stemming from the practical human sciences, such as those related to successful interpersonal communication, with the norms that come from theology, such as the need for pastoral caregivers to embody healing Grace.

Identification of principles – that is, dependable guidelines for practice – for effective pastoral caregiving in interfaith situations. Finally, the pragmatic and strategic dimension of our work called for specific responses to the question,

---

Directions in Practical Theology. Essays in Honor of James W. Fowler (St. Louis: Chalice Press, 2003), 1–11.

"what are the guidelines for effective and faithful practice that we can identify and promote in order to enhance the art of spiritual care in interfaith situations?" Therefore, we came back full circle to the existential and practical questions involving the very person and the spirituality of the caregivers, their knowledge and competencies, and their wise use of caregiving approaches.

Implementation

The first phase of the project started formally on September 1, 2006. It included a number of activities, such as the review of recent reflective work in the areas of intercultural and interfaith spiritual caregiving, and attending an international conference.[11] We also shared the contours and content of our proposal with a number of colleagues, including hospital chaplains, supervisors of Clinical Pastoral Education (CPE), pastors, pastoral counselors, and a theologian and ethicist, with an eye to enhancing our plan of study. A detailed presentation of the project to the staff of the Division of Pastoral Care, chaplain residents and CPE students of Lutheran Hospital of Indiana (LHI), in Fort Wayne, served as the official launching of the program at LHI. Bi-monthly sessions with the hospital chaplains were held on the campus of Lutheran Hospital. Those sessions, which focused primarily on case study material, dealt with the methodological and interdisciplinary issues highlighted in the previous section.

Presentation and group discussion of case material as well as systematic reflection on the key questions raised by interfaith spiritual caregiving continued during the second phase of the study (January 2 to December 15, 2007). In addition, there were consultations with representatives of other faith traditions. The professional gathering of the CAPPE Conference in Niagara Falls, Ontario

---

[11] Our participation in the international seminar of the Society for Intercultural Pastoral Care & Counseling (SIPCC) in Hamburg, Germany (September 17–22, 2006), provided a special opportunity for further study and work on the project, which was endorsed by the executive committee of the SIPCC at a special session. A version of the research proposal was circulated among several members of the SIPCC who are interested in dialogue and collaborating with us in the project. The overall theme of the Hamburg international seminar – "The Truth Will Make You Free: Spaces of Exchange in Missionary Work and Pastoral Care & Counseling" – was directly relevant to the concerns addressed in the project. See the Seminar program and our participation in it, at www.sipcc.org. During the previous international seminar gathering in Duesseldorf, Germany (October 2–7, 2005) we led a workshop on interfaith spiritual caregiving, the core ideas of which are including in Leah Dawn Bueckert and Daniel S. Schipani, "Interfaith Spiritual Caregiving: The Case for *Language Care*," in Leah Dawn Bueckert and Daniel S. Schipani, eds., *Spiritual Caregiving in the Hospital: Windows to Chaplaincy Ministry* (Kitchener: Pandora Press, 2006), 245–263.

(February 8–11, 2007)[12] provided another opportunity to broaden the vision and to further our research work.

As the project progressed, selected pastoral caregivers from several cultural contexts and Christian denominational and theological traditions from several other countries joined our endeavors in light of the understandings, the purpose, and the methodology indicated above. Our study led to the publication of a book[13] consisting of essays on topics including: biblical, theological, and ethical perspectives; philosophical and human science foundations; interfaith pastoral caregiving as a special form of intercultural pastoral care; case studies of interfaith pastoral caregiving in chaplaincy settings; and implications: guidelines for effective interfaith pastoral caregiving.

Pertinence and broader significance of this study

As previously stated, the study sought to integrate the theological and ministerial contributions stemming from the church and theological education, on the one hand, with the practical and clinical wisdom of spiritual caregivers in the hospital setting, on the other hand. The overall aim of the project was to enhance the practice of Christian pastoral caregivers in the hospital as they encounter the growing plurality of faith traditions and expressions among care receivers and colleagues. At the same time we believe that the results of this study will be meaningful also for other Christian caregivers who serve within as well as beyond the hospital setting, such as pastors, social workers and pastoral counselors and psychotherapists, who deal frequently with the challenges and opportunities of interfaith caregiving. Moreover, we hope that the study will yield the fruits that foster further theological reflection on religious diversity and interfaith dialogue and collaboration.

---

[12] CAPPE: Canadian Association for Pastoral Practice and Education. Chaplains and pastoral counselors from the United States regularly attend the CAPPE meetings. We were invited to present a workshop during the February 2007 gathering, "Interfaith Communication in Spiritual Caregiving: From Naïve Idealism to Therapeutic Competence."

[13] See Daniel S. Schipani and Leah Dawn Bueckert, eds., *Interfaith Spiritual Care: Understandings and Practices* (Kitchener: Pandora Press, 2009). This book, especially endorsed by the Society for Intercultural Pastoral Care and Counseling, includes contributions representing diverse contexts from North America, Europe, Australia, and South America.

Interfaith Pastoral Care in the Hospital

Appendix

Honoring the Care Receiver's Faith:
A Baptist Chaplain Ministers to a Jewish Family[14]

It was Saturday evening when Chaplain Will's pager contact informed him of a need at one of the palliative care units. When he heard the name of the patient, Will immediately suspected that he might be Jewish. When Will arrived at the patient's room, he found it to be filled with family members. The young men were wearing yarmulkes (skullcaps). A woman with grey hair who was standing by the bed looked at Will as he entered the room; Will realized that she was the wife of the dying man. He introduced himself to her and she said, "Pastor, thank you for coming. Jacob is not going to make it, and we appreciate that you are here."

Not that there was much doubt, but the chaplain confirmed with the family that they were Jewish and then asked them if it would be helpful if he contacted a Rabbi for them. Jacob's wife smiled and said, "No, our God is your God, and he hears our prayers."

Will affirmed her statement and, since Jacob was not responding, he asked the woman if Jacob had the assurance of God's love and care in those dying days. She smiled again and said, "Oh, yes, he knew..."

Will was then introduced to every person in the room, and Jacob's wife directed a grandson to get him a chair so that he could sit with her by the bed. Will sat down and invited the people in the room to tell him about Jacob as they knew him. Different ones spoke up, telling him about their relationship with Jacob and sharing something about how special he was to them. There was laughter as those family members remembered things that had happened or lessons they had learned.

An hour passed very quickly, and when the time was appropriate, Chaplain Will stood and told them how special it was for Jacob and his wife to have such a loving family present at such time. He encouraged them to keep telling their stories and to tell Jacob how much he meant to them.

Will usually concluded his visits with a prayer. He wanted to be sensitive to how he, a Baptist chaplain, could best minister to that Jewish family, so he asked them if he could leave them with a prayer and a blessing from the Bible. They agreed that would be very good, so he read to them Psalm 23, offered a prayer, and then blessed them with the benediction from Deuteronomy 31:8: "It is the LORD who goes before you. He will be with you; he will not fail you or forsake you. Do not fear or be dismayed."

As he rode the elevator to the lobby, Will was very much aware that he had just experienced a special moment unlike any he had ever experienced before. He had been able to facilitate a meaningful closure with people whose religious experiences were in some ways similar and yet very different from his own. At the same time, he had been

---

[14] Adapted from William H. Griffith, *Lessons in Care-Giving for the Dying: More than a Parting Prayer* (Valley Forge: Judson Press, 2004), 56–57.

blessed by the Jewish family. It was affirming to know that being sensitive to the belief system that has given people hope through the years makes it possible to connect with them deeply in a significant way.

The Author

Daniel S. Schipani is Professor of Pastoral Care and Counseling at the Associated Mennonite Biblical Seminary in Elkhart, IN., USA. An ordained minister of the Mennonite Church, he also serves as a pastoral counselor (volunteer) at a local community health care center for economically vulnerable care seekers. Schipani's research and teaching interests include formation and transformation processes and intercultural and interfaith pastoral care and counseling. He is the author or editor of over twenty books on education and practical and pastoral theology, including *The Way of Wisdom in Pastoral Counseling*, *Spiritual Caregiving in the Hospital: Windows to Chaplaincy Ministry*, and *Interfaith Spiritual Care: Understandings and Practices*. He lectures widely in Latin America. Schipani holds a Dr. of Psychology degree from Universidad Católica Argentina, and a Ph.D. in Practical Theology from Princeton Theological Seminary.

Tabitha Walther

Interfaith Chaplaincy: Pastoral Care for all Religions and all Faiths. A New Perspective for Clinical Pastoral Care in 21st Century Western Europe? A Swiss Protestant view[1]

1. Introduction

Hospitals in Switzerland have become multi-religious institutions. Numerous encounters at the hospital bed are encounters between members of different religious communities or no religion.

In Switzerland hospital chaplains are ordained theologians of the mainline Protestant Church or qualified assigned theologians of the Catholic Church. In most cases they work in close ecumenical co-operation. The mainline churches, Catholic and Protestant, make up 75% of the Swiss population. While the membership of mainline churches has declined significantly since 1970, all other denominations and religious communities have increased their numbers. The Islamic population for example has almost doubled. In Basel people with no confession are the biggest minority, followed by Catholics and Protestants. The Muslim population has increased from 463 in 1970 to 12643 in the year 2000.[2] Although the situation in our pluralistic society poses a challenge to all areas of practical work of ministers and professionals, I will exemplarily focus on the chaplain's situation in the hospital alone.

In the North American context *Interfaith* stands for inter-denominational as well as inter-religious. Interfaith Chaplaincy means Pastoral Care for Non-Christians or Christians of a different denomination or different religiosity. Another term for Interfaith Chaplaincy could be *Pastoral Care for all Religions and all Faiths*.

Interfaith Chaplaincy inevitably happens in the everyday practice of the Swiss hospital chaplain. *How* can it be done in a professional and theologically responsible way? How shall the mainline churches respond to the request for Interfaith Chaplaincy within the public institution *hospital*?

This paper will focus on three issues:

---

[1] This is the slightly shortened and revised text of the presented paper at IAPT Berlin 2007. Special thanks for their inputs goes to my colleagues and mentors at Basel University Nadja Müller, David Plüss, Christine Lienemann, Albrecht Grözinger, and Katrin Kusmierz who have had significant impact on this presentation and to Reinhold Bernhardt who put my attention on crucial literature.

[2] See http://www.statistik-bs.ch/themen/16/sprachen/confession.

416 Tabitha Walther

- Where does critical research on Interfaith Chaplaincy in the German-speaking context stand and what is missing at the moment?

- The paper will give a description of the U.S. American chaplaincy model at the Stanford University Hospital and Clinics, where chaplains are trained as Interfaith Ministers.

- The paper will give a critical reflection on the Stanford model in the context of Switzerland.

2. A critical research report on Interfaith Chaplaincy in the German speaking world

In the German speaking context Interfaith Chaplaincy is located within the wider field of inter-cultural counseling.[3] While inter-cultural chaplaincy focuses on the different cultural background of patient and chaplain, Interfaith Chaplaincy goes further and focuses on cultural and especially *religious and spiritual* difference. I will now briefly outline the research done on those two aspects of chaplaincy.

2.1 Inter-Cultural Pastoral Care

In 2001, the book of Christoph Schneider-Harpprecht on inter-cultural pastoral care and counseling (*Interkulturelle Seelsorge*) set a milestone in the German speaking academic debate on inter-cultural Pastoral Care, especially by linking it to the US American discussion of our subject.[4] Only one year later a Handbook on inter-cultural pastoral care and counseling was published.[5] Since then, the subject seems to be established in the German speaking practical theological scientific community.[6] According to Schneider-Harpprecht inter-cultural pastoral care and counseling are conceptualized as culturally sensible Christian aid for Christians **and non-Christians**.[7] As well the preface of the Handbook points out inter-cultural encounters are often inter-religious encounters.[8] Still, the specific questions and problems raised by inter-religious pastoral care and counseling are not discussed in more detail. It indicates and leaves an open space for further research. It describes a space that needs to be systematized, theorized and explored theologically.

---

[3] For inter-cultural counseling in North America: Augsburger 1986.
[4] Schneider-Harpprecht 2001.
[5] Federschmidt 2002.
[6] For a brief history on Inter-cultural Chaplaincy compare Schneider-Harpprecht, Christoph, Was ist Interkulturelle Seelsorge? in: Federschmidt 2002, 44–47.
[7] Compare Schneider-Harpprecht 2002, 44–50, especially 50.
[8] Federschmidt 2002, 14.

2.2 Inter-Religious Pastoral Care

There has been some literature on inter-religious pastoral care and counseling and its practical implications, for example with regard to pastoral care for Muslim patients[9], but there is no conceptualized systematic reflection on the issue. The only practical-theological publications on inter-religious Chaplaincy I know are the book 'Ethik und Praxis des Helfens in verschiedenen Religionen' from 2005[10] and a "grey literature" booklet from 1999.[11] The booklet is a translation and abbreviation of one edition of the journal Christian Bio-ethics from 1999, supplemented by a systematic-theological article. It takes the US American and the German context into consideration and puts the focus precisely on matters of inter-religious encounters in hospital. It explores generic chaplaincy (*allgemeine Seelsorge*) versus confessional, so called 'brand name chaplaincy' in a post-Christian age.[12] Furthermore, the booklet illustrates a German Protestant view on inter-religious chaplaincy in the hospital[13] and searches for Christian criteria in a pastoral encounter with members of other religions than Christian.[14]

2.3 What is missing?

In publications on Interfaith Chaplaincy a shift from a sheer utilitarian "everything-goes-as-long-as-it-helps" mentality to a more differentiated perspective can be observed, which shows awareness of the tension between practices and theory and between different religious faith traditions. Interfaith Chaplaincy takes place between truth and tolerance. The theological abyss is Christological soteriology: What is not abrogated (German: "aufgehoben") in Christ? Here the theology of Karl Barth read from a liberal, not neo-orthodox (!) perspective might be a helpful concept to work with.

---

[9] See: http://www.ekd.de/download/ekd_texte_86.pdf and Schmidt, Kurt/Egler, Gisela, Den Christen ein Christ, den Muslimen ein Muslim? Überlegungen zu einer protestantischen Sicht interreligiöser Seelsorge im Krankenhaus, in: Schmidt 1999, 19–42 and Hewer, Cris, Generic Hospital Chaplaincy. Some points to a on-going discussion, in: Schmidt 1999, 59–68.

[10] Weiss 2005.

[11] Schmidt 1999.

[12] Engelhardt, Tristram, Ein Seelsorger für alle Glaubensrichtungen? Zur spirituellen Versorgung im post-christlichen Zeitalter, in: Schmidt 1999, 9–17.

[13] Schmidt/Egler 1999, 19–42.

[14] Bernhardt, Reinhold, Wer kann der weisere Richter sein? Kriterien des Christlichen in der seelsorgerlichen Begegnung mit Angehörigen nichtchristlicher Religionen, in: Schmidt 1999, 69–90. Landmarks for further investigations in a diagnosis of the present are the essays from Grözinger and Gestrich in the journal Wege zum Menschen 47 (1995), 389–400 and 400–412.

418 Tabitha Walther

Further we need a close description on how Interfaith Chaplaincy happens in concrete. And we need a conceptualized systematic theological reflection on Interfaith Chaplaincy in Switzerland. We need an educational concept at the university and in CPE training that deals practically and systematically with inter-religious issues at the hospital bed.

One of my next steps in research will be to find and overview the scientific discussion on Interfaith Chaplaincy in Northern America, focusing on inter-religious matters.[15] The following description and reflection shall offer a small contribution to a concept of Interfaith Chaplaincy in hospital, embedded in the context of Switzerland.

3. How can Interfaith Chaplaincy be done? The Stanford Model as an example

In this paper the Stanford Model will serve as an illustration and example of an already existing Interfaith Chaplaincy Model in hospital.

The Stanford University Hospital and Clinics are located in the multi-cultural and multi-religious pluralistic society of the San Francisco Bay Area. This area holds an immense spectrum of religious identities and self-conceptions of patients, staff and chaplains. On the admissions sheet for incoming patients, patients are invited to tick a box indicating their religion or denomination. There is an official choice of 42 (!) religious preferences and one box for "other religious preference".

This denominational and religious pluralism at Stanford asks for a distinct chaplaincy model within the hospital.

The terminology used in this religious manifest is most interesting for the Swiss Protestant observer. The pastoral care services are called Spiritual Care Services. The chaplains introduce themselves as Interfaith Chaplains, standing for generic chaplaincy with professional openness to all other faith traditions. The Stanford University Hospital and Clinics employ one Jewish and four Christian full time chaplains. Three part time ministers, one Jewish, one LDS (Latter-Day Saints/Mormon) and one Episcopal are independently contracted chaplains who are financially supported by their own faith groups. The CPE students belong to various denominations, religions and cultures from within and outside the USA. In my group was a so called "music minister". His in-clusion in the educational program was a pilot project at Stanford: His mission was music, his language was his guitar, his spiritual resources were songs and

---

[15] I am very grateful to the connections established at the IAPT conference 2007 in Berlin, especially to Daniel S. Schipani, USA and Neil Pembroke, Australia who helped me to connect with the English speaking scientific discussion.

Interfaith Chaplaincy: Pastoral Care for all Religions and all Faiths   419

plays, rhythm and tones. In addition over 240 volunteers of the Spiritual Care Department represent most of the 42 religious preferences as given on the admissions sheet.

The hospital chaplains and the CPE students are responsible for medical units. They belong to the medical team. The unit is the multi-religious community of the Interfaith Chaplain. Patients with other religious preference than the unit chaplain are also visited by a minister or volunteer of their respective denomination.

The CPE students are trained inter-culturally and inter-religiously. Classes are taught on different religious preferences and their specific needs. The students are trained in interfaith ministry during on-call duty during the night and on weekends, when they are the only hospital chaplain present on stage. Different pastoral services can be offered by the Christian interfaith minister: The chaplain is free to offer what ever is possible within his vocation and faith standard. The patient is free to ask for or accept what fits his spiritual needs. She or he can also request a chaplain of her own faith group to be called into the hospital. In that case the Interfaith Chaplain is responsible for triaging the request adequately.

For further investigation on the lived religion in the Stanford hospital I will conduct qualitative interviews with hospital chaplains at Stanford. I will do the same in Switzerland. This will provide a close description and a certain empirical and sociological ground for my thesis.

4. A critical reflection on the Stanford Model [16]

The Stanford model is a pragmatic model of spiritual care giving. It has grown organically out of the needs of the hospital. The concept is not per se filled with religious content, but with techniques and methods. A mature chaplain is aware of his confessional imprints and has developed his religious profile as a major resource for spiritual care giving. It seams a clear confessional stand is not only helpful but crucial for interfaith work.

This pragmatic model at Stanford functions surprisingly efficient. It can offer its service to everyone who is willing to receive support, no matter what religious affiliation. It can provide a high quantitative service. But, in many cases, it provides precariously low qualitative service. Often this is due to marginal and superficial or no knowledge of the other faith traditions and due to an uncritical approach towards religion and spirituality as such. It is not surprising then, that Stanford provides no inter-religious concept. It leaves the question of

---

[16] Due to the shortness of this paper it is only possible to mention a few points here that need further exploration.

420 Tabitha Walther

the theological framing of the inter-religious interaction to the chaplain's own truth claim and exclusively to the individual chaplain.

Maybe it is a European need to have a practical model being sustained and founded by an inter-religious theory that holds the mission of the Spiritual Care Services. Still, to have this model implemented into a European context practicality cannot be the only criterion. It also needs a critical theory of the inter-religious practices at the hospital bed.

5. A Swiss Interfaith Model?

The Stanford model cannot be transferred to the Swiss hospital as such. However, the Stanford model can be translated into the religious landscape of Switzerland in terms of a transfer of experience. As shown above, an explicit theological reflection is not communicated and needs further elaboration.

I would suggest that sensitivity for religious difference should be part of the training right from the beginning of a chaplaincy career in a Swiss hospital. Other than Catholic and Protestant ministers should be proactively invited to the CPE education, for example Jewish chaplains, theologians or Rabbis. It is not that a Protestant or Catholic chaplain cannot serve the religiously different, but they provide not the only and exclusive fruitful ministry to meet the spiritual needs of patients nowadays – furthermost to non-Christians.

For the most intimate inter-religious encounter at the bedside Protestant ministers need *both*: compassion for the human being who is religiously rooted in another religious system than her own *and* awareness for the unsolved and not understood difference of the stranger. Here tolerance is truly put to test: The chaplain has to abide the inner conflict between the own religious identity and respect for the Otherness of the Other. A "we-are-all-the-same"-theology misses the heart of the Christian and maybe any religion. We can let go a lot – if not all – soteriological tension into Christ's open arms. But there might be individual religious and spiritual boundaries and limits that should not be crossed for the sake of the other or oneself. These limits become most relevant in prayer, rituals and sacraments. Here again, empirical research needs to be done. Case studies and qualitative interviews with spiritual care givers could explore the sameness, overlap and otherness in Interfaith Chaplaincy encounters.

To my own experience as spiritual care giver, inter-religious encounters at the bedside can make the religiously different intuitively understandable. In an encounter with the Stranger, the Holy can be encountered.[17] Every inter-religious encounter bears the risk of things being created anew and of human existence being changed.

---

[17] Compare also Sundermeier 1996 and Walz 2003.

Interfaith Chaplaincy: Pastoral Care for all Religions and all Faiths 421

Moving practically from inter-cultural towards interfaith pastoral care an inter-religious concept for Swiss and other Western European hospital chaplains is needed. I could imagine a Trinitarian concept of the inter-religious encounter: pastoral aid for non-Christians, culturally sensible and inter-religiously aware, that helps patients to explore their own spiritual roots and resources. It would be a Trinitarian concept because it sets the diversity and difference of person-hood – as metaphorically given in the concept of the Trinity – in analogy to the three personhoods of God: The notion of difference is not the exception in human encounters but the transcendental necessity for human identity.

6. Closure: Interfaith Chaplaincy: A new perspective for clinical pastoral care in the 21st century? Some theses

Does Interfaith Chaplaincy become a new perspective for clinical pastoral care and counseling in the 21st century? That was the question we began with. I assume that it will due to our increasingly multi-spiritual and multi-religious society. At least for the Swiss context a reflected confessional rooting is wanted and needed – not a generic chaplaincy model with low profile chaplains. For the Swiss context we need a new structural openness to serve people other than mainline churches and other than Christian and not religious. We need to serve them as Christians in the name and mission of our religious community but with true respect for their spirituality and tradition and without a desire to missionize. The soteriological question though wants to be kept eschatologically open.[18] The Christological vocation to care for the other must be taken radically serious. An Interfaith Chaplaincy concept from a Swiss Protestant perspective includes both: awareness of the consequences of one's own faith towards non-Christians and awareness of the inter-religious en-counter as an encounter with the Holy that has the potential to change Christian existence.

References

Augsburger, David W., Pastoral Counseling Across Cultures, Philadelphia 1986

Barth, Karl, Kirchliche Dogmatik (Studienausgabe), Zürich 1986–1993

Federschmidt, Karl et al. (ed.), Handbuch Interkulturelle Seelsorge, Neukirchen-Vluyn 2002

Gestrich, Reinhold, Gedanken über die Seelsorge im multireligiösen Krankenhaus und einige praktische Hinweise, WzM 47 (1995), 400–412

---

[18] Compare Janowski ²2000.

Grözinger, Albrecht, Differenz-Erfahrung. Seelsorge in der multikulturellen Gesellschaft, Waltrop 1995

Grözinger, Albrecht, Seelsorge im multikulturellen Krankenhaus, WzM 47 (1995), 389–400

Interkulturelle Seelsorge und Beratung (engl. Ausgabe: Intercultural Pastoral care and counseling), Schriftenreihe der Gesellschaft für Interkulturelle Seelsorge und Beratung e. V., Nr. 1–11, Düsseldorf 1996–2003

Janowski, Christine, Allerlösung. Annäherungen an eine entdualisierte Eschatologie, Neukirchen-Vluyn ²2000

Kayales, Christina, Interkulturelle Seelsorge und Beratung. Brücken zu Menschen aus fremden Kulturen, in: Pohl-Patalong, Uta et al. (ed.), Seelsorge im Plural, Hamburg 1999, 63–73

Schmidt, Kurt (ed.), (Klinik-)Seelsorge im multireligiösen Kontext, Frankfurt a.M. 1999

Schneider-Harpprecht, Christoph, Interkulturelle Seelsorge, Göttingen 2001

Steinacker, Peter, Die Kirche im Dialog der Religionen. Die postpluralistische Theologie der Religionen auf der Suche nach einem neuen Paradigma, ZfM (1997), 166–183

Sundermeier, Theo, Den Fremden verstehen. Eine praktische Hermeneutik, Göttingen 1996

Walz, Heike et al. (ed.), Als hätten sie uns neu erfunden. Beobachtungen zu Fremdheit und Geschlecht, Luzern 2003

Weiss, Helmut et al. (ed.), Ethik und Praxis des Helfens in verschiedenen Religionen. Anregungen zum interreligiösen Gespräch in Seelsorge und Beratung, Neukirchen-Vluyn 2005

The Author

Tabitha Walther, lic. theol., Rev. and Hospital Chaplain, born 1975, is scientific assistant and lecturer at the Faculty of Theology at the University of Basel, Institute of Practical Theology, Switzerland. Member of MTE AG (Medizinisch-Theologisch-Ethnologische Arbeitsgemeinschaft) of Basel University. Research interests: Pastoral Care, Clinical Pastoral Education, Interfaith Chaplaincy, Religion and Pluralistic Societies, Church and Globalization, Theology of Religions, Karl Barth, Liberal Theology in 20th Century Swiss Church History, Theology and Gender, Empirical Sociology of Religion.

International Practical Theology

edited by Prof. Dr. Chris Hermans (Nijmegen), Prof. Dr. Maureen Junker-Kenny (Dublin), Prof. Dr. Richard Osmer (Princeton), Prof. Dr. Friedrich Schweitzer (Tübingen), Prof. Dr. Hans-Georg Ziebertz (Würzburg) in cooperation with the International Academy of Practical Theology (IAPT), represented by Ruard Ganzevoort (President) and Claire Wofteich (Vice President)

Mechteld Jansen; Hijme Stoffels (Eds.)
A Moving God
Immigrant Churches in the Netherlands
This volume focuses on Christian immigrants and their churches in the Netherlands, with a special emphasis on the Amsterdam area. Many immigrants join one of the new immigrant churches that have originated in recent decades, while others attend Dutch Roman Catholic or Protestant congregations with a special ministry to immigrants. Immigrant churches form an exciting and multifaceted phenomenon in the Netherlands, just as they do in other parts of Europe and in North America. This volume is a joint effort of practical theologians and social scientists from VU University Amsterdam.
Bd. 8, 2008, 248 S., 24,90 €, br., ISBN 978-3-8258-0802-0

LIT Verlag Berlin – Münster – Wien – Zürich – London
Auslieferung Deutschland / Österreich / Schweiz: siehe Impressumsseite

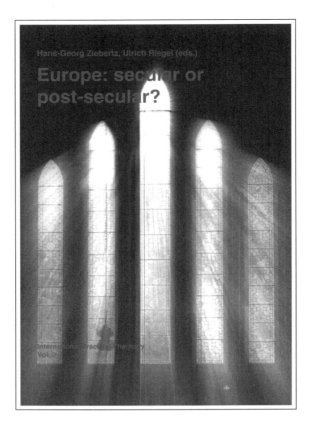

Hans-Georg Ziebertz; Ulrich Riegel (Eds.)
Europe: secular or post-secular?
Religion is back on the agenda. Western societies are searching for an adequate understanding of religion. Media move religion into focus as a resource of significance in modern societies, but also as a source of tension and conflict. Politics is testing how to manage religious pluralism. Education is developing concepts of interreligious dialogue in order to promote a better intercultural understanding. The book discusses if the concept post-secularity allows a suitable understanding of the public presence of religion.
Bd. 9, 2008, 216 S., 19,90 €, br., ISBN 978-3-8258-1578-3

LIT Verlag Berlin – Münster – Wien – Zürich – London
Auslieferung Deutschland / Österreich / Schweiz: siehe Impressumsseite